ISBN 978-1-333-00122-3
PIBN 10448589

1 MONTH OF
FREE
READING

at

www.ForgottenBooks.com

By purchasing this book you are eligible for one month membership to ForgottenBooks.com, giving you unlimited access to our entire collection of over 700,000 titles via our web site and mobile apps.

To claim your free month visit:
www.forgottenbooks.com/free448589

English
Français
Deutsche
Italiano
Español
Português

www.forgottenbooks.com

Mythology Photography **Fiction**
Fishing Christianity **Art** Cooking
Essays Buddhism Freemasonry
Medicine **Biology** Music **Ancient**
Egypt Evolution Carpentry Physics
Dance Geology **Mathematics** Fitness
Shakespeare **Folklore** Yoga Marketing
Confidence Immortality Biographies
Poetry **Psychology** Witchcraft
Electronics Chemistry History **Law**
Accounting **Philosophy** Anthropology
Alchemy Drama Quantum Mechanics
Atheism Sexual Health **Ancient History**
Entrepreneurship Languages Sport
Paleontology Needlework Islam
Metaphysics Investment Archaeology
Parenting Statistics Criminology
Motivational

THE

Being a Pictorial Record of the Great War.

PARTS 1—12.   (June 14th, 1916, to August 30th, 1916.)

Published by the ILLUSTRATED LONDON NEWS AND SKETCH, Ltd.,
172, Strand, London, W.C.

LONDON:
THE ILLUSTRATED LONDON NEWS AND SKETCH, LIMITED,
172, STRAND, LONDON. W.C.

The Illustrated War News, June 14, 1916.— Part I., New Series

The Illustrated War News

WITH ONLY ITS TAIL-FINS SHOWING: AN UNEXPLODED AIR-TORPEDO BURIED IN THE GROUND.

Photograph by Wyndham.

THE GREAT WAR.

IN a general situation growing daily more momentous has come the great tragedy of Lord Kitchener's death. His abrupt and unexpected passing on the smitten *Hampshire* gave greater poignancy to the blow that deprived us of a personality which has had our staunchest regard and has been our surest strength since the outbreak of the war. The position of Lord Kitchener was not merely official ; it was national. His employment as Secretary for War was inevitable. There may be reason to debate upon his worth as a leader in strategy and tactics, but there is no doubt at all that popular imagination found in him its one natural military leader and adviser in the time of crisis. And, having elected him as such, was prepared to — and, in fact, actually did — accomplish all he asked. That this unequivocal reliance had reason behind it is also true. Lord Kitchener's reputation as an organiser, as a person supremely capable of making bricks with very little straw, rests not merely upon his work in his past campaigns, but is proved up to the hilt by his brilliant feat of bringing into being out of nothing, and in spite of an entanglement of difficulties, the tremendous armies we now possess. This was, indeed, his work and office, as this it is that makes his untimely death a tragedy rather than a calamity. There was, perhaps, great work for his gift of organisation to . do ; but the chief work was already done. Even if he had lived, the success or failure of this war depends upon what has already been done, and this was his doing. He died fittingly, as he had lived, in harness, still working on the great cause to which duty had

LORD KITCHENER AS A BABY ON HIS MOTHER'S LAP, WITH HIS ELDER BROTHER AND HIS SISTER : A PHOTOGRAPH FROM A FAMILY ALBUM.

Lord Kitchener's mother was a daughter of the Rev. John Chevallier, D.D., of Aspall Hall, Suffolk. She married Lieut.-Colonel H. H. Kitchener, of Cossington, Leicestershire, and Lord Kitchener was her second son. He was born and spent his youth in Ireland. We reproduce this photograph by permission of the "Illustrated London News," from that paper's special Kitchener Memorial Number, which contains numerous other unpublished early portraits and a full pictorial record of Lord Kitchener's career, together with a large photogravure presentation-plate.

called him. Even though he has died, his work goes on—the end of the war will be of his fashioning.

It is a coincidence of meaning that it was to Russia that he was travelling, for Russia on the very day of his death was beginning to develop that line of great offensive which, perhaps, he had joined with others to plan. On the Monday of last week it became apparent that General Brusiloff was inaugurating the most powerful assault Russia has yet shown, and over a great front. This line of attack runs from the Pripet swamps to the Roumanian border—some 250 miles — and is being carried out not only with the usual Slavic dash and courage, but with the happiest omens of strength in men and guns. The artillery play is, indeed, the most satisfactory note of the movement. The Germans speak of it as something almost unexpected; and the Austrians, who are bearing the brunt of the thrust, have been appalled and intimidated by it. Trenches that were considered impregnable against anything Russia could fire upon them have simply been battered to ruin. Over these shattered fortifications the Russian infantry have swept with irresistible spirit. The Austrian line has been broken at several points, but so badly in the Lutsk area that the Austrians have retreated twenty miles and more, Lutsk has fallen with startling rapidity, and the Russians are pressing along the Styr and are holding out a threat to Kovel, a town of importance on the rail and communication routes. The actual break here is over one hundred miles, and the advance is being carried on in such a fashion that our

Ally is becoming a real menace to the flanks of the line that stretches northward from Pripet.

Further south, on the Strypa, the Russians are also going forward, and have brought their front beyond the river, especially in the Jazloviec sector below Trembovla. The whole offensive has an uncomfortable proximity to Lemberg, and not only eastern Galicia may be over-run; but the goodwill of the Roumanians may be involved in the fighting. In actual cost of battling the Austrians have lost some 107,000 prisoners and an amount of booty as yet uncounted; with wounds and deaths, the whole of the casualties to the Central Powers may well be 200,000 men, a tale of loss that should have decided effect in other fields of the war. It seems possible that such an offensive has been of excellent service to the Italians who are facing the great Austrian drive in the Tyrol; and it is possible, too, that it will force the hand of

LEADER OF THE GREAT RUSSIAN OFFENSIVE AGAINST THE AUSTRIANS: GENERAL ALEXIS BRUSSILOFF, COMMANDING THE SOUTHERN ARMIES.
Photograph by Record Press.

German commanders on other parts of the line, and lead them to inaugurate offensive movements for the relief of the Austrians. There are indications that help is being demanded from Hindenburg; there are suggestions that an attack might be launched against the Dvinsk front. But, so far, in energy and spirit, the initiative is entirely with the Russians. Hindenburg has been credited with saying of the Russians that next time they come on they will mean business. He is probably right.

In the West, the fighting about Verdun has been concentrated into a determined struggle to capture the fort of Vaux. The Germans have spent a costly week accomplishing this end, and only succeeded in gaining the broken works after terrible fighting

that completed the physical exhaustion of an already sorely tried garrison. To attain this end the concentration of artillery fire was again appalling, and the loss of men in the incessant attacks dismaying. Fort Vaux, like Fort Donaumont, was but a point in the system of defence. The approaches are still held by the French, and they must be won at the cost of extravagant effort. Even behind this uncaptured line is the strong main defence of Belleville—Tavannes, with the prospects of months of carnage before the Germans have any hope of winning through. Following the capture of Vaux Fort, the enemy is showing his determined line of advance by hammering at those works covering the Fleury gap, which is a road downward towards Verdun. Notably they have been busy against the Thiaumont Farm front and that in the Caillette woods. Small points have been won, but the defence has not yet been gravely strained. An infantry and flame-jet attack west of the Meuse—against Hill 304—broke down.

The brisk fighting that has been going on west and south-west of the British hold at Ypres seems to be showing no determinate purpose. Following the German attack between Hooge and the Ypres - Menin railway that took place last week, the enemy has again shown an aggressive temper to the north of Hooge. On Tuesday a series of mines were exploded over a front of 2000 yards, and infantry assaults were launched. The majority of these attacks were failures, but at Hooge itself and a little to the north some ground was gained. On our part, we have been carrying out a great deal of raiding, the Australians at Bois Grenier and the Gloucester

DROWNED WITH HIS CHIEF, LORD KITCHENER: THE COFFIN OF COLONEL FITZGERALD, IN ST. MATTHEW'S CHURCH, WESTMINSTER.
The body of Lieut.-Col. O. A. G. FitzGerald, Lord Kitchener's personal military secretary, was recovered from the sea and brought to London. The coffin was placed in All Souls' Chapel of St. Matthew's Church in Great Peter Street, Westminster.—[Photo. by L.N.A.]

Regiment at Neuve Chapelle doing particularly well. Mining and gunnery activity is playing a great part in the fighting just now, and from neutrals and unofficials we learn that the general tendency of the actions are severe. The British, however, are showing a wise patience, and their effort, when it comes, will certainly be at a time of their own choosing.

The stamp of our own truth has been shown by the acknowledged falsehood of the Germans with regard to the Jutland battle. We can see now how well the severity of our own Admiralty statements stands the test in view of the mendacity of those of the enemy. We can see that the " military necessity " of proclaiming a victory led the Germans to suppress the fact that two more at least of their ships had been sunk. It does not increase the good opinion of neutrals to learn that one of those ships was—curiously —one of the latest and best of the German battle-cruisers. The *Lutzow* was the sister-ship to the *Derfflinger*, a 28,000-ton boat, finished only last year. The *Rostock* was a smaller vessel of the light-cruiser type. What the disclosure of this duplicity may mean to Germany we cannot say, but among the neutrals and among ourselves the feeling that the official German statements about the battle are deliberately false has received confirmation. Germany, too, has placed herself in a hopeless position. After she has shown that she is ready to make reports read to her own advantage it will be impossible to convince outsiders that she is not still doing this.

The very reticence of the British official and semi-official communiqués is in itself gradually proving that the sea battle was all to our favour. After all, to take the German way of looking at

things—that is, the outlook that works out victory by means of tonnage—we can, with their own mathematics, place the victory very certainly on our side. The Germans say they won because— in official reports—they sank a greater number of tons than we did. The way we should look at it is not in tons lost, but in tons remaining—that is, tons which still have to be sunk. Even taking German reports as veracious as well as our own—that is, crediting the Germans with only eleven ships sunk instead of our estimate of eighteen—it is obvious that a process of attrition that loses eleven good vessels in order to sink fourteen of ours leaves the enemy very much on the debit side against our greater preponderance. In Italy the Austrian assault, though still vehement, has shown signs of slowing up in movement. The Russian advance, no less than the new Italian line of defence, appears to be taking the sting out of the enemy invasion. Affairs in Greece appear to be critical. There have, apparently, been some advance encounters with the Bulgarians, but nothing of definite nature. Politically the Allies appear to feel that they have come to the end of their patience with the Greek Government, and General Sarrail is handling matters firmly in Salonika. The surrender of Greek territory to the Bulgarians, too, has led the Allies to take precautionary measures. and a stringency verging on a blockade has been brought to bear on Greek ports. On their side the Greeks are said to have demobilised all but four of their classes. Whether this was done to placate the Allies is not positive. The situation is certainly unsettled, and developments may be interesting.

LONDON: JUNE 12, 1916.   W. DOUGLAS NEWTON.

"IRON DUKE",

30th May, 1916.

Dear Mrs. Quirk,

I am forwarding herewith a box of cigarettes for which you asked my in your letter of the 24th instant.

I trust that the "Fag Day" will be a very great success. One cannot do too much for the comfort and well-being of wounded soldiers and sailors who have done their all for the country.

Yours very truly,

ADMIRAL JELLICOE'S EVE-OF-BATTLE GIFT FOR THE WOUNDED : A LETTER SOLD FOR 17 GUINEAS FOR THE FUNDS OF "FAG DAY.
The letter is dated May 30. The battle began on May 31.
Photograph by News. Illustrations Co.

A SOUVENIR OF THE GREAT NAVAL BATTLE : FRAGMENTS OF A GERMAN SHELL WHICH LANDED ON A BRITISH SHIP BUT DID LITTLE DAMAGE.
Photograph by C.N.

Life-Belt Drill on Board a British Transport.

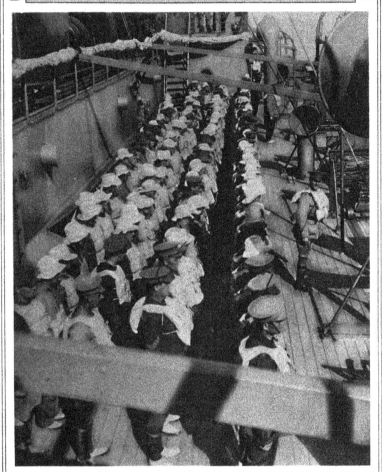

A WISE PRECAUTION, DESPITE OUR MASTERY OF THE SEA: TRAINING TROOPS TO BE READY.

Life-belt drill on board a British transport, as shewn here, is the regularly established custom at sea for all ships. A modified form of it has long been the usage on board passenger-ships of certain lines. It used to be a weekly practice on board the former-day Indian troop-ships (the "Serapis," "Malabar," etc.), in accordance with the naval custom, the Navy in those days "running" the troopers for the War Office. A canvas cover containing cork comprises the life-belt. Securely as Britain holds the command of the sea—more assuredly than ever now, since the battle off Jutland—accidents from collision, fire, incidentally (in war-time) from submarines—must occur from time to time, and the precautionary measure shown is only in the natural order of things. — [Photo. by C.N.]

Gilbert the Airman's Escape: His Arrival in Paris.

A LUCKY THIRD TRY: THE FAMOUS FRENCH AIRMAN GILBERT ON ESCAPING FROM INTERNMENT.

In the upper illustration Gilbert is seen in front, on the steps of a taxi in Paris, amidst a crowd of spectators. In the lower illustration he is seen wearing his decorations, after reporting himself at the War Ministry. Last summer Eugène Gilbert had made a successful bombing-raid on the Zeppelin building-sheds by Lake Constance, when machine trouble made him descend in Swiss territory. He was interned and first escaped last August; but, owing to a technical irregularity as to the time of giving back his parole, the French authorities sent him back. Last February he escaped again, disguised as an old woman, but was recaptured. Though watched night and day, he escaped the third time successfully on May 24.—[Photo. by C.N.]

The Price of Air Supremacy Paid by a British Airman.

HOW OUR ALLIES UNITE IN HONOURING OUR HEROES : AT THE FUNERAL OF ONE OF OUR AIRMEN.

A French escort of honour of infantry head the procession, marching in advance of the funeral car, which bears wreaths from British and French on the coffin and displays both the British and French flags. After the small band of mourners is seen, marching with arms reversed, the khaki-garbed party of British soldiers who, at the graveside, will form the firing-party for the three final volleys. The British airman whose funeral procession it is died in a hospital in a French town a little way in rear of the firing trenches, from the wounds that he had received in action with an enemy's airman. At all military funerals of British officers and men who die in hospital in France, our French allies jointly render the last honours.—[Photo. by C.N.]   .

Zeppelin "L 85" as a Warning and Trophy at Salonika.

SALVING THE WRECKAGE IN THE VARDAR MARSHES: SERBIAN SOLDIERS REMOVING BOMBS.

A French non-commissioned officer, and men of a Serbian fatigue-party who assisted, are seen in the upper illustration removing bombs from among the débris of Zeppelin "L 85," which was brought down by gun-fire of the war-ships in Salonika harbour on May 5. In the lower illustration, one of the Serbians is seen taking his mid-day siesta, the soldier's head pillowed on one bomb and with two others lying on the mud at either side of him. The Zeppelin fell in the marshes at the mouth of the Vardar a few miles to the west of Salonika, and was reduced to a tangled mass of steel girders and lattice-work. The Zeppelin was beaten off before the Germans had had time to drop most of their bombs, and these the Allies set to work to recover for conveyance to

[Continued opposite.

Zeppelin "L 85" as a Warning and Trophy at Salonika.

REBUILDING THE AIRSHIP'S FRAME ON A QUAY AT SALONIKA : ERECTING GIRDERS

[Continued.] Salonika, with the framework of the airship for setting up prominently as a trophy and object-lesson and warning to all whom it might concern. The illustration on this page shows the work of reconstruction in progress. It was taken in hand by French mechanics, the site selected for the rebuilding being at the side of one of the quays, in full view of the shipping in the harbour, on the open space round the White Tower of Salonika, the great central object of interest of the city. The wreckage of the aluminium framework of the Zeppelin was got up with considerable difficulty from the mud of the Vardar marshes and transported round to Salonika in barges.—[Press Bureau Photograph ; supplied by Central Press.]

THE BEGINNINGS OF WAR-MACHINES : SUBMARINE MINES.

THE first development of this form of attack took place about 1777, when David Bushnell, inventor of an early submarine-boat, constructed several ingenious contrivances for attacking the British Fleet blockading the American coast.

Fig. 1 shows a slight modification of one of this inventor's weapons. A wooden barrel or cask (b) was charged with gunpowder, after being coated with pitch to make it watertight. Conical ends (c c) built from light timber were attached to the ends of the barrel, and sensitive percussion fuses (f) screwed into the upper portion. The ends of these fuses projected sufficiently far to make contact with a ship's bottom if the vessel touched the mine when passing over it. The contrivance was moored to an anchor weight at the desired depth below the surface.

Fig. 2 illustrates a method of fixing a group of mines in a frame, for use in shallow waters, the mines themselves (m) being attached to the upper ends of a number of wooden beams whose lower ends rested on the river bottom and were made secure there. Several of such mines placed in échelon (Fig. 8) formed a very effective obstruction in a narrow waterway, and were extensively used as such in the American Civil War (1863). The mines of the device shown in Fig. 3 consisted of cast-iron cones with suitable "feet" for bolting down to the wooden beams, fired by a contact-fuse.

A submarine-mine designed by Robert Fulton is shown in Fig. 4., the mooring cable of which passed through an eyelet (e) in a 50-lb. weight, in order to maintain a horizontal pull on the anchor regardless of the swing of the mine under the influence of the tide (see broken lines). The explosive charge was contained in a hollow drum supported by cork floats attached to its sides. On the top of the drum was fixed a box containing

FIG. 8. — AN AMERICAN CIVIL WAR TYPE : FRAME MINES LAID ACROSS A CHANNEL.

the firing device, operated on the contact of an upstanding lever (l) with a ship's bottom. In the absence of any current, the mine floated vertically (v), but assumed a sloping position during other tide conditions (see arrows).

Fig. 5 shows a mine designed to resist destruction or removal by mine-sweepers. The explosive chamber of this contrivance was attached to the top end of a vertical stem (s), the lower end of which was secured to an anchor weight (w) by means of a "universal" joint, enabling the mine to oscillate freely in any direction. A length of cable (c) connected the anchor weight with the fuse of a second explosive chamber lying on the sea-bottom, called the "Devil Circumventor" (D C). If the trawl of a mine-sweeper came in contact with the stem of this mine the upper end of the latter was pulled over by the trawl until the cable slipped over it, and so freed itself. If the mine was observed and hauled to the surface, the fuse in the "Devil Circumventor" was pulled and an explosion occurred to damage the boat trying to remove the mine.

Fig. 6 shows Singer's Mechanical Mine, a sheet-metal conical explosive-chamber anchored to the sea-bottom, having a detachable weight (w) balanced on the top of it, connected with a firing device by means of a short length of cable (c). Contact with a passing vessel displaced the weight, which fired the mine during its fall by a pull on the cable. A safety-pin (p) received the pull instead of the fuse if the weight were displaced.

Fig. 7 shows a section of a cylindrical explosive-chamber with a firing-pin passing along its axis. The inner end of this firing-pin was dressed with fulminate, whilst its outer end was attached to drift-wood to foul the propeller of a passing vessel. The firing-pin being pulled, the mine exploded.

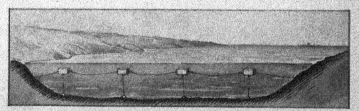

FIG. 9.—AN AMERICAN CIVIL WAR TYPE : SHALLOW CHANNEL "ANTI-GUN-BOAT" MINES.
A ship passing between the mines would foul the connecting-wire and draw the two adjacent mines against her bows, with a resulting explosion.

Beginnings of Modern War-Machines: Submarine Mines.

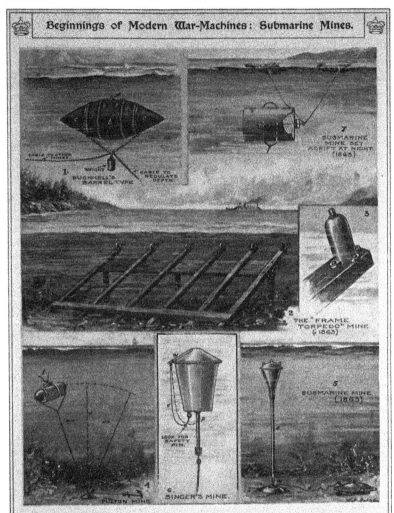

1. BUSHNELL'S BARREL TYPE. — CABLE TO OTHER MINES. WEIGHT. CABLE TO REGULATE DEPTH.

7. SUBMARINE MINE SET ADRIFT AT NIGHT. (1843)

3. THE "FRAME TORPEDO" MINE (1863)

5. SUBMARINE MINE (1863)

4. FULTON MINE.

6. SINGER'S MINE. LOOP FOR SAFETY PIN.

IN IDEA, SUGGESTING SOME MODERN TYPES: DEVELOPMENTS DURING NINETY YEARS.

A remarkably curious and instructive feature of certain of these illustrations—of the submarine-mine types that they show—is their general resemblance in regard to details of the appliances for exploding the mines to modern submarine-mine appliances. Particularly is this traceable in connection with some of the earlier anchored mines. The Bushnell type of a century and a-half ago, and the Fulton type of just over a hundred years ago, have, for example, strikers meant to detonate on being collided with, just like the "horns" of the modern mines which the Germans scatter broadcast. The German "linked mine" method can similarly be traced back directly to the American Civil War device of 1862, illustrated as Fig. 9 on the previous page.

The Australian Premier Sees His Own Men in France.

MR. HUGHES'S VISIT TO THE AUSTRALIANS IN FRANCE: THE INSPECTION AND MARCH-PAST.

The Prime Minister of the Australian Commonwealth, the Hon. W. M. Hughes, is seen in the upper illustration on the occasion of an inspection of the Australian troops in France held during his recent visit to the Commonwealth Contingent on the Western Front. He crossed to France in the last week of May. The Australian Premier, with members of the "Anzac" headquarters' staff, and other officers, is passing along the front of the line drawn up in review formation in open order, officers in front, on the parade ground, which was an orchard on the outskirts of a small town in Northern France. In the lower illustration one of the regiments of the contingent is seen marching past the Premier along the high road.—[Press Bureau Photograph; supplied by News. Illus.]

Lady Angela Forbes' Bath-House at the front.

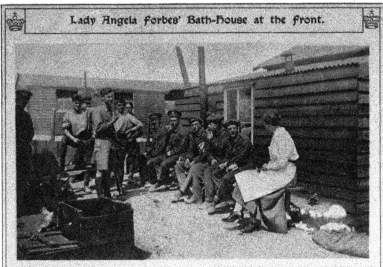

LADY ANGELA'S ENTERPRISE: AT HER BATH-HOUSE WITHIN SOUND OF THE GUNS.

Our first photograph shows Lady Angela Forbes sitting outside the bath-house in France, which is one of the various efforts to help our soldiers for which she is working, chatting cheerily with the men who are waiting their turn. Our second photograph also shows her talking to the soldiers, amongst whom is a lad so eager to do something for his country that he smuggled himself in with a draft although he is only fifteen. His zeal was appreciated, and some work has been found for him as a helper in the buffet. Lady Angela Forbes is a sister of Millicent, Duchess of Sutherland, and also of the Earl of Rosslyn, and is always a willing and energetic helper when any works of benevolence are to the fore, as in the case illustrated in our photographs.—[Photos. by C.N.]

ROMANCES OF THE REGIMENTS : No. I.—THE ROYAL ENGINEERS.

THE PARTING OF TWO FAMOUS SAPPERS.

THERE is a minor incident in the annals of the Royal Engineers, quite apart from the regiment's long and famous record of military exploits, which, although a quiet personal happening, is as romantic as any story of siege or assault. Although remembered, for the most part, only by specialists in military history, this event may claim a place among the world's famous partings, for it has in it that pathos and finality, touched with the sense of coming doom, which marks such scenes as the farewell of Hector and Andromache, or that last episode at Toledo Bridge, when the student-admirer of Cervantes took leave for ever of his dying master "the All-Famous and Joy of the Muses," and sadly turned aside to go round by the bridge leading to Segovia. Akin to such human documents is the parting of two illustrious Engineer officers, Graham and Gordon.

Colonel (afterwards Lieutenant-General) Sir Gerald Graham, and General Gordon were very old friends, comrades in the Crimea and in China. It was a curious chance, entirely in accordance with the eternal fitness of things, that the last glimpse of the hero of Khartoum, before he plunged into the desert from which he was never to return, should have been vouchsafed to a brother Sapper, whose sense of the picturesque significance of the moment

ONE OF OUR "ANZACS" ON THE WESTERN FRONT : EXPERIMENTING WITH A MODEL AEROPLANE CONSTRUCTED WHILE IN THE TRENCHES.
Official Press Bureau Photograph ; supplied by L.N.A.

enabled him to do it justice in a simple but adequate record. Graham, who had served with great distinction through the first Egyptian Campaign, was in Cairo, commanding an infantry brigade of the Army of Occupation, when Gordon came out on his mission to the Soudan in January 1884. During Gordon's brief halt in Cairo the two men saw as much of each other as possible, and when the time came for Gordon to push southward, Graham decided to see him on his way as far as Korosko.

The caravan set out about eight o'clock in the morning. Gordon mounted his camel and bade Graham "good-bye," but the latter,

reluctant to say the last word so soon, still walked on by his friend's side. Seeing this, Gordon dismounted, and for a time the two went on together on foot. Graham took minute notice of the accessories of the scene, and has left an account of details which add to its picturesqueness. At the head of the caravan rode a son of the Sheikh of Berber, armed with the great cross-hilted sword and the shield of rhinoceros hide familiar in pictures of Soudan warfare. Another son of the Sheikh's, Ahmed, a handsome young man, was similarly armed; and both the Arab brothers carried very old flint-lock double-barrelled pistols, the only weapons borne by the party, with the exception of Stewart's revolver. Gordon himself carried no arms, and the unwarlike equipment of the expedition was altogether in accordance with the spirit in which the chief had undertaken his mission on that evening at Charing Cross not long before, when, without ceremony and unobserved, he shook hands with the Duke of Connaught and stepped quietly into the train for Dover. Another unwarlike touch was shortly afterwards added to the incident, a touch almost serio-comic, and quaintly reminiscent of that cane which was Gordon's only weapon in the tightest places in China long ago. Just at the last moment, he presented Graham with a silver-mounted kourbash, the long, heavy Soudan riding-whip of hippopotamus hide : "Take it," he said ; "and say that it is a token that the reign of the kourbash in the Soudan is over."

Then, as if to emphasise his intention to carry into the Soudan not a sword, but peace, Gordon took, in exchange for the kourbash, Graham's umbrella ! He had lost his own. He had now remounted, and beside him rode young Ahmed, on a beautiful white camel. A little farther, and it was time for Graham to turn back.

He has left a careful account of the place where he last saw Gordon. It was wild and

[Continued overleaf.]

The Clergyman V.C. of the Great War on Leave.

FROM THE BATTLEFIELD OF ST. ELOI TO ST. PAUL'S, DEPTFORD : THE REV. E. N. MELLISH, V.C.

It was on Easter Monday that the General Officer Commanding the Division to which the Rev. Edward Noel Mellish is attached, pinned upon his breast the ribbon of the Victoria Cross, awarded for his courage and devotion in succouring the wounded at St. Eloi. On June 4 the brave curate of St. Paul's, Deptford, returned to his church on leave ; and our photograph shows him the following morning at St. Paul's, where he conducted a special children's service. Mr. Mellish is more than six feet in height and very popular, especially with children, to whom he is notably gentle. He has seen both service and adventure in South Africa, where he was in Baden-Powell's Police, and served in the South African War.—[Photo. by Illustrations Bureau.]

desolate, amid desert covered with a series of volcanic hills. Scott, Stewart's aide-de-camp, compared it to a miniature Switzerland. But Graham noted the incompleteness of that comparison, for there, he wrote, were no fertile valleys, no bright sun-clad peaks, no thriving population—nothing between the hills but black basins, or ravines, dry, dark and desolate of all vegetation, looking like separate entrances to the pit, where those who entered might leave hope behind. The forbidding features of the region accorded well with Graham's mood at the moment, and drove his thoughts back to Hicks Pasha with his doomed army coming into such a ravine after forty days in the wilderness, utterly spent and worn out, only to find the dark crests of the surrounding heights lined with a fierce, exultant enemy.

Still unwilling to lose sight of his friend, Graham climbed the highest of the hills with Scott, and through a glass watched Gordon and the little caravan, as his camels threaded their way along a sandy valley. "I watched, hoping that he would turn round, so that I might give him one more

sign; but he rode on until he turned the dark side of one of the hills and I saw him no more. Sadly we returned to our steamer, and I felt a gloomy foreboding that I should never see Gordon again."

Graham's intuition was right. It was his everlasting regret that he did not on his own responsibility send troops to Berber, to relieve the pressure on Khartoum, as he could have done after Tamai. But the Government vetoed his request for permission to advance. "Though not allowed," Graham writes, " the honour of being Gordon's deliverer, though sorrowing with all England, with the added grief of one who has lost a dear friend, it is yet some consolation to me to know that Gordon, in the midst of his bitter reflections when alone at Khartoum, acquitted me, and the gallant little force I had the honour to command, of all unreadiness or disinclination to advance to his rescue." In a triple sense Khartoum is a Sapper's romance, for it was another great Sapper who, years later, retook the town, avenged Gordon, and true to Gordon's spirit, gave him a memorial after his own heart—the college that bears his name.

WITH OUR MEN IN MESOPOTAMIA : AN AFTERNOON'S OFF-DUTY RIVER-OUTING IN A "BELLUM."

Bellum " is the local name on the Shatt-el-Arab, in Lower Mesopotamia, for the commonest type of native paddling craft. As seen here, it has amidships much the same "tippy" look as has a Thames Canadian canoe; with ends that seem vaguely suggestive of a Venetian gondola.—[Photo. by C.N.]

WITH THE ROYAL FLYING CORPS IN MESOPOTAMIA : ARAB COOLIES CARRYING-IN AN AEROPLANE WING-FRAME FOR REPAIRS.

For the necessary fetching and carrying between the hangars and the British mechanics' repairing-shops, or sheds, hired Arabs from the villages are employed as coolies to save our men from unnecessary toil and fatigue. They have hard enough work as it is.--[Photo. by C.N.]

Mourning for Lord Kitchener: Changing the Guard.

"OFFICERS ARE TO WEAR CRAPE ON THE LEFT ARM": AT BUCKINGHAM PALACE, JUNE 7, 1916.

On June 6 an Army Order was issued in the following terms: "Death of Lord Kitchener—Orders for Mourning. His Majesty the King commands that Officers of the Army shall wear mourning with their uniforms on the melancholy occasion of the death of the late Field-Marshal the Right Honourable H. H. Earl Kitchener of Khartoum, K.G., K.P., G.C.B., O.M., G.C.S.I., G.C.M.G., G.C.I.E.,

Colonel Commandant Royal Engineers, Colonel Irish Guards, Secretary of State for War, for a period of one week commencing 7th day of June, 1916. Officers are to wear crape on the left arm of the uniform and of the great-coat. By Command of the Army Council, R. H. Brade." Our photograph shows officers when changing guard at Buckingham Palace on June 7.—[Photo. by Topical.]

Lord Kitchener's Country Seat, Broome Park, Kent.

WHERE LORD KITCHENER ENTERTAINED WOUNDED SOLDIERS: THE MAIN APPROACH TO THE HOUSE.

Broome Park, Lord Kitchener's country seat, is a Kentish mansion at Denton, about midway between Canterbury and Folkestone. Lord Kitchener purchased the property some five years ago, and had spent a considerable sum on its restoration and renovation. Whenever he had a brief interval off duty from the toil of White-hall, since the war began, he liked to go down to Broome Park, where on several occasions he received parties of wounded soldiers, mostly from Folkestone. He took special pains to make the men feel at home, and proved an ideal host. Only a few days before leaving England for the last time, Lord Kitchener entertained a large party of wounded soldiers with nurses, and was photographed among them.—[Photos. by S. and G. and G.P.U.]

The Last Photograph taken of Lord Kitchener.

LORD KITCHENER'S LAST LONDON APPEARANCE: GOING TO MEET M.P.'S AT WESTMINSTER.

This is the last photograph taken of Lord Kitchener while in London. It was taken on June 2, the day on which Lord Kitchener met, by a special arrangement, a number (about two hundred) of Members of Parliament desirous of information it was not in the public interest to discuss publicly in the House of Commons. In the words of the brief officially issued report, he "made a statement reviewing certain aspects of the war, and replying to certain criticisms of Army administration. Subsequently he answered a number of questions put to him." Within a few hours of the unprecedented gathering, he had left London, with his personal staff, and was on his way to take ship for Russia on board the cruiser "Hampshire."—[*Photo. Farringdon Photo. Co.*]

d by the Nation and her Allies : Lord Kitchener

FIELD-MARSHAL EARL KITCHENER OF KHARTOUM AND OF BROOME: BORN, JUNE 24, 1850; DIED, JUNE 5, 1916.

Field-Marshal Horatio Herbert Kitchener, K.G., P.C., O.M., etc., first Earl Kitchener of Khartoum and of Broome, was son of the late Lieut.-Colonel Henry Horatio Kitchener (13th Dragoons), of Cossington, Leicester. He was born on June 24, 1850, educated at the Royal Military Academy, Woolwich, and entered the Royal Engineers, 1871. He served in the Soudan Campaign, 1883-5; at Handoub, 1888 (severely wounded); Dongola Expedition, 1896; Nile Expedition, 1897-8; Soudan Campaign, 1898 (Khedive's medal, with five clasps, peerage, G.C.B., specially thanked by both Houses of Parliament, granted £30,000); and in S. Africa, 1899-1902, first as Chief of the Staff, and subsequently as Commander-in-Chief (thanked by Parliament, promoted General, created Viscount, granted £50,000), and acted as High Commissioner of S. Africa and Administrator of Transvaal and of Orange River Colony, 1901; was A.D.C. to Queen Victoria, 1888-96; Sirdar of Egyptian Army, 1892-99; Governor-General of the Soudan, 1899, and Commander-in-Chief in India, 1902-9; Agent and Consul-General in Egypt, 1911, and Secretary of State for War, 1914.

Lord Kitchener's Dardanelles Visit of Inspection.

THE BRITISH WAR MINISTER'S CRITICAL EXAMINATION : AT EACH END OF THE POSITION.

In the upper of these illustrations Lord Kitchener is seen, during his tour of inspection to the Dardanelles, visiting the interior of Fort Sedd-ul-Bahr, one of the Gallipoli Peninsula forts guarding the entrance to the Straits, which was taken during an early naval bombardment. Marks of the British shells may be observed on some of the fort buildings. In the lower illustration, Lord Kitchener (the second from the right) is seen in one of the advanced trenches on the side of Anzac and Suvla Bay. The War Minister's visit, it will be remembered, was specially undertaken with the object of obtaining first-hand information as to the actual conditions on Gallipoli, and the evacuation was decided on by the Cabinet on Lord Kitchener's return.—[Photos. by C.N.]

Lord Kitchener and the Allies—France.

BRITISH WAR MINISTER AND FRENCH GENERALISSIMO: LORD KITCHENER AND GENERAL JOFFRE.

Lord Kitchener is seen, on the occasion of General Joffre's visit to London last October, leaving the War Office with his distinguished guest. After the war began, Lord Kitchener paid at least five visits to the French front, and saw the Commander-in-Chief of the Allies, both there and in Paris, and also at Calais. With General Joffre, he inspected one of the French Armies; also some of our troops in France, and jointly reviewed troops of all arms of both Armies. It was at General Joffre's hands also that Lord Kitchener received the prized decoration of the French war medal of 1870, specially awarded him for his service as a Volunteer in France with Chanzy's Gardes Mobiles. Frank cordiality existed between Lord Kitchener and General Joffre.—*[Photo. by Newspaper Illustrations.]*

Lord Kitchener and the Allies—Italy.

THE BRITISH WAR MINISTER AND THE ITALIAN GENERALISSIMO: KITCHENER AND CADORNA.

Lord Kitchener is seen here at his meeting in London with General Cadorna, the leader of the Italian Armies, which took place last March. It was their second meeting during the war. The first was at the time of Lord Kitchener's visit of inspection to the Dardanelles. On his way back to England, he paid a visit to the Italian Army, and, after being met by General Cadorna in Rome, accompanied him on a tour of inspection along portions of the Italian front. On a third occasion, at one of the general War Councils of the Allied Commanders and War Ministers held in France, Lord Kitchener and General Cadorna also met. On other occasions Lord Kitchener held counsel with the Italian War Council delegate, General Porro.—[Photo. by S. and G.]

Lord Kitchener with the Allies—Russia.

IN LONDON : LORD KITCHENER INSPECTING THE RUSSIAN CONTINGENT ON SPECIAL DUTY HERE.

In this photograph Lord Kitchener is seen holding his inspection in London of the men of the contingent of Russian soldiers who some weeks ago came to England in connection, it was stated, with certain munitions arrangements. It was while on his way to visit the Russian Army Headquarters on a "special mission to the Emperor of Russia," as the King's message to the Army states, and at the particular invitation, it is also said, of the Emperor Nicholas, that Lord Kitchener met his death in the disaster to the cruiser "Hampshire." Both in London and in Paris during the past six months, Lord Kitchener met the Russian special delegate to the War Council of the Allies, General Jilinski, one of the Heads of the Imperial General Staff.—[*Photo. by C.N.*]

THINGS DONE : I.—THE ROYAL HORSE AND FIELD ARTILLERY.

A WISE and fearless man can, even now, divide the functions of the Royal Regiment of Artillery into two groups, though it must be confessed that, in the time before war went to earth and stayed there, one felt easier and less daring in insisting upon the fact that artillery was light and mobile, as well as heavy and more or less fixed in position. However, even to-day, when strange and censored guns and groupings are making their appearances in the *culs-de-sac* of war, the laws that govern the administration of Army groups help us, and we can say, with the War Office behind us, that the Royal Regiment is separated into two corps—the Horse and Field (the light and mobile) and the Garrison Artillery, which is the slow and heavy. In the latter grouping might be included the Howitzer Batteries, though, until war came to confuse us, these were usually brigaded with the Field. To place trench-mortars, bomb-throwers, and aerial-torpedo casters must be left to the military historian of the future. He is sure to be a fellow heroic in his attack on knotty problems. Of the Royal Regiment, the corps of Horse and Field gunners takes the pride of place. They do this not merely

ONE OF THE GUNS FOR WHICH MUNITION-WORKERS ARE ASKED TO DO THEIR BEST; A HEAVY BRITISH HOWITZER IN ACTION ON THE WESTERN FRONT; WITH ITS SHELLS AND CARTRIDGES IN REAR.

Press Bureau Photograph; supplied by Central Press.

because one of the branches—the Royal Horse—has won for itself the honour of the first in precedence, "The Right of Line," but because in those times when war is reasonable they are inevitably into the battle with the first of the fighting.

The characteristic of the Horse and Field Artillery is mobility, and of the Horse Artillery itself an even greater mobility. With moving troops, cavalry and infantry, the office of the R.H.A. is to march with the cavalry. Wherever a horseman can go, the R.H.A. is expected to go—and, also, it goes. Over rough ground or smooth ground, with flying reconnaissance or rapid turning movement, the Horse gunners ride to give the squadrons their moral and metallic support. It is the same in retirement. Where the swifter, more fluent cavalry are used to cover retreat, the R.H.A. remain to cover all.

To this end the R.H.A. is built light. It has six guns to a battery, as the R.F.A.; but its gun is lighter than the R.F.A. 18-pounder gun, for it is a 13-pounder, and the weight of the piece is 3 cwt.

ANOTHER OF OUR HEAVY HOWITZERS DOING ITS "BIT" ON THE WESTERN FRONT; THE ARRIVAL OF SHELLS BY TRENCH-RAILWAY.

Press Bureau Photograph; supplied by Central Press.

lighter than the 9 cwt. of the R.F.A. Also it mounts all its men, and does not carry them on the limbers. Some people seem to think that the

[Continued overleaf.]

Switzerland's Welcome to Exchanged British Prisoners.

OVERWHELMED WITH KINDNESS : THE FIRST TRAIN WITH EXCHANGED BRITISH PRISONERS AT ZÜRICH.

Both these photographs were taken in the station at Zürich, during the half-hour's halt of the first train bringing exchanged British prisoners of war from Germany to be interned in Switzerland. In our last number, it may be recalled, we gave a photograph of their place of internment, Château d'Oex, near Montreux. From the moment of their arrival on Swiss territory the train-load of disabled British soldiers and sailors received a most hearty and generous welcome. At Zürich, and at every other station where they halted, presents of flowers, cigars and cigarettes, sweets, papers, and so on, were showered upon them. It was a triumphal progress, and our men were deeply touched by the kindness of the Swiss people, which was beyond anything they had expected.—[Photos. by Alof.]

fact that the R.H.A. does not carry gunners on the limbers is the chief difference between Horse and Field batteries. This is not quite the truth. The difference lies in the fact that the R.H.A. cannot afford to risk carrying gunners on the limbers. Watch the corps charging headlong, teams stretching, traces taut (as is the resolute

WORK THEY FOUND ALMOST IMPOSSIBLE ON THE ROCK-BOUND PLATEAU OF GALLIPOLI : AUSTRALIAN PIONEERS FILLING SANDBAGS IN REAR OF THE TRENCHES ON THE WESTERN FRONT.

Press Bureau Photograph ; supplied by Central Press.

etiquette), and guns bumping along behind like toys over ground that would ruin the constitution of a dray, and the point of this will be realised at once.

The Royal Field Artillery is more leisurely, but still swift. The R.F.A. conforms to the movement of armies rather than outposts, yet a high degree of movement is required of it. It must be well up in the first moments of the engagement. It must be ready to move swiftly, so as to concentrate upon given points of the fight ; it must be as ready to race off to strengthen a flanking thrust as to meet unexpected pressure at a distant part of the field. It must go into battle close up to the line of assaulting battalions, and keep on moving up with those battalions through all the stages of advance. It must be as ready to fall back as the most swiftly retiring ranks of infantry.

The special functions of this horsed and mobile artillery gives it special methods and special means of striking. Its objects and ambitions do not lie in the direction of battering fortresses—or even, if it can help itself, smashing trenches—for that is the object of the " Heavies," but in

smashing the ranks of the enemy facing it—that is, killing men. Therefore its natural means of striking is a man-killing shell, a shrapnel shell. Both Horse and Field guns use shrapnel almost exclusively, and they use it against regiments rather than against placements. Shrapnel is a shell which, bursting at a given range, drives from three to four hundred bullets into an enemy gathered in mass. These shells, with their hundreds of potential deaths, are fired against the enemy when his ranks are holding firm and his resistance must be broken, or when his ranks are coming on strongly either to reinforce or to attack and must be checked. The shells are also fired to support our own infantry in defence by keeping down the energy either of the opposing infantry or of opposing gunners, and also to support our own infantry attacks by breaking down the opposition and weakening any possible resistance to an effective charge. The best work of the Horse and Field Artillery is thus done against troops in the open, but they also do good service against troops under cover, either by keeping them pinned down to their lines, or by spreading a zone of shrapnel behind the lines and preventing supports from coming up, or by firing on moving trains, convoys, parked *matériel*—guns, munitions, food stuff—

READY AT A MOMENT'S NOTICE TO FALL IN AND MAN THE PARAPETS : AUSTRALIANS OFF DUTY IN A SAND-BAG-BUILT TRENCH IN FLANDERS.

Press Bureau Photograph ; supplied by Central Press.

marching troops, or anything else that would, but for them, be used in action against us. But primarily they are the friends, comrades, and protectors of mobile troops.—W. DOUGLAS NEWTON.

Battle-Scars from the Great Sea-fight.

AFTER THE GREAT NAVAL BATTLE OFF JUTLAND : MARKS OF GERMAN SHELLS ON BRITISH WAR-SHIPS.

The upper photograph shows the battle-scarred side of a British war-ship which took part in the great sea-fight. The shell-hole on the left is seen stopped up with bedding. An enlarged view of this shell-hole is given on another page in this number. The lower photograph shows the mast and upper works of a British war-ship also damaged. All the British battle-cruisers which emerged from the encounter, it is said, bear marks of the enemy's shot, but the damage was comparatively slight in view of the fact that the heaviest guns in the German Navy had been turned on them for hours in overwhelming force. It appears certain, on the other hand, that the German ships suffered very heavily from our fire, apart from those which were actually sunk.—[Photos. by C.N.]

Marks of the Great Battle on British War-Ships.

BRITISH WAR-SHIPS SCARRED IN THE GREAT NAVAL BATTLE: SHOT-HOLES AND DÉBRIS ON DECK.

The upper photograph shows the deck of a British war-ship which participated in the great naval battle. Among other signs of conflict may be noted a tank riddled with shot. In the lower photograph is seen a heap of débris, also on the deck of a British ship that fought in the action. As some of our other photographs show, bedding was used to stop up shell-holes torn in the sides of our ships. The general consensus of naval opinion, as expressed in public, seems to make it certain that those enemy ships which survived the battle suffered more heavily than our own. One gunnery officer has compared their plight to that of "a pugilist leaving the ring with both eyes closed, his nose broken, and the wind knocked out of him."—[Photos. by C.N.]

A War-Ship's Wound "Dressed" with Bedding.

"WOUNDED" IN THE GREAT NAVAL BATTLE: A GERMAN SHELL-HOLE IN A BRITISH WAR-SHIP'S SIDE.

When a shell penetrates the side of a war-ship, the hole is usually stopped up with mats or shot-plugs, or anything that is handy. In the present case a pile of bedding has been used for the purpose. Another photograph in this number shows the position of this particular shell-hole on the side of the ship. It was above the water-line, and was therefore the less dangerous. The stopping-up of holes torn by shells or otherwise at or below the water-line is, of course, a matter of much greater importance. For below-water injuries "collision mats" are provided. In spite of some damage, the British Fleet was ready to put to sea again the day after the battle. Admiral Beatty has said : "The Battle-Cruiser Fleet is alive, and has got a very big kick in her."—[Photo. by C.N.]

At the Camp of the Russians in France.

A RED-LETTER DAY FOR THE EASTERN ALLY: M. POINCARÉ'S REVIEW—NEWLY UNIFORMED RUSSIANS.

In the upper illustration on this page, President Poincaré is seen arriving to hold a review at the camp of the Russian Contingent in France, which is within easy distance of the Front. The President is the figure on the dais at the saluting-point nearest (left) to the standard-pole. A Russian General is also seen in the photograph. In the lower illustration are Russian soldiers in the new Western Front uniform and fighting-kit which has been served out to them since their arrival in France. The new equipment differs in details from the field uniform worn by the regiments of the armies on the Eastern Front. Steel helmets of the French pattern have been supplied to the Russians, and they are now armed with the French Lebel rifle in place of their own

[Continued opposite.

The New Fighting Kit of the Russians in France.

WITH FRENCH HELMET AND LEBEL RIFLE, LIKE THE FRENCH: A RUSSIAN PRIVATE.

Continued.]

service weapon, a common-sense measure adopted owing to the difference in calibre between the rifles of the French and Russian Armies, to prevent any shortage of ammunition when the Russians in France come into action. As seen in the illustration of a private in marching order on this page, the Russians continue to carry their great-coats en bandorole, according to the Russian Army usage, over short blouse-jackets fastened after the Russian way with hooks and eyes, and wear French Army gaiters in place of the Russian knee-boot, also for practical reasons. The Russian soldiers on the French front will, no doubt, fight all the better for hearing of the splendid victory won by their comrades in the east over the Austrians in Galicia.—*[Photos. by Illus. Bureau.]*

WOMEN AND THE WAR.

"THE women are splendid," said Mr. Lloyd George some time ago. As if women did not know that before. They are not surprised, though a great many men seem to be, that the hand that uses the powder-puff can also help to rule the world—or at least to help England at her task in preventing Germany ruling it — and there is ample testimony to the value of women's services in this direction. Seriously, it is not altogether a compliment, this perpetual astonishment of the male publicist that the women should have proved themselves worth their salt in the great emergency of the war.

It is the object of these articles to sketch the activities of women in various directions connected with the great struggle. The full story must be left till later. When it is told it will astonish England—and Germany too. For Germany made not the least coarse of her mistakes when she imagined that because Englishwomen were not dull, fat, and housewifey in and out of season, like the German frau, they are merely frivolous and giddy. We do not know what Fräulein Schmidt and Frau Schultz are doing. Their best, no doubt. But one may be sure it is a dull, uninventive, routine sort of best as compared with the energetic and creative work of Englishwomen.

We are always being accused of a want of system in our everyday conduct of affairs. A notion was current at one time that women were wanting in initiative and organising

THE GREAT "WAR FAIR" AT THE CALEDONIAN MARKET, JUNE 6 AND 7 : MRS. JOHN ASTOR SELLS ANTIQUES FOR THE WOUNDED.
Photograph by Newspaper Illustrations.

ability. That notion has been dispelled by the events of the war. The frivolities in which women engaged in pre-war days, the freakish entertainments to which they gave their patronage, their presence at what were once considered essentially masculine entertainments, were amongst the arguments advanced by the undiscerning to prove that they were incapable of sustained effort in serious work. The truth was, of course, that the gay, pleasure - loving Englishwoman of two years ago was no more indifferent to the interests of her country than Drake when he played bowls at Plymouth with the Spanish Armada sailing to destroy our Fleet.

Everybody knows that it is not the woman of society, but the lady's maid, who grumbles most and is most helpless in a wreck or siege. It is, indeed, just the joy of life, the freedom of thought and action that she has enjoyed, that makes the Englishwoman so adaptable ; and when the great crisis came on Aug. 4, 1914, she was able at once to throw aside frivolity and devote herself without reserve to the service of her country.

Women knew directly war was declared that their services would be required in capacities other than those of a nurse, though no one had any idea of the extent to which they would be employed in the national interest. They were not idle long. Within two days of the declaration of war the Women's Emergency Corps came into being, with the object of organising

THE GREAT "WAR FAIR" AT THE CALEDONIAN MARKET, JUNE 6 AND 7 : LADY MARKHAM, WHO HAD 20,000 TONS OF COAL TO SELL FOR THE WOUNDED.
Lady Markham is the wife of Sir Arthur Markham, M.P. for the Mansfield Division of Notts, the Member who "wants to know."—[Photo. by Newspaper Illustrations.]

[Continued overleaf.

A Caledonian Market for the Wounded Allies.

BOUQUETS AND BENEVOLENCE: HOW LADIES PLAYED THE FLOWER-GIRL FOR THE WOUNDED.

Our first photograph shows a picturesque group of helpers (with coster's barrow) at the great so-called "Jumble Sale," held at the Caledonian Market, Islington, on Tuesday and Wednesday, June 6 and 7, to swell the funds of the Wounded Allies' Relief Committee, when thousands of things were offered for sale, from jewellery and antiques, autographed books and objets d'art, to bouquets and buttonholes, motor-cars and tons of coal. Nothing was too great, nothing too small, to play its part in helping the funds for the Wounded Allies, the attendance was enormous, and the results should prove in the highest degree satisfactory. The "Fair" was a clever idea. Our second picture is of a charming group of amateur flower-sellers.—[Photos. by C.N.]

women's help to deal effectively with whatever emergencies might arise, and to co-operate with the authorities in any way that might be desired.

Millicent Duchess of Sutherland, the Duchess of Marlborough, the Marchioness of Londonderry,

WOMEN'S WORK FOR THE WAR: LORD KITCHENER'S SISTER AND THE SIGNALLERS CORPS.

Lord Kitchener's sister, Mrs. Parker, has from the first shown keen interest in various forms of war-work undertaken by women, and our photograph shows her at an inspection of that useful body, the Women Signallers Corps.—[Photo. by Photopress.]

the Countess of Essex, and the Countess of Selborne were a few of the many leaders of Society whose names were connected with the enterprise. Women of all classes flocked to enroll their names in the nation's army of helpers. Within two weeks the corps dealt with over ten thousand offers of personal service from volunteers ready to serve as doctors, dispensers, trained nurses, interpreters, chauffeurs, gardeners, tram and omnibus conductors, lift-attendants, and in various other capacities. This early list is particularly interesting now when "Woman's Sphere" is being enlarged in every direction at the express invitation of many who two years ago would have been the first to oppose their employment.

The first business of the Corps, having enrolled the workers, was to bring them into touch with agencies through which their services could be used to the best advantage, for it was no part of the organisation's plan to overlap with existing institutions, but rather to co-operate with them in every possible way.

New schemes were devised to meet emergencies outside the scope of normal peace machinery. Work-rooms were opened to help unemployed women. The knitting department opened soon after the outbreak of war expanded quickly. Toy-making employed others; the National Guild of Housecraft gave training in domestic work.

The influx of Belgian refugees gave an opportunity of which the Corps took full advantage. Interpreters met the unfortunate victims of German barbarity, armed with lists of lodgings and offers of free hospitality. The clothing department supplied necessary garments, the kitchen section the requisite food. These were but a few of the activities of the W.E.C., numerous branches of which were started in the United Kingdom.

Later, initial emergencies having been dealt with, changes in organisation were made. Schemes that had served their turn were "scrapped," others developed into independent institutions. The work, however, is still going on. The Corps remains true to its original idea of being ready

FRENCHWOMEN WORKING FOR SOLDIERS AT THE FRONT: RED CROSS HELPERS.

Our photograph shows a scene to be found in many parts of France, of constant and patient workers for the Red Cross, who help to keep up the immense store of necessaries for the use of the wounded.

to meet any emergency, and women of leisure are invited to enroll in the Handy Women's department. It is impossible in a single article to do justice to the services rendered by this body.   CLAUDINE CLEAVE.

The Funeral of Lord Kitchener's Secretary—Col. FitzGerald.

THE CORTÈGE, HEALED BY A BAND OF WOUNDED, PASSING THROUGH EASTBOURNE.

Our first photograph shows the coffin being conveyed from Eastbourne station to All Saints' Church, where the first service was held, before the procession made its way to Ocklynge Cemetery, where the interment took place, on Saturday last, with full military honours. Our second photograph shows the coffin, draped with the Union Jack, and followed by British representatives and the Attachés of the Allies. His Majesty the King was represented by Lieut.-Colonel Clive Wigram. Colonel FitzGerald was the personal military secretary of Lord Kitchener, and also a personal friend of the great soldier, with whom he was travelling to Russia on the "Hampshire" when that vessel struck a mine and went down off the Orkneys.—[Photos. by L.N.A.

Hospital - Ship Work after the North Sea Battle.

THE TRANSFER OF WOUNDED TO THE HOSPITAL-SHIPS: COMING ALONGSIDE; AND ON BOARD.

In the upper illustration wounded from the battle off Jutland are seen being transferred after the close of the fighting from ships in action to the hospital-ships. Auxiliary light craft took the men on board and, running alongside the hospital-ships, slung the cots up the side while men able to help themselves went on board. The upper deck of one of these, with bandaged men and cot-cases, is shown. In the lower illustration, a cheerful group of less seriously wounded, with members of the sick-berth staff, are seen on the upper deck of a hospital-ship. At daylight on Thursday (June 1), while the guns of the pursuing cruisers and destroyers could still be heard in the distance, the hospital-ships had begun taking in the wounded.—[Photos. by C.N.]

Heroic Defenders of Kut who are now in Safety.

SHOWING SIGNS OF PRIVATIONS: SICK AND WOUNDED FROM THE KUT GARRISON.

The first photograph shows "walking cases" assisted down the gangway by a line of helpers; the second shows a British soldier from Kut talking to friends on arriving in the British lines. The third photograph shows a file of Indian soldiers from Kut going on board a hospital-steamer at Basra en route for India. The War Office announced on May 10: "The fourth party of sick and wounded from Kut, consisting of 281, reached the Headquarters of the Tigris Corps on the evening of May 6, and the fifth party, consisting of 172, on the evening of May 7. The total number of sick and wounded evacuated from Kut in these five parties is 1073. The hospital-ship started for Kut again on the morning of May 8 to bring back the sixth and last party."—[Photos. by C.N.]

In the Canadian Lines, Close Up at the Front.

NEAR YPRES, WHERE THE CANADIANS FOUGHT . A CAMP THOROUGHFARE ; AND THE KITCHEN.

Two camp scenes in Flanders, where some of the Canadians are quartered, close up against the fighting-line at Ypres, are seen above. The upper photograph shows a camp thoroughfare with men off duty. The second shows a section of the lines where the mobile field-kitchen cookers, which accompany the troops on the march and do cooking for the men in camp, are ranged. The Canadians are " in the limelight " again in connection with the display of endurance they have been—and are still—making—at Ypres. It was in the great battle there, just a year ago, when the Germans first used poison gas, that the Canadian Contingent won its fame for intrepidity. It is adding to that fame by the stand at Ypres now.—[Canadian Official Photograph ; supplied by C.N.]

The Illustrated War News, June 21, 1916.—Part 2, New Series.

The Illustrated War News

LORD FRENCH REVIEWING VOLUNTEERS IN HYDE PARK: "EYES LEFT" AT THE SALUTING-BASE.

Photograph by L.N.A.

THE GREAT WAR.

By W. DOUGLAS NEWTON.

THE Russian victory, which is also an Austrian rout, continues without any perceptible sign of abatement in vigour. The first fine speed of the movement has become a trifle slower, but progress yet goes on steadily, and the determined success of the fighting is showing—if only in the enormous hauls of prisoners that are being brought in every day. At the time of writing these men captured number close upon 170,000, but the total increases so rapidly and so vastly that this might easily be a division or so out of verity by the time of publication.

These enormous captures seem to prove that the Russians have the Austrians completely out-manœuvred, and that only by the most speedy and extravagant tactics westward can they hope to save their forces from a complete disaster. It is probably true, also, that this counsel of swiftness has saved them in another way, for their retreat must have outstripped the movement of the Russian heavy artillery. The need for getting up the less mobile howitzers explains the apparent slackening—not of the advance, but of the swiftness of the advance. With the threat of being overpowered by the heavy shells removed — and the heaviness of the Russian shelling appears to have been remarkable— the enemy have been able to offer some resistance in rearguard actions, though even these actions have not prevailed against the advance.

The Russians in their thrust are employing the now well-recognised method of double-flanking attack. This was Foch's method at the Marne, and the habitual German method during the great Russian drive of last autumn. By breaching the enemy line at two points and driving resolutely forward, the centre position is threatened from above and below, and must give if the breaching strokes are carried onward with success. In this case the Russians are driving forward in the Lutsk area, and, on the southern flank, along the Pruth and Dniester. If both these movements are continued with power and victory, it will be found that the apparently strong defence of the enemy along the Strypa— that is, the defence which bars the direct road to Lemberg—will collapse, and the Russian centre will make an exceedingly rapid movement, bringing the front, perhaps, up to or beyond Lemberg itself. This movement will also imperil the enemy forces fighting in Bukovina, for, if the Austrians are not careful, they will be pinned against the Carpathians. To the north, the Germans—and particularly Prince Leopold of Bavaria's army, which holds this part of the line— will be in danger of a movement which will get behind their flank. The Russians, indeed, have already brought the Germans uneasiness, for the sureness of their movement has caused the enemy line to bend back at Kolki in order to keep in touch with Austrian forces forced towards Kovel.

The Russian advance here has been a mighty affair. A breach of thirty miles has been pushed to a depth of forty miles. In the direction of Kovel the pressure seems to be meeting

"THERE NEVER WAS A NOBLER ACT": THE MEMORIAL UNVEILED IN MEMORY OF ADMIRAL SIR CHRISTOPHER CRADOCK, IN YORK MINSTER.

The memorial to Rear-Admiral Sir Christopher Cradock—a native of Yorkshire, who with self-sacrificing heroism fought and died facing heavy odds in the battle off Coronel on November 1, 1914, was unveiled in York Minster, by the Marquess of Zetland, on June 16. Mr. Balfour, as First Lord of the Admiralty, with the First Sea Lord, attended the ceremony and delivered an address. In the course of it, Mr. Balfour said: "There never was a nobler act" than that Admiral Cradock performed.—[Photo. by Topical.]

resistance on the River Stokhod, but above this point the Russian line is swinging forward, and the defence may be turned from the direction of Kolki. Below the Stokhod the advance has gone on some thirty miles west of Lutzk, where the front is pressing towards the Bug. In the Czernovitz area the Russians, in spite of strong fighting by the enemy at Buczacz, are pushing well forward along the Dniester, and between the Dniester and the Pruth. The direct railway line between Czernóvitz and Lemberg was cut early in the week when our Ally took Sniatyn, and Czernovitz itself was hemmed on three sides and its suburbs the ground of battle from the beginning of this movement. Its fall was inevitable. The Russians have plenty of strategic points to aim at here, for the important junctions at Kolomea and Stanislau are delicate cogs in the machinery of defence, and the Austrian line is bound to react under threat to them. The fighting, however, must be hard and strenuous, for the steep banks of the Dniester give good footholds for defence, and for their lives the enemy must make good use of them.

Our Ally's wisdom in directing the main power of his attack against the weaker of the enemy partners, with the object of inaugurating a process of disintegration more surely, is made obvious both by facts and its success. The armour of the Central Powers is most vulnerable through Austria, and it has always been recognised that the death-wound might be struck through her. It is probable that the Germans will endeavour to create some diversion to save their Ally—and, indeed, they have already attempted something in their attacks on the northern front near Riga and at Kevo. Directly above the Russian point of advance the counter-irritant movements have been pushed heavily. At Baranovitchi, north of Pinsk, there has been a good deal of fluctuating fighting. Though it is difficult to know whether the initial move came from the Germans or our Ally, the Germans certainly appear to be fighting in strength, and to have made advances and captured prisoners. It is true this engagement may be a Russian manœuvre to pin down the enemy while Russians further south press on towards Kovel; but it is more likely that the Germans consider that pressure here would have a great effect on the position lower down, and are fighting to distract energy to themselves. German attempts should be hampered not only by the energy of the Russians, but by their own present distribution of reserves. The enemy has been caught —and deliberately caught—at a moment when his forces are heavily concentrated in distant spheres: before Verdun and our lines at Ypres, for example, and in front of the Italians in the Trentino. These things will not make the Austro-German defence of Galicia and Poland an easy and a happy affair.

Of the Verdun fighting a good tone is apparent. The Germans, with some pauses, have

A TRIBUTE TO GORDON'S AVENGER PLACED ON GORDON'S EFFIGY : THE MEMORIAL WREATH FOR LORD KITCHENER FROM THE WOMEN WORKERS OF THE WAR OFFICE.

This splendid wreath of laurel, lilies, and scarlet carnations, "a last tribute of respect and remembrance from the women workers' of the War Office," was placed appropriately on Gordon's effigy in St. Paul's on the occasion of the Memorial Service to Lord Kitchener.—[Photo. by Illustrations Bureau.]

THE GHOULISH EFFECT OF THE ANTI-GAS RESPIRATOR : A PARTY OF FRENCH ARTILLERYMEN MASKED AGAINST GERMAN POISON.

been hammering away at the defences in the Thiaumont area in the hope of pushing through by the Fleury Gap, and to this end their most determined assaults have been driven forward in the Caillette Woods above Fleury, and against Hill 321, which guards the left flank of the Thiaumont line. These attacks have been broken, and, more than this, the French have been able to counter and win elements of German works on Hill 321, these being held in spite of all Teutonic offensives. On the west bank of the Meuse the French also made some ground on the Mort Homme, and have held it in spite of attacks of most desperate nature all along this front. On the rest of the French line there has been considerable activity at many points—on the Somme, in the Champagne, in the Argonne, and in the Vosges. On the British front there are growing signs of energy. The Canadians have brilliantly regained all the lost ground south-east of Zillebeke. Following this, the enemy indulged his spirit in heavy bombardments, and on Friday endeavoured to force matters by sending forward two gas-clouds west of the Messines-Wytschaete ridge ; the clouds were ineffectual, and were not followed up by infantry assaults. Bombing, mining, and artillery work complete a tale of somewhat unusual activity, and, coupled with the hints thrown out by the usually laconic Paris reports, we have reason to view the general work

THE CANADIAN POSTMASTER-GENERAL'S WIFE : MME. CASGRAIN.

Mme. Casgrain, who has come on a short visit to France and England, has brought out a memoir of Madeleine de Verchères, with a frontis-piece by Princess Patricia, to be sold for the Red Cross. Copies may be obtained by sending subscriptions to Mme. Casgrain, c.o. the High Commissioner of Canada, 19, Victoria Street, S.W.—[Photo. by C.N.]

on the Western front with much interest and attention within the next few weeks.

The Austrian offensive in the Trentino has been engineered at a most unfortunate time. Already there are signs that the impulse of aggression has died—advances have stopped, and the Italians are working their way back over conquered ground about Asiago and in the Lagarina Valley. In Greece, artillery duels are reported between the Allies and the mystical troops — we cannot say whether they are Bulgars, Germans, or Austrians — opposing them. Greece itself is apparently a prey to mental uncertainty, accelerated

COMMANDING A BRITISH COLUMN WHICH RECENTLY ENTERED KERMAN, IN SOUTHERN PERSIA : BRIG.-GEN. SIR PERCY SYKES.

Sir Percy Sykes, author of a " History of Persia," was recently sent to organise a Military Police Force in Southern Persia, for the Persian Government, to rid the country of German and Turkish rebels. He and his troops were received most cordially at Kerman.—[Photo. by Elliott and Fry.]

by the determination of the Allies to handle the matter decisively. The shipping restrictions enforced by us are pressing heavily. A decisive success either in the East or the West will settle Grecian opinion once and for all.

General Smuts's steady campaign in German South-West Africa continues excellently. The force acting in the east of the colony has taken the town of Wilhemstal, the capital of Usambara ; and a column under Brigadier-General Hannyngton has done the same for Korogwe. This latter town is but forty miles from the port of Tanga, which is said to be clear of the enemy. The Belgians moving up from Lake Tanganyika have not merely taken Usumbara, the chief port on the lake, but have pushed inland over 120 miles. On Lake Victoria Nyanza the British have secured the island of Ukerewe, and two Krupp guns on it, and are now in a position to direct their threat against the port of Mwanza, on the mainland. In the Kilimanjaro district another British column is moving in strength against the Germans entrenched about the water supply at Handeni.

On the sea there has been little to note. The British destroyer Eden was sunk in collision in the Channel, and most of her crew, apparently, lost. In the Baltic, on the other hand, a German convoy was attacked and roughly handled by a Russian flotilla ; several ships were sunk.

LONDON: JUNE 19, 1916.

Vaux Church, Wrecked in the Battle of Verdun.

NEAR VAUX FORT, CAPTURED BY THE GERMANS AFTER BOMBARDMENT: RUINS OF VAUX CHURCH.

The village of Vaux, which lies about half a mile north of the Fort, has been laid in ruins during the terrific struggle round that part of the defences of Verdun. A French communiqué of June 8 announced that "after seven days' desperate fighting against assaulting troops renewed incessantly, the garrison of the Fort of Vaux, which had reached the limit of its strength, was unable to prevent the enemy from occupying the work, which had been completely ruined by furious bombardment." The Fort had withstood direct attack for ninety days, and on it, latterly, had been concentrated an immense weight and volume of artillery fire. The Vaux position was not vital, and the losses sustained by the Germans there were altogether incommensurate with the gain.—[Photo. C.N.]

British Wounded Happy in a Playground of Europe.

OUR EXCHANGED PRISONERS FROM GERMANY TRANSFERRED TO SWITZERLAND : AT CHÂTEAU D'OEX.

The first photograph shows a party of British wounded in Switzerland off for a trip on a mountain railway. In the second a British soldier, of an industrious turn of mind, is seen helping two Swiss women with their washing in a public square. The change from a German prison camp and its attendant miseries to the delightful hospitality of Switzerland has seemed, to the men lucky enough to be chosen, like passing into Paradise from a region less alluring. The second convoy of wounded British soldiers from Germany arrived at Château d'Oex, near Montreux, on the Lake of Geneva, about twenty-four hours after the first ; and from the moment of crossing the frontier of Switzerland they received a no less hearty welcome.—[Photos. by Sport and General.]

With the Heroic Canadians on the Western Front.

MEN OF AN ARMY ONCE MORE FIGHTING MAGNIFICENTLY NEAR YPRES : CANADIANS IN RESERVE.

The first photograph shows a Winnipeg battalion held in reserve near the Western front ; the second a Canadian soldier in charge of a field post-office. In the new battle of Ypres, which began on June 2, the Canadian troops have again shown the same magnificent heroism as when they withstood the first German attacks with poison-gas, and thus saved the Allied line. In the recent fighting, it is said, not only the men in the advance trenches, but even those in the wooded positions behind, came under a terrific bombardment from the German artillery. They had their revenge, however, in their "gallant and successful assault" near Zillebeke, where they captured a position and took 123 German prisoners.—[Canadian Official Photos. ; supplied by C.N. Crown Copyright reserved.]

The Loyalty of France's West African Mahomedans.

AT BONDOUKOU, CAPITAL OF THE "IVORY COAST": THE COLLECTING BOOTH ON "POILUS' DAY."

This illustration affords a useful glimpse behind the scenes of war in an out-of-the-way part of the world—evidence of the sterling loyalty to France of the Mahomedan peoples in French colonial possessions. Bondoukou, where the photograph was taken, is the capital of the French West African colony, the "Ivory Coast." The vast Mahomedan population of the region, which adjoins and forms part of the French Soudan territory, have subscribed liberally ever since the war began to aid the French Army's sick and wounded. They also raised a contingent of "tirailleurs." Bondoukou itself had a special "Soldiers' Day," "La Journée du Poilu." The living representation of the poster by Poulbot, as arranged outside the collection booth, is seen above.

Shelled and Stormed : In a Captured German Trench.

ARTILLERY WORK COMPLETED WITH THE BAYONET : FRENCH VICTORS AFTER AN ASSAULT.

A realistic idea of the scene of chaotic disruption and havoc that a trench presents after having been subjected to a protracted shelling and then taken by storm is afforded by this illustration. It is a photograph of one of the German trenches, in a locality that has to be nameless just at present, immediately after the victorious French in the neighbourhood had overwhelmed the section with continuous salvos of high-explosive shells, and then followed up the artillery devastation by charging in among the battered and shapeless ridges and mounds of earth, to seize and occupy the position. Everywhere the surface of the ground is seen to be littered with torn and tangled wire, broken stumps, German rifles, clothing and accoutrements.—[Photo. by Alfieri.]

whose name history records as the — father — of — torpedo —

steam propulsion for marine work, came over from America with the object of persuading the British Government to adopt one or other of his schemes for blowing up enemy vessels by means of explosives applied to their bottoms. To demonstrate the possibilities of this mode of attack, he destroyed the brig *Dorothea* off Walmer (Fig. 10) by exploding 180 lb. of gunpowder under her. The British Admiralty refused to adopt any of Fulton's inventions, and he returned to America. Continuing his experiments there, he, in 1810, invented the Harpoon Torpedo (Figs. 1 and 2). In this device a harpoon (*H*) fired from a musket

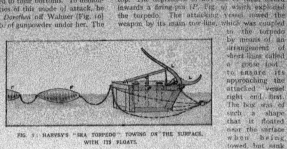

FIG. 9: HARVEY'S "SEA TORPEDO" TOWING ON THE SURFACE, WITH ITS FLOATS.

(*M*) was intended to embed itself in the side of the attacked vessel (*B*, Fig. 2). A canister (*C*) containing the explosive charge, supported a few feet below the surface by a cork float (*P*), was attached to the harpoon by a short length of cable (50 feet). When the current, due to the vessel's motion or to the tide, caused the canister to strike the ship's bottom, a spring gun-lock was released to explode the charge. The gun - lock was cocked by a safety-line when the musket shooting the harpoon was discharged.

Fig. 3 shows a small boat designed in 1863 for the Confederate States of America for the purpose of attacking Federal ships blocking the Southern ports during the American Civil War. The vessel shown was propelled by steam (though hand-power was employed in some cases), and made its attack whilst almost submerged. A spar-torpedo (*T T*) carried at its bow was its only weapon. These little boats were nicknamed "Davids." The head of another type of spar-torpedo is illustrated in Fig. 4. The contact-fuses (*F*) in its forward end are clearly shown,

The method of using Harvey's "Sea Torpedo" is shown in Figs. 5 and 6. This device was a wooden box (Fig. 6) containing the explosive, fitted with a system of levers (*L*, Fig. 6) on its top. The depression of any one of them forced inwards a firing-pin (*P*, Fig. 6) which exploded the torpedo. The attacking vessel towed the weapon by its main tow-line, which was coupled to the torpedo by means of an arrangement of short lines called a goose foot, to ensure its approaching the attacked vessel right end first. The box was of such a shape that it floated near the surface when being towed, but sank when the tow-line was slack. The lines comprising the "goose foot" were also attached in such a manner that the torpedo took a course considerably to one side of that of the towing vessel. A line having a number of floats (*F T*) attached to it like the tail of a kite was employed with the same object in view. When towed across the bow of an enemy ship, its tow-line was slacked away at the correct moment by means of a windlass on the deck of the attacking vessel just before the torpedo made contact with the attacked ship's side and exploded there (Figs. 5 and 6 — positions *B*).

The Simms Edison torpedo (Fig. 7) was electrically controlled by a wire (*C*) from the shore, the cable being coiled on a drum inside the torpedo itself. The Lay torpedo (Fig. 8) was propelled by liquefied gas inside, being similarly controlled from shore.

The Brennan torpedo, constructed in 1882, was also controlled from outside, but in this case its propeller was revolved by uncoiling piano-wire from drums mounted on its shaft.

FIG. 10: FULTON'S EXPERIMENTAL BLOWING - UP OF THE DANISH BRIG "DOROTHEA" OFF WALMER CASTLE IN 1805.

The above is a sketch from a contemporary drawing. The brig was a vessel of 200 tons, formerly captured by the British from the Danes, and British property. She was specially anchored for the experiment.

The Beginnings of War Machines: Early Torpedoes.

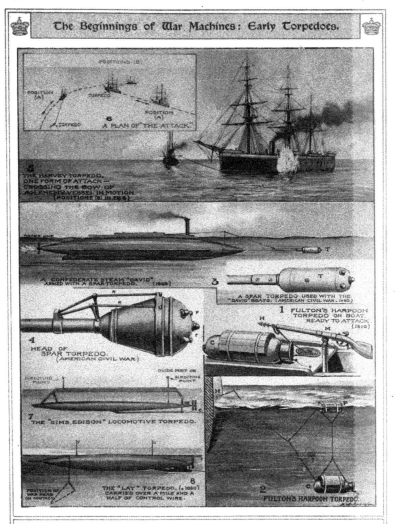

POSITION (B)

POSITION (A)   TORPEDO   POSITION (A)

TORPEDO   6   A PLAN OF "THE ATTACK".

5
THE HARVEY TORPEDO.
ONE FORM OF ATTACK—
CROSSING THE BOW OF
AN ENEMY VESSEL IN MOTION
(POSITIONS (B) IN FIG 6)

A CONFEDERATE STEAM "DAVID"
ARMED WITH A SPAR TORPEDO. (1863)

3
A SPAR TORPEDO USED WITH THE
"DAVID" BOATS. (AMERICAN CIVIL WAR. 1863.)

1
FULTON'S HARPOON
TORPEDO ON BOAT,
READY TO ATTACK.
(1810)

4
HEAD OF
SPAR TORPEDO.
(AMERICAN CIVIL WAR.)

GUIDE POST OR
DIRECTING POINT

7
THE "SIMS EDISON" LOCOMOTIVE TORPEDO.

POSITION OF
WAR HEAD
ON CONTACT

8
THE "LAY" TORPEDO, (c.1880)
CARRIED OVER A MILE AND A
HALF OF CONTROL WIRE.

2
FULTON'S HARPOON TORPEDO.

EARLY TYPES PREVIOUS TO THE AUTOMOBILE WHITEHEAD: DEPENDENT ON HUMAN CONTROL.

The diagrams above bring out incidentally what was necessarily the governing feature in all torpedo designs until the invention of the automobile Whitehead type (about 1870) revolutionised the system of under-water warfare. All the earlier devices, as explained on the page opposite and illustrated here, were dependent for their manipulation on active human agency on board the

attacking craft. Controllable torpedoes were dependent in like manner on human operation throughout. Spar and towing torpedoes were in use during the American Civil War, and Confederate vessels were sunk by them. The British Navy employed both forms during the 'seventies of last century. The masted iron-clad men-of-war seen in Diagrams Nos. 5 and 6 are of that date.

Outpost Incidents in Western Egypt.

WHERE WATCH IS EVER MAINTAINED : ARMOURED CARS ; AND SOUDANESE CAMEL CORPS TROOPERS.

If the operations on the Western Egypt frontier are complete, yet watch is still kept there. In the first illustration one of our armoured cars, a brigade of which rendered effective service in the campaign against the Senussi, is seen heading out to communicate with a patrol in the desert. The second illustration shows Soudanese Camel Corps troopers, who garrison the desert stations, moving from one post to another, with their families. The leading camel trooper has his wife riding behind on a pillion. The wife is riding the second camel which the soldier is leading. The third man is holding his wife on. In the lower illustration Staff armoured cars going at speed along a desert highway are seen passing a Camel Corps column on the march.—[Press Photo. Agency.]

"Jocund-Hearted" Wounded in Grosvenor Square.

"HAPPY, HAPPY WOUNDED MAN!" MEN WHO HAVE "DONE THEIR BIT" ENJOYING HERO-WORSHIP.

These photographs show wounded soldiers enjoying the fruits of patriotism on the balcony of the Coulter Hospital, in Grosvenor Square. It is right that men who have risked their lives for the benefit and protection of those at home should receive abundant gratitude. May the public solicitude for their welfare last through the years ahead when their hurts may disable them for the long battle of life! Meantime, the "happy, happy wounded man" (to quote some recent verses) is well content in the consciousness of having "done his bit" and escaped the greater peril. The milieu of our photographs recalls some older lines to a "jocund-hearted grinder," of whom the poet sang: "As they love thee in St. Giles's, Thou art loved in Grosvenor Square."—[Photos. by C.N.]

ROMANCES OF THE REGIMENTS : No. II.—THE RIFLE BRIGADE.

THE BRIDE OF BADAJOS.

A FAMOUS officer of the Rifle Brigade, recalling, in his later years, the story of Badajos, turns away from the grimmer details of that memorable fight to relate the romance which came to him out of that field of carnage. " This scene," he says, " however cruel to many, to me has been the solace and whole happiness of my life for thirty-three years." For at Badajos, Captain, afterwards Lieutenant-General, Sir Harry Smith found the lady who became his wife, and may almost be named a recruit to the Rifle Brigade, whose fortunes she followed in the field for many a day to come. Both husband and wife wrote their names large in the military annals of Great Britain, and Lady Smith stood godmother to that South African town which is for ever associated with heroic memories.

It was on the day following the capture of Badajos, when the regrettable excesses of the victorious troops had not yet been entirely quelled by their commanders (many of whom had been wounded in the attempt to restore order), that Smith and his friend Kincaid, a brother Rifleman, talking together at the door of Captain Smith's tent, saw two ladies approaching them from the city. The ladies made directly for the British officers, who noticed that both were young and both evidently Spaniards. As they came within speaking distance, the elder of the pair threw back her mantilla, revealing a face of great beauty, although her sallow, sunburnt, and careworn appearance told an unmistakable story of hardship and terror. But there was no mistaking the spirit of the Spanish aristocrat in the bearing of the fugitives, who introduced themselves as the last

of an ancient and honourable house, and gave sufficient guarantees that they were what they professed to be.

The elder of the two girls, for they were only in their 'teens, was the wife of a Spanish officer, or possibly his widow, for she did not know her husband's fate. She and her sister were homeless, their house had been wrecked during the previous day's disturbances; they were starving, and had only the clothes they stood up in. If they had escaped the worst outrage, they had still suffered cruelty and indignity, and their bleeding ears showed how their ear-rings had been wrenched through the flesh by the plunderers, who would not take the trouble to unclasp the ornaments.

For herself the Señora said she cared nothing, but for her sister, not yet fourteen, and only lately returned from a convent school, she was in despair, and declared that she saw no security except to throw herself upon the protection of some British officer. She apologised charmingly for the apparent indelicacy of her action, but so great, she said, was her faith in our national

A FRENCH SOLDIER FROM THE FAR EAST AT SALONIKA : ONE OF THE COLONIAL MARINE INFANTRY FROM COCHIN-CHINA RECENTLY LANDED THERE.

Official Photograph, issued by the Press Bureau ; supplied by Central Press.

character that she felt sure her appeal would not be made in vain, nor the confidence abused. She had reason ; and fortune had sent her to two exceptionally chivalrous and sympathetic men. For her own sake the officers would have done everything in their power to help her, but the little sister added an overwhelming argument. Kincaid in later life could still rhapsodise about her, for he, although not destined to be the lucky man, had experienced also the *coup de foudre.*

" A being more transcendently lovely," he writes, " I had never before seen—one more

[Continued overleaf.

On the Watch in our Lines at Salonika.

IN THE BRITISH TRENCHES AT SALONIKA: A SERGEANT USING HIS PERISCOPE.

Interesting news regarding the position in the Balkans came in a despatch dated June 10, from Mr. G. Ward Price. "Already," he said, "there exists much nearer to the enemy than the works round Salonika a strong line of defence, where fresh trenches and more barbed wire are daily appearing. White German aeroplanes, so high that you can hardly see them, go droning across the sky, watching long sections of open road below them covered by black echelons of advancing troops ; Bulgarian field-officers focus their telescopes upon the working parties they can see from their own advance-trenches, and sometimes order a few shells to be fired, though the distance is really beyond the effective range of the guns the enemy has."—(Official Photograph supplied by C.N.)

amiable I have never yet known ! Fourteen summers had not yet passed over her youthful countenance, which was of a delicate freshness—more English than Spanish ; her face, although not perhaps rigidly beautiful, was nevertheless so remarkably handsome, and so irresistibly attractive, surmounting a figure cast in Nature's fairest mould, that to look at her was to love her ; and I did love her, but I never told my love, and in the meantime another and a more impudent fellow stepped in and won her ! "

Sir Harry Smith, with excellent humour, quotes his friend Kincaid's words in his Autobiography, adding, " I confess myself to be ' the more impudent fellow,' " and Kincaid, for his part, says he was happy, for in Harry Smith, Señorita Juana Maria de los Dolores de Leon found a husband in every way worthy of her. They were married in the field, just after Juana had passed her fourteenth birthday, which is fully marriageable age for a Spanish woman. Captain Smith was then twenty - four. Their romance never faded. " From that day to this," wrote Sir Harry in 1844, " she has been my ' guardian angel. She has shared with me the dangers and privations, the hardships and fatigues of a restless life of war in every quarter of the globe. Already inured to war (she had seen three sieges of Badajos before her marriage) she followed the Rifle Brigade all through the rest of the Peninsular struggle, and was the veritable daughter

PRECAUTIONS AGAINST VIOLENCE AT A VENIZELIST MEETING AT SALONIKA : POLICE SEARCHING EVERY PERSON ENTERING, FOR CONCEALED WEAPONS.

of the regiment, behaving with a courage worthy of her ancestor, Ponce Juan de Leon, the Knight of Romance." Kincaid tells how one day when the battalion was moving into action, he passed Juana's lodging, which was so near the outposts that he never doubted but that she had been already removed to some place of greater safety. Consequently he did not trouble to look out for her. " But just as I passed the door, I found my hand suddenly grasped in hers. She gave it a gentle pressure, and without uttering a word, had rushed back into the house again. Throughout the remainder of that long and trying day I felt a lightness of heart and buoyancy of spirit which, in such a situation, was no less new than delightful." Sir Harry's account of those Peninsular days, when his young wife was the idol of the regiment, reads more like a chapter of " Charles O'Malley " than serious history. She went through Salamanca and Vimiera, and three years later saw thrilling adventures at Waterloo. Her mad ride to Antwerp and her frenzied return to the field on a rumour of her husband's death, to search, happily without reason, for his body, were recorded by Lady Smith herself (possibly with her husband's help) in a delightfully human document, which modern soldiers' wives have little chance of rivalling, for they may no longer take that personal share in campaigning which fell a century ago to the Lady of the Rifle Brigade.

WHERE THE ALLIES RECENTLY PROCLAIMED MARTIAL LAW : POLICE AT SALONIKA SEARCHING ALL WHO ATTENDED A VENIZELIST MEETING.

Official Photographs, issued by the Press Bureau ; supplied by Central Press.

A Royal Boy Scout: The Italian Crown Prince.

A SOLEMN CEREMONY IN ROME : PRINCE HUMBERT SWEARS LOYALTY TO HIS COUNTRY.

Our first photograph shows Humbert, Prince of Piedmont, Heir to the Throne of Italy, as a Boy Scout, at the base of the statue of his grandfather, King Victor Emmanuel II., which was raised in Rome in 1911, to celebrate the fiftieth year of Italian unity. He stands, a gallant young figure, as he vows fidelity to his country. Our second photograph shows him waiting to attach his signature to the document spread upon the table. In our third illustration he is seen affixing to the flag of the Boy Scouts, or Jeunes Explorateurs, of Verona, the gold medal which was awarded in memory and honour of those who lost their lives by an air-raid on Verona by Austro-Hungarians, who, like their allies, do not heed that most of their victims are civilians.—[Photos. by C.N.]

The Memorial Service to Lord Kitchener, June 13, 1916.

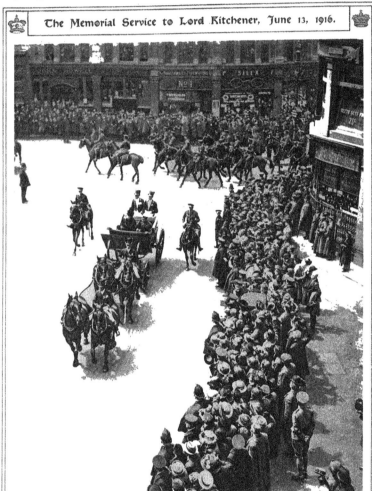

A ROYAL TRIBUTE TO A GREAT SOLDIER : THE KING AND QUEEN ON THEIR WAY TO ST. PAUL'S.

Our illustration shows their Majesties the King and Queen driving to St. Paul's for the Memorial Service to Lord Kitchener. The King was attended by a captain's escort, and was in khaki. Queen Mary was in black. The route was crowded with spectators, who silently played their part in the tribute to the splendid soldier whose loss is mourned by the whole Empire.

The solemn and impressive service was conducted by the Archbishop of Canterbury and the Bishop of London, Dr. Winnington Ingram. Stately and beautiful in every word and note, the great tribute to the splendid soldier and gallant gentleman proceeded step by step until the buglers sounded the pathetic and appealing notes of the Last Post.—[Photo. by Newspaper Illustrations.]

French Colonial Troops Fighting for the Tricolour.

FROM FAR EAST TO EUROPEAN BATTLE-GROUNDS : AN ANNAMITE BATTALION ; AND RED CROSS PARTY.

In normal times, the troops in the upper illustration are infantry of an Annamite regiment of the Cochin-China garrison. They have recently made their appearance in Europe, to join the other colonial corps, from the French West African possessions and elsewhere, who are fighting for the Tricolour. The battalion seen here is one that has joined the Allies at a certain camp. Others of the Annamite troops, as the papers have announced, marched through Paris the other day, "perfectly equipped and formed into regular companies." The hats the men are wearing are made of light cane, covered with greyish khaki cloth. The lower illustration shows an Annamite Red Cross ambulance party.—[Official Press Bureau Photograph; supplied by Central Press.]

Theatrical Talent in the Russian Army: 1

ONE WAY IN WHICH RUSSIAN SOLDIERS RELIEVE THE TEDIUM OF TRENCH LIFE:

In the Russian Army, as in all those now at war, the men keep up their spirits by various recreations. Dramatic entertainmen are popular with the Russian soldiers, and, as our photograph shows, the men possess ingenuity and originality in improvisin tableaux with the scanty "properties" available in the field. Reading is also a favourite amusement, as indicated by several lette

ableau Arranged by Troops in the Field.

LEGORICAL TABLEAU, "THE APOTHEOSIS OF RUSSIA," PERFORMED NEAR THE FRONT.

om Russian soldiers recently published. "Beautiful spring," says one, "has set in ; we have become at ease and free ; we have come t of our earthen refuges in which we passed the winter and the cold, and now it has grown warm, and it is possible to sit where e wishes, alongside a bush, to read some story or novel, or legend, which our illustrious writers have composed."—[*Photo. Korsakoff.*]

With the Victorious Russians on the Eastern Front.

ON THE EVE OF THE GREAT SPRING ADVANCE : BIVOUAC AND CAMP SCENES.

Russian infantry soldiers bivouacking in a farmyard on an early spring afternoon, during a halt of the column to which they belong, are shown in the upper illustration. Shelter-tents, of the pattern seen, are carried on the march by Russian infantry, one to each section of four men. Each of the men carries a part of the tent equipment as his own share—the sheets, poles, ropes, and pegs—which is worn strapped at the back of the rolled-up over-coat. Even with tent-gear added, the weight a Russian soldier carries, including ammunition, kit, water-bottle, cooking-tin, and entrenching-tool, is kept under sixty pounds. In the illustration below are seen Russian soldiers engaged in doing regimental tailoring work in a camp.—[Photos. by Choubsky Korsakoff.]

With the Victorious Russians on the Eastern Front.

FRONTIER SCENES: CONVALESCENT RUSSIAN SOLDIERS ENTERTAINED; AND GERMAN PRISONERS.

In the upper illustration a party of convalescent Russian soldiers is seen while being entertained at tea in a farmhouse garden by a Russian family living near a hospital on the frontier. One of the band of Sisters of Mercy who are attached to every field hospital unit of the Russian Army as part of the staff, is seen among the patients; also hospital orderlies and visiting comrades of the wounded. In the lower illustration a gang of German prisoners are seen while being marched off to their internment camp under an armed Russian escort. In physique there is apparently little to choose between the captives and their guards. The sullen and dejected look that most of the German prisoners show is noteworthy, by the way.—[Photos. by Chomlsky Korsakoff.]

With our Victorious Ally on the Eastern Front.

IN A CAMP OF ONE OF THE RUSSIAN ARMIES: CAMERA-NOTES AMONG THE LINES.

A Russian field-service church-tent, with its roof and cross partially decked with boughs, is seen in the first illustration. In accordance with the religious spirit innate in every Russian, every regiment has a priest-chaplain, who accompanies the unit on campaign, and wherever camp is formed the church-tent is pitched. The second illustration shows the new pattern gas-mask adopted by the Russians. The mouth and nostrils are protected by a rubber attachment connected with a small flask holding anti-gas chemicals, and worn slung round the neck. In the third illustration a Russian airman is seen with his lion-cub mascot. The man in front is Lieut. Efimoff, a pilot noted for daring.—[Photo. by Underwood and Underwood.]

A Unique Aeroplane Episode of the War.

HOW KUT GARRISON WAS FED BY FLYING-MACHINE : READY FOR FLIGHT WITH BAGS OF GRAIN.

An airman's feat which must reckon as one of the most interesting episodes of the air operations during the war is illustrated in this photograph from the Mesopotamia front. It shows a British aeroplane ready for flight to Kut with bags of grain to be dropped in General Townshend's camp in order to help the garrison to hold out as long as possible during the last weeks of the siege.

During these last weeks of the siege, while the relieving force was held up on the flooded front at Sanna-i-Yat, stores were dropped into Kut by aeroplane, chiefly salt, atta, flour, and tea. Earlier aeroplanes had also dropped various light articles—rifle-cleaners, spare parts for wireless, nets for fishing, and, at one time, cigarettes and tobacco.

fabulous weights of the fabulous 16-inch Skoda howitzer used by Austria. The more enormous the weight, the greater the use against heavily fortified works, until such thick concrete and steel as went to the building of the Belgian and Polish forts simply crumble like dry earth under its fearful impact. The heavier the shell, however, the heavier and less mobile the howitzer. The light 5-inch piece can be pulled anywhere by a small team of stout horses; heavier guns demand heavier teams, and as many as forty horses are needed to move some of the smallest of the brutes. Motor traction has helped here. Heavy trolleys, guns cunningly divided into two sections, and mounted on "caterpillar wheels" to ease the strain and save the road from the weight, have partly solved the difficulty. But even when they arrive mounting is slow, for solid platforms of beams, concrete, and steel have to be built to take the recoil-thrust. Heavy guns proper were born in the South African War. The Boers introduced us to them when they astonished us with "Long Tom." But we had a repartee in the naval 4·7-inch. The Heavy gun is of the genus

of field-gun, but heavier and more cumbersome in build, and capable of firing a heavier charge a greater distance. Its vocation is accurate long-range fire and big shell-power; and, besides being of notable service against fortified places and shielded guns, it is used to bring enfilade and cross fire to bear on the enemy. For instance, because of their inordinate range, they can fire over one face of a salient and shell the rear of another face. The 60-pounder guns of the Heavies were used with great effect at the Marne, where they could fire across the bends of rivers into the flanks of Germans holding tight on opposite banks. Part of the Garrison Artillery's job is, of course, coast defence. The work and the method of this is simple. It is merely the work of guns of the 60-lb. and heavier type employed to fire from fortified positions at enemy ships venturesome enough to raid. Under this heading, too, must rank the Mountain Batteries, Kipling's " screw guns," the infants of artillery, and jointed at that. They are 10-pound pieces that can be unjointed and slung on mule-back, and do their best service high up against the sky.   W. DOUGLAS NEWTON.

KING ALBERT IN A STEEL HELMET: HIS MAJESTY INSPECTING TRENCHES AT THE FRONT.

Photograph by C.N.

" ANZACS " FROM YPRES ON LEAVE IN LONDON : GIVING THREE CHEERS FOR KING AND COUNTRY.

Five officers and sixty men of two Australian battalions who recently made a dashing trench-raid near Ypres were rewarded with special leave. They were entertained here by the Australian Natives' Association to a luncheon at the Anzac Buffet and a motor-trip round London and thence to Kew and Richmond.—[Photo. by Topical.]

With the British Expedition in Mesopotamia.

CAMPAIGN SCENES : ARAB COOLIES LADING FODDER IN NATIVE BARGES ; BRITISH CROSSING A BRIDGE.

In the upper illustration is shown an every-day scene on the Shatt-el-Arab, at one of the places along the river in the neighbourhood of Basra where a base-camp for the Mesopotamia Expedition has been established. Steamers from overseas, laden with commissariet stores and munitions, as well as transports with men, can navigate for some way up the lower reaches of the stream and its estuary from the Persian Gulf, beyond the outer bars, crossing by way of deeper channels. On arrival at the destinations, the stores are unladen into native craft (by local Arabs employed as coolies) for towing up-stream. In the lower illustration a detachment of British infantry is seen crossing a bridge after traversing a narrow thoroughfare.—[Photos. by C.N.]

With the British Expedition in Mesopotamia.

'THE HELPING HAND : A BRITISH ARMY POLICEMAN PILOTING A BLIND ARAB BEGGAR.

The illustration represents a homely incident, but one typical of the kindly treatment of the natives by our men which has undoubtedly gone a long way towards creating a feeling of goodwill towards the Expeditionary troops on the part of the inhabitants of Lower Mesopotamia. A British soldier-policeman on duty for regulating the military traffic near a British-built road-bridge in a town is seen piloting a blind Arab beggar safely through the traffic on a bridge. After their past experience of the rigorous measures dealt out to the native Arab, inhabitants of Lower Mesopotamia by the enemy, the humane attitude of the British authorities of all grades has brought about a marked change in the demeanour of the natives.—[Photo. by C.N.]

With the British Expedition in Mesopotamia.

ON THE LINE OF COMMUNICATIONS : IN AN INDIAN REGIMENT'S CAMP BESIDE THE TIGRIS.

In the upper illustration the men of a company from an Indian infantry battalion are seen, on arrival at a camp on the Tigris, being told off to the quarters that they are to occupy—so many men with their huts to each hut. The huts are of the materials of which the natives' huts in the Arab villages along the banks of the Tigris are built—structures of reed or cane, roofed over with rush-matting. The walls of the upper part of the residence of the former Turkish governor of the district are seen beyond. The illustration below shows a camp bazaar. The regimental bazaar is an integral feature in the lines of Indian troops, and in it shops they make purchases to supplement their rations. Shopping is quite a favourite occupation of the troops when occasion serves.

With the British Expedition in Mesopotamia.

ON THE LINE OF MARCH: AN INDIAN DRAUGHT TRANSPORT-TRAIN PASSING BETWEEN CAMPS.

An Indian Army mule-transport train is seen here, on the line of march beside a palm-grove on the Lower Tigris. The mule-transport service of the Indian Army is one of the most efficiently organised departments of any army. Lord Roberts and Lord Kitchener, during their terms of holding the chief command of the Indian Army, may be considered as having been largely responsible for the placing of the departments connected with army and regimental transport on the satisfactory basis of the present war. The heterogeneous mixture of pack animals, mostly weedy ponies, and camels, which, with bullock-wagons, constituted the transport in former Indian Army campaigns, has been systematically replaced by mule transport, both draught and pack.—[Photo. by C.N.]

With the British Expedition in Mesopotamia.

CAMPAIGN NOTES : A REGIMENTAL BAGGAGE-TRAIN ; BUILDING AN ICE-FACTORY FOR HOSPITALS.

A section of an Indian regimental baggage transport-train is shown in the upper illustration carrying details of camp equipment for its battalion along a wide road in a certain town (called by our men, "The Strand") beside one of the canals that branch off from the Shatt-el-Arab in Lower Mesopotamia. The hardy, thick-skinned, and hard-working mule, a beast that requires little grooming and can exist, if not thrive, on almost any kind of provender, has proved itself the most adaptable and easily managed of transport animals in the present campaign. In the lower illustration we have a scene at Busreh—the erection by Arab coolie labour, under Royal Engineer supervision, of the plant for an ice-making factory for the hospitals.—[Photos. by C.N.]

WOMEN AND THE WAR.

THE history of woman's work in the war is really the record of the mobilisation of a sex. The highest and the lowest have vied with each other in the service of the country. This splendid solidarity, which seems now a commonplace, could not have been achieved without one gracious inspiration. It is impossible to exaggerate the influence of her Majesty the Queen on the enrolment of the army of women that stands behind the army of men.

If you go through Colour Court, which is in St. James's Palace, and turn to the right, a walk of a very few yards will bring you to the headquarters of Queen Mary's Needlework Guild ; and Queen Mary's Needlework Guild is one of the largest and most all-embracing of those organisations that have come into being as a result of the war. The vanguard of our "contemptible little army" had scarcely arrived on French soil before her Majesty, with rare imaginative sympathy, translated into action the unspoken desire of her feminine subjects and issued a public call for service to the women of Great Britain. It took

WOMEN AND THE WAR : LANCASHIRE LASSES WORKING AT AN ARMATURE.
Photograph by Illustrations Bureau.

the form of an appeal for clothes for soldiers and sailors, for their families, for the inmates of naval and military hospitals, and for such others as might suffer through the war. It was in this way that Queen Mary's Needlework Guild came into being ; and its headquarters at Friary Court, St. James's Palace, is a vast sorting and clearing house for the work sent in by a nation of women at the needle.

A wave of industry swept over the country. Even bridge lost its charm. For the moment its problems proved less engrossing than those presented by the refractory heel of a sock or the inexplicable obstinacy of a flannel shirt. Athletics lost their savour, ousted by the superior attractions of making flannel bed-jackets and striped pyjamas ; and, if the golfer did not exactly beat her niblick

into knitting-needles, she did at least invest in and employ herself to some purpose with those indispensable articles.

Ever since it was founded, a steady stream of parcels has flowed to the Guild headquarters. The value of the goods handled each week amounts to several thousands of pounds. The rooms at the Palace, once the scene of brilliant levées, are now piled high with mountains of swabs and miles of bandages, with pillows that come from China and pyjamas from Peru. Here, shelf on shelf of gauze bandages tells of the sympathy of New Brunswick, and 20,000 cardigans convey the good-will of Boston. There, barrels of disinfectant and a goodly number of kegs of soap form part of a vast United States contribution. Here, too, is cotton-wool from Chile; and a consignment of cases awaiting packing and classification is pointed out as gifts from our Allies farthest East. Perak is represented ; Thursday Island has done its share. From Trembuland and the Transvaal, Malakand and Manchuria, Hongkong and Siam, Oporto and Nova Scotia, and every corner of the civilised world have come proofs of the sympathy felt with the Allied Cause. Not long ago the Queen received a parcel which on being opened was found to contain some very finely embroidered towels, and a note saying that the contents were the work of some Russian peasants, and asking that they might be sold and the money expended on behalf of British soldiers, for whom the givers expressed the warmest admiration. Parcels with similar requests enclosed have been sent by Zulu chiefs. The Queen's appeal has gone far beyond the limits of the Empire, and the generosity of the world-wide response has touched and pleased her Majesty not a little.

Day after day the work of sorting and classifying goes on under the personal direction of the Hon. Lady Lawley, who has acted as Hon.
[Continued overleaf.

New Work for Women: At a Lancashire Glass Works.

AT ST. HELENS: DIGGING CLAY; AND MOVING A HUGE SHEET OF GLASS.

Our first photograph shows a number of women engaged in work somewhat, in appearance, like that of the women who are working on agricultural land; but those shewn are digging clay for use in the glass works in which they are employed. The particular glass industry in question was, until the war, largely in the hands of the Belgians, but now that enemy guns have levelled so many factories to the ground, the industry is being more largely undertaken in this country. Our second photograph shows a number of other Lancashire women workers moving, with studious care, a big and costly sheet of glass. They make a particularly interesting picture, their poses graceful, their sense of responsibility to be read in their faces.—[Photos. by Illustrations Bureau.]

Organising Secretary from the outset. Day after day bales and packages of medical requisites, clothing, and the " comforts " that the men so

WOMEN WORKERS IN A GLASS-FACTORY : A SCENE AT ST. HELENS.

It is not surprising that the women war-workers seen in our picture look determined, for they are working an overhead crane in a Lancashire glass-factory, and evidently have a due sense of their responsibilities.—[Photo. by Illustrations Bureau.]

dearly love are sent to our hospitals at home or abroad. Patients in France and Flanders, Belgium and Egypt, Salonika and East Africa, Persia and Malta, have reason to be grateful to the Queen's army of workers. In the general distribution the needs of our Allies have not been overlooked, for the sympathies of the Guild in this respect are as catholic as its friends are widespread.

About two-and-a-half million articles have been received since the Guild was founded, and almost that number have been sent out in 5000 grants, more or less. Every article received is entered in the stock-book ; each one despatched must be shown in the requisition volume. I have seen those books. They are a revelation of what faultless organisation can achieve in the way of record-keeping.

It all sounds very easy and simple, but the work of running a huge organisation—the Guild has more than 240 branches at home and abroad—is not all tea and talk by any means. There is hard work to do, and plenty of it. Lady Lawley and her helpers,

included amongst whom are Lady Dawson, Miss Welch, Miss Manning, Mrs. Mullins, and Miss Douglas - Pennant, are incessantly busy. The Marchesa Imperiali, Countess Greppi, Mrs. Page, Lady Wemyss, Lady Sandhurst, Lady Fitzwilliam, and Mrs. Arthur James are others who render help. The Queen, whose interest in this scheme of her own creation has never waned, is a constant visitor at Friary Court. Those visits are unannounced and entirely free from ceremony. Work goes on as usual whilst the President makes her round, examining parcels,, inspecting gifts, and gleaning information on the latest details of working. As a president her Majesty is nothing if not practical, and a daily bulletin of work accomplished is forwarded to Buckingham Palace from Friary Court. The gigantic amount of work accomplished by the Guild and its friends is, of course, merely a fraction of the service women are rendering. Much of the work it has done has been made possible by the generous co-operation of sympathisers the world over, but not a little of the success achieved is due to the royal and gracious lady to whose kindly personal interest in all that affects the welfare of her subjects the institution owes its origin. CLAUDINE CLEAVE.

LANCASHIRE LASSES WORKING FOR THE WAR : MOVING SHEETS OF GLASS IN A FACTORY.

These busy workers are helpers in the manufacture of glass, in St. Helens, and are seen moving great sheets along in a trolley. It is a new industry for them, but they have taken readily to their task.—[Photo. by Illustrations Bureau.]

Making British Snipers at the Front.

MARKSMANSHIP TRAINING AT THE FRONT: AN OFFICERS' CLASS; AND AN "INTERNATIONAL MATCH."

In the upper illustration, a squad of officers, whose qualifications as marksmen may be assumed, are seen aiming through loopholes while undergoing instruction in sniping. To learn how to "snipe" is a branch of military training that stands by itself in its methods. Unwearying patience, alertness of hand and eye, in combination with rapidity of decision and steadiness of nerve, are qualities the ideal sniper should possess, and the training of natural faculties requires exceptional qualifications. In the lower illustration we have an instance of the interest in good shooting taken at the front. It shows in progress an "International Match" between Canadians, Australians, New Zealanders, South Africans, and Mother Country corps.— [Official Canadian Photographs; supplied by C.N.]

Grand Fleet Officers at Play after the Day's Work.

IN AN OFF-DUTY HOUR : JUNIOR OFFICERS AT HOCKEY ABOARD A SHIP OF THE GRAND FLEET.

It is in general at the end of the afternoon, or getting on towards the early evening, Dog Watch time, after four o'clock Divisions' muster, and the last fleet exercise, or ship's drill, is done for the day, that scenes such as those shown above may often be witnessed on board ship. The officers' "dress for mess" bugle—if that peace-time call be still sounded—has not yet gone. The lower-deck hands, except for the men on watch and ever vigilant look-outs on the bridge, or right forward, or at the mast-head, are taking life easily, or "sky-larking," according to the usage of the ship. The "First Dog," say, between five and six p.m., and sometimes for half an hour or so later, is the playtime of the fleet by immemorial custom.—[Photos. by C.N.]

A Tribute to a Great Sailor: Admiral Cradock.

THE UNVEILING OF THE CRADOCK MEMORIAL : AN IMPRESSIVE CEREMONY AT YORK MINSTER.

Our photograph shows Admiral Sir Francis Bridgman committing the Memorial to Admiral Cradock to the custody of the Dean and Chapter of York Minster, on June 16. The ceremony of unveiling was performed by the Marquess of Zetland, who said of Admiral Cradock that " he did not employ such tactics as sheltering under cover of darkness," but " upheld the best traditions of the British Navy." Admiral Cradock, it will be remembered, went down with his ship, the " Good Hope," in the battle off Coronel, Nov. 1, 1914, when he attacked a German squadron, under conditions which made his action heroic, and broke the German Admiral's power, which, as Mr. Balfour said, would have been " great for evil while he remained untouched."—[Photo. by L.N.A.]

The Volunteers now "Part of His Majesty's Forces."

BEFORE THE REVIEW: THE NATIONAL GUARD AT THE HORSE GUARDS' AND "SWEARING IN."

The upper photograph shows the City of London National Guard drawn up on the Horse Guards' Parade, just before marching to Hyde Park to join in the great review of London Volunteers by Lord French, on Saturday, June 17. In the lower photograph, the Lord Mayor, Sir Charles Wakefield, is seen administering the oath to members of the corps, of whom over 1500 were enrolled, in the Guildhall, before they assembled at the Horse Guards. The Lord Mayor said that during his recent visit to the front he heard high praise of the National Guard and the service they had rendered at London stations to men on leave from the front. At the inspection, Lord French said : "The Volunteer Force now forms part of His Majesty's Forces."—[Photos. by Topical.]

The Illustrated War News

ITALY'S ALPINE WAR WITH AUSTRIA: IN A SHELLED CHURCH AT GORIZIA.

From a Painting by Ludovico Pogliaghi in the Collection of War Pictures by Italian Artists at the Leicester Galleries, Leicester Square.

THE GREAT WAR.

By W. DOUGLAS NEWTON.

THE paramount struggle of the week has been the very earnest effort of the Germans to save the vital military post of Kovel. The retarded pace of the Russians in this district is first-hand evidence that the Germans are fighting with the energy of anxiety, but there are other signs that the enemy has not put his trust in Austrians, and is rushing up reserves at a lively pace, in the hope of putting the brake on the fine impetuosity of the Russian advance. There are reports that von Mackensen has lent himself to the defence ; there is the certainty that von Linsengen, with strong forces, has been hurried to the immediate Kovel front, and that he is fighting desperately to bar the way. Further north, along the Dvina and below it, Hindenburg is employing the weight of his army and his prestige to distract the Russians and to dress the line. Berlin hails as a victory a powerful attack that penetrated the Russian line south of Smorgon ; but the Berlin version is apparently only half a truth, for the Russians, while admitting the strength of the attack, also mention that it was frustrated. The same can be said for another Hindenburg . victory in the Vilna zone, at Dubatovka. Here the German mass was able to penetrate, and, having penetrated, the communiqué was promptly despatched to the waiting heart of Germany. Meanwhile, the Russian reserves had come up, and the penetration was finished and the penetrators driven back to their own line. At the same time, the condition of

DECORATING A WOUNDED LIEUTENANT : THE CROWN PRINCE OF ITALY AT A CEREMONY IN ROME.

Photograph by Alfieri.

SERBIA'S NEW SEA FORCES : THE FIRST SERBIAN NAVAL CAPTAIN (ON THE LEFT).

It was stated on May 2 that Serbia had acquired her first naval unit—a destroyer named the "Velika Serbia "—for escorting transports. Each of the Allies, it was added, would present Serbia with two units to form the nucleus of a Serbian Navy.

von Linsengen is less equivocal. He is certainly giving our Ally a very stern fight, though, on the whole, the movement is favouring the Russians. From Kolki, the enemy line has been forced back until quite another fifty miles of front have been added to German tribulations. The fighting in this area has been mainly counter-attacks from the Germans, and these have all been rendered inutile with the greatest loss. Lower down, the River Stokhod has been crossed, and fighting of a particularly ferocious nature is going on. The Germans here have been making use of explosive bullets, and have received a very drastic reprisal for their criminality, the angry Slavs having refused to give quarter. In the early days of the week our Ally was able to extend the breach in the enemy line by carrying his front towards Brody ; but the defence has pulled itself together, and the movement became slower. At the Austrian centre the defence has weakened a little, and the Russians have been able to force some advances north of Buczacz.

In the Bukovina the Austrian " cave " has been as startling as anything observed in this great new offensive. Czernowitz had hardly fallen before the Russian cavalry was pressing the retreat with a most swift determination. The Czernowitz army seems to . have been very badly handled, and to have been divided by General Letchitsky's fine handling of the cavalry : one portion of this force appears to have been driven to the Carpathians, the other harried to the south in such a fashion that it is in imminent danger of being engulfed by the advance or driven over the Roumanian frontier and into internment. The rapidity of this movement is remarkable.

QUEEN ALEXANDRA AND SOLDIERS AND SAILORS: AT THE OPENING OF THE NEW Y.M.C.A. ALDWYCH HUT.

Queen Alexandra paid a special visit to Aldwych to open a new Y.M.C.A. Hostel for soldiers and sailors. Her Majesty, after inspecting the building, presided over the tea-bar and personally served tea to a number of wounded men.—[Photo. by Photopress.]

In a few days the Russians had forced their way down to Radautz (30 miles due south of Czernowitz), and a day later to Gura Humora, which is 20 miles further on, as well as Kuty, more directly west. Here, once again, our Ally's troops have come within marching distance of the Kirlibaba Pass, the gate of Austrian Transylvania, and from here they might well open out into an invasion of the Hungarian plain, a movement that should have immense significance to the Allies fighting in the south-eastern theatres of Europe, that might have real meaning to Roumania, and which, already, may have had some moral bearing upon the attitude of Greece. In the other spheres of the Bukovina fighting, the Russians have yet to make decisive movement towards Kolomea or Stanislau. As far as mental strategy goes, however, it is obvious that their victories have had disturbing effect on the defenders of those two important points, no less than the defenders of Lemberg. There are palpable

signs of uneasiness among our enemies, particularly among our Austrian enemies, and the disturbing effects are bound to have reaction in other spheres.

It is fairly certain, for instance, that Austria's Trentino adventure has been robbed of some of its vitality by the Russian menace. Austria has ceased to report victories in Italy, while, on the other hand, the Italians can show some good movements to their credit. On the Asiago Plateau our Ally is pressing forward in the face of a strong Austrian defence, that remains, practically, no more than a defence; on the ground between Lake Garda and the Astico, the Italians have been making captures, and the whole tone has a healthy suggestion in favour of the Entente. There are also suggestions that the Austrians have been obliged to relinquish their hold on Albania, the troops being required for the Trent and Galician fronts. In the Balkans the situation has become better, thanks to the emphatic attitude of the Allies. Greece, after a great deal of gentleness, has been handled with decisive action. The three protecting Powers, Great Britain, France, and Russia, presented a final Note to Athens on Wednesday last demanding complete demobilisation of the Greek Army, the establishment of a Government which would guarantee benevolent neutrality in fact as well as in theory, the dissolution of the Skouloudis Chamber, and the dismissal of those police officials whose neutral benevolence was all in favour of Germany. The determination of the attitude met with prompt acceptance, all the demands were conceded by King Constantine, M. Zaimis took over the formation of a new Cabinet in the place of M. Skouloudis, and there is every prospect that the Greek people, having elected a Government in favour of the Allies, will now be permitted to be

TO WIN THE TOY TRADE FOR ENGLAND : MISS "NELL FOY" IN HER CHELSEA FACTORY.

Miss Berthwick, niece of Lord Borthwick—otherwise Miss "Nell Foy," the sculptor—has established a doll-factory in Chelsea. It is run entirely by women, to free men for service and also to help in capturing a trade annexed by Germany. Miss Borthwick knows all the German toy centres.—[Photo. by L.N.A.]

ruled by that Government, and not by methods that have been inherently unconstitutional. The acceptance of the Allied demands brought Greece its own relief, for the embargo on shipping has been lifted and the menace of a dangerous food-shortage removed. The action should be beneficial

AN EMPIRE DAY CELEBRATION AT TOKYO : THE BRITISH ASSOCIATION TEA-PARTY.
Empire Day was celebrated by the Tokyo branch of the British Association by a tea-party in the garden of the British Embassy. Members of the British colony at Tokyo and their families were invited.—*Photo. by The Meiji Seihanjo.*

to the Greeks and the Allies ; it should end a period of distrust that has made the situation at Salonika difficult and vexatious.

The main development in the West has been a formidable German effort against the north-eastern lines of Verdun. After battering the defences out of all form and shape, the masses of infantry have been able to press for-ward and occupy the devas-tated ground. They have thus been able to make ad-vances on Hill 321 and Hill 320, and west and south of Fort Vaux in the woods of Chenois and Fumin. Late in the week, after a pause, a terrible battle developed. Thanks to their power of guns and their prodigality in lives, advances were made on the half-circle from Hill 321 to Fleury. Thiaumont was apparently forced, and Fleury itself captured. The French retort to this was an immediate and very spirited counter. Ground on Hills 321 and 320 was won back, though Thiaumont still re-mained in German hands ; the village of Fleury was cleared as far as the fringes, and gains made by the enemy in Chenois and Fumin Woods were retaken. The battle is still raging, and the losses are ex-ceedingly heavy, especially among the Germans.

On the west bank of the Meuse there have been a number of unsuccessful attacks by the enemy, and a like fate befel an attack in the Champagne, where two German assaults near Mont Tetu were shattered, and a third only succeeded in getting into a trench in order to be flung out with the bayonet. On the British front the Germans were able to follow up a mine explosion near Givenchy and enter our line. They were promptly attacked by the Welsh Fusi-liers, and routed in very quick time. On all the sectors of the West there has been a great deal of artillery work, and also a significant amount of air fighting, in which the French and British aviators have dealt out punishment both to opposing pilots and strategic towns.

One of the most interest-ing side-issues of the war has been the revolt of the Grand Sherif of Mecca against Otto-man rule. The Grand Sherif has had the support of the Arab tribes of West and Cen-tral Arabia, who had grown weary of the inaction and maladministration of Turkey, and the rising swiftly met with success. Jeddah, the Red Sea port, as well as Mecca, has been captured, with the Turk-ish garrisons ; and, save for garrisons holding out in two small forts, Taif has fallen also ; while Medina, the terminus of the Hedjaz Railway, is

THE NEW RUSSIAN AMBASSADOR TO JAPAN : M. KRUPENSKY ARRIVING AT TOKYO STATION.
The new Russian Ambassador to Japan, M. Krupensky, made his *entrée* at Tokyo in the quietest and most unobtrusive way. He arrived as an ordinary passenger by train, and only some of the Embassy officials met him at the station.—[*Photo. by The Meiji Seihanjo.*]

under close siege. The capture of Jeddah opens up trade routes with the Arabian littoral, as well as giving access to the Holy Places of Mecca.

LONDON : JUNE 26, 1916.

Both Brought Down?—Germany's Most Lauded Airmen.

ENEMY AIR-FIGHTERS: CAPTAIN BOELCKE; WITH THE LATE FIRST LIEUTENANT IMMELMANN.

First-Lieutenant Immelmann, whose death in action is reported from Berlin, is seen here (right), in a photograph reproduced from a German paper, with the Kaiser's other "star-turn" airman, Captain Boelcke. Both wear the "Ordre pour le Mérite" and the Iron Cross. Immelmann is stated to have been killed on June 20, and "his death has created a profound sensation in Germany." He was of Saxon birth, twenty-six years old, and was credited with having brought down 15 Allied aeroplanes, 9 of them, as claimed by Immelmann himself, British. His tactics were to rise to an immense height and swoop down diagonally, shooting at close quarters. Boelcke was reported — erroneously, it is now said—to have been killed previously.

More French Trophies at the Invalides.

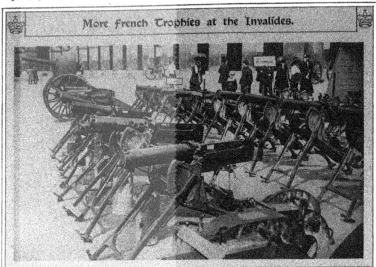

A COLLECTION THAT IS GROWING CONSTANTLY: HOWITZERS AND TRENCH ARTILLERY.

Captured German guns form the greater number of the war trophies at the Invalides, in Paris, and the specimens on exhibition are being constantly added to by fresh trophies, mostly from the Champagne area of operations. In the upper illustration an array of captured German machine-guns is seen as at present displayed in the Grand Court. In the lower illustration, the two pieces in the foreground are (right) a German mortar of old type, apparently sent to the trenches from some arsenal; and (left) a medium-sized modern howitzer. The Krupp wedge-block has been removed from the breech and the aperture for its insertion is seen open. In the second row of trophies a German position-gun stands on the right of the row of smaller pieces of different patterns.

More French Trophies at the Invalides.

EXHIBITS THAT DRAW CROWDS: A BIG GUN; AEROPLANES; AND A "77" FIELD GUN.

In the upper of the illustrations on this page, in addition to the captured German "position-guns," there are shown, elevated on cone-shaped pylons, portions of two captured aeroplanes; to be seen to the right and left. There are several German aeroplanes among the trophies at the Invalides, most of them belonging to the earlier period of the war. Indoors, within the galleries are displayed in glass cases the twelve or so German regimental battle-standards which the French took previously to and at the Battle of the Marne. Since that time the Germans have given up carrying their colours into action. In the illustration below, a German "77," a 77-mm. field-gun of the ordinary Krupp pattern used by the German artillery, is seen.

After the Jutland Battle—Shell Damage.

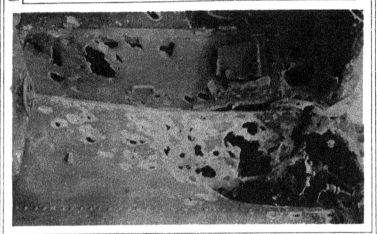

ON THE NAVIGATING BRIDGE OF A BRITISH SHIP : OUTSIDE AND INSIDE THE CHART-HOUSE.

The smashed and riddled thin metal of the door of the chart-house in a British ship after the battle off Jutland is shown in the upper illustration, the effects of shell-splinters. For the safety, during action, of the navigation party, whose habitat the chart-house ordinarily is, the conning-tower, behind thickly armoured walls, is provided. In the lower illustration, we have an interior view, within the chart-house. It shows the damage shell-fragments did to the steering-wheel, voice-pipe apparatus, and engine-room telegraphs which are installed on the chart-house bridge for every-day use. Duplicate steering-gear, voice-pipes, telephones and telegraphs to all parts of the ship, turrets, q.f. gun positions, engine-rooms, are in the conning-tower.—[*Photos. by C.N.*]

The Hunting-Down of Enemy Submarines.

ALONGSIDE A BRITISH DESTROYER: A GERMAN SUBMARINE'S RESCUED CREW BROUGHT ABOARD.

A British destroyer's whaler, or principal boat, is seen here just after coming alongside the ship on returning with the crew of a German submarine as prisoners after the destroyer had settled accounts with the enemy vessel. The officer in charge of the whaler is seen standing up with, in front of him, the captain of the German submarine. Our destroyers are the principal dread of the German submarine—they pounce on them at sight, just as a dragon-fly "hawks" at a wasp. Gun-fire is one form of attack commonly employed for a submarine sighted on the surface at any distance; aiming at the submarine's superstructure. Another is to go full speed at and ram the submarine before it can submerge; when the enemy is within speedy reach.—[Photo. by C.N.]

THE BEGINNINGS OF WAR-MACHINES : THE DIRIGIBLE.

IN 1670, Francisco Lana, a Jesuit priest, designed a "flying boat" which was to be supported in the air by light copper spheres from which the air had been exhausted (Fig. 14). It is obvious that this could never have succeeded, as the weight of the copper spheres, if strong enough to withstand the resultant unbalanced air-pressure, would be such as to counteract the lifting power of the vacuum within them. In 1709, a Portuguese friar, Laurence de Guzman, designed a wonderful "flying ship." From the description, the inventor seems to have provided contrivances to enable the ship to do everything except fly. In the year 1783 the brothers Montgolfier tried some buoyancy experiments by filling paper bags with heated air (Fig. 1). The results of these experiments they developed in the "Montgolfier" fire-balloon, in which air within the envelope was heated by a fire burning in a brazier below the opening in its neck. One of these vessels (Fig. 2) was the first balloon to make a free ascent.

FIG. 14.—A SEVENTEENTH - CENTURY JESUIT'S DESIGN FOR A FLYING-BOAT : A DIAGRAM OF LANA'S PROPOSED CRAFT.

The danger caused by the proximity of fire to the envelope induced research in the direction of buoyancy without heat, the best medium being found in hydrogen gas. The difference in weight between hydrogen and air is such that 35,000 cubic feet of the former gas will lift a weight of about one ton. This first balloon filled with hydrogen as a buoyancy agent ascended in Paris on Aug. 27, 1783 (Fig. 3). In September of the same year a Montgolfier fire-balloon (Fig. 4) was sent up at Versailles carrying a cock, a sheep, and a duck, none of which was injured when the balloon descended. Two Frenchmen, Pilâtre de Rozier and the Marquis d'Arlandes, made the first free ascent in a fire-balloon (Fig. 5) from Paris on Nov. 24, 1783.

The first ascent in a "manned" gas-balloon (Fig. 6) took place in Paris on Dec. 4, 1783, when MM. Charles and Robert made a voyage of twenty-seven miles. In this case hydrogen gas was used. The first ascent in a "manned" balloon using coal-gas instead of hydrogen took place about 1820. Coal-gas, though not so light as hydrogen, is used in cases where great lifting capacity for volume is not required. Its lifting capacity is about half that of hydrogen. In 1784 the first attempts at steering were made. Fig. 7 shows Blanchard's balloon, which was provided with a parachute, to break its fall when landing with a collapsed envelope, and wings with which it was proposed to steer it. These latter were, of course, quite useless for that purpose—as, any steering contrivance must be when fitted to a balloon which drifts with the air-current and has no "steerage way."

On June 30, 1784, a Montgolfier balloon (Fig. 8), also fitted with a useless rudder, ascended from Paris in charge of l'Abbé Miollan, but was caught in a tree in its descent and burnt.

Fig. 9 shows a more business-like attempt at a dirigible balloon, but in this case also the inventor provided a totally inadequate means of propulsion by oars. As, however, he expected to propel his vessel by means of these oars, he was justified in fitting a rudder for the purpose of steering it.

One of the first mechanically propelled dirigible balloons was that constructed by Henri Giffard in 1850. The vessel was 144 feet long and 39 feet in diameter. It was propelled by a steam-engine acting on a screw propeller. The inventor made an ascent in Paris in 1852 (Fig. 10), and obtained a speed between 4½ and 7 miles per hour.

The next illustration (Fig. 11) is that of M. Dupuy de Lôme's dirigible balloon, commenced during the siege of Paris and finished in 1872. This balloon had a capacity of 120,000 cubic feet, was 118 feet long, and 48 feet in diameter. Its screw-propeller was operated by eight men, and it made a speed of about 6½ miles per hour.

Tissandier's dirigible balloon (Fig. 12) made use of electric power as a means of propulsion. This machine was constructed in 1883, and was 91 feet long by 30 feet in diameter. Driven by storage batteries, it was well under control, and was a very promising experiment.

(Continued opposite.)

AN EARLY TYPE OF SUSPENDED BASKET FOR BOMB - DROPPING : GALE'S BALLOON, 1847.

Mr. Gale ascended at Peckham on April 7, 1847. At a great altitude he went from one basket to the other. About the same time Coxwell demonstrated before military authorities at Berlin in a similar balloon, with a second basket 40 ft. below, and *dropped bombs !*

Beginnings of Modern War-Machines: Dirigibles.

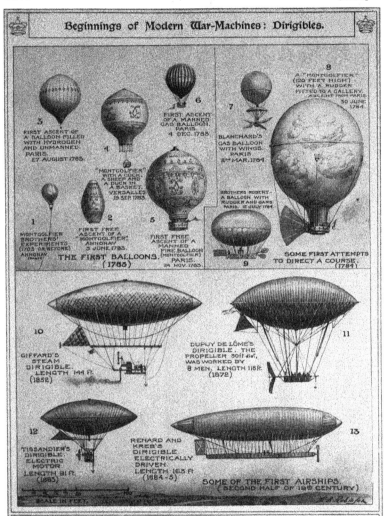

ANCESTORS OF THE ZEPPELIN: EARLY TYPES OF DIRIGIBLE AIRSHIPS.

[Continued.]
A dirigible balloon (Fig. 13) 165 feet long and 27 feet diameter, of a shape much more in keeping with modern practice, was tried by Renard and Krebs in 1884. This machine was also electrically driven, and did some very good work, considering its date of production. It made two trips from Paris for some distance and back, and attained a speed of about twelve miles per hour.

In the year 1900 Count Zeppelin's first airship ascended from Lake Constance. This vessel was 420 feet long by 40 feet diameter, and the envelope was divided into seventeen separate compartments. It was driven by two 16-h.p. Daimler motors. Only three flights were made with this dirigible of 1900, and the results were fairly satisfactory.

"Roses, Roses, All the Way!" Alexandra Day.

THE "DAY" OF "DAYS" IN LONDON : HOW SOME OF THE 30,000,000 ALEXANDRA ROSES WERE SOLD.

The first photograph shows a rose-seller, greatly daring, offering her wares to the statuesque equestrian figure of a Life Guard on duty at the Horse Guards. In the second, a party of wounded soldiers out motoring have chosen a favourable moment to stop their car and buy roses. The third photograph shows three soldiers at Victoria Station, about to return to the front, duly decorated with the emblem. In the case of the Highlander, the rose may be said to have joined the thistle. Alexandra Day (June 21) this year was a huge success,' in spite of the many "flag" and other "days" that preceded it. The weather was fine, and nearly 15,000 dainty rose-sellers were busy in London alone.—[Photos. by Sport and General and L.N.A.]

An "Anzac" helps to Sell Roses on Alexandra Day.

A TALL AUSTRALIAN ASSISTS IN SELLING ROSES TO WOUNDED SOLDIERS: A ROSE DAY INCIDENT.

The problem was to effect communication between the rose-seller and the would-be purchasers, convalescent wounded soldiers at the Fourth London General Hospital. A tall member of the Australian Military Police solved it in the manner shown. The dog, by the way, is an Australian mascot, and wears an identification-disc. In her letter of thanks to the Duchess of Portland, Queen Alexandra said: "'Alexandra Day' . . . is now celebrated not only in the United Kingdom, but in most parts of our great dominions overseas. . . . This year roses have been sent to Canada, Australia, New Zealand, South Africa, and the West Indies, and to our soldiers at the front; also we have our Australian, New Zealand, and Canadian sections working in London."—[*Photo. by C.N.*]

ROMANCES OF THE REGIMENTS : No. III.—THE K.O.Y.L.I.

THE EXPLOITS OF ENSIGN DYAS.

THE old 51st, which with the 105th Regiment is now the King's Own Yorkshire Light Infantry, had among its Peninsular heroes a certain Ensign Dyas, who covered himself with glory and yet contrived for a long time to escape any substantial recognition of his services. Even at the last, when his merit was tardily rewarded, a perverse fortune cheated him of the full fruition of his bravery, and he died a half-pay Captain. But he was remembered by Grattan, the historian of the Connaught Rangers, who went a little out of his way to do justice to the memory of this gallant officer of another regiment.

Joseph Dyas first came into notice during the second siege of Badajos. On June 6, 1811, the British batteries had so far overcome the fire of the San Christoval Fort that an assault was considered practicable, and a hundred men of the 7th Division, commanded by Major Macintosh of the 85th, were detached to storm the breach. Ensign Dyas begged permission to lead the forlorn hope of six volunteers who headed the attack. With them went an Engineer officer, who fell in the first rush, leaving Dyas in sole command, for Macintosh and the main body failed to plant the scaling-ladders and had to retire, believing that the forlorn hope had died to a man. A little later, when Macintosh was seated in his tent regretting the failure of the attack and the loss of so many brave fellows, who should walk in but Dyas, not even scratched !

"WATCHING FOR THE ENEMY" DURING MANŒUVRES AT SALONIKA : SCOTTISH TROOPS.

Official Photograph, issued by the Press Bureau ; supplied by C.P.

Nearly all his men had fallen, but still the Ensign hung on in the breach, until he heard the enemy entering the ditch by the sally-port. Then, and not till then, he withdrew, determined to repair his luck, if possible, on the next opportunity.

Three days later he had another chance. A new attack was ordered. The party advanced under the fire of every gun that San Christoval could bring to bear upon them. They did all that men could do, but their numbers thinned rapidly, and again the assault failed. Dyas was wounded in the forehead and fell upon his face, but he sprang up and rallied his few remaining followers. In vain. A second time he had to retire. As before, he was the last to leave the ditch, from which he escaped by a curious chance. One of the ladders, which could not be placed upright, still hung from the glacis on the palisades. Up this he sprang, and immediately flung himself on his face on the top of the glacis. At that moment the enemy had delivered a volley, and, seeing Dyas fall, they shouted "He's dead ; that 's the last of them." Hearing these words, the Ensign lay perfectly still for a few minutes, and shortly afterwards the enemy slackened their fire. Dyas seized his chance, and reached the British batteries in safety.

DURING MANŒUVRES AT SALONIKA : A HIGHLAND BATTALION ON THE MARCH.

Official Photograph, issued by the Press Bureau ; supplied by C.P.

In the first affair, his conduct had been sufficiently gallant, but the authorities blamed him for too hastily pronouncing the breach impracticable to twelve-foot ladders. When

[Continued overleaf.

Canadian Contingent Notes: Behind the Lines.

FOR BATTLE AND AFTERWARDS : A GRENADE TESTING-HOUSE ; AND A FIELD-HOSPITAL WARD.

The upper illustration shows a building that has been specially fitted up for the testing of bombs and grenades. Testing is necessary before the projectiles are served out, in order to ensure their being safe for handling by those to whom they are issued. To keep off inquisitive persons, wire fencing surrounds the building. The piled-up sand-bags act as anti-splinter screens, to prevent fragments from a bomb, or grenade, which may explode while undergoing its testing, flying outside the building and harming any persons within reach. Every possible precaution is taken against accidents within the buildings and without. The lower illustration shows men in a field-ambulance ward—a contented-looking group.—(*Canadian Official Photographs ; supplied by C.N.*)

he volunteered the second time, General Houston refused, remarking that Dyas had already done enough, and that it would be unfair that he should again bear the brunt of the attack. Dyas modestly referred to the doubts cast upon his opinion, and begged that, although he still believed the breach to be impracticable, he might again lead the party. Houston would not yield, whereupon Dyas exclaimed,"General Houston, I hope you will not refuse my request, because I am determined, if you order the fort to be stormed forty times, to lead the advance as long as I have life." This argument succeeded. Dyas did his work with admirable skill, but the encountering of unexpected obstacles led to the second failure.

In reconnaissance, however, as well as in attack, Dyas was a cool and capable hand. The night before the second attack he had been sent out with fifteen men to observe the communications between Badajos and San Christoval. All through an unusually still summer night the party lay in a hollow, within point-blank shot of the fort. Day broke, and they had no order to retire. Dyas became anxious, and expected every moment to be observed. He sent back a trusty Irishman to ask for instructions. If they were to retire, the messenger was to hoist his cap on his musket. The long minutes passed, and at length the signal came. Dyas, telling his fifteen that their lives depended on strict adherence to orders, started them singly to different parts of the British lines, and, although it was daylight, not a man was hit. His splendid, if

FISHING UNDER THE WATCHFUL EYE OF THE BRITISH ARMY, ON A LAKE NEAR SALONIKA: FISHERMEN HAILED BY A MOTOR PATROL-BOAT AND ASKED TO PRODUCE THEIR PERMIT.

Official Photograph; supplied by Newspaper Illustrations.

unsuccessful, service before San Christoval was brought to Wellington's notice; but, by some oversight or mischance, nothing came of the recommendation, and Dyas served all through the Peninsular War, and afterwards at Waterloo, without rising higher than Lieutenant. Nearly ten years passed, and then, in 1820, he was suddenly remembered. In that year Sir Henry Torrens, happening to inspect the 51st at Hampton Court, heard of Dyas's exploits from Colonel Gurwood, of the 10th Hussars, Colonel Ponsonby, and Lord Wiltshire (all, curiously enough, personally unacquainted with the gallant Lieutenant), and Torrens made it his business, on returning to London, to look up the documents, and drew the Duke of York's attention to the matter. The Duke recognised the merits of the case, and at once had Dyas gazetted to a company in the 1st Ceylon Regiment, and when the Lieutenant called to thank him the Commander-in-Chief took care to express his regret that promotion had in this instance been so slow. His Royal Highness then asked what leave of absence Captain Dyas would require before he joined his regiment. "Six months," Dyas replied, "if your Royal Highness does not think that too long." "Perhaps," said the Duke, "you would prefer two years." The hero, who had certainly not enjoyed much leave for many a day, was delighted, and may have indulged visions of further promotion after a well-earned holiday. But it was not to be. Dyas got no further in his profession, and before long had to retire on the half-pay of his Company.

EXAMINING PERMITS : THE OFFICER IN COMMAND OF A BRITISH MOTOR PATROL-BOAT ON A LAKE NEAR SALONIKA QUESTIONING FISHERMEN.

Official Photograph; supplied by Newspaper Illustrations.

With the Indian Contingent at Salonika.

A CAMP GYMKHANA MEETING : A COUPLED - MULE RACE ; AND MOUNTED TUG-OF-WAR.

Two very sporting "events" on the card at a recent camp gym-khana meeting at or near Salonika are shown here; and soldiers of the Indian Contingent who are serving with the Army under General Sarrail figure in them. In the upper illustration we have a coupled-mule race incident, which made everybody on the course laugh heartily. The competing mules, each with a rider, had to race fastened two and two. What happened at one of the jumps with one pair, where one of the mules took the leap, and the other jibbed, is depicted. The lower illustration shows another mirth-provoking "event" of the afternoon, a tug-of-war on mules between Indian competitors, each man stripped to the skin and riding bare-back.—[Press Bureau Photograph ; supplied by Newspaper Illustrations.]

With the British Red Cross on the Tigris.

AT AMARA MILITARY HOSPITAL : A HOT OR COLD FOOD APPARATUS, AND A HOSPITAL TENT.

In the upper illustration is shown an ingenious contrivance (in use at the Military Hospital at Amara, on the Tigris) designed for keeping invalids' food either hot or cold, as may be required. Its value is obvious for keeping food cool in the hot season of the year which prevails in Mesopotamia from April to the autumn rains. Ice is not procurable except by artificial means. As illustrated in a recent issue of " The War News," it is not very long since the very first ice-factory in the country began to be built at Basra, by British Engineers and coolie labour, primarily for the use of the hospitals. In the lower illustration, the interior of a hospital-tent at Amara, with men at a meal, is seen. The netting is to keep the flies off the food.—[Photos. by C.N.]

With the British Red Cross on the Tigris.

AT AMARA MILITARY HOSPITAL : ONE OF THE OUTSIDE WARDS, AND THE CONVALESCENTS' VERANDAH.

The upper illustration shows one of the smaller temporary structures, an erection with walls of the woven rush-matting used in native buildings, in the compound, or enclosure, of the large military hospital at Amara. It is used as a ward for minor cases. More serious cases are housed in a large permanent brick building, formerly the residence of the Turkish official in charge of the Amara district. Its verandah overlooks the Tigris, and a convalescent patient is reading and resting while an orderly fans him. Amara, shown in the lower illustration, is a largish town on the Tigris, about midway between Basra and Bagdad, and its position marked it out for a hospital centre and headquarters station. Kut-el-Amara is many miles off.—[Photos. by C.N.]

When the Tide Rises Over No I

ASSAULTING THE ENEMY'S TRENCHES AFTER ARTILLERY PREPARATION AND MINE-EX

An infantry assault in force upon the enemy's trenches has always to be preceded by "artillery preparation" in the form of sustained and violent bombardment with high-explosive shells, and generally also by the detonation of mines, in order to shatte his defences and make the way comparatively clear for the advancing troops. As soon as this preparation is considered to hav

's Land: "Waves" of Assault.

AN INFANTRY ADVANCE IN SUCCESSIVE LINES—A FRENCH ARTIST'S IMPRESSION.

sufficient, the signal is given, and the troops surge forward to the assault in successive "waves." The object of the first "wave" is to sweep over the enemy's front line of trenches and pass on to attack those beyond. Then the next "wave" follows, consolidates the position in the front line of enemy trenches, and so on.—[From the Drawing by André Devambez.]

Battlefield Scenes on the Italian Front.

IN THE CARSO COCKPIT: A STORMED AUSTRIAN TRENCH AT SELTZ, AND THE TOWN.

In the upper illustration is seen what remained of an Austrian trench section on the Isonzo front after its bombardment and storming by the Italians. Describing the locality, a correspondent says this: "Each one of these hills is nothing but a chaotic mass of rocks and stones, flat and open, recalling a Dante scene. The effect of shells falling on this rocky ground is terrible. Each shell, as it bursts on the rocks, scatters them into a thousand splinters, which are as deadly as bullets. Seltz—the ruins of which heavily bombarded township in the valley of the same—is on the Carso front. It was the scene of a brilliant Italian victory a few weeks ago, and the Austrian guns from a distance have continued to shell the place ever since."

General Cadorna on the Italian Front.

GLIMPSES OF THE ITALIAN GENERALISSIMO : DESCENDING FROM A TREE AND ENJOYING A JOKE.

The world was favoured recently with a German war-correspondent's story of how the Kaiser spent a Sunday morning up a tree in Alsace with members of his General Staff, scanning the French lines through a telescope. In the upper illustration General Cadorna, with some of his Staff, is seen coming down from a similar observation post. An interesting precedent is recorded of Napoleon.

Napoleon, it is told, in one of his earlier battles, while still a slim young Republican General, "spotted" from up a tree the tell-tale dust of an important enemy 'move far off, and, countering it, won the day. In the lower illustration, General Cadorna is seen much amused at something told him. The "bonne histoire" is a welcome relief in war-time.—[Photos. by Topical.]

By a Raemaekers of Italy: Sachetti War Cartoons.

ITALIAN WAR-CARTOONS AT THE LEICESTER GALLERIES: SOME EXAMPLES BY SIGNOR E. SACHETTI.

Cartoon No. 1 on this page shows a German soldier saying "Teach the child German? It is unnecessary. He will lie soon enough." No. 2 is entitled simply, "A Boche," and No. 3, "Those who spread Kultur." These caricatures represent Teuton types familiar in photographs of German prisoners. No. 4 is called "The Censor in Belgium," and shows a German soldier who has pre-vented the spread of unfavourable news by the simple expedient of killing the newsboy. These cartoons, with those on the opposite page, form part of the interesting collection of Italian war-drawings brought together by a Belgian gentleman, and recently placed on view at the Leicester Galleries in Leicester Square. Those on this page are all by Signor E. Sachetti.—[Photos. by C.N.]

By a Max Beerbohm of Italy: Tirelli War Cartoons.

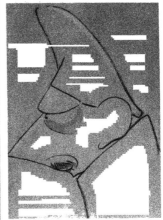

ITALIAN WAR-CARTOONS AT THE LEICESTER GALLERIES: EXAMPLES BY SIGNOR UMBERTO TIRELLI.

Cartoon No. 1 on this page is called "A Kaiser"; No. 2, "A Crown Prince"; No. 3, "A Czar"; and No. 4, "An Emperor." They represent respectively, of course, the Kaiser and his heir— the German Crown Prince; Czar Ferdinand of Bulgaria; and the Emperor Francis Joseph of Austria, and they hit off very cleverly the characteristics popularly associated with the several subjects— arrogance, imbecility, craftiness, and dotage. Signor Tirelli's work in caricature has been compared with that of Max Beerbohm, who similarly gets his humorous effects by emphasising points of facial expression with an element of distortion. Another striking Tirelli cartoon at the Leicester Galleries, called "Miss Kronprinzins," shows the Crown Prince as a smirking circus rider.—[Photos. by C.N.]

THINGS DONE : III.—CAVALRY.

SHRAPNEL, machine gunnery, magazine rifles, armoured cars, aeroplanes, and the theoretical experts who sit at home and settle large and little destinies with the stroke of a fountain pen have played havoc with the function and worth of the cavalry. But the cavalry still goes on. Between the South African War and this war, even between the Franco-German War and this, few men considered themselves *ex cathedra* experts unless they said solemnly and often that " the day of cavalry was over." But the cavalry still went on. Armageddon 1914 came, exhibiting its shocking capacity for shattering the moral fibres of both theories and theorists; and one of the theories that received a bad compound fracture was that accepted one about the *arme blanche.* In the beginning—that is, while there

forming the manoeuvre of pursuit, when a swiftly moving and mobile force is absolutely a necessity, we have seen that in the battle of the Marne, no less than in the latest splendidly rapid Russian advance in Poland and Galicia, cavalry has been able to fulfil all that was desired of it in practical fact.

The functions of the cavalry squadrons are the functions of mobility. Their business in life is to see quickly, to hit quickly, and to parry quickly and flexibly; it is also their habit to raise a dust by the volatility of their movements, and the object of that dust is to get into the other people's eyes. The last attribute is linked with the first; while they see as much as they can themselves, they must do their best to make the enemy see as little as possible.

HOW THE ALLIES DO EVERYTHING POSSIBLE FOR THEIR PRISONERS : A MASS FOR AUSTRIAN PRISONERS IN AN ITALIAN INTERNMENT CAMP.

Everywhere—in England, in France, in Russia, in Italy—the Allies have set an example of humanity and consideration for their prisoners which contrasts as light and darkness with the vile cruelties and atrocious barbarities which the two Central Powers deliberately inflict on the men in their hands. The illustration of how the Italian Government goes out of the way to show consideration for the religious creed of its Austrian prisoners is, in this regard, instructive.—[*Photo. by Topical.*]

was movement in war—the one profoundly certain thing about the cavalry was that it was doing most of those things the theorists said it would not do. It did excellently in scouting; it formed, especially in the case of the Germans, an admirable screen to veil the advance of armies; it showed sound propensities for covering flanks and attacking them; and of our own cavalry even yet not enough has been said of the magnificent skill and courage with which the retreat was covered. When opportunities showed, shock tactics were employed with effect, and, in per-

This scouting and screening faculty of the cavalry is, in modern war, perhaps the most vital duty. The cavalry go out to find, to feel, and to see the strength of the enemy. The face of any army in movement must be protected by numberless sensitive antennæ, and these antennæ must send back facts of position, movement, and power of the force opposing. Aeroplanes, cyclists, and motorists have taken from the cavalry patrols much of their value as scouts, but not even the advance of modern science has been able to beat the horse and horsemen in this.

(Continued overleaf.)

An Ill-Fated Air-Attack on King Albert.

DESTROYED IN AN ATTEMPT TO BOMB KING ALBERT'S RESIDENCE: AN AVIATIK BROUGHT DOWN.

The upper photograph was taken, from above, at the moment when a German Aviatik biplane, brought down by a Belgian warplane at La Pagne, was falling into the sea. The lower photograph shows the wreckage of the machine being hauled up on to the beach. Both the pilot and the observer were drowned. Their object, it is stated, was to drop bombs on the residence of the King and Queen of the Belgians. It will be noted that some of the soldiers are wearing steel helmets. King Albert has also adopted this form of head-gear for use at the front. Queen Elizabeth was last month presented with the French "Croix de Guerre" by President Poincaré, when he visited the Belgian troops near Nieuport Ville and Ramscapelle.—[Photographs by C.N.]

Cycles and automobiles are things of frail virtue on rough ground and in roadless tracts; and where there are troop-covering trees and valleys the airman is lost; and the enemy can bluff him, in any case, with dummy positions, or carefully screened guns and forces. Amid trees and over rough country, then, the horsemen come into their own. They find out the enemy by actual contact and the effect of arms. This

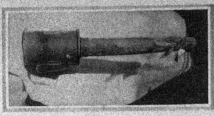

AN ENEMY TRENCH PROJECTILE FROM THE WESTERN FRONT:
A GERMAN HAND-GRENADE.

The hand-grenade, with its throwing-shaft, has a tag of tape attached at the upper end. The hook seen fixed on the metal case of the grenade itself is to hold the grenade, with the explosive head uppermost, on the soldier's belt. Fire and a-half seconds are allowed for the flinging; between the pulling of the tag and the explosion taking place.

advance screen of horsemen has the second advantage of hiding the movements of troops behind from the screen of equally anxious scouts pushed out by the foe. By attacking and driving in enemy cavalry patrols, certain numbers of the enemy's are put out. Even the progress of the enemy can be hampered by making swift raids on communications, against railways and railway bridges with an aim to destruction, or upon convoys and outposts insufficiently protected.

In the actual battle the cavalry waits on tip-toe ready to seize opportunities. Its office is to lunge a swift and slogging blow when, for a moment, the opposing guard has weakened or lost alertness. If it can catch artillery unguarded or in a moment of flurry, or infantry in a moment of sixes and sevens, or if it can swing on to enemy cavalry when that cavalry is unable to counter, that is the horsemen's chance. The abrupt smash of the charge is to break, throw into confusion and to scatter enemy units by the swiftness and fire of the stroke. In this way the cavalry is best at home in a flanking attack, when its rapidity of movement, its mobility, enables it to get round the enemy, threaten his rear, and roll up his line.

In retreat the cavalry lives to harry and to hold. If, fortunately, it is the enemy who retreats, then the horsemen fill his soul with the

love of speed and urgency. The cavalry breaks up the enemy's retiring line and keeps it moving and broken. All attempts to stand are shattered, and amongst the broken regiments the quick, raiding charges beget panic and stop all hope of reforming with courage. If, unfortunately, the enemy is pursuing, the cavalry and their horse-batteries form a thin wall to protect the retreating columns. The cavalry can do this because its greater speed enables it to fall back more swiftly, and its greater mobility enables it to move about to those points where effective defence will hold back the most aspiring of the pursuers.

The British cavalry can perform this office admirably, because the British cavalry has been trained to fight with equal *insouciance* on foot as well as mounted. Continental cavalry—except, in some degree, the Russian—do not do this as well, because the trooper has been taught to fight as a horse soldier pure and simple.

The Continent, however, had no South African War; if the South African War led us to place too much trust in shrapnel, it also taught us that a man and a rifle, plus a horse, form something more valuable than a decorative unit of shock-tactics design, that the added mobility gave the man and a rifle immense effectiveness both in advance and retreat. We have no mounted infantry now,

AN ENEMY TRENCH-PROJECTILE FROM THE WESTERN FRONT:
A GERMAN "CRAB" HAND-BOMB.

The crab bomb, which is shaped like the upper and under shells of a crab, is shown with its safety-pin (to be pulled out at the moment of flinging) still fixed in position for safe carrying. Before throwing, the soldier pulls out the pin, using the ring seen, and the bomb explodes on striking, by means of an internal detonator.

as we had in South Africa, but that is only because every cavalryman is also a mounted infantryman.   W. DOUGLAS NEWTON.

At the Front in German East Africa.

WITH ONE OF OUR COLUMNS : ON THE MARCH ; AND COOKING AN EVENING MEAL.

The pair of illustrations which are shown here are campaign notes taken with one of the British columns now fighting in German East Africa. Their progress, according to the telegraphic despatches from General Smuts and his Brigadiers, is meeting ever with more and more success. Alike on the northern or Kilimanjaro side, and in the south-west of the German colony in the Lake Tangan-

yika quarter, our troops, British, Indians, South Africans, Rhodesians, are all advancing and striking hard. In the upper illustration is seen a marching column of strapping fellows in shirt-sleeves and shorts because of the intense heat of the country at this time of year. In the lower illustration men are seen during a halt, cooking an evening meal.—[Photos. by Realistic Travels.]

With a British Unit Serving in Russia.

WHERE OUR MEN LANDED IN THE FAR NORTH: ARCTIC TRANSPORT AND A PARADE MUSTER.

The Emperor of Russia has conferred the Order and Medal of St. Anne on some of the officers and men of a British unit in Russia for "meritorious work." The unit comprises various contingents, it would appear; one a large armoured motor-car section. They landed some time ago and spent some time at Alexandrovsk, on the Kola Peninsula, between the White Sea and the Arctic Ocean, a glimpse of which in winter time is given in the upper illustration, when reindeer-drawn sledges perform the ordinary transport traffic. In the contingents of the unit, seen in the lower illustration on parade "somewhere" in Russia, are men who have seen service in Belgium, Northern France, Gallipoli, and Africa, and practically the whole Empire is represented.

Russia in the Field; and On a Visit to Italy.

FIELD GUNS IN THE SNOW; AND THE DUMA DEPUTATION: INCIDENTS ON TWO FRONTS.

While England was experiencing cold winds from the north-east in mid-May, the same winds, according to Petrograd telegrams, were bringing a recurrence of heavy snow along the Russian front. There was, however, no cessation of artillery activity anywhere, and at several places, facing Marshal Hindenburg's group of armies, the Russians pushed home attacks against points of vantage held by the enemy. Russian field artillery moving forward through the snow are seen in the upper illustration. In the lower we have an incident during the visit of the Duma Deputies to the Italian front. They have visited England and France. Prince Lobanoff, Chairman of the Empire Council, is seen returning a popular greeting in the war zone.—[Photos. by Illustrations Bureau and S. and G.]

With our Indian Cavalry in France.

KEEPING UP THEIR TRAINING : A JODHPUR LANCER PATROL AT A FIELD DAY.

A patrol of Jodhpur Lancers—one of the highly trained and disciplined cavalry corps of Indian Imperial Service troops which the patriotism of its native Prince sent to Europe as a unit of the Indian Contingent—is seen in the upper illustration. The patrol is shown at a field day such as are of constant occurrence at the cavalry camps in rear of the trench front, for keeping men and horses fit and in hard training. An alarm that hostile forces are approaching has just been given, and several of the Lancers are seen dismounting or already on foot, hastening off to hold a certain point. In the lower illustration the Sowars of the troop are seen lying down under cover of a bush-grown hedge-row ready to open fire as the enemy appear.—[Photos. by Realistic Travels.]

With the Indian Contingent in France.

AT WORK AT FIELD ENGINEERING : LAYING AN OVERHEAD TELEPHONE WIRE IN A VILLAGE.

Men of a section of Indian pioneer infantry on signalling service are seen in the illustration above at a village in Northern France engaged in running an overhead field-telephone wire connecting headquarters with some point. As shown, one of the linesmen is up the ladder fastening the insulator on the upper part of a brick-walled house, and affixing the telephone wire to it. Another sepoy on the ground is holding up the length of wire with a guiding fork and regulating the strain on it as it comes off the reel which two other men in the background are holding. Telephone wires over military roads are fixed as high as possible where there is traffic. The chief risk they run is of being cut by stray shrapnel bullets.—[Photo. by Realistic Travels.]

WOMEN AND THE WAR.

WAR, we are told, is the business of men. But there is at least one section of the feminine community officially linked with the profession of arms on land and sea. Wherever the British soldier goes in any numbers there goes the grey-clad, scarlet-caped figure of the Army nurse. In war or peace the fortunes of the members of Queen Alexandra's Imperial Military Nursing Service are closely linked with the fortunes of Thomas Atkins. The first hint of definite "trouble" that sends him cheering into the barrack square sends her to her post, alert and ready to meet any emergency that may arise.

When the Fleet mobilises and clears for action, the members of Queen Alexandra's Royal Naval Nursing Service, metaphorically speaking, "pull up their socks," call up their reserves, and prepare for developments. Amongst other duties that fall to their lot is helping to "man" the hospital-ships attached to the Fleet. It is a task to which the Hun, with his studied disregard for the laws of humanity and the Geneva Convention, has added not a few anxieties.

The ambition of the Army nurse is to be sent on active service; and our quarrel with Germany was not many hours old before Miss Becher,

THE "WAR BROWNIES" ON THE LAND: A CHEERFUL GROUP OF WOMEN RETURNING FROM WORK.
"War Brownies" is the name given to women workers on the land at Evesham. They have been so nicknamed on account of their earth-brown breeches and smocks.—[Photograph by C.N.]

R.R.C., Matron-in-Chief at the War Office, had called up her reserves and was well on with the work of transforming her army of matrons, sisters, and staff nurses from its peace footing of rather less than three hundred to its war complement of about as many thousand. A few days later the first batch of English nurses—military nurses, at any rate—had left London for the "Front" on general service with the Allied troops. Like the British Army, the Nursing Service attached to it was definitely caught up in the great war machine.

Those early nurses had a stirring time. When the fog of war definitely lifts, their adventures will make interesting reading. We do know, though, that the rapid advance of the Germans entailed an equally rapid retreat on the part of the staffs attached to hospitals barely in working order before the order to "move on" was received. First one and then another building had to be abandoned. But the nurses were "wonderful." Wherever, for the moment, they happened to find themselves, the work of preparing for the patients went methodically forward. If the necessary furniture was lacking, it was improvised from the best materials that came to hand. Stately homes became in less than twenty-four hours

[Continued overleaf.

"FARM-WORK FOR WOMEN": A DEMONSTRATION AT KELMSCOTT, OXFORD.
Photograph by Dennis Moss.

The "War-Brownies" at Work on a Farm.

WOMEN ON THE LAND: SOME INTERESTING SCENES AT EVESHAM.

Our first photograph shows women workers watering marrows; our second shows other women-workers filling a barn. They form part of the little army of some two hundred women now at regular work on the land at Evesham. The first party of women fruit-pickers sent out by the National Land Council, seen in other pictures, arrived at Evesham last week. It included cheery, enthusiastic women, daughters of clergymen, professional and business men, some artists, a teacher, and some girls who prefer to exchange office work for life in the open air. They joined the "Brownies," so nicknamed because of their earth-brown breeches and smocks. They also wear high boots and "boots they wear in the trenches."—[Photo. by C.N.]

up-to-date hospitals, with their furniture and fittings put to strange uses, and into these the wounded poured in one continuous stream of dirty, tired, hungry, half-naked, and indescribably mangled humanity. Later on the nurses in the hospital-ships had an equally strenuous time.

THE "WAR BROWNIES" DOING MEN'S WORK : FILLING WATER-BARRELS FROM THE RIVER AVON.

The workers shown here have undertaken a heavy task—witness the huge butt on wheels—but are showing that they have the strength of a man when occasion calls.

Photograph by C.N.

Queen Alexandra's Military Nursing Service, however, is only one branch of the great organisation whose business it is to attend to the sick and wounded in war time. Behind it in readiness for emergencies is the Territorial Force Nursing Service, founded ten years ago at the instance of Miss Haldane, with Miss Sidney Browne, R.R.C., as Matron-in-Chief. In peace it is a " paper" service, and " Preparedness " can properly be called its motto. Never was motto more apt. From the Matron-in-Chief working ceaselessly at the War Office, the twenty-three principal matrons enrolled on its books—fully trained nurses, as are all the members of the Force—received their mobilisation orders the day after war was declared. They in their turn summoned their staffs. A few days later the three thousand Territorial nurses scattered throughout England, Scotland, and Wales were ready for service, and the twenty-three Territorial General Hospitals were ready too. Since then the number of nurses has risen to over five thousand, and an additional hospital has been formed in London, and four hospitals staffed for service at the Front. The members, on mobilisation, come directly under the War Office, and at the moment

nearly a thousand are on foreign service scattered abroad in France, Egypt, and other distant theatres of war.

Incidentally, this calling-up of the Territorial Force Nursing Service has given another proof of the sacrifices women are ready to make in the cause of their country. In not a few instances the women who responded to the call of the War Office gave up good posts to do it. Many of these positions will not be open to them when they return to civil life. But almost without exception the " called-up " nurse has stuck to her job.

From the farthest corners of the Empire and beyond it, women have flocked to serve under the sign of the Red Cross. A hospital-ship came from the Begum of Bhopal. Canada supplied its nursing contingent ; so did Australia, so did South Africa. Japan sent a fully equipped Red Cross unit.

Magnificent as the military nursing organisation is, without outside help it would have been wholly inadequate to meet the gigantic needs created by the war. The history of what private effort has accomplished in the direction of

THE "WAR BROWNIES" AS FRUIT-PICKERS : PLUCKING GOOSEBERRIES.

Our photograph suggests that this form of work demands something of the nerve of those who are told to "grasp the nettle " like a man and it "soft as silk remains."

Photograph by C.N.

hospital work would fill a volume. Nor must the efforts of the British Red Cross Society and the Order of St. John be overlooked. These will be described later. CLAUDINE CLEVE.

A Religious Service Amid Glaciers.

ITALY'S ALPINE WAR WITH AUSTRIA : MASS BEING CELEBRATED ON A MOUNTAIN-SIDE.

This picture by Ludovico Pogliaghi is one of the series of battle-paintings in the Italian Exhibition at the Leicester Galleries, Leicester Square. It illustrates the almost incredible difficulties of terrain and climate with which the Italian armies have had and have to contend. The incident of a mountain-side Mass, near an Alpini camp, with the celebrant priest at an altar set up on a steep slope, evidences also the devotional character of the Italian soldier, to whom the war against Austria for the recovery of " Unredeemed Italy " is a Crusade. The surroundings of sheer crags where rock-fissures and ledges between glaciers afford the only foothold, with dark masses of vapour rolling overhead, are everyday concomitants of an Alpine battlefield. The pictures should be seen.

A Campaign that was Brilliantly Successful.

ON THE WESTERN EGYPT FRONTIER: A BIG GUN; AND GIFTS FROM AUSTRALIA ARRIVING.

In the upper illustration a heavy position gun, for service with the Western Egypt Frontier Force and strengthening certain defences, is seen on disembarkation. The gun is starting for its destination in charge of a section of the Australian transport train. Sir John Maxwell, in his recent despatch on the Egyptian operations, speaks of the Australian train as having "worked splendidly." The landing of heavy *matériel* was under control of the Navy, a transport of which is seen in the background. "I wish to emphasise the unvarying and whole-hearted support accorded throughout by the Royal Navy," writes Sir John Maxwell. In the lower illustration an incidental naval service in the safeguarding of vessels from Australia to. Egypt is suggested.—[*Photos. by C.N.*]

A Campaign that was Brilliantly Successful.

ON THE WESTERN EGYPT FRONTIER: A FLOODED AUSTRALIAN CAMP; AND BEDOUIN PRISONERS.

Australians digging trenches in a swamped desert camp to drain off the flood water during the Western Egyptian Frontier campaign are seen in the upper illustration. It may be true that rain never falls in the Nile valley, but it certainly does to the west, towards the Tripolitan border along the shores of the Mediterranean. On the occasion illustrated, rain-storms swept the camp for days on end. Sir John Maxwell, in his recently published despatch, speaks of "torrential rains which continued with rare breaks for a week, the country becoming a sea of mud." A party of Bedouin enemy captured by an Australian patrol while escaping after a battle across the desert, are seen with their captors in the lower illustration.—[Photos. by C.N.]

The Tsar and His Victorious General at the Front.

THE VICTORIES IN THE BUKOVINA : THE EMPEROR OF RUSSIA AND GENERAL BRUSSILOFF.

It was ＿＿＿ on the 26th that the Russians had conquered the whole of the Bukovina, thus adding to the Tsar's dominions a territory of 4000 square miles. Further north, near Lutsk, they had ＿een slightly checked by the Germans in their advance towards the important railway centre of Kovel, but had since regained some of the ground. Speaking of his recent great victories to Mr. Stanley

Washburn, General Brussiloff said : "The sweeping successes attained by my armies are not the product of chance, or of Austrian weakness, but represent the application of all the lessons which we have learnt in two years of bitter warfare against the Germans. . . . If we are able to take Kovel . . . the whole Eastern front will be obliged to fall back."—[Photo. by C.N.]

The Illustrated War News, July 5, 1916.—Part 4, New Series.

The Illustrated War News

LEADER OF THE BRITISH ADVANCE ON THE WESTERN FRONT: GENERAL SIR DOUGLAS HAIG.

Photograph by Elliott and Fry.

THE GREAT WAR

By W. DOUGLAS NEWTON.

THERE has come a quickening on practically the whole of the great girdle of war that encircles the strength of the German Powers. It is a sense of movement which we of the Allies have not experienced before, though it was expected in the spring of last year. Not merely its novelty and its obvious strength, but even more its indication of sure unanimity among the Allied forces, carries to us a hope of great significance. The Allied Powers have given us optimism by the strength of this co-operative initiative, but as much as anything we have gained that good feeling by the knowledge, now made obvious, of the greater strength that made the co-operative reticence that went before. During the past few months the patience of the different army groups has been undergoing a great strain. It is clear that the German movement upon Verdun must have been watched with anxiety, for the most natural mode of relieving the pressure there would be to set up a counter-irritant by large attacks on the German fronts elsewhere. It is not easy for powerful forces to stand idle while the enemy is winning ground elsewhere, and undoubtedly part of the German intention was to force that imperative desire "to do-something" into activity, and so upset our plans by causing our premature action. It says much for the strength of the Allies that their Commanders were determined enough to take the risks, and abide by a plan of their own making. The results

QUEEN ALEXANDRA AND A CHILD COLLECTOR OF £1100: HER MAJESTY INSPECTING THE "YOUNG KITCHENER'S" MOTOR AMBULANCE.
Little Miss Jeannie Jackson, the daughter of a Burnley miner, has collected £1100 in coppers in the streets of Burnley during the past twelve months. With £450 of the money the "Young Kitchener's" Motor Ambulance was provided.—[Photo. by C.N.]

A WAR-GIFT FROM INDIA: A BATTLEPLANE PRESENTED BY RESIDENTS IN THE PUNJAB ABOUT TO LEAVE ENGLAND FOR FRANCE.
Official-photograph issued by the Press Bureau; supplied by Topical.

have so far justified the plan. Germany has involved herself in a huge local encounter, in which her interest has been prolonged considerably beyond her schedule, and in which her losses have been at least equal, and probably greater, than the French. She has concentrated her effort against France, and in so doing has left two of her chief enemies almost intact. Having allowed Germany to concentrate on France, Russia and England (and in a measure Italy), following the set plan, are now going to war with Germany, when, obviously, she must be suffering in some degree from exhaustion. Russia is making big movements; the British front has broken into a state of activity that is full of real menace to the Central Powers, and may develop to calamity; Italy, after allowing the Austrian to expend his vigour against an equable retreat, is countering with a vehemence which is telling on the tired opponent; and France, calling together again her splendid reserves of power after her truly wonderful defence, is thrusting at the enemy line. The whole of the fronts are quickening; the enemy, after months of heavy fighting, is being called upon, not to rest, but to fight with greater heaviness. This may not be the end, or even the beginning of the end yet, but the patience, the strength, and the freshness of the Allied movement place all the advantages with us. The auspicious note of Allied co-ordination is that, side by side with the Russians and the Italians, the Western forces have entered upon an offensive of power. This big movement was begun on the morning of July 1, and the zone of pressure embraced a front of some twenty-five miles. About sixteen miles of this front lies within the British sphere between Gommecourt and the Somme; the remainder is on the French line running down from the Somme, probably to somewhere in the Chaulnes area. The line of attack seems to be an admirable one. The face of this great curve that turns over the Oise to the Aisne line, and stretches upward from the Somme in the long curtain of Arras, Ypres, and the Yser, protects the most delicate of strategic communications. A deep penetration would not merely mean the retirement of the German front—it would uncover great flanks and rears to the right and left, and would demand

working magnificently in conjunction along this line. The first German trenches were swiftly carried, the British reaching Contalmaison, two miles in front of our line; Mametz, and Montauban, and practically isolating the Germans at Fricourt. The French, pushing up on our right, took Hardecourt, the outskirts of Curlu, and, further to the south, the villages of Dompierre, Becquincourt, Bussu, and Fay. North of Albert we have broken into the Gommecourt salient, and are making fighting advance north of the Ancre Valley. Here the Germans resisted strenuously, and we were not able to hold all the ground we captured at first. Still, the trend of the fighting is carrying us forward, and we are penetrating on the whole of our sixteen miles of front. It is useless yet to note down specific gains of ground, because each

QUEEN ALEXANDRA AND THE GIFT OF THE BRITISH SPORTSMEN'S AMBULANCE FUND: HER MAJESTY INSPECTING
MOTOR-AMBULANCES, WITH LORD LONSDALE.
Queen Alexandra inspected at Marlborough House the other day 16 motor-ambulances provided by the British Sportsmen's Ambulance Fund, of which Lord Lonsdale is President. Her Majesty presented the vehicles, on their behalf, to the Wounded Allies Relief Committee and the Sir Arthur Du Cros Ambulance Convoy. Lord Lonsdale said the Fund hoped to raise £50,000 and provide 100 cars.
Photograph by Central Press.

that violent readjustment of enemy fronts for which the Germans seem to be aiming at Verdun. The attack, which was not unexpected by those who had followed the communiqués closely, began in spirited fashion. A great deal of trench-raiding and reconnaissance work and heavy bombarding had filled the seven days preceding July 1. The Germans spoke of our excessive zeal in artillery in the Somme area, especially before Albert. The attack itself was heralded by a particularly heavy bombardment, and the movement of the infantry, which followed at 7.30, was thus able to attain some of its initial gains with few casualties. The main line of the assault appears to be in the direction of Bapaume, and perhaps Peronne, the French and the British

fresh day may bring some change. All that need be said is that the Allies in the West appear to have entered upon an undertaking that will not be lightly relinquished.

At Verdun the French have changed their mode of defence from the resolutely passive to the resolutely aggressive. They have been countering heavily and have won back ground, including the Thiaumont works. A swaying battle is taking place, the Germans alternately capturing and being evicted from Thiaumont.

Not the least august of the movements to record this week are those of the Russians and the Italians. Of the former, it may be said that, after a short and anticipated pause, the advance has again broken forward. This advance has been on the Russian left wing, where General Lechitsky, after over-running Bukovina between the Roumanian border and the Carpathians, is pressing forward along the Pruth beyond Kolomea. Here, between the Pruth and the Dniester, and in country that is conspicuously more easy for defence than attack, our Ally struck his blow on a line running from the Dniester to Kuty, gained three sets of trenches, and added another 10,000 men captured to his spoils. Kolomea fell quickly, and its capture took one of the primary converging points out of enemy hands; its fall weakens the whole of the defensive system — even, perhaps, to Kovel. On the right of the offensive — that is, on the Lutsk front—the Germans are still fighting strenuously to save Kovel. Here the Russians appear to be waiting calmly for the exhaustion of the German counter-efforts, breaking every attack as it is sent out against them. The Germans claim to have made certain gains, but these appear to have been so small as not to have made a very tangible impression on the battle. On the Riga and Dvinsk fronts there are signs that the Germans are feeling for an opportunity to attack heavily. Heavy bombardments and gas discharges have been brought into play, but the Russians have been able to hold the enemy at most points.

Arsiero and Asiago, and their invasion appeared well on towards the subjection of the Venetian plain and the damage of the Isonzo communications. General Cadorna was, however, able to master the enemy in brilliant fashion, to hold him, and then to drive him back in a manner entirely unequivocal. The fighting in Galicia and Poland must have had effect on the Austrian

A SCHOOL O.T.C. BATTALION WITH A FAMOUS NAME: THE "MARLBOROUGHS" MARCHING TO THE REVIEW GROUND.

strength, if it only starved the movement of reserves; but the new victory owes quite as much to the skill and the dash of the Italian soldiers.

The front of invasion has been rolled back along its entire line, and in a couple of days our Ally has been able to regain quite half of what the Austrians had taken in their whole campaign. Such strong positions as the Asiago and Arsiero defences, and the works on Mounts Priafora, Cengio, Trappola, and on Monte Maggio were carried with extraordinary swiftness, until the line in the centre has advanced well up the Astico towards Tonezza. The right is making good and steady progress in the Val Sugana; but the left is facing heavy counter-attacks, though pressing upward in the Monte Zugna and Pasubio areas. The Austrians have the strength of the ground in their favour, and the Italians have a hard task; they are attacking it with great spirit and with exceedingly well-equipped armies. Some excellent work is being accomplished on the road to Tarvis and in the Isonzo area generally, where an Italian offensive is meeting with success.

A SCHOOL O.T.C. BATTALION WITH A FAMOUS NAME: LIEUT.-COL. STEWART INSPECTING MARLBOROUGH COLLEGE O.T.C.

Marlborough College, as becomes the great public school at the town whence the great captain in the first great war on the Continent in which the British Army took part received his title, has been one of the strongest supporters of the O.T.C. At the outset of the war, in August 1914, it possessed an O.T.C. battalion of six companies; and the corps is stronger still, with its *esprit de corps* raised to the highest pitch by what former members serving with the Armies in the Field have done and the distinctions that they have won.—[*Photo. by S. and G.*]

The Italian counter in the Tyrol has been only less startling than the Russian offensive. The Austrian attack had carried them to a line beyond

LONDON: JULY 3. 1916.

A British Officer's "House-Boat" on the Tigris.

WITH A HEN-COOP ON THE ROOF! A TRANSPORT OFFICER'S MESOPOTAMIA HEADQUARTERS.

One of the native river-craft of the Tigris, turned to war service in the capacity of a house-boat, as the floating headquarters of the officer in charge of the local transport arrangements at a British riverside camp, is seen in the above illustration. The open-boat hull of the vessel has been housed over by means of a timber framework structure, covered on the roof and at the sides with rush, or cocoanut, matting, over which is drawn, as a protective awning against the fierce heat of the sun, a canvas-screen covering, the outer fly of a tent. There are on earth few hotter places—if any—than Lower Mesopotamia between May and August. The crate on the roof is a hen-coop, to provide the "Murghi-roast" (roast fowl), the Indian mess khansamah's staple dish.—[Photo. C.N.]

A Fancy Fair for War Funds in Tokyo.

JAPANESE AND EUROPEANS IN TOKYO WORK FOR SERBIAN, FRENCH, AND BELGIAN SUFFERERS.

Our first photograph shows the Belgian booth at the very attractive and admirably managed bazaar, held in Tokyo on May 18, 19, and 20, which was promoted by foreign residents and realised a very substantial and welcome addition to the much-needed war funds on behalf of which it was got up. It was held at Mitsukoshi Store, Niponbashi, Tokyo; and a large number of sympathetic and open-handed purchasers came from Yokohama. Our second picture shows some pretty, white-clad girls selling flowers; and in our third is seen Count Okuma talking to a lady at a stall. Many other notabilities were present, among them being Princess Mori, Princess Nabeshima, Baron and Baroness Mitsui, Baron Iwasaki, and other distinguished personages.—[*Photos. by C.N.*]

Queen Mary Visits the National Economy Exhibition.

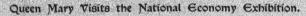

ROYAL AND CIVIC INTEREST IN THE HOME : THE QUEEN AND LORD MAYOR STUDY ECONOMY.

The practical value of the National Economy Exhibition at Prince's Skating Club, Knightsbridge, appeals to all ; the interest shown in it by high and low has been most marked, and it has conclusively proved that economy does not necessarily imply discomfort. Queen Mary, an expert in everything connected with home life, has taken much interest in the Exhibition. Our first photograph shows her Majesty leaving Prince's after paying a visit to the Exhibition on Tuesday, June 27, prior to the official opening by the Lord Mayor. Our second photograph shows the Lord Mayor, Sir Charles Wakefield, arriving to open the Exhibition. Our third picture shows Sir Charles purchasing a War Loan certificate.—[Photos. Nos. 1 and 2, by Photopress ; No. 3, by Illustrations Bureau.]

With the British Gunners on the Western Front.

A HEAVY GUN ON A RAILWAY MOUNTING : RAMMING THE SHELL HOME ; A GUN FIRING.

In the upper illustration, a heavy gun team is seen loading a big gun on a railway mounting. The gunners are shown in the act of ramming home into the breech of the gun one of the heavy projectiles fired by ordnance of the class. The shell is, of course, inserted first into the rear end of the gun-barrel immediately forward of the chamber in which the cartridge with the charge of propellant is placed. The charge lodged, the breech is closed, and the gun is ready for firing. In the lower illustration a howitzer on a railway mounting is seen at the moment of firing—with the fumes of the smokeless powder from the discharge still hanging round in the air, and the gunners getting ready for the next round.—[Official Photograph ; supplied by C.N.]

With the British Gunners on the Western Front.

IN ONE OF THE "STRAFING" BATTERIES: A HEAVY GUN IN ACTION; A MESSAGE TO "FRITZ."

A British heavy gun in time of action is seen in the upper illustration. Its "long, lean barrel," as Mr. Kipling somewhere says when speaking of the appearance of a long-range piece of heavy ordnance, differentiates it at a glance, at first sight, from a howitzer, the barrel of which weapon is short, stumpy, and squat-looking, whatever the calibre. To the left are seen ammuni-tion-cases in which the charges are conveyed, also some projectiles of different classes, each of which is known by the marking on the tip of the shell. In the lower illustration a shell labelled for the enemy with words of a sort that gunners in all armies rather like writing, is seen ready for insertion in the breech.—[*Official Photographs; supplied by C.N.*]

THE BEGINNINGS OF WAR-MACHINES: ARTILLERY.

THE beginnings of artillery, in the modern acceptation, may be said to date from the early part of the fourteenth century. Gunpowder, as it is known to-day, then began to be used as the propelling charge, and by the middle of the century the employment of firearms in Central and Western Europe was considerable.

"Crakys of War" were employed by Edward III. against the Scots in 1327, but no authentic description of the pieces exists. Cannon were used by the French, in 1338, at the Siege of Puy Guillaume, and two years later by the English at the Siege of Quesnoy. "Bombards," as they were called, were used at Crecy in 1346, the first occasion on which the English used such weapons in the field. A contemporary historian (Villani) says that the English king had, intermixed with his archers, "bombs which by means of fire darted small iron balls, for the purpose of affrighting and destroying the horses; and this kind of missile caused so much noise and tremour that it seemed like thunder from heaven, whilst it produced great slaughter amongst the soldiery and the overthrow of their horses." In 1347 cannon were used by Edward III. at the Siege of Calais, "arrows bound with leather," in addition to round metal shot, being fired from these weapons.

The early cannon, or bombard, was built up by means of wrought-iron bars bound together with iron hoops, and was larger in diameter at the muzzle than at the breech. An example is shown in Fig. 4 amongst the fifteenth-century weapons illustrated. In the chamber at the breech a charge of powder was exploded behind a missile placed in the barrel. The tapered bore of the latter accommodated a variety of sizes of shot, which at first took the form of stone balls, but these were afterwards superseded by iron balls. Fig. 5 shows a number of small bombards mounted

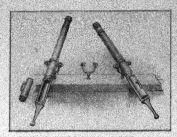

SIXTEENTH-CENTURY BREECH-LOADERS: ENGLISH NAVAL SWIVEL GUNS.

on the same carriage. This device appears to have been an attempt to produce a "quick-firing" weapon. Fig. 2 shows a bombard much resembling a mortar, mounted on a primitive carriage and fitted with an elevating device in its trail. An early breech-loader is illustrated in Fig. 3, the barrel being fixed in a wooden cradle whose rear end was turned up at right angles to the bed to form a breech-block holding in position the powder-chamber whilst the gun was fired. This powder-chamber was contained in a detachable section of the barrel, which, after receiving the powder charge, was wedged in between the breech end of the barrel proper and the breech-block abutment on the cradle. Fig. 1 shows a pair of fourteenth-century bombards, one of which is being fired by the artilleryman with a red-hot iron applied to its touch-hole, the iron having been heated in the brazier or fire-bucket kept burning alongside the weapon for this purpose. Bombards were replaced by guns of cast-iron and brass at the end of the fifteenth century.

In the sixteenth century the question of mobility seems to have received consideration, and we find cannon of that period in some cases mounted on serviceable travelling wheels and moved by horse-traction. Fig. 6 shows a French culverin of about 1550 so fitted. An ammunition-wagon of ten years later is seen in Fig. 7.

A sixteenth-century breech-loader (Fig. 8) has a detachable breech-block which is kept in position by a primitive form of wedge action. The same principle is used for that purpose in the German q.f. field-gun of to-day. A vehicle for carrying two light guns called "Petrieroes" is shown in Fig. 9. This machine was in use in the fifteenth and sixteenth centuries, and appears to have been designed to act in addition as a gun-shield for the protection of the artillerymen.

A "BOMBARD" OF HISTORY: MONS MEG OF EDINBURGH CASTLE.

"Meg" as the gun was familiarly called, was made in the fifteenth century, at Mons, whence the name. It is said to have been used at the siege of Dumbarton in 1489, and fired granite shot of about 325 lb. weight.

The Beginnings of War-Machines : Artillery.

PROTOTYPES OF WEAPONS IN THE GREAT WAR: BOMBARDS; CULVERINS; PETRIEROES.

The bombard in its giant calibre and heavy projectile may, in a sense, be spoken of as the lineal ancestor of the type of ordnance the employment of which has specially been the epoch-making event of the present Great War. The idea of its first makers in producing such a monster piece was the same as that in the minds of Herr Krupp and the Directors of the Austrian Skoda Factory—

to bring into existence a weapon absolutely to be relied upon for battering down the most formidable fortifications of the age by means of the huge and tremendously powerful projectile that it threw. A typical "roaring culverin" of Macaulay's "Ivry" is shown in Fig. 6 above—exactly, also, of the same period—just such a gun, indeed, as was used at the date and in the battle.

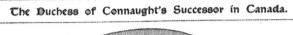

The Duchess of Connaught's Successor in Canada.

THE NEW "VICEREINE" OF THE DOMINION: THE DUCHESS OF DEVONSHIRE.

The Duchess of Devonshire is the eldest daughter of the Marquess of Lansdowne, and before her marriage, in 1892, to Mr. Victor Cavendish (as the Duke of Devonshire then was), was Lady Evelyn Emily Mary Fitzmaurice. The Duchess of Devonshire has been Mistress of the Robes to Queen Mary since 1910. The Duke and Duchess of Devonshire have two sons and five daughters. The eldest son, and heir to the Dukedom, the Marquess of Hartington, is in the Army and serving at the Front. He joined as an officer of the Derbyshire Yeomanry, and has been an A.D.C. to the Brigadier-General Commanding the South Midland Mounted Brigade. The Duchess of Devonshire has interested herself greatly in war-work for the wounded soldiers.—[Photo. by Whitlock.]

The Duke of Connaught's Successor in Canada.

THE NEW GOVERNOR-GENERAL : THE DUKE OF DEVONSHIRE, K.G., K.C.V.O.

The Duke of Devonshire, whose appointment to succeed the Duke of Connaught as Governor-General and Commander-in-Chief in Canada was officially announced on June 28, has been a Civil Lord of the Admiralty since the formation of the Coalition Ministry. He held office under the Administrations of the late Lord Salisbury and Mr. Balfour, as Treasurer of the Household and as Financial Secretary of the Treasury. He is a grandson of the seventh Duke, and a nephew of the late Duke, who was for so many years one of our leading statesmen, while Marquess of Hartington. The Duke of Devonshire is forty-eight years of age. As Mr. Victor Cavendish he sat in the House of Commons for upwards of seventeen years.—[Photo. by Downey.]

ROMANCES OF THE REGIMENTS : No. IV.—THE 2ND OXFORDSHIRE LIGHT INFANTRY.

GURWOOD AND THE GOVERNOR.

AT the period of the following story, the 2nd Oxfordshire Light Infantry was known as the 52nd Regiment of Foot, and during the Peninsular War one of its young Lieutenants, Gurwood, afterwards that Colonel Gurwood who edited the Duke of Wellington's despatches, made his reputation and his fortune by his gallant conduct at Ciudad Rodrigo. With a touch almost of superstition, he attributed his success in life to a mascot, which came into his possession at the storming of that stronghold, and his own account of his exploit is coloured by a curious vein of fatalism. His credit in the adventure was, it is true, challenged by another officer, and in the

to his battalion and asked leave of the Battalion Commandant to go alone to El Bodon, the cantonment of the 52nd. During a long and toilsome walk he still pondered the chances of death or distinction, in the event of an assault on Ciudad Rodrigo, and the probability of the Light Division being ordered for such service, and decided to volunteer for the forlorn hope.

At headquarters he spoke to Major Napier, brother of the historian, who said he too would volunteer ; and together they went to Colonel Colborne, their chief, who approved of the plan, but bade them keep it secret. He forwarded the proposal in writing to General Crauford, and either

ONE OF THE FORCE THAT HAS DISTINGUISHED ITSELF IN RECENT TRENCH-RAIDS AT THE BRITISH FRONT : AN "ANZAC" ON SENTRY DUTY.

Official Photograph ; supplied by Alfieri.

'forties a belated controversy raged in the Press and in certain memoirs over the affair, without a satisfactory conclusion. But Gurwood's rival spoke too late, and the first claimant's name bears the honours of a remarkable adventure.

On the night of Jan. 17, 1812, Lieutenant Gurwood was on duty on the midnight relief, advancing a sap. Towards the end of his four hours' spell, while he was anxiously awaiting the stroke of four o'clock from the tower of the cathedral not two hundred yards distant from the works, the thought of the probable assault of the town flashed across his mind. This still occupied him when the relief came on, and after snatching a few hours' sleep on an epaulement—for he was too much fatigued to quit the trenches—he returned

he or Wellington himself—Gurwood never heard which—consented. Early on the morning of the 19th, orders for the attack and a call for 300 volunteers arrived by the hands of Lord March, and it was made known that Major Napier and Lieutenant Gurwood "had their positions already allotted."

Lord March, knowing the full meaning of the cryptic phrase, came to Gurwood and shook hands with him. There followed a little wrangle about precedence, another Lieutenant, Mackie of the 43rd (the subsequent claimant), having also volunteered ; but reference to the Army List settled Gurwood's seniority, and his post was confirmed. Gurwood now began to live at high tension ; he kept on eating, principally bread, and carefully controlled his thirst, knowing how

[Continued overleaf.

Far Eastern "Bantams" Fighting for France.

MEN OF THE ANNAMITE CONTINGENT: HOME SERVICE KIT (LEFT); WAR FRONT KIT (RIGHT).

Two Annamite soldiers of the French Colonial contingent from the Far East now serving in Europe are shown here. On the left is a private in the uniform worn in Indo-China, where the corps is recruited. He is wearing the conical, lamp-shade shaped hat worn by natives in the Far East. It is of straw or bamboo-fibre, and with the troops is covered with grey cloth. The fan carried is an indispensable adjunct of life among Far-Eastern peoples. The Annamites arrived wearing these hats, and with fans, but both have been discarded, the fans entirely. Neither will be resumed until the Annamites embark for home again at the conclusion of the war. A soldier in the new hat, a *béret* of the Alpine Chasseurs pattern, is on the right.— [*Official French Photographs; supplied by C.N.*]

insatiable that becomes under nervous excitement. Meanwhile, Wellington, Crauford, Napier, and Gurwood climbed the tower of a neighbouring convent and carefully examined the point of attack, Gurwood being told to make very sure of his ground and direction. The storming party, drawn from the 43rd, the 52nd, and the 95th, was

A SERBIAN REGIMENTAL CELEBRATION AT SALONIKA : THE RELIGIOUS
PART OF THE CEREMONY.

The Serbian 15th Regiment of Infantry at Salonika celebrated its regimental name-day recently. After a religious ceremony in memory of 37 officers and 1665 men of the regiment killed in action, there were songs, dances, and gymnastic displays. The Allied commanders and their staffs attended.—[Photo. by L.N.A.]

now assembling, and March carried Gurwood, Napier, and others off to discuss a turkey-pie. Some spoke of horses, others of other things ; but, in joke, Gurwood said to Lord March, " I will bring you the Governor."

He little dreamed how his jest would be turned to earnest. As soon as darkness had fallen, the Light Division moved off, headed by the 300 volunteers. Of these, the forlorn hope was to number not more than thirty. Gurwood detached thirteen file and told them simply to follow him.

Three guns from the batteries gave the signal for the attack.

He missed the main breach, which was his objective, but by a neat piece of scaling mounted and turned a smaller breach in the faussebraie, which was at once abandoned by the defenders. The forlorn hope then made for the main breach, which the rest of the 300 carried after a terrific struggle. Gurwood was knocked over by a stone shot, and for a while lay stunned, but picked himself up, and was then wounded in the back of the head.

He pushed on, however, and dropped down into the town, which he knew well. There was now a lull in the firing, and Gurwood, with Sergeant MacIntyre and Corporal Lowe, made for La Tour Carrée, about which, by strange luck, a French officer whom they had captured told them something particularly interesting. Gurwood summoned the place to surrender, on pain of instant death to all the garrison, and a voice cried from within, " *Je ne me rendrai qu' au Général-en-chef.*" Gurwood answered that the *Général-en-chef* would not trouble to come there, but if the door was not opened he would blow the tower up.

After a time they were admitted, and in the darkness someone fell on the Lieutenant's neck, and, kissing him, cried, " *Je suis le Gouverneur de la place, le Général Barrié. Je suis votre prisonnier.*"

The fortunate captor received the prisoner's sword and led him to the Governor's house. The victorious troops were now pouring into Ciudad Rodrigo, and as he went along Gurwood kept shouting " Lord Wellington, Lord Wellington." Picton heard him, and gruffly bade him rejoin at once ; but Gurwood risked disobedience and went on, still shouting for the Commander-in-Chief. At last a well-known voice answered out of the confusion, " Who wants me ? "

On the rampart Gurwood presented the Governor to his Commander. " Did you take him ? " Wellington asked.

" Yes, Sir ; I took him in the Citadel above the Almeida Gate."

Whereupon Wellington handed Gurwood the Governor's sword, saying, " Take it ; you are the

A MEMORIAL FORMED OF MACHINE-GUNS AND RIFLES : A SERBIAN REGIMENT
AT SALONIKA COMMEMORATING ITS DEAD.

Photograph by L.N.A.

proper person to wear it." Gurwood wore it ever after, and considered it his luck-bringer,

And so the Lieutenant kept his word and brought back the Governor.

Woman for the Watering-Cart: New War-Work.

AN IRISH SPORTSWOMAN WORKING A WATERING-CART: MISS M. K. McVEAGH, AT FINCHLEY.

War-work for women is branching out in new directions every day, and our photograph shows what is perhaps the latest innovation. Two young ladies well known in Irish sporting circles, Miss M. K. McVeagh and Miss N. M. Loughrey, are employed by the Finchley Urban Council in watering the roads. Miss McVeagh is here seen preparing to load up the cart with water. The term war-work includes, of course, not only work done directly for the Services, but every form of industry by which women are able to release men for combatant duties. Thus hundreds of women are now engaged in agriculture and in factories, also as clerks, van-drivers, 'bus-conductors, milk-carriers, postal messengers, window-cleaners— to mention but a few of their activities.—[Photo. by L.N.A.]

Ready for the Hour of "La Revanche!"

BELGIUM'S REORGANISED AND HIGHLY EFFICIENT ARMY: A BATTALION WITH MACHINE-GUNS.

In the illustration, a battalion of Belgian infantry is seen on the march in hilly country "somewhere" near the front, with its equipment of machine-guns. The Belgian Army, it has been stated in the papers, is now numerically stronger than the entire force that King Albert could put into the field in 1914. It is immeasurably more powerful in every other respect, in *moral* and in *matériel*. The men are all in khaki and have been furnished with steel helmets (as seen above). They had no field uniform in 1914, and had to fight in their conspicuous dark-coloured peace-time uniforms. Their artillery has been reorganised and is provided with powerful pieces, both field guns and heavy ordnance. Their cavalry is in fine form.—[Photo. by C.N.]

Wounded British Soldiers Taking a "'Busman's Holiday."

RISKS OF THE AIR AS A DIVERSION AFTER THE TRENCHES! WOUNDED SOLDIERS TAKING AIR-TRIPS.

Some of the wounded British soldiers who were recently exchanged from prison-camps in Germany, and returned to this country, have been enjoying their freedom in a manner suggestive of the proverbial "busman's holiday." Having survived the perils of the trenches, they tempted the risks of the air the other day when they were taken for an outing to a British aerodrome. A "joy-ride" in an aeroplane was evidently very much to their taste, judging by our photograph, which shows one of them seated behind the pilot and talking to his comrades just before the ascent. The experience would no doubt be very interesting to men who must have watched many a thrilling aeroplane flight at the front, under less tranquil conditions.—[Photo. by Central Press.]

The Stricken Field of Verdun : A Sc

HEROIC DEFENDERS OF FRANCE FIGHTING AMID A SCENE OF DEATH AND DEVASTATION

The long-drawn-out struggle for Verdun has now lasted more than four months. It began with the first German onslaught on February 21, and, up to the time of writing, although they have here and there had to yield ground, as at Douaumont, Vaux, and Thiaumont, they are still heroically holding the main defences and dealing effective counter-blows. A semi-official French statement

# of Superb Fighting by the French.

CH INFANTRY ADVANCING ALONG A TRENCH TO ATTACK BEFORE FORT DOUAUMONT.

June 26 said: "During the night a German attack against our positions west of the Thiaumont works . . . was absolutely cked. . . . A *coup-de-main* between the Fumin and the Chenois Woods gave us back some ground. . . . The Germans may be mentarily exhausted by the violent effort . . . which has cost them sanguinary losses."—[*From the Drawing by Georges Scott.*]

Nurses Decorated by the King at Buckingham Palace.

NOW ELIGIBLE ALSO FOR THE MILITARY MEDAL : NURSES WHO RECEIVED THE ROYAL RED CROSS.

The first of these photographs, taken outside Buckingham Palace at the Investiture held by his Majesty on June 27, shows some of the nurses decorated leaving the Palace. In the second, two Canadian sisters, Miss Dorothy Winter and Miss Kathleen Lambkin, are seen showing their decorations to an officer. In the centre of the third photograph is Miss Annie Farrington, a staff nurse of one of the Civil Hospitals, among a group of wounded soldiers from the hospital where she is serving. All the ladies mentioned received the Royal Red Cross of the Second Class. It is announced, by Royal Warrant, that the Military Medal may now be awarded to women who have shown devotion under fire, on the recommendation of a Commander-in-Chief in the Field.—[Photos. by C.N.]

The Trench Warfare in Mesopotamia.

ON THE TIGRIS: FILING ALONG A COMMUNICATION-TRENCH BETWEEN FIRE AND SUPPORT TRENCHES.

Some of our men on the Mesopotamia front, wearing their sun-helmets and neck-coverings, are seen passing between the fire-trenches and the support-trenches by way of one of the zig-zagged communication-trenches. In its essential features, modern warfare has to be conducted on the same general lines everywhere. The trench system is the same in Mesopotamia as in Flanders. As in Flanders, the *terrain* along the Tigris is flat and open. Hardly an elevation shows above the wide-stretching level of the plain higher than a sand hillock, and these only here and there. Thus digging-in or trench tactics are imposed on both sides. Exposure in the open to machine-gun and magazine-rifle fire means anni-hilation to the combatants.—[Photo. by C.N.]

Bees Provide an Industry for Maimed Soldiers.

BEE-KEEPING INSTRUCTION UNDER LORD EGLINTON'S SCHEME : FUMIGATION, AND COMB-EXAMINATION.

On this page, a number of wounded soldiers are shown being instructed in details connected with bee-keeping and the production of honey for market. That industry is one in which the Earl of Eglinton is specially interested, as offering a ready and profitable means of livelihood for disabled and maimed soldiers. Lord Eglinton has put his scheme into operation, and is having it conducted on practical working lines at Borland House, Kilmarnock, where tuition in the methods of bee-keeping is being given to wounded men. In the upper illustration a group of soldiers, some in civilian dress and others in uniform, are seen being taught the best method of fumigating bees. In the lower illustration men are being shown how best to examine the combs.—[Photos. by C.N.]

Bees Provide an Industry for Maimed Soldiers.

BEE-KEEPING INSTRUCTION UNDER LORD EGLINTON'S SCHEME : A MASKED CLASS AT THE HIVES.

On this page some of the wounded soldiers who are being taught bee-keeping and hive management as a future means of earning a living, at Borland House, Kilmarnock, under Lord Eglinton's scheme of training (illustrated also on the adjoining page), are seen engaged in undergoing instruction in another of the working details of the industry—adding a section to a hive. They are shown here wearing hive-masks of gauze netting which to some of them no doubt will recall the wearing of other masks against a more noxious foe than stinging bees during days at the Front. In regard to the originator of the scheme, Lord Eglinton was himself formerly in the Army, and is at the present time President of the Ayrshire Territorial Force Association.—[Photo. by C.N.]

THINGS DONE: IV.—INFANTRY.

IN these days it would be an easier task to set down the things the Infantry does not do, but that is a cowardly way to evade a topic. In a general sense, the Infantry does everything in the military line you can think of, and, in these days, a few more on top of that. The Infantry-man has increased his scope; he always does. Once upon a time he was a skirmisher and an outpost, the man who guarded convoys, the man who sat tight behind his rifle, and the man who went in and finished things with his bayonet. He was also the man who marched, who garrisoned communication lines, and the man who held towns and forts. In these days he is a general utility fellow, sometimes a prestidigitator with bombs, sometimes a troglodyte, sometimes a sort of nimble night-hawk with a club and a ready way of killing in a trench. At all times, before and now and after, he is the backbone and the bulk, the sinew and the substance, of the Army. The Cavalry and the Artillery can argue how they like, but as far as armies and war go the Infantryman is It.

Infantry forms the solid stuff of battles. All other arms minister and support it in the actual shock of war. The Cavalry seeks out the enemy so that the Infantry can fight him, or covers up the retreat so that the Infantry can get away whole for another day. The Artillery mauls the enemy so that the Infantry can get in with a final and unequivocal blow, or holds the enemy in check so that the Infantry can preserve itself for a crucial effort. The Engineers, the Army Service Corps, the Army Ordnance Corps, all serve and make smooth the way of the Infantry. The Infantry is the weapon that kills and wins, or that holds and saves. The Germans call Infantry "cannon-fodder"; what they should really explain is that cannon had to be invented in order to cope with multitudinous, well-handled infantry. And cannon has never yet succeeded in coping with it.

The Infantry battalion is a mass of one thousand men divided into four companies, and the companies divided into platoons. A battalion is not a regiment, but only a part of it. It would be easy to explain a regiment in pre-war terms, but now it is not so easy. In pre-war days a regiment had three, and occasionally more, battalions—one serving at home and sending drafts to one serving abroad, and a Territorial battalion tacked on to these two regular units. Nowadays regiments go on accumulating battalions until the mind grows dizzy, and these battalions go to positions and even lands miles
(Continued overleaf.)

FRIENDLY ARABS OF MESOPOTAMIA VISITING A BRITISH WAR-SHIP: THE SHEIK OF MOHAMMERAH'S BODYGUARD ON BOARD H.M.S. "ESPIÈGLE."
Photograph by C.N.

BRITISH MOTOR-AMBULANCES FOR VERDUN INSPECTED BY THE KING: THE CONVOY APPROACHING BUCKINGHAM PALACE.
The King inspected on June 24 a convoy of motor-ambulances presented to the French Army for use at Verdun, out of a sum of £40,000 subscribed by members of Lloyd's.—[Photo. by Newspaper Illustrations.]

A Great Indian Prince at the Western Front.

A FAMOUS VETERAN: SIR PERTAB SINGH, WITH GENERAL JOFFRE AND SIR DOUGLAS HAIG.

The veteran Indian Prince, the Maharajah Sir Pertab Singh, formerly Regent of Jodhpur and Ruler of Idar (left), is seen in conversation with General Joffre (right) and Sir Douglas Haig. Sir Pertab, who is a Lieut.-General in the Army, is one of the most famous of the Princes of India—a *chevalier sans peur et sans reproche*. He came to Europe with the Indian Contingent, returned home on urgent private affairs for a short time, and then came back to the front. Sir Pertab is seventy-one, and has seen service with the British on the Indian frontier, and in China. He was wounded in action on the frontier, but concealed the wound until a British officer accidentally discovered it, in time to prevent blood-poisoning.—[*Official Photograph; supplied by C.N.*]

away from other battalions of the same regiment; this is why it is that you read that a certain regiment is fighting in Flanders,

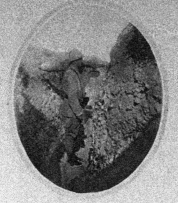

HOW THE LARGEST KIND OF TRENCH-BOMB IS BROUGHT UP TO THE FIRING LINE: A FRENCH SOLDIER IN A COMMUNICATION - TRENCH CARRYING AN AIR - TORPEDO.
Photograph by Rol.

whereas the next column of the paper makes out that it is also fighting in Mesopotamia.

The function of an Infantry battalion is to fight in mass. Usually its entrance into fighting means that this fighting is a battle. When, by the grace of Germany, the war is one of movement, the infantry comes up to fight when the cavalry has picked up the enemy, and has found that that enemy is strong and is showing a rigid determination to hold his ground. The Infantry battalions move up to positions in column formation, then the column formation breaks and a thin screen of skirmishers move out to get in touch with the enemy and to cover the movement of the main body. The main body also moves up in lines—the firing line; then, at an interval, the supports; then, further behind, the reserve. The movement is carried out in open order—that is, with wide spaces between each man, so that the effect of the enemy's fire shall be minimised. There are special advancing formations too, in order to counteract artillery fire and machine-gun fire. Drawing near the point of attack, the lines converge, the supports come up to thicken the first rank, and the charge is attempted.

The Germans at least taught us the value of hurling masses of men against lines without any preliminaries such as skirmishers. This gives to the attack some of the values of surprise. The trenches are battered flat, and then in a mass the assaulting Infantry is swung at the breach in battering-ram fashion. In the same way trench warfare, while accumulating the tools of the infantryman's trade has robbed the old weapons of some of their effectiveness. Thus a regimental charge is now something like a workshop moving in a hurry. All the instruments needed for cutting or bridging barbed wire, for making parapets of sand-bags and filling the sand-bags, and for bridging trenches, have to be carried, as well as the rifle for defending the trenches, and the specialised weapons—the trench-knife, the trench-club, and the grenade—for clearing up communication works and staving off enemy bombing parties.

For infantry fighting after the old style has given place to excavation and construction work. After a brisk few minutes with knife and bomb—the rifle and bayonet are too cumbersome for ditches—the building is taken up; while the bombers (who must be called grenadiers) work along the trenches, driving the Germans further back, or finishing off any Germans who yet hold sections of the captured trenches. If they can, the rest of the infantry follow the grenadiers, and push on and on into enemy territory; but always, as they go, digging and building and fortifying captured works. If they cannot press forward, the captured trench is made as strong as possible, and defence of it is assumed. Here at last the rifle, and that highest common multiple of the rifle—the machine-gun—are brought into play, and the Infantry, after their old manner but with a new method, hold tight and beat the enemy back with the bullet.   W. DOUGLAS NEWTON.

MOUNTING A NEW TYPE OF AIRCRAFT *MITRAILLEUSE*: ONE OF THE FRENCH ARMY'S FAST AND POWERFUL DOUBLE - ENGINED AEROPLANES.
Photograph by C.N.

Presentation Aeroplanes Ready to Cross Overseas.

AWAITING ORDERS TO START: NEWEST-TYPE BIPLANES; AND CROSS-CHANNEL PILOTS.

Fifteen presentation aeroplanes, gifts from various quarters, are seen in the upper illustration. They are shown as when recently assembled in readiness for flight overseas to the Front. All are completely equipped in every detail, down to the painting of the red, white, and blue concentric circles on the planes and tricolour bands on the vertical rudders, recognition-marks common to both British and French machines. There is hardly an outlying dependency or Crown Colony within the radius of the Empire which has not presented to the Royal Flying Corps aeroplanes provided by public subscription. In the lower illustration are seen a number of cross-Channel pilots, both military and naval, awaiting orders to start.—[Press Bureau Photograph; supplied by Topical.]

A French Infantry Attack Photographed from the Air.

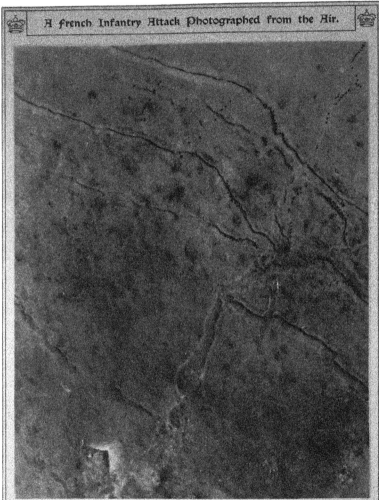

TAKEN FROM AN AEROPLANE: FRENCH INFANTRY ADVANCING TO ATTACK AT FORT DOUAUMONT.

This photograph of Fort Douaumont, near Verdun, was taken from a French aeroplane during the recapture of the fort from the Germans on May 22. The direction of the fort is towards the right of the photograph. The dark, irregular curving lines, which somewhat resemble the markings on a photograph of the moon, are trenches. Following these lines in the upper half of the photograph may be discerned, on close inspection, a number of dark dots in rows or little groups. These are French infantrymen advancing to assault the fort. The French, it may be recalled, were temporarily successful in recapturing the greater part of the fort, but on May 24 the Germans again dislodged them from it.—[Photo. by the Photographic Section of the French Army.]

A Famous Verdun Position Photographed from the Air.

TAKEN FROM A FRENCH AEROPLANE : DOUAUMONT FORT AFTER A THREE-DAYS' STRUGGLE.

This photograph, taken, like the one opposite, from a French aeroplane, shows the Fort of Douaumont as it appeared from the air after the three days of fighting from May 22 to 24, during which the French temporarily recovered it. In the middle of the photograph, just within the lower side of the fort (which shows white), may be descried the curving line of new French trenches established on May 23 within the rectangular enclosure. These trenches show dark, and in shape resemble a wriggling snake, or the course of a winding river on a map. On the right-hand side, at the top, are a number of German tracks or pathways leading through the north-east corner of the fort.—[Photo. by the Photographic Section of the French Army.]

Sporting Events of Camp and Trench.

TWO KINDS OF SPORTS : AN ATHLETIC COMPETITION ; AND A "REHEARSAL" AT THE FRONT.

An event at a recent camp athletic meeting is shown in the upper illustration. The sports were held at a training camp of the Irish Guards, and the programme included, as in these times is the case at similar gatherings, a number of competitions of a class which might prove of utility in war, on the battlefield, such as that here seen. Sport, in another sense, is seen in the second illustration. The incident playfully reproduces the sort of thing that may happen just now nightly during our trench-raids. One of the two British soldiers (left) is wearing a German officer's field cap, the man to the right has on the German pattern of trench-helmet (which is of interest in comparison with the British and French patterns)—both trophies.—[Photos. Photopress and C.N.]

Sport as Training for the Battlefield.

AT A RECENT ARMY ATHLETIC SPORTS MEETING: THE "GAS-MASK" OBSTACLE RACE.

In the above illustration is seen an obstacle-race incident at a recent camp athletic-sports meeting. A soldier is shown, masked and carrying his rifle as in a charge in action in Flanders, taking a post-and-rail fence. It is, of course, impossible to say too much in regard to the immense benefit that such athletic sports are to the British soldier. He owes to them in no small degree that physique which has so surprised and pleased our Allies across the Channel. The robust physique and alert athletic bearing of the men of the British Army have been among the things which, as innumerable letters during the war have recorded, have almost above everything else struck the French people with admiration and wonder.—[Photo. by Underwood and Underwood.]

WOMEN AND THE WAR.

HOW many women are now engaged in occupations generally regarded as men's? There are exact figures available, but the total must run into millions. Every week sees their number increased, as the men get weeded out from the offices and shops and warehouses. The supply of women is generally looked on as inexhaustible. Everybody writes and talks as if women could be called from the vasty deep whenever Ministers or a managing-director wants them. But is this so? There are, of course, plenty of feeble and useless women left in a country which, before the war, was inclined to treat its womenfolk either as drudges or as playthings. But the physically strong women are being very rapidly absorbed. For the able and educated woman capable of organising and enforcing discipline, the demand is at least as great, if not greater than, the supply. It is possible, if the war lasts long enough, that a Civil Service (Women's) Bill may supplement the Military Service Acts.

Those in authority at some of the organisations specially connected with getting voluntary helpers for the war, hint at difficulties to come. They depend already in some cases largely on women already hard at work in business and professional pursuits, who can only give a limited

A SNAPSHOT IN THE WEST END : WOMEN WINDOW-CLEANERS.
The woman window-cleaner is a practical addition to our army of war - workers. Clad in sensible brown "over - alls," she has something of the look of the French workman, and she does her work expeditiously and well.—[Photo. by Sport and General.]

ROSALINDS OF RUSSELL SQUARE ; WOMEN AMBULANCE DRIVERS AND ATTENDANTS.
The adaptability of women to work hitherto accepted as a masculine monopoly is one of the changes brought about by war. Our photograph shows an attendant and driver, employees of the London County Council, at the new Ambulance Station, Bloomsbury.—[Photo. by C.N.]

amount of time. The work itself, however, is without limit, and there are already the hints of an agitation that people of comfortable means

and no occupation should be conscripted, if they fail to volunteer. The number of women absolutely uninterested in the war is, of course, very small. There are few who have not done "their bit." The "bit," however, is often not particularly useful. The want is felt of some authority to decide what is and what is not worth doing. For example, some conscientious maid or matron may make herself thoroughly tired sending lavender water to the soldiers in hospital; but then Tommy is not really very much given to lavender water, and transport might be unnecessarily blocked by the packages. The woman, too, who laboriously "sewed shirts for soldiers" 36 inches round the neck and long enough for the funeral shroud of a Gargantua, must be regarded as a miracle of undisciplined energy. Yet she is no figment of the imagination. She does exist, though not, perhaps, in such great numbers as in the early days. The writer has vivid memories of the face of the wounded soldier who put on one of these garments on his first day of convalescence. "Seems a sort of hoss-cloth for the King of Siam's number one elephant" was his comment.

The truth is that women are wanted everywhere for work—real, hard, soulless, unromantic work, and not for the amateurish busybodiness that satisfies conscience without doing anybody much good. It is no question of incapacity. Women have shown, in jobs that are paid for, that they can manage most things as well as men.

(Continued overleaf.

War-Time Pastorals: Women on the Land.

PICTURESQUE WAR-WORK: THE LADY SHEPHERD; AND CORNELIA LADY WIMBORNE'S RABBITRY.

Something of the pastoral peace of a painting by Jean François Millet is suggested in the beautiful picture which we give of a lady shepherd, picturesquely garbed in smock and soft hat, tending her flock as they make their way homeward in the light of the setting sun. An artist could not wish for a more charmingly "composed" subject than this page from the scrap-book of Nature. Our second photograph shows a cheery scene at Cornelia, Lady Wimborne's "rabbitry" at Canford, Dorset. With a view to encouraging rabbit breeding, Cornelia Lady Wimborne has had several greenhouses filled with hutches. Our photograph shows the lady gardener feeding the rabbits. A greenhouse stocked with hutches is seen in the background.—[*Photos. by C.N.*]

The office girl is, on the whole, better than the office boy, and a good deal more cleanly and decorative. We may laugh at her spending part of her week's money on face massage or manicure, but she runs about briskly and gives messages with intelligence. And the " conductorette " and ticket - collector, the chauffeuse and the lift-girl—are they not standing (or sitting) witnesses to the adaptability of the sex ? But there is

HARD WORK, BUT WILLING WORKERS : WOMEN STACKING BRICKS FOR THE PRESS.

These women workers in South Wales make pretty figures in a prosaic setting. Stacking bricks is cheerfully undertaken by the girls and women who have taken the men's places.

Photograph by Illustrations Bureau.

a want of women for work that is no less necessary but which is not paid and demands rather higher thinking capacity. One hears a good deal about this need among those who direct various war organisations, and a regret that so much energy is directed to things less essential— things too much on the lines of peace-time charity work.

No such criticism, however, can attach to the scheme—originated by the Duchess of Somerset, in aid of which a series of concerts, matinées, and other entertainments is given in London this week. It is called the "Women's Tribute," and its object is to crystallise, as it were, for all time women's desire to care for those who · have been broken in the war, by raising a tribute in money from all women of the Empire with the idea of permanently placing on a sound footing those institutions which give help to soldiers and sailors, and particularly to those wholly or partially disabled on active service. The Women's Tribute is to stand to existing organisations concerned in much the same relation as King Edward's Hospital Fund does to the hospitals. Queen Alexandra, who takes a keen

interest in anything connected with the welfare of the sailors and soldiers, is patron. The Duchess of Somerset is president.

For the first time in two years the Royal Opera House at Covent Garden has opened its doors for public entertainments; and promenade concerts by celebrated military bands, theatrical entertainments organised and performed by particularly bright " stars," a special interlude, " An Extraordinary General Meeting," representing women's services in the war, by Louis N. Parker, are some of the features of Tribute Week in London.

Every woman who contributes, whether the sum be one shilling or a thousand pounds, will receive a pledge card. ·This is the pledge—

TO THE SAILORS AND SOLDIERS OF THE GREAT WAR.

Inspired by gratitude for your Heroic Defence of All we Hold Dear, Admiration of your Gallantry and Valour, and Sympathy for your Suffering and Sacrifice ; I pledge myself to make the welfare of our disabled Sailors and Soldiers, now and always, 'my special care.

Date   Signed.

Of course, there is no obligation to sign the pledge. It is merely meant to act as a reminder to the women in years to come, when the war is a memory, of their debt

WOMEN'S WORK IN BRICKFIELDS : CLOSING UP A LOADED TRUCK.

Women workers in South Wales, where concrete bricks are being made on scientific lines.

Photograph by Illustrations Bureau.

to the men, and as a help to make their gratitude a warm and pleasant and ever-present · thing, and the address at which it can be obtained is 8A, New Cavendish Street.   CLAUDINE CLEVE.·

The Head of the Army and the Chief of Staff.

THE KING'S INTEREST IN HIS ARMY: HIS MAJESTY WITH SIR WILLIAM ROBERTSON AT ALDERSHOT.

This photograph, taken a few days ago in the grounds of the Royal Pavilion at Aldershot, affords another example of the King's untiring interest in the doings of the Services. Only recently, it will be remembered, he returned from inspecting the Grand Fleet, and now we find him, at the first opportunity, hurrying off to renew his first-hand acquaintance with the progress of the Army. With the Queen, his Majesty remained at Aldershot for several days, and during that time they received a visit from General Sir William Robertson. Since Lord Kitchener's death, Sir William Robertson, as Chief of the Imperial General Staff, has occupied the first position of responsibility for the military side of the War Office administration.— [Official Photograph; supplied by Newspaper Illus.]

Honour to the flags of H.M.S. "Kent."

THE FLAGS OF THE "KENT" BEING BORNE TO THEIR RESTING-PLACE IN CANTERBURY CATHEDRAL.

Our first photograph shows the arrival at Canterbury Cathedral, on July 1, of the flags flown by H.M.S. "Kent" in the victory off the Falkland Islands, December 8, 1914. Our second shows the procession in which they were borne from the station to the Cathedral. The flags were presented to the ship by the ladies of Kent. They were badly rent during the battle, but the fragments were collected by Captain Allen and restored by the Ladies' Committee of the Association of the Men of Kent and Kentish Men. Beneath them is a plate bearing a record of the action, and the names of men who fell. Seamen formed a guard of honour. Captain Allen was on duty with his ship, but Mrs. Allen was present. [Photo. No. 1 by C.N.; No. 2 by Newspaper Illustrations.]

Helping a German Kite-Balloon Observer to Land.

DESCENT OF A "SAUSAGE": HAULING THE BALLOON DOWN AND "UNPACKING" THE OBSERVER.

In the upper photograph German air-service men are hurrying to the spot where a kite-balloon is descending, some holding ropes attached to a winch for hauling it down. Below, the observer is seen being divested of his thick and cumbersome attire. Kite-balloons shared in the great British offensive. Sir Douglas Haig said in his despatch of July 2: "Our kite-balloons were in the air the whole day," and Mr. W. Beach Thomas writes: "Scores of our great kite-balloons hung like clothes on an invisible washing line, at a commanding level along all the battle front. I counted exactly 22 to my right, and could not detect a single German with the strongest glasses." A British despatch on June 25 records the destruction of 3 German kite-balloons.—[Photos. by Baudouin.]

Serbian Soldiers Ready to Win Back Their Country.

AT EXERCISE, AND A RELIGIOUS CEREMONY : SERBIA'S REORGANISED SOLDIERS AT SALONIKA.

The upper photograph shows Serbian soldiers going through physical exercises ; the lower one, a religious service held on Holy Thursday. At the table, it will be noticed, is a priest wearing a stole over his uniform as the only outward mark of his sacred office. By the end of May the Serbian Army had been transferred from Corfu to Salonika. "Now they are all here," writes Mr. G. Ward Price, "hard-bitten, war-seasoned veterans, both young and old. What strikes one about them chiefly is their good-humour and simplicity—brawny, 15-stone men with the heart and spirits of a child. . . . The Serbian camps stretch for miles. · · · Here they are putting the last touches to their training, though they need little, for all are veterans."—[Photos. by Baudouin.]

The Illustrated War News, July 12, 1916.—Part 5, New Series

The Illustrated War News

GREAT BRITAIN'S NEW AND POWERFUL ARTILLERY: A HEAVY HOWITZER IN ACTION.

Official Photograph issued by the Press Bureau; supplied by L.N.A.

THE GREAT WAR,

By W. DOUGLAS NEWTON.

THIS has been a week of progress on all fronts. There has been that steady and deliberate motion on the three centres of assault which gives to the present offensive its enduring and determined character. The French and the British have pressed on, the French rather more swiftly than the British, but both in a manner suggesting that a plan is being followed · justly and that there is no thought of halting. The Italians are pushing the Austrians back from point to point in unhesitant fashion ; and the Russians, after their deliberate pause before Kovel, have shown their capacity for progress by a new effort here and on the Lake Narotch-Baranovitch line ; while in their advance on the southern wing there has been at no time the slightest hesitation. The concentric squeeze of the Allies follows its natural, patient and inflexible course. It seems to me

HONOURING A FORMER CHORISTER KILLED IN ACTION : A MEMORIAL WREATH IN ST. MICHAEL'S, BEDFORD PARK.

The wreath is placed over the seat formerly occupied by Mr. Kenneth Hallward, of the Worcestershire Regiment, who was recently killed in action. Before joining the Army he was in the choir at St. Michael's.

Photograph by Photopress.

that there is no need for any of us to bolster up our hope in regard to the Western advance by a constant repetition of " All is well," because the very tone of the official reports carries with it that atmosphere. The calmness and reticence of the British statements give one the impression that there is really nothing to worry about, or even to enthuse about, because the work is going on all right, and that it will be time enough to shout about things when this job is through. Just

as there is no advertisement of heady victories, so there is no hint of any unexpected setback. The cool tone of the communiqués seems to me to be especially stimulating : it seems to be the outcome of a resolve equally cool to finish off this business without any nonsense. It is not the reticence of ambiguity either, since, for those who are sceptical (if there are any), the German reports provide a running annotation to our own in which one can note — sometimes through a rush of candour, and sometimes through the deliberate fog of German ambiguities — that the enemy is not at all satisfied with the Franco-British advance, and is inclined to show his nerves over it.

It will be found, upon examination, that this advance has varied in extent and texture in a manner proper to the ground over which it passes and the circumstances of its encounters. We have learnt from the French, (not from our men) that of the great tasks before them that of the British was the more difficult, and that this is the reason why our movement appears slower. The British had to face the most intricate and powerful terrain. Before them at Thiepval, Ovillers, and in the La Boisselle-Contalmaison area, the ground rose up to give the Germans the full benefit of the positions. Also, and again with the ground in

A FAMOUS ARMY CHAPLAIN BURIED : THE FUNERAL OF BISHOP BRINDLE, D.S.O., ROMAN CATHOLIC BISHOP OF NOTTINGHAM.

Bishop Brindle, who died near Sheffield on June 27, was buried at Nottingham, with military honours, on July 5. As an Army Chaplain he served from 1874 to 1899, was at Omdurman, and officiated at the Gordon Memorial Service at Khartoum.

Photograph by Photopress.

their favour, the Germans had anticipated that the offensive would be directed against the positions occupying the ground on the Gommecourt-Fricourt front, and were thus well prepared to cope with the aggressive when it came. This explains in a particular way why progress has not developed on the Gommecourt-Serre-Thiepval line with the success attained elsewhere. At the same time, it must not be thought that advances have not been made ; apparently, the first German line has fallen into our hands, and, if there is no perceptible further progress, this front is doing good work in breaking and exhausting German counterstrokes against us. At Thiepval, after a good deal of fighting, our advance is pushing well on to the plateau which ranks as the highest ground in this area. The same forward progress up-hill is to be observed at Ovillers ; and part, if not all, of the village is now in our grasp. La Boisselle, also on

was made at most other points mentioned, and heavy German attacks—even one by the Prussian Guard—have been able to make little or no impression. In captures the toll is steadily mounting, 16,000 men and 96 guns having already fallen to the Anglo-French troops.

The French have, as has been said, made splendid progress. North of the Somme they have pushed out beyond Curlu and Hem, taking both places, and are driving forward towards Clery. South of the river, with the ground a little in their favour, they have gone on through the woods and over the flat, swampy levels with notable sureness and swiftness. Frise, Feuillères, together with all the ground contained by the arm of the Somme Canal as far as the Sormont Farm at the the bend of the canal and river, have been taken, and the front browbeats Peronne from a distance of no more than three-quarters of a mile. From

A MOUNTAIN OF PARCELS FOR INTERNED SOLDIERS IN SWITZERLAND : A SPECIAL DEPARTMENT
OF THE GENERAL POST OFFICE AT BERNE.

The Swiss postal officials at Berne have organised a special department for dealing with letters and parcels for British, French, and German prisoners of war interned in Switzerland. There are some 500 British, at Château d'Oex, Leysin, and elsewhere. Most of the parcels shown in the photograph have been re-directed from German prison-camps.

the rise, was the seat of a severe tussle ; but our men won the exchanges, and passed still further up the slopes. From here the line bends deep into the German defences in excellent fashion. The Bois de Mametz has been reached, and our hold secured there in spite of counter-effort. Fricourt, that held out with some tenacity, has now come entirely into our grasp, so that, with the capture of Montauban, we have secured all the ground well forward in a straightish line from the Wood of Mametz to the Wood of Bernafay, where we turn south to link up with the French at Hardecourt. On this last sector more progress was made in a renewed offensive begun last Friday, the French and British, acting in conjunction, being able to force their way forward north of Hardecourt, taking a knoll and extending their gains in the Bois de Trones. Progress

Sormont downward, the French enclose, in a wide line that bends sharply west from Belloy to Estrées, a great area of country, containing many villages, that has fallen to their assault. It is a big slice slashed out of the German front, and its occupation was the result both of brilliant fighting and curiously few casualties. Some of the villages were entered apparently without battle ; others were fought for with desperation, and had to be held against the heaviest assault. On all fronts, both French and British, there is considerable activity in evidence, apart from the advance. British and Germans are showing much energy at Hulluch, La Bassée, and elsewhere ; and French and Germans are strongly engaged at Verdun, especially at Damloup. On all fronts the note of confidence is with us.

The offensive has yet to show any specific

tactical or strategic intention, save that the French have been able to reach within shelling distance of the Peronne-Combles railway, which serves a portion of the Somme front. But, though it does not do this, the reason seems to lie in the fact that the major objective is yet far distant,

A NEW TYPE OF HEAD-GEAR FOR BRITISH SOLDIERS : MEN WEARING HATS
OF A KIND RECENTLY ADOPTED.
Photograph by Sport and General.

and that the present fighting is little more than the initial move towards a larger end. This end may well be—as I suggested last week—the breaking of the great Western salient and the turning of the German flanks both south and south-east, as well as north and north-west. It is well to keep in mind that, the larger the scope of a manœuvre, the less easy is it to see the ultimate objective. This is probably so here, and, since it is, it is a matter for intense congratulation. It signifies that the Western Allies have at last the means to initiate a huge campaign after the fashion of the Germans—in the manner, for example, of the Polish advances—and that we are entering upon war on that large scale which will give large results.

In the East, too, the Russians have also once more taken up the attitude of advance. The new break is above the big Lutsk bulge, running downward into it, and the line of pressure is in the Styr country from a point above Rafalovka and running west of Chartoryisk to Kolki—that is, the front is some thirty miles long. Working forward in the now accepted manner, the Russians were able first to shatter the defence, and then to rush it with cavalry until they have driven forward to the Stokhod and even over it above Kovel. The number of prisoners taken is again bewilderingly

great. North of the Pripet the Russians have also made a move that must embarrass Germany. Allowing von Hindenburg to spend himself, they have retorted in force along a line running from Lake Narotch to Baranovitch, and have broken forward at several points. In Galicia, the pressure of General Lechitsky is already having effect on the enemy right wing. Von Bothmer has already begun to fall back along the Dniester, and has suffered a bad mauling in the process at Koropiec, where again the haul of prisoners was large. As the Russians gain rapid control over the strategic railways, the retirement is bound to be sure and hurried, and this is the process which is going on.

The Italian offensive must not be overlooked either in the great spate of events, for they have not only been able to exert pressure on the whole of their line, but they have made useful progress. In the Astico area they have patiently won back ground, carrying the crest of Monte Seluggio and advancing at the Rio Freddo, as well as other points. On the Sette Communi Plateau the defence works are coming into their hands one by one, and in the Campelle Valley (north of Val Sugana) they are forcing the Austrians out of very strong positions. All the time a vigorous activity is going forward on the Isonzo, and good gains are being registered. With the Russians, the French, and the British, the Italians are not

WOMEN AS POLICE : NEWLY ENROLLED RECRUITS PARADING AT THE LONDON
HEADQUARTERS BEFORE RECEIVING THEIR UNIFORMS.
Police-women are doing very good service ; they are much in request at munition-factories,
and are employed at many places throughout the country.
Photograph by L.N.A.

only threatening the enemy by advances, they are also embarrassing his dispositions and reserves to an unpleasant degree.   LONDON: JULY 10, 1916.

The British Artillery Surprise in the Great Offensive.

"GRANDMOTHER"—THE ENEMY'S DREAD: GETTING UP 15-INCH SHELLS FROM A CONCEALED MAGAZINE.

This photograph, like others in the present issue, is one of the official series taken on July 1, while the great Anglo-French offensive on the Western Front was in progress on its opening day. It shows some of the gigantic 15-inch shells used in the British bombardment of the enemy's position at Beaumont Hamel, a village in the northern sector of the British attack, lying about a mile south-west of Serre, and about the same distance north-west of the River Ancre. In that district severe infantry fighting afterwards developed. The giant guns for which shells are being unearthed in their hiding-place from German airmen are each known individually as "Grandmother." Their tremendous boom is audible far and wide.- [Press Bureau Photograph; supplied by Topical.]

The British Western Offensive—Our Opening Bombardment.

CLEARING THE WAY FOR THE INFANTRY ONSET : BRITISH SHELLS DESTROYING THE GERMAN TRENCHES.

The preliminary bombardment of La Boisselle (a village two miles from Albert) and the German trenches (shown as white chalk-soil furrows across the middle distance) is seen taking place. The photographs were taken immediately before the attack on July 1. Albert is the town where the Virgin and Child statue still remains, horizontally outstretched over the cathedral ruins. "I could see," relates Mr. Philip Gibbs, who was present as a war-correspondent, "our shells falling on the German line by Thiépval and La Boisselle, and further by Mametz, and southwards over Fricourt. High explosives were tossing up . . black smoke and earth. Shrapnel was pouring upon these places and leaving curly white clouds which clung to the ground."—[*Press Bureau Photograph ; supplied by Topical.*]

The Master Weapon on the British Front.

PREPARERS OF THE GREAT OFFENSIVE: NEW GIANT HOWITZERS IN AND BEFORE ACTION.

In the upper illustration one of the heavy British howitzers is seen in action in the bombardment of the German lines preceding the attack on July 1. A similar howitzer is shown at closer quarters in the lower illustration. There is enemy testimony to the terrifying effect of the British fire. "One man," relates Mr. Philip Gibbs, in mentioning how he spoke to some of the prisoners, "told me that most of his comrades and himself had been without food and water for several days, as our intense fire made it impossible to get supplies. . . . About the bombardment, he raised his hands and eyes a moment—eyes full of a remembered horror—and said, 'Es war schrecklich'—'it was horrible.'"—
[Press Bureau Photograph; supplied by Topical.]

The Great Anglo-French Offensive—First Results.

ALREADY NUMBERING THOUSANDS : GERMAN PRISONERS TAKEN IN THE OPENING INFANTRY CHARGE.

Some of the prisoners made in our opening onsweep on the morning of July 1 over the battered mounds of the German first-line trenches are seen in these two illustrations. In the upper one the prisoners are shown, as shepherded in batches of 50 or 100, on their arrival within the British second line. Mr. Philip Gibbs speaks of many of them as "wounded and nerve-shaken in the great bombardment. . . . Some of them, on halting, lay on the ground all bloody and mangled; . . . But the English soldiers gave them water, and one of our officers emptied his cigarette-case and gave them all he had to smoke." Prisoners are seen below on the march—those on the left were mere lads, as they appear.—[Press Bureau Photograph ; supplied by Topical.]

German Prisoners from the Great Offensive.

A BATCH OF PRISONERS TAKEN BY THE BRITISH : ON THE MARCH TO THE REAR.

The first batch of German prisoners taken during the opening of the fighting on July 1 are shown here while being marched to the rear during the battle. They are men who had surrendered in dug-outs and amid the wreckage of the German first-line trenches. Most of them were unnerved and dazed by the fearful ordeal of the incessant bombardment before the infantry assault, and gave themselves up after in most cases offering little fight. Some held out for a time, but, as more of our men came charging up, the German resistance at these points collapsed and surrenders became numerous. The first day's fighting, according to the latest accounts, left 4000 prisoners in our hands. The numbers have since increased to 6000.—[*Press Bureau Photograph; supplied by Topical.*]

THE BEGINNINGS OF WAR - MACHINES : NAVAL GUNS.

WHILST arrows and spears were thrown by the fighting men carried on war vessels as early as 600 B.C., these could scarcely be considered as the beginnings of naval artillery, in that they were employed to destroy the crew rather than to damage the vessel. The advent of cannon early in the fourteenth century may therefore be looked upon as the serious beginning of this branch of warfare, though catapults throwing heavy stones were used in the intermediate period.

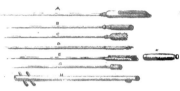

FIG. 9.—A SEVENTEENTH-CENTURY NAVAL GUNNER'S OUTFIT : CHARGING IMPLEMENTS.

The various implements, reproduced from Sir Jonas Morris's treatise on artillery (1685), are explained in the accompanying article.

In A.D. 1338 three vessels—*Christopher of the Tower*, *Mary of the Tower*, and *Bernard of the Tower*—were armed with iron and brass cannon, but such weapons were not common in the Navy until about 1373. A breech-loading naval gun was produced about 1398.

The Venetian Navy used cannon at sea in 1380, one of their vessels being taken in that year at Sluys having a number of these weapons on board. Fig. 2 shows one type of fourteenth-century 13.6 gun.

Fig. 4 shows the barrel of a hooped iron gun of the sixteenth century ; and Fig. 1 quaint breech-loaders of two centuries earlier, in which a detachable breech-block, shown alongside the gun, was removed to load the piece. " Bombards " were carried by trading vessels towards the end of the fifteenth century, at which date each recognised size of gun had its own name—*e.g.*, an 8-in. gun was called a " Cannon," a 5½-in. a " Culverin," a 3½-in. a " Saker," a 2½-in. a " Falcon," a 2-in. a " Serpentine," etc.

During the fifteenth century artillery of all sorts was placed on the upper deck, but about 1500 a Frenchman named Descharges hit upon the idea of mounting guns on the lower decks also, by means of port-holes. Port-holes as first made were circular and little larger than the gun-muzzle, but this involved a fixed position for the gun. The round port-holes were therefore quickly superseded. This improvement contributed largely to the success of the English against the Spanish Armada, as the Spaniards had the old-fashioned port-holes, and so could not make the best of their fire, whilst the English were more up-to-date in that respect. In the reign of Henry.VIII. artillery had attained some importance, and

the Venetian Ambassador is said to have informed his Government that the English King had "cannon enough to conquer Hell." The *Henri Grace à Dieu*, launched at Woolwich in 1515, carried 21 heavy guns and about 230 smaller pieces.

Some interesting information as to sixteenth-century ordnance was obtained about the middle of last century, when some guns were recovered from the wreck of the *Mary Rose*, which capsized and sank in 1545, owing, it is suggested, to the weight of her own ordnance (Figs. 3 and 5). Fig. 3 illustrates one of these recovered guns. Leather has been used at times instead of iron in the construction of cannon, and a weapon made of this material was fired in 1788 at Edinburgh.

In Nelson's day the largest gun in common use at sea was the long 32-pounder, of which the *Victory* carried 30 on her lower deck at Trafalgar. This gun (Fig. 6) consisted of a simple cast-iron tube mounted on trunnions fixed to a wooden carriage. The gun-muzzle was lowered by hand-spikes inserted below the breech and retained, by wedges or " quoins " driven under the breech end, at any desired elevation. Lateral training was effected by moving the carriage bodily, recoil being kept within bounds by a cable passing through an eye at the breech of the gun, the ends of which were fastened to the side of the vessel. The gun was loaded through the muzzle, and fired through a touch-hole near the breech. Fig. 9 shows a number of tools used in the manipulation of muzzle-loading cannon of the seventeenth century and later, consisting of (A) a ladle for inserting a charge of loose powder ; (E) a similar instrument for insert-

FIG. 10.—INVENTED AT THE CARRON FOUNDRY IN 1779 : AN EARLY "CARRONADE."

ing a cartridge (F) ; a rammer (B) for driving home the shot ; a sponge (C) for cleaning the gun ; a wad-hook or " worm " (D), for withdrawing a charge ; and a " driver " (H), or heavy type of rammer, having a small wheel under its forward end to roll along the bottom of the gun's bore. A good grip of the after end was obtained by means of suitable transverse handles.

[Continued opposite.]

The Beginnings of War-Machines: Early Naval Guns.

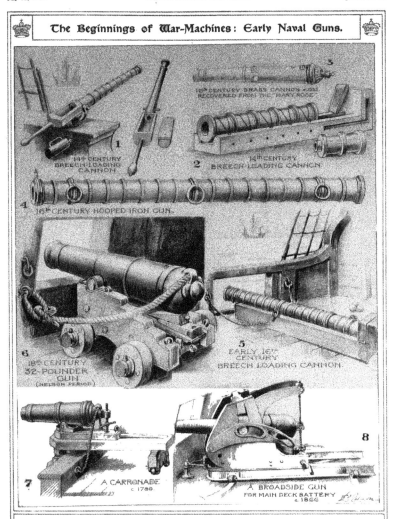

FROM THE FOURTEENTH CENTURY TO NELSON'S TIME: THE EVOLUTION OF NAVAL GUNS.

Continued.] In 1779 the Carron Foundry in Stirlingshire produced a short cast-iron gun afterwards called a "Carronade." This weapon (Fig. 7) was much shorter and lighter than the existing gun of the same calibre, and as its smashing power at the short range, then usual in sea-fights, was equal to that of the heavier and more clumsy weapon, it soon became very popular. Fig. 10 shows an early type of Carronade, in which the barrel is fixed to a wooden carriage by means of an eye-bolt. Fig. 8 shows a much more elaborate weapon, forming a unit of a main deck battery, 1865 to 1867. In this case lateral training is obtained by swivelling the carriage round a centre-pin situated as nearly below the centre of the porthole as possible.

Captured in Our Advance: German Prisoners in England.

SOME OF THE 6000 GERMANS TAKEN IN OUR OFFENSIVE : PRISONERS MARCHED THROUGH SOUTHAMPTON.

These photographs show some of the first batch of German prisoners brought to this country, after being captured in the opening stages of the British offensive. They were landed at Southampton on July 4, and marched along the esplanade and through the streets to their temporary quarters. There were over 30 officers among them and more than 1500 rank and file, mostly seasoned troops. Many were without caps, and a number of these wore handkerchiefs tied over their close-cropped heads. Numbers of women lined the streets to see them pass. An official despatch from the British Headquarters in France on July 5 stated : " . . . The total number of prisoners taken in the last five days now amounts to over 6000."—[Photos. by Central Press.]

German Prisoners Marched through Southampton.

CAPTURED BY AN ARMY NEITHER "LITTLE" NOR "CONTEMPTIBLE": GERMAN PRISONERS.

As mentioned on the opposite page, more than 1530 German prisoners, captured by the British Army in the great offensive begun on July 1, were landed three days later at Southampton. They were only a first instalment, for by July 4 the total number captured by our troops had exceeded 6000. By the same date the French on our right flank had taken over 9000, making a total for the first four days of the Allied offensive of about 15,500. Most of the Germans brought to Southampton looked dejected or indifferent. In some places the enemy's troops had given themselves up in large batches. A British official despatch of July 4 said : "The remainder of a whole German battalion surrendered in the vicinity of Fricourt yesterday."—{Photo. by Central Press.}

ROMANCES OF THE REGIMENTS : V.—THE 14TH (KING'S) HUSSARS.

HOW BROTHERTON KNOCKED UP WELLINGTON.

THERE was a moment during the Peninsular War when it was a case of touch-and-go with the British Army. But the dash and energy of a single horseman, and afterwards his persist-ence in overcoming certain natural scruples of the Staff, saved the situation. It is very well known that Napoleon's officers feared to waken the great man when he was asleep ; it is less known that a similar reluc-tance to arouse Wellington once nearly cost the British arms very dear. Yet such is the fact. The credit of the affair lies with General Sir Thomas William Brotherton, who was at the time a Captain in the 14th Light Dra-goons, now the 14th (King's) Hussars.

Brotherton had joined the Army in 1800 as an Ensign in the Coldstream Guards, and seven years later, as Captain, exchanged into the 14th Light Dragoons. He was a stirring fellow, up to any adventure and the hero of many, for adventures, saith the old platitude, are to the adventurous. Seven clasps on his Peninsular medal marked his share in the battles of Busaco, Fuentes d'Onor, Salamanca, Vit-toria, the Pyre-nees, Nivelle, and Nive. He was twice wounded, and once taken prisoner in cir-cumstances that form another romance ; and, besides, there was not a skirmish in which the 14th was concerned where Brotherton was not to the fore with credit

A TROPHY OF ITALIAN ANTI - AIRCRAFT ARTILLERY MARKSMANSHIP : AN AUSTRIAN AEROPLANE SHOT DOWN BY THE ITALIAN GUNNERS AND LYING NEAR A CAMP.

An Italian Army gendarme is seen to the left. The Austrian aeroplane is marked exactly as are all German aircraft, with the German Iron Cross badge.

Photograph by Underwood and Underwood.

A FALLEN FOKKER IN FRENCH HANDS : SOLDIERS EXAMINING THE CARTRIDGE - BELT AND FIRING - MECHANISM OF THE MACHINE - GUN.

One of the features of the opening stage of the Great Attack now in progress has been the success that attended the French air-service. " While the attack was proceeding, our aeroplanes were masters of the Front," says a French official despatch.—[Photo. by C.N.]

to the regiment and to himself. In the case here noted he did his country yeoman service and saved Portugal from a second invasion.

Wellington lay at Govea in the north of Portugal, near Castello Branco, the key of the country in that direction. The enemy was massed on the frontier in supe-rior force, and it fell to the 14th, together with an alien corps of a nationality whose alliance with Britain is now for ever, impos-sible, to take the advanced post and watch all hostile move-ments. Suddenly, at dead of night, the enemy moved, and the Allied forces were in instant peril unless a strong counter-movement should be immediately undertaken. Wellington's headquarters lay eight leagues distant from the force of observation, a serious matter in those days of slow communica-tion. To-day the field - telephone laughs at such comparatively trifling distances. Then, it was a case of good horse-flesh or failure. The good horse-flesh was forth-coming, and the bold horseman. Brotherton was chosen to carry the message to the Chief. He took his best mount, a valu-able thorough-bred which his father had re-cently sent him from England. The horse had been purchased at the sale of the King's stud, and the elder Brotherton had trained him himself, which gave the animal additional

[Continued overleaf.

The Patriotic Spirit of Young Italy.

GIRL GUIDES AND SCOUTS AT THE BRITISH EMBASSY, ROME : AN ADDRESS ; AND CAMP COOKING.

In the upper illustration a party of Italian Girl Guides and Boy Scouts, with their leaders, scout-masters, and Army friends, are seen being addressed on what patriotism requires of them at a fête in the grounds of the British Embassy, Rome. There is little need, though, to say much to members of the organisation on such a subject just now. The British Ambassador, Sir Rennell Rodd, is seen standing beside the speaker, on the left. Seated on the extemporised dais (beside the speaker on the right) is Lady Rennell Rodd. A party of Italian Girl Guides, who correspond in essentials of training with our own Girl Guides, the model of all bodies of the kind, are seen in the lower illustration, giving a display of camp cooking.—[Photos. by S. and G.]

value to his owner. The beast went well, but no consideration was possible; and Captain Brotherton, against his will, had to force the pace to such an extent that before he had got half-way the poor brute dropped dead under him. Luckily, he fell near a cavalry regiment on the road, and from that corps Brotherton borrowed a troop-horse and went forward ventre-à-terre. The second mount just lasted out the distance, but no more. It was already half-dead when the rider drew rein in the darkness before dawn outside the old convent where Wellington had his headquarters.

No one was about except one sentry, who was greatly surprised when the headlong rider dismounted and assailed the door with furious knocking. It was long before Brotherton succeeded in gaining admittance. He then had to find his way alone in the dark to one of the bedrooms, where he aroused an aide-de-camp. This was Captain, afterwards Major-General, Fremantle, rather a favourite of the Chief's and well versed in his ways, for which he had a wholesome respect. Fremantle did not at first take in the full significance of Brotherton's errand, and demurred about awaking Wellington, who had gone to bed very tired and in no very pleasant temper. Temper or none, the messenger knew that the risk must be taken. Fremantle still refused, whereupon Brotherton said he must do the job himself, if Fremantle would have the goodness to point out Lord Wellington's room.

Nothing would move the aide-de-camp, so at last Brotherton took the law into his own hands, found the Chief's room, knocked, and was bidden enter.

ON THE RUSSIAN FRONT IN BUKOWINA : AN AUSTRIAN BAGGAGE TRANSPORT WAGON ABANDONED AND SET ON FIRE DURING THE ENEMY'S HEADLONG FLIGHT.
Photograph by C.N.

ON THE ITALIAN FRONT : HELMETED REGIMENTAL TAILORS AND COBBLERS AT WORK WITHIN SOUND OF THE GUNS NEAR THE SUPPORT-LINES.
Photograph by S. and G.

No sooner had the messenger told his story than Wellington began to make things hum. As usual, he had grasped the situation in a flash. He ordered his visitor to go at once and awaken the Quartermaster-General, Sir George Murray, and bring him back instantly to the Chief's room. Headquarters immediately got astir with the liveliest bustle, orderlies and aides-de-camp were sent out in every direction, and a general movement of the Army was commanded. But for the timely alarm, only just in time, the position at Castello Branco would have been turned, and the enemy would have re-entered Portugal. As it was, Wellington's sudden counter-dispositions rendered the movement futile.

To one regret, and one only, Brotherton confessed over the brilliant little affair. He never received adequate compensation for the loss of his good horse. The authorities allowed him the bare regulation price of £35 : small consolation, seeing that he had lately refused three hundred guineas which Lord Londonderry had offered him for his mount. But he grinned and bore it cheerfully, for the honour of the Service and the safety of the Army counted with him far beyond mere filthy lucre. It is not recorded that his feat brought him any special distinction—it was before the days of D.S.O.'s and the like thronging honours—but Brotherton's list of decorations and rewards for a long life of service is as fine as any in the records of the 14th Light Dragoons. And he had it to his everlasting credit that he woke Wellington with impunity.

The Romance and Pathos of the War.

A TRIBUTE TO THE BRAVE: A "ROLL OF HONOUR," FLOWER-DECORATED, IN A LONDON STREET.

Nowhere in London has the price of war been paid more freely than in the East, more than a hundred men, for instance, voluntarily enlisting from Palace Road, Hackney. Of these, many have already given their lives for King and Country. The names of men at the front are written in a framed Roll of Honour. To these little "shrines" women bring their offerings of flowers, and a brave note is struck by the flags with which the wall is decorated. It is a strange and touching tribute of sympathy and remembrance to be found in such prosaic surroundings, but the war has brought to the surface things besides "Man's inhumanity to man," and has created an awakening of sympathy, of courage, of patriotism, which will long be an influence for good.—[Photo. by Sport and General.]

The Russian Army's Munition Supply from France.

AN IMPERIAL HONOUR FOR FRENCH FACTORY WORKERS: GENERAL GILINSKI DECORATING MEN.

General Gilinski is shown here pinning the Emperor of Russia's special decoration for the munition-workers of France on the breasts of a number of factory workmen. Both men and women workers are receiving it, as the photographs on this page and on that opposite show. The Russian General, it may be recalled, is the specially appointed representative of the Russian Army at the War Council of the Allies. He is one of the principal officers of the Imperial War Council at Petrograd, and on the Headquarters Staff. He came to Western Europe with a mission in connection with the co-ordination of operations between the Allies. General Gilinski has paid several visits to London.—[French Official Photograph; supplied by Newspaper Illustrations.]

The Russian Army's Munition Supply from France.

AN IMPERIAL HONOUR FOR FRENCH WORKERS: GENERAL GILINSKI DECORATING WOMEN.

In both the above illustrations the Russian General Gilinski, of the Imperial General Staff, is seen decorating female munition-workers in France. The decorations were specially sent by the Emperor as a testimony to the valuable aid that the French munition-workers have been rendering to the Russian armies. In addition to manufacturing munitions for their own Army, the French factories have turned out an immense quantity for Russia. In the upper illustration some of the decorated women are seen lined up in the presence of their co-workers. The General is seen in the lower illustration bestowing the decoration, while just behind him stands a French officer with a decoration ready for the next.—[French Official Photographs; supplied by Newspaper Illustrations.]

The Glorious Defence of Verdun : Heroic

THE SHATTERING EFFECT OF HEAVY GUNS : THE CRUMBLED RUINS OF FORT DO

This remarkable photograph was taken within the enclosure of the Fort of Douaumont, near Verdun, three hours after a succe
French assault. It shows French infantrymen and engineers at the south-west corner of the fort, holding a trench which they
hastily dug round the masonry structure, within which the enemy had taken refuge and installed machine-guns. A French commu

...ch Troops Holding the Ruins of a Fort.

...S OF FOR.T, OCCUPIED BY FRENCH INFANTRY AND ENGINEERS WHO HAD JUST RECAPTURED IT.

...cribing the enemy's counter-attacks, said : " The Haudromont-Douaumont region was all day the theatre of a murderous struggle. The Germans multiplied their assaults, which were on each occasion preceded by very powerful artillery preparations. In spite of all their efforts, the positions won by us yesterday were held in their entirety, particularly in the Fort of Douaumont."

Gunnery Aboard a British Cruiser.

ON THE QUARTER-DECK: SIX-INCH GUNS' CREWS OF BLUEJACKETS AND MARINES.

A gun-crew of bluejackets on board a cruiser is shown in the upper Illustration, at practice with a 6-inch gun on the quarter-deck. The gun is mounted (as is also shown in the photograph) behind a stoutly armoured shield, to save the gun-crew from harm by the splinters of enemy shells. In the lower Illustration, a gun-crew of marines is seen at practice with a similar quick-firing gun to that shown above. On board ship the marines man certain guns as well as the bluejackets, and the rivalry between the two services for the credit of their gun is very keen at all times, as the annual Admiralty gun-practice returns of the days before the war often showed. The national watchword, "Fear God. Honour the King," may be observed blazoned on the bulkhead.

Gunnery Aboard a British Cruiser.

THE IDEAL WEAPON FOR SWIFT AND HARD-HITTING CRAFT: A SIX-INCH GUN.

The 6-inch quick-firing gun has for years past formed the principal armament in our cruisers, in particular of the swift and lighter-armoured types. It is the biggest gun of the quick-firing class, the reason being that the shell it fires, weighing 100 lb., is the heaviest that can be conveniently "man-handled," or loaded by hand without the employment of machinery. The range of the gun is considerable, and the penetrative power and explosive destructiveness of its projectile are sufficient for the special purposes for which our fast cruisers are designed. Also the rapidity with which the gun can discharge a succession of shells is one of its most important properties—as has been shown in recent actions in which our cruisers have taken part.

"The Conduct of Officers and Me

THE KING AND OUR JUTLAND BATTLE VICTORS: HIS MAJES

Men of the Grand Fleet's ships' companies who won the Action off Jutland Bank, as the Admiralty designate the battle of May 31,
are seen here being addressed by the King, who inspected the Fleet on its return to port. In the background is seen the "Warspite."
The King is seen standing, while he is addressing the men, on the draped platform which appears in the background to the left.

cers and Mens Entirely Beyond Praise."

DDESSING GRAND FLEET CREWS—H.M.S. "WARSPITE" IN THE BACKGROUND.

cers, almost in front of one of the funnels of the "Warspite." "The conduct of officers and men," records Sir John Jellicoe in a despatch on the victory, "was entirely beyond praise. No words of mine could do them justice. On all sides it is epted to me that the glorious traditions of the past were most worthily upheld."—[Official Photo. supplied by S. and G.]

THINGS DONE : V.—THE ENGINEERS.

THE Engineer is the bold fellow who carries a rifle and fifty rounds of ammunition, and never has time to use them. Even in his most dramatic moments, when he is doing his best to push a pontoon bridge across an ungrateful river, and the enemy has other ideas about the matter, the last thing an Engineer hopes to handle is a rifle; and as for the fifty rounds, they are but a dream. For the Engineer has no time for fighting ; set in another sense, he has no time for anything else. His method of fighting is a little different from the accepted ideal, that is all. His fighting, in fact, is frequently no more than inspired plumbing, and the weapons he employs are every kind of weapon— save, perhaps, the rifle—from a tack-hammer to a ton of explosive. He makes such deadly use of his tools, however, that all other arms bow down to him, and find him lots of work

THE DRINKING-WATER SUPPLY FOR OUR MEN IN THE TRENCHES : "ANZACS" TAKING A CASK TO THE FIRING-LINE.

Official Press Bureau Photograph ; supplied by Alfieri.

to do. The man who invented the proverb " A woman's work is never done " was really thinking of the Engineers, only he couldn't mention the Engineers because the proverb would have sounded too indolent a thing in the face of the amount, variety, and continuity of the Engineers'

tasks. As with women, nobody really realises how much the Engineers do until something happens to the entanglements or to a pump-washer. It is only when one telephones along and finds that the line is blocked for two hours and a half that one grasps the fact that every other telephone in the line is calling up the Engineers, demanding that a man be sent along at once to mend or build or destroy something. At these times one perceives that the life of an Engineer has plenty of interest.

In fact, the Engineer's life *has* plenty of interest. He is the general-utility man of armies. That spectacular rôle of his—the building of pontoon or trestle or lock bridges under fire, and even the driving of mine-galleries through earth that is half water to some point from which the enemy's trench can be blown sky-high— are but things of glowing incident in his arduous and laborious existence. The solid, Martha-like grind he puts into his daily round is more natural to him, and quite as important to warfare as the building of bridges, with the destruction of them too, and the tunnelling of mines. It is also something even more marvellous.

[*Continued overleaf.*]

WEARING STEEL TRENCH-HELMETS AND READY FOR IMMEDIATE ACTION : A RELIEF PARTY OF "ANZACS" MARCHING IN SINGLE FILE TO TAKE THEIR TURN IN THE FIRE-TRENCHES.

Official Press Bureau Photograph ; supplied by Alfieri.

A Turkish Air Raid on the Egyptian Frontier.

DURING AN ATTACK: AN ATTACKING ENEMY, AND A BRITISH AIRMAN RISING TO PURSUE.

A Turkish aeroplane appears in the upper illustration, while attempting to raid an Egyptian frontier post from across the Sinai desert. The Turks, it is stated, make "somewhat reckless airmen." In the lower illustration a British airman is seen rising in pursuit of a daring Turkish air-raider. As stated in an official despatch in June, the Turks had an aerodrome at a camp at El

Arish (95 miles east of the Canal), which was bombed by us. An enemy Fokker attacked our machines, but was driven down. Turkish air-attacks have been made at Serapeum, north of the Bitter Lakes; on shipping in the Canal, and at Kantara. Only negligible damage was done; "by bombs and machine-gun fire," the enemy being driven off by gun-fire and aircraft.

It is the Engineer who sets the scenes of war. It was he who plotted the ground of it, and who, through his Survey Companies, drew up the exquisite and elaborate maps of hostile and allied countries upon which the Generals base their plans. As the war progresses, it is his work that is the basis of battles. He is constantly producing maps, from surveys by his own comrades

ON THE WAY TO HELP IN BREAKING THROUGH THE GERMAN FRONT: ONE OF FRANCE'S NEW GIANT GUNS ON THE RAILWAY.
t has now been allowed to become generally known that the equipment of the French Army at the Front includes a large number of heavy guns yet bigger and more powerful than any the Germans are known to have.—[Photo. by Photopress.]

or by other officers and men in the field, that show at a glance the shift and change of fronts and dispositions. Skilled, rapid, wondrous work this, by which every conformation of ground and trench in the German line can be drawn perfectly from rough notes, etched, and returned to Headquarters in a thousand copies after but a few hours of time.

And · as they map the country, so the Engineers also bend it to their wills. They change the face of the land not merely by excavating or building up to their needs, but by driving roads through it, constructing railways, filling or turning rivers, and running up bridges as the powers that command require. Roads and railways are, perhaps, the most striking items of their virtuosity. They take over existing lines and run trains to their own time-tables, just as capably as they string out light field railways for the conveyance of troops, guns, and ammunition. And they re-set the old main roads, just as easily as they put down heavy or light tracks of metal or rough beams to take the horse and foot traffic of armies across a diffident country. Their gift in bridging, too, is superb. They will put up anything from an iron cantilever to a rope-walk

across a ravine ; and, no matter how in earnest an enemy may have been in the destruction of a viaduct, they will mend it with their timber, or, if it is past mending, erect, with an air almost of derision, a new structure of their own alongside.

Occupied with making smooth the way of armies, it also makes easy the means of intercourse. The Corps, in addition to other things, is a portable and highly efficient G.P.O. ; telegraphs, telephones—their laying, upkeep, and repair—as well as letter and parcel deliveries, form part of the Engineers' daily grind. The Corps must be just as ready to send a message under shell-fire as to mend the wire that carries the message. More often than not the dug-out or hut that forms the telephone or telegraph-box was first built by the Engineers. The attribute of building is, indeed, very much in the Engineers' schedule of existence. It is the Engineer who is called in to build the most responsible kind of redoubt and fieldwork, and to baffle the enemy with the most deadly sort of craft. Behind the front line there is no doubt at all who does the building. The hutments and camps that the Engineers have built stretch from County Mayo to the Somme, and, after a discreet interval, go on from Salonika to the Tigris, and on again through India to the last far-flung outpost at Tsing-tao, Sydney, and beyond. And as camps

ANOTHER DETAIL OF THE EXCELLENCE OF FRENCH ORGANISATION : A TRAVELLING FIELD-KITCHEN PASSING THROUGH A VILLAGE TO THE BATTLE FRONT.
Photograph by Photopress.

and hutments and barracks, and the Headquarter château, infantry billets and fire-trench dug-outs, experience the wear and tear of war, it is the Engineer who is called in to repair and make good. One of these days the Engineer hopes to do a little fighting for a rest. -W. DOUGLAS NEWTON.

With the Enemy in the Adriatic—According to Himself!

GAS-MASKS IN NAVAL FIGHTING: ON BOARD AN AUSTRIAN WAR-SHIP.

The three ghost (or masquerade)-like figures seen in the above illustration (reproduced from a German paper) are those of sailors on board an Austro-Hungarian war-ship. They are upper-deck hands, and are seen coming down from the navigation-bridge to take their places at the guns, apparently just before action. The goggled masks that the men wear—in general appearance not unlike those worn by some of the French and our own soldiers in the trenches on the Western Front—are for protection against the noxious fumes which are given off by mélinite and lyddite high-explosive charges of shells, on bursting after impact with the upper works of the ship. The fumes from the chemical substances used in high explosives are somewhat poisonous in their effect.

War-Time Life in the British Submarine Service.

PATROLLING FOR PETROL-CARRYING ENEMY CRAFT : ABOUT TO OVERHAUL A COASTER.

A British submarine is seen in the above illustration in the act of stopping an apparently harmless sailing-coaster for the purpose of overhauling her, and "rummaging" for contraband—in particular, to see if she is carrying cans of petrol. It is notorious that enemy submarines are in the habit of surreptitiously obtaining supplies of petrol from similar coasters, as well as from other innocent-looking craft of different kinds. They employ both steam and sailing vessels which navigate under various neutral flags, or even under sham British flags, and pose as ordinary trading or fishing craft. In addition to the patrol and torpedo-boats told off for the inspection of coasting vessels, some of our submarines are at times so employed.—[Press Bureau Photograph ; supplied by Alfieri.]

War-Time Life in the British Submarine Service.

AFTER A RUN BELOW THE SURFACE: THE CREW ON DECK TO GET FRESH AIR.

Some of the crew of one of our submarines just come up "on deck" for a blow of fresh air after cruising submerged for some time are seen here. While under water, the necessary supply of breathing air is ordinarily derived either from large steel cylinders containing air in a highly compressed state, or from flasks of oxygen. Conversely, the carbonic acid gas of the respired air is at the same time chemically absorbed. The drinking-water supply is kept stored in special tanks, and the food for the submarine's crew is cooked by electricity, the power which propels and lights the ship when submerged. It may be added that the temperature while a submarine is under water is little above that of a ship's engine-room.—[Press Bureau Photograph; supplied by Alfieri.]

Before Our Bombardment : Photographed from an Aeroplane.

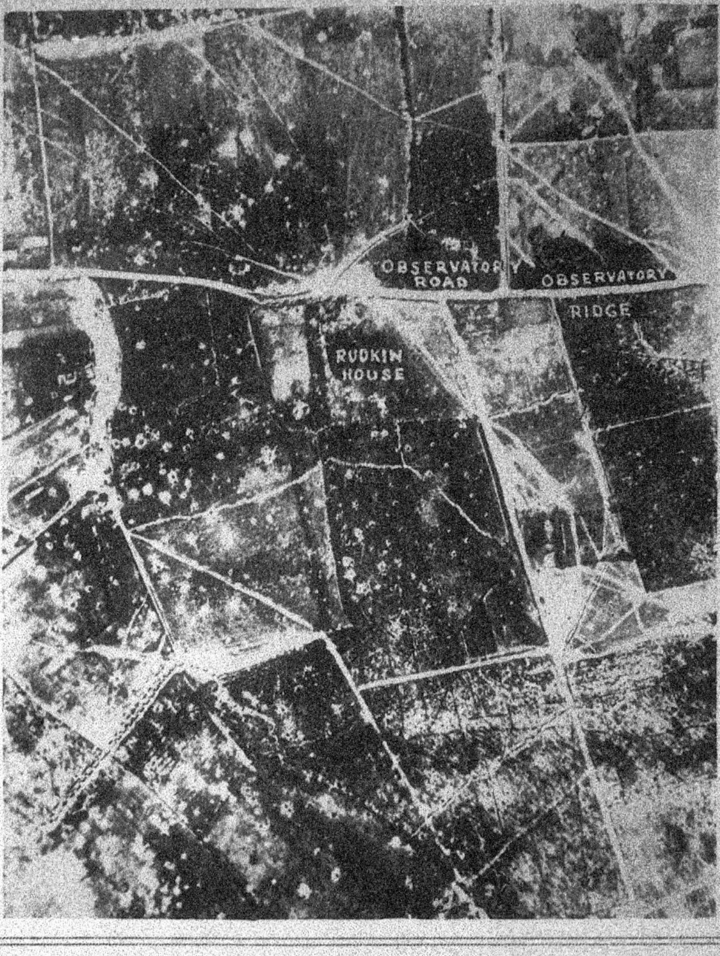

OBSERVATORY ROAD

OBSERVATORY RIDGE

RUDKIN HOUSE

SHOWING ROADS AND TRENCHES CLEARLY : GERMAN POSITIONS BEFORE OUR BOMBARDMENT.

Striking proof of the immensely destructive effect of the heavy guns now possessed by our Army is afforded by comparing the above photograph with that on the opposite page. Both were taken from a British aeroplane scouting above the enemy's lines, the one on this page shortly before a British bombardment, and the other shortly after. The former shows the lines of roads, paths, and trenches clearly defined, while in the latter everything is blurred and indistinct, all the outlines of the German defences having been obliterated in the havoc wrought by our shells. The whole place had become a mass of craters some 15 ft. deep in which it was impossible to recognise the former features of the ground.—[Official Photograph issued by the Press Bureau; supplied by Central Press.]

After Our Bombardment : Photographed from an Aeroplane.

WITH OUTLINES OBLITERATED : THE AREA SHOWN OPPOSITE, AFTER BOMBARDMENT.

This photograph shows the same positions as those opposite after they had been bombarded by our guns. The district is that round Observatory Ridge and Armagh Wood, near Ypres, where the Germans temporarily gained some ground last month, and the Canadians gallantly recaptured it. Their assault was preceded, as usual, by artillery preparation. "What happened," writes Mr. Philip Gibbs, "is a very strong proof that when our guns get to work in a combined effort with plenty of ammunition they can be as frightful in destruction as the enemy's. . . . The Canadian guns were but a small part of the great orchestra of heavies and field-batteries which played the devil's tattoo.—[Official Photograph issued by the Press Bureau ; supplied by Central Press.]

WOMEN AND THE WAR.

ONE after another, the old shibboleths concerning women's sphere are being ruthlessly demolished by the war. In peace time they were constantly being told that such-and-such an occupation on which they had set their hearts was "unsuitable." But that hard-worked weapon in the verbal armoury of those "agin" women's progress in any direction seems to have been definitely laid on the shelf. And that is one of the few good results of the war.

In less serious times men's touching confidence in women's capacity to perform any and every job that wants doing would be distinctly humorous. Who, for instance, would imagine that the War Office would so far lay aside tradition and red tape as to invite women to become Government hay and forage inspectors? But several hundred women are employed in this way, and do their work very well too.

There are, in fact, very few things these days, short of actual fighting, at which women are not willingly, or almost willingly, allowed to try their hand. But though there is no recognised place for women in the firing line, the official announcement the other day that the Military Medal might, in exceptional circumstances, and on the special recommendation of a Commander-in-Chief in the field, be given to women for bravery and devotion under fire shows that, when occasion requires, women are ready and willing to "face

WOMEN'S WORK IN NOTTINGHAM: A WILLING WORKER IN A FLOUR - MILL. With all due care in retaining men for the heavier work, women are being successfully employed as millers. The worker seen in our photograph is obviously well contented and well able to discharge her new and unusual duties.
Photograph by Illustrations Bureau.

the music." This mark of appreciation of women's services is rather specially gratifying, because decorations for women are very much the exception in England. And now that a start has been made, why should not a medal be instituted for valour in the fields of domesticity? After all, with prices up and household allowances down, to make both ends meet involves a real struggle, and it requires a good deal of courage — moral courage, which is much more difficult than the other kind—to adopt economy on a wholesale scale.

But, domesticity apart, active war-work involves the performance of endless duties which, dull though they are, are cheerfully undertaken by women anxious to help in the great cause. The members of the various Voluntary Aid Detachments are a case in point.

The Women's Voluntary Aid Detachments were, as a good many people know, attached to Territorial units in peace, and spent their spare time learning to prepare emergency hospitals and acquainting themselves with the best ways of preparing food for sick soldiers, so that in the event of invasion they would be equal to the task of acting as a link between the field and the base hospitals.

Organised by the British Red Cross Society and the Order of St. John, they learned also the elements of Home Nursing and First Aid, and, on occasion, improvised hospitals and nursed and dosed and
(Continued overleaf.)

A HAMMER-AND-NAIL CONTEST FOR NURSES: "DOMINION DAY" IN A CONVALESCENT HOME AT DULWICH.

characteristically cheery party of convalescent Canadian soldiers celebrated "Dominion Day" at the Massey-Harris Convalescent Home, Kingswood, Dulwich. The nurses entered cordially into the sports. Our photograph shows Sister Oram (centre), winner of the Hammer-and-Nail contest, and Sister Wilson, second (on the right).—[*Photo. by Sport and General.*]

New Work for Women: Merry Millers of Nottingham.

A PICTURESQUE GROUP OF WOMEN WORKERS: MAIDS IN A MILL IN NOTTINGHAM.

War-time, with its hitherto unheard-of conditions, has convinced even the most bigoted that the nature of womanhood is chameleonic. Just as the chameleon develops the colour of his surroundings, so does the woman of to-day adapt herself to the calls of the labour market with characteristic ability and ready goodwill. Milling is not light work, but it has been taken up successfully and cheerfully by the workers seen in our photographs. The first shows a girl lifting a sack on to a trolley; the second shows a row of eight girls in white overalls and caps, looking as though they were playing at work instead of working seriously, as they do. The girls attend to the grinding machines, weighing and tying up the sacks; but the heaviest part is still done by men.—[Photos. by Illus. Bureau.]

bandaged " patients " under the eye of an examining War Office magnate, to the amusement of the public, who audibly wondered " what was the good of it all.

But the war upset the homekeeping character of the V.A.D.'s, many of whose members are now serving abroad, sent thither by the authorities at Devonshire House, where, for the period of the war, the Order of St. John and the British Red Cross Society are working as one organisation.

The V.A.D. worker's sphere of activities is as wide as her willingness is unlimited, though her efforts are necessarily confined to activities connected with the care of the sick and wounded in war. She may be sent to help in a regular military hospital, where she is very small fry indeed, or to one of the auxiliary institutions served by the Voluntary Aid Detachments, in which case she feels less of a worm and more of a woman, and rises to the height of applying simple dressings and bandaging by way of variation on the scrubbing, cleaning, dusting,

THE WOMAN SILVERSMITH AT WORK : IN THE "PEASANT ARTS" SHOP, NOTTING HILL.

The adaptability of women to the delicate craft of the silversmith is not a matter for surprise, and our picture, taken at the "Peasant Arts" shop, in Notting Hill, shows how seriously intent upon her work the woman silversmith can be.—[Photo. by Alfieri.]

polishing, and washing-up that fall plentifully to her lot.

But the usefulness of the V.A.D. worker is far from being confined to nursing. She may be a cook, or a clerk, or an X-ray assistant, or a motor - ambulance driver, a storekeeper, or a telephone - operator ; for it is her business to do just whatever work requires doing. There is, for instance, a home " somewhere in France " for nurses, and a hostel for the relations of the wounded on the danger list. There the domestic staff is composed entirely of these voluntary workers, educated women all of them, who interpret the call to " do their bit " in the widest possible sense.

And if the V.A.D. worker is doing none of these things, you will find her, may be, at one of the rest stations or Red Cross hostelries where wounded men taken from the train are cared for till the ambulance arrives, or sick men on their way to hospital are fed, and many other things are done to mitigate those hardships of war that are none the less real because less well known.   CLAUDINE CLEVE.

WOMEN WORKERS AT PLAY : A TUG OF WAR.

The energy with which the workers at play in our photograph enter into the spirit of the tug of war speaks well for the conditions under which they carry out their tasks as munition - workers at Messrs. Thornycroft's, where our photograph was taken on Saturday at the sports held by the Athletic Club of the firm.—[Photo by Topical.]

"faithful Unto Death": The "Chester's" Boy-Hero.

"WITH JUST HIS OWN BRAVE HEART AND GOD'S HELP TO SUPPORT HIM": JOHN T. CORNWELL.

The Battle of Jutland Bank saw many acts of heroism, but none finer than that of the sixteen-year-old boy whose portrait we give. Admiral Beatty said: "A report from the Commanding Officer of 'Chester' gives a splendid instance of devotion to duty. Boy (1st class) John Travers Cornwell, of 'Chester,' was mortally wounded early in the action. He nevertheless remained standing alone at a most exposed post, quietly awaiting orders till the end of the action, with the gun's crew dead and wounded all round him. His age was under 16½ years. I regret that he has since died, but I recommend his case for special recognition in justice to his memory, and as an acknowledgment of the high example set by him."—[Photo. by C.N.]

The Great British Offensive in Progress.

THE STEADY, RESISTLESS, CONFIDENT ADVANCE OF OUR MEN : GOING FORWARD TO THE ATTACK.

In the two illustrations here some of our men are seen going forward at a certain point during one of the opening phases of the great British offensive, to attack through the curtain of powder-smoke and mist that lay over the battle area, and turned later on to pouring rain. Across the front is seen stretching the battered and apparently abandoned line of an advanced German trench, reduced to a ragged length of mounds of earth, untenable by anything alive, by the British preliminary artillery bombardment. Our men are seen advancing in extended order by sections and platoons, moving steadily forward in calm, assured confidence across the open, exposed ground—some with rifles carried at the trail, others with arms sloped.—[*Official Photographs; supplied by L.N.A.*]

German Prisoners Taken in the Great British Offensive.

SOME OF THE THOUSANDS CAPTURED BY OUR TROOPS; GERMAN PRISONERS IN BRITISH HANDS.

The upper photograph shows 1700 German prisoners at Méaulte, near Albert, who were captured in the British advance. In the lower photograph are seen a further batch. Altogether, several thousand Germans fell into our hands in the first few days of the offensive which began on July 1. An official despatch of the 5th gave the total as over 6000, and this figure has since received considerable additions. On the 7th it was stated in another despatch : " About 10 a.m. the Prussian Guard were thrown into the fight east of Contalmaison . . . but the attack was crushed by our fire. The enemy subsequently fell back northwards, leaving 700 prisoners of various regiments in our hands."—[Official Photographs issued by the Press Bureau ; supplied by Central Press.]

Woman as Recipient and Giver of Decorations.

A FRENCH HERO'S WIFE; AND A BRITISH PRINCESS: TWO NOTABLE MILITARY OCCASIONS.

The upper photograph shows Mme. Raynal, wife of the heroic defender of Fort Vaux, near Verdun, receiving from General Cousin, at the Invalides, in Paris, the decoration awarded to her husband, that of a Commander of the Legion of Honour. Major Raynal, who is a prisoner at Mainz, has been treated with honour by the Germans, who gave him his sword and a copy of General Joffre's Order congratulating him on his defence. He was also allowed to take his dog with him.——The lower photograph shows Princess Louise Duchess of Argyll, presenting colours and a silver shield to the General Officer Commanding the Canadian Forces, Major-General Steele. The presentation was made outside Kensington Palace.—— [Photos. by Rol and C.N.]

The Illustrated War News

CAPTURED BY THE FRENCH IN THE GREAT SOMME OFFENSIVE : A GERMAN 15-CM. SIEGE-GUN.

Official French War Office Photograph.

THE GREAT WAR.

By W. DOUGLAS NEWTON.

THE fighting of the Allies continues in its admirable compact and progressive fashion. Pressure is being exerted not only evenly upon the opposing lines, but being exerted evenly through all the days. It is easily to be observed that at all times our full weight is straining against the enemy's front, and this only gives place to those occasions when we give that necessary heave which carries the labouring enemy back still further. The enemy is having no breathing space ; he is engaged all the time against a movement unceasing and implacable. This is observable on both the Western and Eastern fronts, both the Russian and the Franco-British forces being ready to allow the Germans to fight themselves to exhaustion, until the enemy's fatigue as well as their own striking power gives them the opportunity of breaking forward once more. Thus the line of progress is indubitably inward on all fronts, in spite of all pauses.

The most impressive of the fighting in the West this week has fallen to the lot of the British. It has been stern stuff, concerned mainly with the consolidation of difficult positions in the face of very game counter-assaults driven forward by the enemy, and concerned, too, towards the end of the week, with another deliberative push forward that has won more ground of important nature and has helped to damage the enemy both morally and materially along his line. The heaviest of the engagements have taken place at the village of Contalmaison and for possession of the woods of Mametz and Trones. Contalmaison was taken by us in the first hours of the advance on July 1, but

THE WIFE OF A GERMAN POPULAR IDOL : FRAU VON HINDENBURG.
From a Drawing in a German Paper.

the Germans, having the advantage of the ground with them, were able to push us out. After staunch effort we succeeded in fighting our way over the hills, and on Wednesday the village was completely in our grasp ; while a succession of powerful counter-strokes directed against it during the following days were beaten off. In the Mametz and Trones Woods a fluctuating battle has been going on during all the week, The Germans attacked with the greatest urgency, particularly against Trones, and, though most of the assaults were broken, some succeeded, and the Germans were able to gain place into the woods. We have at no time left the enemy in idle security, and our own determination won back the Wood of Mametz in very quick time, while we pushed ahead in the Wood of Trones. This was the situation up to Friday ; but on Friday, at dawn, the British offensive opened out again into a state of new and admirable vigour. The German second line, which had held its own with some show of tenacity up to this, was swept away under the astonishing double impact of shells and men, and in unexpectedly quick time our men were able to force their way ahead through the five-mile gap they had torn in the German front as far as the outskirts of Pozières on the left, to the woods of Bazentin le Petit and Foureaux in the centre, and the village of Longueval and the woods of Delville on the right. The advance is even more auspicious than that which gave us the victories of July 1. In practical asset, it gives us control of ground ' four miles beyond the German first - line

"FOOD" FOR THE TRENCH-MORTARS DURING THE BRITISH ADVANCE : PILING BOMBS IN READINESS BEHIND THE LINES.
Trench - mortars played an important part in the British advance, and the photograph suggests that there was no lack of ammunition for them.
Official Photograph issued by the Press Bureau.

positions at Fricourt and Mametz, it has carried as well beyond the debatable Bois de Trones, has given us command in addition of such advanced woods as those of Delville and Bazentin le Petit ; while we have captured the rather significant

FIGHTERS IN THE GREAT BRITISH OFFENSIVE : BANDSMEN OF A ROYAL
SCOTS BATTALION AT THEIR HUT.

A bandsmen group of Royal Scots, who are taking part in the fighting line in the Great Offensive on the Western Front, are seen in the above illustration at their hut in the British lines. Their regiment, the former-day 1st of the Line, won its first victories with the British Army Just two hundred and twenty-two years ago over the same tract of country where the Royal Scots are now fighting.—[Press Bureau Photograph.]

village of Longueval, as well as the villages of Bazantin le Grand and le Petit. Moreover, we ho'd out real menace to Pozières, a village of critical value on the Bapaume road ; and there are indications that we are working forward to the right of that village and are threatening Martinpuich, which is slightly in its rear. In this way we must be making uncomfortable the German line holding at Thiepval and Authuille. Better than any news is that which tells us that we actually penetrated into the enemy's third line in the Bois de Foureaux, though we have since relinquished th.s point. Beyond this position the country is apparently more open, and our troops should be able to gain greater play to push a finely successful advance. That the attack is obtaining some mobility seems certain by the particular attention drawn to the fact that our cavalry has, after nearly two years, been able to indulge in mounted action, and has come into contact with and defeated a detachment of the enemy. It is certain that Sir Douglas Haig is alert to the uses that cavalry can be put in even modern and

p:culiar circumstances of war, and that, like the Russians, he hopes to make them responsible for the swift power of an advance if the slightest chance is offered. With our men already hammering at and into the German third line, we have reason to expect events of great interest ; at the same time, we must not minimise the defensive faculty of the enemy. He has had ample time to be prepared for just such an attack, and he owes it to his very existence to make the most of his opportunities. A point of really notable excellence is the way this second lunge has been handled. It is one thing to prepare through months to smash the first line of the enemy ; it is quite another thing to prepare in the course of a few days only, and over ground that must be badly torn up, to smash in the second line. Not the least honourable part of this second victory is the admirable staffing that has passed the guns and supplies up so smoothly and swiftly that the renewed assault has gone so well.

The French, though they have been quieter during the week, have also been extending their own front where it joins with our own in the Hardecourt area, showing sign of pushing east towards Maurepas, which would give them a good advantage north of the Somme. South of the river they have carried their line to Biaches and Barleux, and, what is

BRITISH SPOIL TAKEN IN THE GREAT OFFENSIVE : GERMAN MINING AND
DUG-OUT ELECTRIC APPARATUS.

In addition to captures of German guns and howitzers with ammunition—which, as Sir Douglas Haig says, in a despatch, will be available against the enemy—quantities of other useful spoil have fallen into our hands during the Great Offensive. Mining apparatus and electric gear for dug-outs, found at Carnoy and Mametz, are shown displayed above.—[Press Bureau Photograph.]

more, have taken the Maisonette work on Hill 97—a point which gives them command of the river and Peronne itself, not more than 1000 yards away. The capture of this point was a brilliant piece of work, well in keeping with the excellence of the fighting that is showing on the whole of the Western front.

It might be said, too, that a great deal of fighting has occupied the rest of the Western line during the time under review. There has been a great deal of raiding going on, a little by the Germans and more than a little by ourselves, and this has kept the West in a high state of tension. Our own raids took place in the Loos salient, and those of the French were placed in the Champagne ; these were successful. The Germans raided at La Bassée and in Lorraine, the first being a failure, the second giving them command of a short section of line. At Verdun the attack has been actuating spasmodically. There has been more bombardment than infantry assault so far, but the infantry assaults have certainly made a little progress towards the Souville line in and about the Chapitre, Chenois, and Fumin woods. Also, after heavy fighting and heavy losses, the Germans were able to force their way into the Damloup Battery, where they cling to a precarious foothold.

To a great extent the Russians have halted their lines this week to hold off the heavy German counter-assaults that have been flung against the advancing faces of the Slav attack. The most vehement of these attacks have been placed in the Baranovitchi sector, and they have followed a Russian thrust in the middle of the week which carried them over the Stokhod at several points and won back river crossings at Svidniki. Following this threat, the Germans have been fighting north of the

A RELIC OF A ZEPPELIN RAID : ONE OF A NUMBER OF ASH-TRAYS MADE FROM A DROPPED PETROL-TANK AND SOLD FOR THE RED CROSS.
A number of ash-trays made from part of a Zeppelin petrol-tank picked up in the eastern counties are being sold for the Red Cross.—[Photo. by Waddell.]

A " MEAT-LESS " AMERICAN BANQUET IN BERLIN : A SIGNIFICANT MENU.
We have no wish to exaggerate the alleged food shortage in Germany, but the menu here reproduced is certainly interesting. It suggests at least that July 4 was a "meatless" day in Berlin. The Hotel Adlon is one of the most fashionable in the city.—[Photo. by Topical.]

village of Skrobova, and by their furious determination have striven to blunt the power of the Russian drive. An offensive, too, has been engineered to the south-east of Riga in the Frantz centre. Notwithstanding the excessive losses of the enemy at both places, no success was gained, and there is little hope of relief for the hard-tried German lines, since the Russians are only waiting their tim to come forward again. Meanwhile, though the front in Poland and Galicia has been quieter during the week, the campaign in the Caucasus, which has been for some time obscured by a cloud of peculiarly Turkish reports, has again developed interest, and developed it to Russian success. In their advance from Erzerum to Erzinghan the Russians have once more been able to break the Turks, turning them out of the strongly-planned positions that held the heights east of Baiburt. This victory was completed by the capture of that important depôt town. In battles south-east of Mamakhatun and south-east of Mush the Russians have also been victorious, and have driven the Turks in some haste towards Diarbekir. This news will add some further distraction to the none too concentrated forces of the enemy. Italy, on her front, continues in the rôle of progress ; strong and difficult positions in the Posina Valley and in the Tofana have now been reached and passed, and the Austrian resistance, though obstinate, has not yet reached a solid halting-place.

In East Africa, General Smuts has reached the coast at Tanga, capturing the railway port, thus cutting the Germans off from one of their very few points of concentration and reinforcement. Generally, then, the week has been an excellent one for the Allies all round.

LONDON: JULY 17, 1916.

Gas-Masks in an Eastern Front Action.

WEARING THEIR GAS-MASKS : RUSSIAN INFANTRY IN A FOREST BATTLE.

The above photograph from the Eastern Front shows something of the kind of country over which our Russian allies are operating. It illustrates a battle-incident, characteristic in details, of the infantry fighting now proceeding along great parts of the Russian front from the neighbourhood of Dvinsk to the Carpathians. A detachment of Russians, entrenched in a fir copse, are seen in action wearing gas-masks. The combat is taking place amidst typical natural surroundings in a little wood of close-growing trees. Such woods constitute the prevailing natural feature in the forest region which extends across the swamps of the Great Plain of Eastern Europe in Galicia and Poland. Strips of open moor and patches of marsh intersect the forest belt.

A Public Tribute to an Intrepid Airman.

HONOURING A ZEPPELIN-DESTROYER : A MEMORIAL TO FLIGHT SUB-LT. R. A. J. WARNEFORD, V.C.

In unveiling, on June 11, the memorial in Brompton Cemetery, to Flight Sub-Lieut. R. A. J. Warneford, V.C., R.N., who destroyed a Zeppelin, Lord Derby, Under-Secretary of State for War, paid a stirring tribute to the courage of the airman. Lord Derby referred to the way in which the imagination was appealed to by the spectacle of "a man, single-handed, taking on a great opponent, knowing full well that in doing so the odds against his surviving were indeed small, but counting it not for one minute in his determination to do what was right by his country, and by the corps to which he belonged." Among those present were Mr. Warneford's mother, Lieut.-General Sir E. Bethune, and Commodore Murray Sueter.—[Photo. by C.N.]

The Victor over Immelmann: A Gallant Airman.

THE BRITISH PILOT WHO CONQUERED GERMANY'S MOST FAMOUS AIRMAN: SEC. LIEUT. McCUBBINS.

The bringing down of the famous German airman, Immelmann, was due to the pluck and skill of the brave young pilot whose portrait we give. He is a Johannesburg man, who joined the Royal Flying Corps this year, as a mechanic, but quickly won promotion. On the morning of his achievement he saw two Fokkers dropping upon the machine of his comrade, Lieut. Savage (who was killed), and plunged down 3500 feet. His observer fired and brought Immelmann down. Our pilot was unharmed, but wounded in another encounter, and is now in hospital in France. Airmen recognise the courage and skill of their opponents ; and at the squadron aerodrome were seen two wreaths, one for Lieut. Savage, the other for Immelmann.—[Photo. passed by the Press Bureau ; supplied by C.N.]

"fishing"— by Explosives and for Explosives.

TWO FORMS OF "FISHING" IN WAR-TIME : A CATCH BY GUN-COTTON ; AND MINE-SWEEPERS.

The upper photograph, taken in Egypt, shows a quantity of fish that have been blown up by gun-cotton ; the lower one shows two motor-boats of the British Navy engaged in mine-sweeping. The use of explosives to catch fish is not exactly a discovery of the war—it has been heard of occasionally in the past—but the war has probably caused it to be more prevalent. Sometimes fish are killed in this way accidentally in the course of naval engagements ; at other times the explosive method is employed on purpose, in order to replenish the larder. Mine-sweeping is also known as "fishing" among the thousands of daring men of the auxiliary fleet who are daily risking their lives in this most perilous form of "sport."

Back in "Blighty": Wounded Soldiers at Home Again.

HEROES OF "THE GREAT PUSH": SOMME SOLDIERS ON A HOSPITAL "ROOF-GARDEN."

The roof-garden, which was originally an American notion, has long been acclimatised in England—when the climate permits—and, as our photographs show, is used now not merely for fashionably unconventional tea or supper parties, but, with excellent effect, for giving our brave soldiers who have returned home, "gashed with honourable scars," a welcome opportunity of resting and recuperating in the open air. Our photographs show the cheery fellows, smiling contentedly despite their array of bandages, of slings, and empty sleeves, all dumbly eloquent of wounds sustained in battle. In the little open-air encampment shown on the roof of a hospital "somewhere" in England, these men are being nursed back to health.—[Photos. by Newspaper Illustrations.]

THE BEGINNINGS OF WAR-MACHINES: AEROPLANES.

IN the year 1480 Leonardo da Vinci produced what were probably the first designs of a "heavier-than-air" flying-machine. The ideas of this inventor involved the use of flapping wings like those of a bird, together with vertical air-propellers to assist in lifting the machine.

In 1617 Veranzio attempted to fly by means of a parachute (Fig. 7), and in 1678 a smith named Besnier constructed a device operated by the arms and legs of the "flying" man with which he expected to be able to soar in the air (Fig. 8). This contrivance was, of course, quite useless in view of the fact that the muscular power of a man is hopelessly inadequate to operate any mechanical contrivance which will raise and carry his weight through the air.

It was not until the year 1810 that any serious attempts were made to investigate the principles underlying flight in "heavier-than-air" machines. In that year Sir George Cayley produced designs of a monoplane to be driven by a steam-engine, after having made a study of the effect of wind-pressure on inclined planes. About the year 1842 an aeroplane was made by one Henson, called the "Aerial" (Fig. 1). This machine was very similar to the modern monoplane, having one pair of fixed planes (P P) or wings, a horizontal rudder-tail (H), a vertical rudder (V), and an under-carriage provided with wheels (W) for landing. The machine did not fly, as its steam-power plant was too heavy. Had the internal-combustion engine been available at that date, it is probable that this inventor would have made the thing a success, as he evidently thoroughly understood the principles involved. In 1843, W. Miller, M.R.C.S., in spite of his presumed

FIG. 7.—AN EARLY SEVEN-TEENTH-CENTURY EXPERIMENT: VERANZIO'S PARACHUTE—FROM A CONTEMPORARY PRINT.

professional knowledge of anatomy, was foolish enough to put his name to a wing-flapping flying-machine to be operated by the arms and legs of the flier. Another "man-power" flying-machine

(Fig. 9) killed its inventor, a Belgian named De Groof, in the year 1874. This accident occurred at Chelsea. The machine, having been taken up by a balloon to an altitude of 3000 feet, was then allowed to fall. The inventor did his best to work the wings, but the whole thing fell quickly to the ground and he was instantly killed.

Much valuable information as to the behaviour of aeroplanes when in operation has been obtained by the use of "gliders." These machines have the supporting wings of the aeroplane proper, but are not provided with any motive power. It is, therefore, necessary to launch them from a high level and allow them to plane down to a lower level under the influence of gravity, the air-pressure under the wings supporting them during the voyage. The first well-known machine of this class (Fig. 2) was produced in 1893 by Otto Lilienthal, a German inventor, who made a series of experiments with it, and was finally killed by it in August 1896 when flying in the province of Brandenburg.

In 1894, Mr. (now Sir Hiram) Maxim built a flying-machine driven by a steam-engine of a very light type specially designed by the inventor for the purpose. It never had a free flight, but its lifting power was demonstrated.

A steam-driven model called by the inventor an "aerodrome" (Fig. 3) was constructed by Professor Langley in 1896, and made several successful flights in America. The total weight of this model was 25 lb., and its length over the wing-tips 14 feet. After travelling about 1000 yards at 22 to 25 miles per hour, its steam reserve was exhausted, and it alighted safely on the surface of the water over which the flight took place.

FIG. 8.—ATTEMPTING THE IMPOSSIBLE: BESNIER THE SMITH, 1678—FROM A SEVENTEENTH-CENTURY SKETCH.

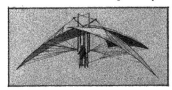

FIG. 9.—A FATAL ATTEMPT TO FLY BY MAN-POWER, IN 1874: DE GROOF'S MACHINE.

Percy Pilcher, an English engineer, built a glider in 1896, but was killed whilst operating it in 1899, although he had made many successful flights. [Continued opposite.

The Beginnings of War-Machines: Early Aeroplanes.

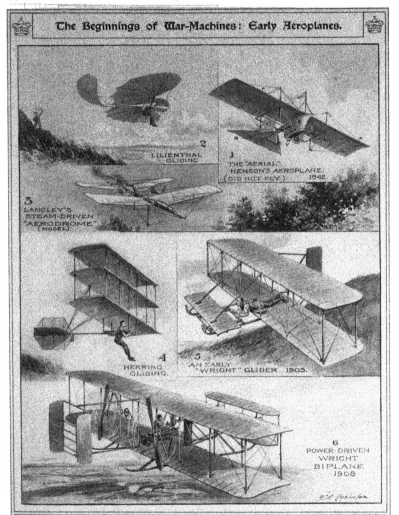

THE EVOLUTION OF HEAVIER-THAN-AIR FLYING MACHINES: ANCESTORS OF THE AEROPLANE.

[Continued.] The Herring Glider shown in Fig. 4 was an American device. The best-known machine of this class is that of the brothers Orville and Wilbur Wright, of California (Fig. 5), whose experiments, commencing about 1900, were carried out with great care and patience, and went a long way towards developing the modern biplane. When these gentlemen, by experiments with the Glider, had become thoroughly familiar with the conditions under which these machines are operated, they turned their attention to a power-driven 'plane, and produced, in 1908, the "Wright" Biplane (Fig. 6), propelled by an internal-combustion engine situated amidships, which operated a pair of "pusher" screw-propellers through the medium of pitch chains.

The Great Offensive in the West: Captured Guns.

SOME PROOFS OF THE ALLIES' SUCCESS: A GERMAN POSITION-GUN AND A "77" FIELD-GUN.

In the upper illustration a German position-gun captured by the French is seen passing through the French reserve lines, drawn by ten horses ridden by helmeted and cloaked French artillery drivers. In the lower illustration a French General, wearing the steel helmet originally designed for trench service, but now the universal battlefield wear, is inspecting the breech mechanism of one of the many German field-artillery 77's which our Allies have captured and continue to capture. The majority are field-pieces, 77's, but heavy pieces and howitzers are also being taken. It is known that, at least in the sector facing the British, the Germans withdrew most of their heavier artillery from the front line before the attack began.—[French Official Photograph; supplied by News. Illus.]

A Picturesque War-fête in a Historic Château.

FOR WAR-CHARITIES OF FRANCE : THE GLORIES OF VERSAILLES REVIVED FOR FRENCH WOUNDED.

There was something curiously suggestive in the recent revival of the ancient beauty of Versailles as it was in the luxurious era of Louis Quatorze and Louis Quinze. The Tableaux were given in aid of soldiers wounded in fighting German invaders of France, and many who cheerfully paid 100 francs for the privilege of witnessing them recalled that it was here that William I., in 1871,

was proclaimed German Emperor, after his entry into Paris. "The whirligig of Time brings in his revenges." The scene, too, was not without its humour, for the contrast between the hooped and flowered skirted dames and demoiselles of the dead centuries and the sturdy, kilted Scots of to-day, who gave an exhibition of their national dances, must have been piquant.—[Photo. by C.N.]

ROMANCES OF THE REGIMENTS : VI.—THE BLACK WATCH.

THE GHOST-STORY OF TICONDEROGA.

IT is an old and well-worn tale, but it will bear retelling once more, although it must be familiar to many readers of Dean Stanley and of Robert Louis Stevenson. Stanley's account of the legend, taken down by him and vouched for by the Campbells of Inverawe, occurs in Parkman's "Montcalm and Wolfe"; and Stevenson, to whose hand it was a subject made, wrought the story into his poem "Ticonderoga," which *Scribner* published in December 1887. The bibliography of the tale is, however, far more considerable than these instances; it has been much traversed by American writers, and will be found also in the works of Sir Thomas Dick Lauder and Lord Archibald Campbell. The curious in psychic lore and in Celtic mysticism will find all the references in Mr. Richards' "The Black Watch at Ticonderoga," a minutely careful monograph to which the present version is much indebted.

On July 7, 1758, the 42nd Highlanders were preparing, in the highest spirits, to attack Montcalm's position on a neck of land that runs out into Lake Champlain. But one of their number did not share the cheerfulness of his comrades, for the discovery of the Indian name of the place, otherwise known as Fort Carillon, was to him a menace of doom. For years past, while he was still unaware that such a place existed, the word "Ticonderoga" had haunted him, for he had heard it once spoken with terribly sinister meaning. To Major Duncan Campbell of Inverawe it signified a. tryst with death.

His thoughts flew back to a strange adventure which had befallen him long ago in the romantic

WITH SCALING-LADDERS (IN THE BACKGROUND) PLACED ACROSS THE TRENCH IN READINESS: BRITISH TROOPS IN A SUPPORT-TRENCH DURING A BOMBARDMENT WAITING TO ATTACK.

Official Photograph issued by the Press Bureau; supplied by L.N.A.

castle of his race, that keep of Inverawe which stands beside the Awe under the shadow of Ben Cruachan, whereby the Campbells swear their binding oath. As he sat alone, late one evening, in the hall of his ancestors, there came a furious knocking at the door, which the laird opened to admit a stranger all tattered and bloody from a recent fray. Breathless with long and hard running, the man begged for shelter and concealment. He had killed a man; the avengers of blood were at his heels. Duncan Campbell, respecting the laws of Highland hospitality, bade the fugitive enter, and, asking no questions, promised to shield him. But the murderer hesitated ; he would have fuller assurance. Little did the laird suspect why his bare word was doubted.

"Swear on your dirk," said the stranger. And Campbell swore, adding, it may be, the family oath by Ben Cruachan.

He led the fugitive to a secret chamber in the innermost part of the castle; but hardly had he got him safely bestowed again the door was assailed with heavy blows. It was a night of unbidden guests at Inverawe. This time, as the laird had surmised, he had to deal with the pursuers; but he was not prepared for their news.

"Your cousin Donald," they said, "has been murdered, and we are looking for the murderer."

Mindful of his oath, Campbell denied all knowledge of the fugitive, and the avengers went on their way.

The laird was now in an unenviable state of mind. For his oath's sake he had done well ;

(Continued overleaf.

The Allies' Western Offensive : Projectiles the French Use.

THREE HIGH-EXPLOSIVE GIANTS : SHELLS WITH WHICH OUR ALLIES ASSAIL THE GERMAN FRONT.

The three French heavy gun, or howitzer, high-explosive projectiles seen above are, reading from left to right, a 420-mm. (or 16·5-in.) shell ; a 360-mm. (or 14-in.) shell ; and a 305-mm. (or 12-in.) shell. They show certain kinds of heavy *matériel* the French gunners have used in the battle on the Somme. The enormous bulk of the two former types of shell, in particular, may be judged from the height of the French soldier standing by. A 16·5-in. shell of the ordinary pattern weighs, loaded, according to the published tables in text-books, 2350 lb. ; a 14-in. shell, 1400 lb. ; and a 12-in. shell, 850 lb. The shells shown are a tribute to the magnificent work of the French munition-factories, whence they come.—[*French War Office Photograph ; supplied by Newspaper Illustrations.*]

but, unwitting, he had come to harbour beneath his own roof one who had shed the blood of his near kindred. Torn with conflicting emotions, he retired to rest in a large dark room, still shown at Inverawe, with its sombre hangings and furniture; and there Campbell tossed until he fell asleep, only to waken to new terrors.

For beside him before cock-crow stood the ghost of the murdered Donald, crying in a hollow voice, "Inverawe, Inverawe, blood has been shed. Shield not the murderer."

At dawn the laird went to the murderer's hiding-place and told him that he could shelter him no longer.

But the man appealed to the oath. "You have sworn on your dirk," he cried; and Inverawe was flung back upon the horns of his dilemma. The blood of the Campbells called aloud for vengeance, yet a Campbell's honour was at stake. Duncan, sorely perplexed, at last resorted to a compromise. Not beneath the Campbells' roof-tree, but in a cave of Ben Cruachan, the murderer might lurk, virtually protected, and yet not entertained—a fine point of casuistry. So to the cave Duncan led his strange guest, and hid him there.

Next night the laird was as unhappy as before; he slept fitfully and in fever, expecting what he

THE OFFICE-WORK SIDE OF A MODERN BATTLE: THE INTERIOR OF A SIGNAL EXCHANGE DURING THE BRITISH ADVANCE.

Official Photograph issued by the Press Bureau; supplied by Alfieri.

"Inverawe, Inverawe, blood has been shed. Shield not the murderer."

At daybreak Campbell, greatly agitated, sought the cave, for what purpose no man knoweth. But the stranger was gone.

No sleep visited the laird's eyes that night either, and again the shape of Donald ghastly pale, stood by him. But the accents were now less stern—more in sorrow than in anger.

"Farewell, Inverawe," said the spectre; "farewell, till we meet at TICONDEROGA!"

Where or what Ticonderoga might be Campbell had no notion; but the strange name dwelt in his memory, and he was horror-stricken when in after years he was ordered to attack the very place. His brother officers, who knew the story well, tried to disarm his fears by telling him they had not yet reached the spot, but were at Fort George.

Their kindness reckoned without the ghost.

For next morning, the day of the fight (July 8), Major Campbell appeared with haggard looks before his comrades. "I have seen him. You have deceived me. He came to my tent last night! This is Ticonderoga! I shall die to-day!"

Not that day in actual fact, but he had his death-wound early in the

CANADIANS REHEARSING A SMOKE-ATTACK: A BOMBING-SCHOOL DEMONSTRATION ON THE WESTERN FRONT.

Official Canadian Photograph issued by C.N. (Canadian Government Copyright reserved.)

hardly dared think upon. And, sure enough, again the shade of the murdered Donald stood by the bedside and again came the adjuration—

disastrous affair, and nine days later Major Duncan Campbell of the Black Watch kept his tryst with death.

After British Mines and Guns had Done their Work.

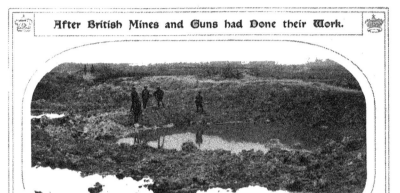

PHOTOGRAPHS TAKEN DURING THE BRITISH ADVANCE: A MINE-CRATER AND RUINED VILLAGE.

The upper photograph shows the enormous upheaval caused by the explosion of a mine underneath the enemy's position at a certain point in the German lines during the British offensive. Several great cavities in the ground have become filled with rain-water, and formed into ponds of considerable size. A group of British officers are seen examining the results, and in the background on the left are two men carrying a stretcher. In the lower photograph is seen all that was left of a village near Mametz after the British bombardment of the German trenches there. The place is in ruins, and scattered about are lengths of rail which perhaps had formed part of a German light railway.—[Official Photograph, issued on behalf of the Press Bureau by Newspaper Illustrations.]

The Western Front Offensive : British Bombarding-Pieces.

WEAPONS THAT CLEAR THE WAY TO VICTORY : A HEAVY GUN AND A HOWITZER.

One of the many similar giant guns along the British front which have been engaged in breaking through the German defence lines, and are still at work with every fresh advance of our unconquerable infantry, is shown in the upper illustration. It appears, after having just fired, a moment or two after going off, and with the cloud of smoke of the discharge still drifting away, as seen to the left. In the lower illustration, and affording an informative contrast between the characteristic features of the two classes of weapon—one long-barrelled, the other dumpy and short—is seen a British heavy howitzer in its firing-pit, with the howitzer team awaiting orders to stand to for action.—[Press Bureau Photographs ; supplied by Newspaper Illustrations.]

The Western Front Offensive: In Our Artillery Line.

IN POSITION, AND PREPARING FOR ACTION : A BRITISH HEAVY GUN, AND A HOWITZER.

A British heavy gun, apparently not long brought up to its place for action to join in the general bombardment of the enemy trench-lines during the different phases of the British attack, is seen in the upper illustration. Placed conveniently in a clearing in a copse, it has already been partially screened from Fokker observation by boughs of leaves, and the gun-team are at work making preparations for getting the gun into firing trim. A newly arrived, or recently moved on, British howitzer is seen in similar circumstances in the lower illustration. To be in the firing position the short barrel of a howitzer has to be elevated at a more or less steep angle, tilted well up so as to give its shells their trajectory-curve according to range.—[Official Photographs ; supplied by L.N.A.]

The Great British Offensive on the W

IMMEDIATELY AFTER THE BRITISH HAD STORMED THE ADVANCED GERMAN TRENCHES

This is the scene on the battlefield at La Boisselle immediately after the British infantry attack which stormed the position been carried through. The photograph was taken from the British front trenches—the original British advanced line and barbed entanglement is in the foreground. Shells from our guns are to be seen bursting ahead, "searching out" parts remaining

rn front: The Battlefield at La Boisselle.

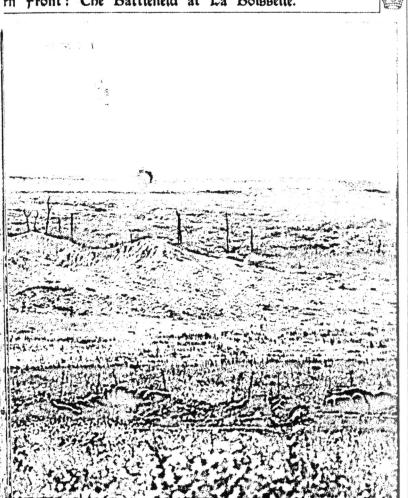

REMAINS OF THE ENEMY'S FRONT LINE, SHOWING A HUGE MINE-CRATER IN THE CENTRE.

pparently intact in the German entrenchments. A wide clearance in the German defences at one point was made by blowing up n immense mine, which had taken our men many days to dig and carry right under the enemy's front. Its crater is seen in he centre ; its resemblance to the crater of a natural volcano is extraordinary.—[*Press Bureau Photograph ; Supplied by Central Press.*]

Effects of British Gun-Fire on German Trenches.

BATTERED OUT OF RECOGNITION: HAVOC WROUGHT IN GERMAN TRENCHES BY BRITISH ARTILLERY.

These and other photographs in this issue show the devastating effects of the British bombardment directed upon the German trenches, as a preparation for the advance of the infantry in the Great Offensive. The scene suggests the havoc of an earthquake or a volcanic eruption. Where formerly there had been orderly and well-constructed trenches, with solidly built parapets and dug-outs, and protected by barbed-wire entanglements, there was nothing but a confused heap of rubble and shattered timber. Everything was blown to pieces by the terrific explosions of our shells. Only thus, under modern conditions, can the way be cleared for assaulting infantry.—[Official Photographs issued on behalf of the Press Bureau, by Newspaper Illustrations.]

On the Canadian Front: Wrecked German Trenches.

DEMOLISHED BY BRITISH SHELLS : GERMAN TRENCHES CAPTURED BY CANADIANS.

The upper photograph shows the havoc wrought by the British artillery fire in a heavily sand-bagged section of German trenches, preparatory to an attack by Canadian troops, who succeeded in capturing the position. In the lower photograph, also showing German trenches taken by the Canadians, it may be noted that, although the trench itself has not been rendered so shapeless as that seen in the other photograph, the barbed-wire entanglements outside the parapet have been thoroughly torn and shattered by the action of our high-explosive shells, making it easier for the Canadians to force their way through. A successful assault was made recently by the Canadians near Ypres.—[Photographs by the Canadian Official Photographer ; supplied by C.N. Canadian Government Copyright reserved.]

The Scene of a Gallant Canadian Counter-Attack.

CANADIAN HEROISM TRIUMPHS : RECAPTURED GUNS ; AND A TRENCH FROM WHICH TROOPS CHARGED.

The upper photograph shows the emplacements of two forward guns in Sanctuary Wood, near Ypres, which were temporarily captured by the Germans but retaken soon afterwards by the Canadians in the course of a vigorous counter-attack. In the lower photograph is seen part of a trench from which the 14th Canadian Regiment charged on this occasion. Describing the event,

Mr. Philip Gibbs writes : " The Canadian troops charged at two o'clock in the morning. Their attack was directed to the part of the line from the southern end of Sanctuary Wood to Mount Sorel, about a mile, which includes Armagh Wood, Observatory Hill, and Mount Sorel itself."—[Canadian Official Photographs ; supplied by C.N. Canadian Government Copyright reserved.]

Captured by the Canadians: Wrecked German Trenches.

GALLANTLY TAKEN BY THE CANADIANS AFTER BOMBARDMENT: GERMAN TRENCHES; AND A DUG-OUT.

The upper photograph shows part of the German trenches after they had been wrecked by a British artillery bombardment prior to a successful counter-attack by Canadian Infantry. The effect, it will be seen, was the same as in other parts of the German front during the British offensive. Parapets were reduced to heaps of rubble, and dug-outs were blocked up with débris. The wreckage at the entrance to one German officer's dug-out is shown in the lower photograph. On the right may be seen the shaft down which either stairs or a ladder led to the chamber below, in most cases some 30 feet beneath the surface. Many Germans were found in their dug-outs, and most surrendered.—[Photos. by the Official Canadian Photographer; supplied by C.N. Canadian Government Copyright reserved.]

THINGS DONE : VI.—THE ARMY SERVICE CORPS.

THERE are some who consider that the existence of the Army Service Corps is all jam—plum-and-apple jam—but this is not quite the case. They have other reasons for existence. They are the people the infantry use in their best jokes, and they are also the people the Army cannot do without. The Army makes jokes about the A.S.C. in the same way that a man lets off pleasant little witticisms about his wife. And the A.S.C. is the wife of the Army, ordering its life to that wifely rule contained in the seraphic counsel "Feed the brute."

The Army Service Corps spends its days feeding the brute, and, on the whole, feeding him with such efficiency that the food

CAPTURED IN THE GERMAN TRENCHES DURING THE BRITISH ADVANCE :
A GERMAN TRENCH-MORTAR (ON THE RIGHT), A GERMAN MACHINE-GUN,
A RUSSIAN MACHINE-GUN, AND AN AUTOMATIC RIFLE.

Official Photograph issued by the Press Bureau ; supplied by Alfieri.

is brought to the fighting men not so much in a series of meals, as in a series of miracles. The A.S.C. is the bringer-up of meals though the heavens fall. Advance or retreat, order or chaos, choked roads or communications strafed, the A.S.C. brings up the plum-and-apple jam, and whatever else is eatable in food and forage or consumable in fuel and light. Men who fight must have their several meals a day, and the A.S.C. is there to see it is done. One of the

marvels of the war has been the thoroughness of the way the A.S.C. has seen to the doing.

The task is an enormous one. It is the sort of task that makes a statistician go mad in an aureole of figures. It is the sort of task that makes men say, "If all the A.S.C. lorries were put end to end they would reach——" But why put lorries end to end ? It is a task that sets men carrying food and fodder in pounds and ounces over roads thousands of miles in extent to men in millions. The vision of the task is a vision of lorries and carts, railway trucks and ships, and lorries and carts again, travelling in an endless circle, travelling forward with loads of food and returning empty, but always moving in that endless chain, as though progressing in some enormous Dantesque circle under the doom of feeding an insatiable maw. The task, and the vision of it, is Gargantuan. But the A.S.C. never seem to notice.

The plan of the A.S.C. task is the plan of the linked chain, and each link is a revolving circle of carts, trains, or ships. The carts go out collecting from different centres all the foodstuffs the huge

(Continued overleaf.

GERMAN HEAD-GEAR, BUT NOT GERMAN FACES ! TROPHIES CAPTURED BY THE SHERWOOD FORESTERS,
INCLUDING A DOG FOUND IN A GERMAN DUG-OUT, DURING THE ADVANCE.

Official Photograph issued by the Press Bureau ; supplied by Alfieri.

The Western Front Offensive: French Big Guns

TWO OF GENERAL JOFFRE'S TITANS: HEAVY PIECES SHELLING THE GERMAN LINES IN PICARDY.

In the upper illustration is shown one of the giant guns that the French use in the great Allied Offensive on the Western Front, and by means of which they are, literally, battering down the German entrenched works in Picardy. Its mounting rests on a field-railway truck. To screen the piece from overhead observation, tree-branches have been laid on the superstructure over the gun, which itself is protectively coloured. In the lower illustration, French artillerymen are shown preparing to get a big gun, just arrived at its firing-point, and still roped down and with tarpaulin muzzle and breech covers on, off the vehicle on which it has been brought to the Front. They work smartly and all is soon clear.— [French Official Photographs ; supplied by Newspaper Illustrations.]

armies require; the foodstuffs are stored in great depôts. From the depôts trains carry the foodstuffs to ports, going full, returning empty. From the ports the ships carry foodstuffs to sea-bases behind the fighting line, where the great caches f food are piled for ever, to be unpiled as quickly

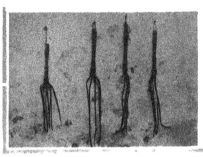

SOME OF MANY SIMILAR IMPLEMENTS FOUND IN THE GERMAN TRENCHES DURING THE BRITISH ADVANCE : GERMAN CAT-O'-NINE-TAILS !

Official Photograph issued by the Press Bureau; supplied by Alfieri.

as they grow. From these bases the radial links circle out to the fronts, by lorry and cart, carrying food up to Corps parks, returning empty. From the Corps parks, the food is taken to the Divisional depôts, the Divisional depôts separate it into Brigade depôts, and to the Brigade depôts the regimental wagons come empty and return full to the trysting-places where the company "grub-fatigues" snatch the life-giving jam and meat and the weekly pepper ration per man for the sake of the privates. Always the links are in motion, the regimental carts always racing back full to the "grub-orderlies," the Brigade lorries always bumping back at high speed to the Brigade depôt to keep large the pile of goods from which the regimental wagons are constantly stealing. The Divisional lorries are always racing back empty to get goods in time before the Brigade fellows have reduced their stores to nothing. And so along the whole chain the A.S.C. is working at top speed to keep pace with the voracity of the demand. And the miracle is the smoothness of the whole thing. The bacon-rasher appears on the end of the bayonet over the trench-brazier without the slightest sign of flurry on its comely countenance, though it has been whirled through

intricacies of miles and men have laboured like giants to bring it to this, its just fruition.

But besides being the provider of food and the carter of every kind of cartable thing between Britain and the front—and the front is as long away as Mesopotamia, remember—the A.S.C. has several other little jobs to do. They are the slaughtermen, butchers, and bakers of the Army also. They catch their meat, drive it to the abattoirs, and kill it, as well as preparing it and sending it to the front. In the same way, they bake the bread that goes along to the firing line, setting up bakeries (as well as butcheries) at the strategic gastronomic points in the lines of communication. Again, not content with training their own motor-men and wagon-drivers, they concern their industrious minds with the problems of remounts, though here they lose some of their Corps distinguishing marks and become admixed with cavalry and artillerymen who join them in training the young horses of the Government in the way they should go. Moreover, the Army Service Corps man is the sort of fellow who is expected to go away at any moment and drive a General or a General's Staff, or even fill up the gaps in the Field Ambulance section. The A.S.C. privates have, therefore, to be versatile; they must know how to handle a four-ton lorry and a high-power touring limousine just as perfectly as they must know how to drive with a delicate hand over a shell-pitted road that would give agony to the wounded in the Red Cross tonneau

CAPTURED IN THE GERMAN TRENCHES DURING THE BRITISH ADVANCE : TWO PERISCOPES WITH CASES, A TELEPHONE, A GAS-HELMET, AND A FIRST-AID OUTFIT FOR DEALING WITH GAS-POISONING.

Official Photograph issued by the Press Bureau; supplied by Alfieri.

behind them. And over all, though they are not, on the whole, fighters, they must know how to fight.   W. DOUGLAS NEWTON.

The Western Front Offensive: Enemy Trench-Destroyers.

FRENCH ARTILLERY GIANTS IN THE SOMME BATTLE : A GUN MOVING BY TRAIN—AND IN POSITION.

A typical specimen of the huge artillery that the French use in the Somme sector of the Great Offensive is seen in the upper illustration, moving to its post. A metal casemate, protectively coloured, roofs in the breech-end. Most of the big guns, both British and French, travel on the battle-front by railway, along the network of light lines which extend everywhere in rear of the Allies' positions. The train is just starting with some of the artillerymen on the gun-truck, one or two jumping on, and others in the vans behind the engine, which serve also to carry spare battery stores and gun gear. The lower illustration shows a gun in position, under a screen of boughs, being prepared for action.—[French Official Photograph ; supplied by Newspaper Illustrations.]

The Western Front Offensive: France's Readiness.

AT A FRENCH AMMUNITION DEPÔT NEAR THE SOMME: SHELLS ARRIVED AND ARRIVING.

These illustrations will give an idea of the output of the French munition-factories, and the strenuous labour of the workers; also of the enormous store of projectiles that the French have amassed in readiness for the Great Offensive in the West now taking place. In the upper photograph is seen one of the many railway sidings in the Somme sector of the French battle-front. Every yard and corner is crammed with shells of all calibres and kinds, unladen from trains which keep continually arriving by day and night. In the lower photograph one of the ammunition-trains is seen on its way, with trucks laden with big high-explosive shells, on one of the network of light railways in the French rear.—[French Official Photograph; supplied by Newspaper Illustrations.]

The Western Offensive: While the Guns are Busy.

THE FRENCH BATTLE LINE: POILU RESERVES IN REAR; OTHERS AWAITING TO ATTACK.

Until the artillery have completed their special work of sufficiently battering to pieces the enemy's trench-lines, and with a storm of projectiles of every calibre—mostly high-explosive shells—have practically swept away the barbed-wire entanglement defences across the front of the enemy's position along the whole space to be attacked, the infantry of the assaulting regiments, front line and supports, have only to stand by and await the order to advance. In the upper illustration French infantrymen held in reserve to support the first attacking line, are seen resting, but ready to go forward at a moment's notice. In the lower illustration, men in the French advanced trench-line are seen at ease under shelter during a lull in the bombardment.—[Photos. by C.N.]

At the Front in German East Africa.

CAMPAIGN NOTES: GERMAN ASKARI PRISONERS; AND A BRITISH SCOUT IN THE BUSH.

In the upper illustration is seen a batch of German native soldiers, seen in uniform, captured during General Smuts' ever-victoriously progressing campaign in German East Africa. They are in a British detention camp at Arusha, one of the places where a prisoners' depôt is established, behind a barbed-wire enclosure with a British soldier on guard. They are generally known as "Askaris," an East African vernacular term in common use, alike in the British and German possessions, for armed levies generally. It includes, in time of peace, the native armed watchmen hired to accompany big-game hunters on safari, or hunting expeditions, who do sentry-go at the camping-grounds. In the lower illustration a British scout is seen.—[Photos. by C.N.]

Italy's Battle-Front amidst Ice and Snow.

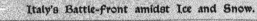

A WAR-AREA WHERE WINTER CONDITIONS HOLD ALL THROUGH THE YEAR: OUR ALLY'S TASK.

Both illustrations on this page are photographs from the Italian Army collection of battle-front photographs which have been added to the Italian War Picture Exhibition at the Leicester Galleries, Leicester Square. In the upper illustration, an Italian field-gun is seen being transported to a firing-point high up on a mountain side, at altitudes where the snow lies all the year round, slung on a wire rope by means of a travelling cradle, to the under-side of which the gun is attached. The method is one that has been successfully employed by the Italians throughout the Alpine campaigns. In the lower illustration is seen the entrance to a gallery tunnelled under ice and snow, among the upper peaks of the Monte Nero range on the Isonzo front.

WOMEN AND THE WAR

THE ex-Minister of Munitions, in one of his outbursts of picturesque oratory, declared that it should "rain shells for forty days and forty nights." So far, there has been no occasion for this very up-to-date form of deluge, though no doubt Mr. Lloyd George would have been as good as his words if needful. We do know, though, that for forty hours, and many more than forty hours, British big guns poured a continuous hail of steel and explosives on the German trenches not so many days ago. The victims of the "Big Push," whether our own men or enemy prisoners, declare that the fire of our guns was terrific, and that nothing like it had ever been known. As for the Germans, they have lately and very painfully acquired a wholesome respect for the might of our artillery, plentifully supplied as it is with stores of shells of every sort and description.

UNDER MILITARY DISCIPLINE : A CAMP 'ORDERLY' IN WORCESTERSHIRE.

The women workers on a farm in Worcester have adopted military discipline and fall in with its rules and methods loyally. Our photograph offers proof of this salutary state of things.

Photograph by L.N.A.

On the face of it, there does not seem to be much direct connection between the women at home and the British advance in France. But the shot and shell symphony given on the fields of France the other day appealed to a wider audience than the Germans cowering in their deep dug-outs, or the British awaiting the moment to advance. In England, thousands of women engaged on their twelve-hour shifts in the munition-factories worked with quickened interest at their tasks of shell-making, cartridge-filling, and kindred jobs as the brief official bulletins recorded the increasing intensity of the

British fire. After all, the great bombardment was in a measure the direct result of their labours ; no wonder that its success is a matter of personal pride to every individual female munition-worker in the country.

Quite early in the war women realised that, even if they could not fight, they could help to provide the means of killing the enemy. But it took quite a long time, and a "right-to-make-munitions" procession into the bargain, to convince the authorities that women's energies could be employed in other spheres than the "work-rooms" so lavishly established after war was first declared. So women were admitted to munition-factories, and now there are few processes connected with the manufacture of the death-dealing devices of modern warfare in which they do not take an active part. Incidentally, though woman has temporarily forsaken home toil for the arsenal, and laid aside the needle in favour of the lathe, there is none of the confusion that Tennyson predicted would result if ever woman should prove herself possessed of head as well as heart. Perhaps the best testimonial to the value of women's work at munitions is found in the fact that in one large institution where 10,000 women are already employed it is proposed to increase the number to 20,000 in the near future. In the same factory, one of the superintendents declared that he had no intention of engaging any more boys. "I dismiss about six a month," he

continued overleaf.

ON THE GREATER SCALE : DOMESTIC DUTIES CARRIED OUT IN UNDOMESTIC SURROUNDINGS.

A humorous writer not long ago gave us a wonderfully funny description of the Horrors of Washing-up. He did not specifically include tea-things, but even they, under conditions, may be not quite the sort of work to obtain which "influence" is sought.—[Photo. by L.N.A.]

[Continued overleaf.]

New Work for the New War-Time Women.

AMONG THE GRAPES: MEMBERS OF THE WOMEN'S DEFENCE RELIEF CORPS PRUNING VINES.

A question cognate to that of the suitability of women for work on the land, in and after war-time, is that of their success in such lighter branches of the work as fruit and flower growing. In these fields of labour it would seem that certain of the more delicate forms of work might be entrusted to women with advantage. Such work, for instance, as that shown in our photograph demands a niceness of touch, a care for detail, a delicacy in handling which come naturally to women workers. Viticulture is an industry demanding close attention to weather and other conditions, neglect of which may destroy a whole crop of grapes in a few hours. The earnings of the workers who seen in our photograph are to be given to the Red Cross Funds.—[Photo. by Alfieri.]

added. " Out of hundreds of women, I have only sent away half-a-dozen in as many months."

From making shell-cases for heavy eighteen-pounder shells to filling blank cartridges used for training horses to stand fire, women are playing their part in the production of munitions of war. A shell-case starts life as a rather thick round metal disc. It is placed on an iron platform covering an unseen furnace. A girl in a khaki overall and a cap turns a handle, down comes a heavy metal rod, the disc crumples like a piece of paper, disappears from sight, and finally emerges in the image of a roughly fashioned finger-bowl. That is one stage. There are about half-a-dozen others, each one of which is noisy, and during each much the same performance is repeated, except that every time the case is lengthened an inch or two, until it finally emerges clean and polished and perfect—the shell-case as we know it, that makes such a perfect dinner-gong when it is empty and such a matchless engine of death when charged with its burden of explosive.

But the charging operation is a part of the business that belongs to the sheds in the " danger " zone, where the workers wear fireproof overalls, and flat leather shoes innocent of heel and free from metal of any kind, where hairpins are anathema and the wearing of rings is sternly discouraged. Here the gigantic " cartridges " are charged with the cordite (which resembles nothing so much as a handful of bristles taken from a carpet-broom) that finally sends the projectile whistling on its death-dealing errand. Here, too, these same projectiles are fitted to the cases,

"THERE'S NOTHING LIKE LEATHER!" ESSENTIAL AIDS TO VICTORY.
Among the industries in which war-time has enlisted many of its recruits from the ranks of women, that of boot-making is one of the most important. Our photograph shows some women workers with "trays" of boots for the use of our troops ready for delivery.—[Photo. by Illustrations Bureau.]

gauged to ensure correctitude of size, and then filled with the innocuous-looking substances that suggest scented soap, whose pleasant appearance

WOMEN WORKERS FOR THE WAR: HOW OUR BRAVE SOLDIERS ARE SHOD.
The substantial and comfortable boots worn by our troops are of immense help to them in the arduous conditions of war, for they, of all men, learn " where the shoe pinches." But, very wisely, the greatest care is taken in the matter of foot-gear for the soldiers, for the matter is one of very real importance.
Photograph by Illustrations Bureau.

entirely belies their explosive reputation. Then the fuse is fitted and screwed on—a delicate business, where careless handling may bring disaster to all concerned—and then the shell is ready for its journey to the gunners " somewhere at the front."

That is just one fraction of the work the women are doing. There is the lighter ammunition for the rifles and the deadly machine-guns; and, while some women spend their time waxing wicked-looking little bullets, others fit the caps into the cartridge-cases, where they are punched into security by machines before being charged. Or, again, there is the tailor's shop that supplies the cartridges with their textile requisites and the workers in danger-buildings with clothes; or there is the paper-factory, where all sorts of things necessary to the interior well-being of shells are turned out; as well as the work on machine-tools. And in most of the buildings there is noise. But through it all the women work steadily, and, if you ask them, they will tell you quite frankly that, while the money is acceptable, the thought that they are helping to avenge our soldiers slain in the field is even more pleasant.—CLAUDINE CLEVE.

The Fourteenth of July Parade in Paris.

THE ALLIES' MARCH-PAST IN PARIS ON THE NATIONAL FÊTE DAY : FRENCH INFANTRY AND "75's."

July 14, the anniversary of the fall of the Bastille in 1789, was celebrated in Paris this year by a deeply impressive military pageant, held at a no less momentous hour in the history of France. Representatives of the French, Belgian, Russian, and British Armies paraded through the city, in such force that they took three-quarters of an hour to pass a given point. The French troops, in their battle-stained blue uniforms, marched to the music of "Mourir pour La Patrie" and Méhul's "Chant de Départ." Several batteries of the famous "Soixante-Quinze" field-guns, decorated with flowers, were greeted with special enthusiasm. The fervour was intense, without "mafficking"; for Paris, though full of confidence, realises that the war is not over.—[Photos. by Topical.]

An Ovation for British and Indians in Paris.

PARIS WELCOMES BRITISH AND INDIAN TROOPS: MARCHING DOWN THE CHAMPS ELYSÉES.

The British contingents that took part in the great parade of Allied troops in Paris on July 14 received a most enthusiastic welcome. They were headed by the pipers of the Scots Guards, and among them were English battalions, Highlanders, Canadians, Australians, and Indians. To all of them the Parisians paid the same hearty tribute, and, as they went by, girls ran out to offer gifts of flowers. Every officer and many of the men received flowers as they passed down the Champs Elysées. In reply to a message from Sir Douglas Haig, President Poincaré said: "Those of your magnificent troops who have to-day paraded in the streets of Paris . . . received throughout their march a striking proof of the public sentiment."—[Photos. by Topical.]

Russians and Annamites in the Great Paris Pageant.

ALLIES AND COLONIAL TROOPS OF FRANCE IN PARIS ON JULY 14 : RUSSIANS AND ANNAMITES.

The upper photograph shows a regiment of the splendid Russian infantry marching past in the Rue Royale during the great parade of Allied troops in Paris on July 14. They marched in long lines of sixteen abreast, singing every now and then their national battle-chants. Their mounted officers saluted with their swords as they passed. President Poincaré, in reply to a message of congratulation from the Emperor, thanked him for having authorised the magnificent Russian troops in France to join in the French national fête. The Russians received a hearty welcome from the crowd. In the lower photograph is seen a contingent of Annamites, French colonial troops from Cochin China, in khaki uniforms and caps of Chasseur Alpin shape.—[Photos. by Topical.]

Belgium's Place of Honour in the Paris Parade.

THE BELGIAN ARMY LEADS THE WAY IN THE MARCH-PAST : INFANTRY AND MACHINE-GUNS.

The upper photograph shows Belgian infantry in the Rue Royale during the great march-past of Allied troops in Paris on July 14. The lower photograph shows a Belgian *mitrailleuse* (machine-gun) section in the Place de la Concorde. Belgium was given the place of honour in leading the procession, just as she held it in the war by being the first to withstand the invader. The well-drilled and well-equipped appearance of the Belgian troops, and their resolute demeanour, evoked general admiration and testified to the successful reorganisation of the Belgian Army. As the Belgians came by, the shower of flowers began. The infantry were followed by the machine-gun parties, cyclist-buglers, Red Cross cyclists, and Belgian Lancers.—[*Photo. by Topical.*]

LONDON: Published Weekly at the Office, 172, Strand, in the Parish of St. Clement Danes, in the County of London, by THE ILLUSTRATED LONDON NEWS AND SKETCH, LTD., 172, Strand, aforesaid; and Printed by THE ILLUSTRATED LONDON NEWS AND SKETCH, LTD., Milford Lane, W.C.—WEDNESDAY, JULY 19, 1916.

The Illustrated War News

TURBAN AND HELMET: INDIAN CAVALRY RECENTLY IN ACTION IN FRANCE—A BATTLEFIELD PHOTOGRAPH.

THE GREAT WAR.

By W. DOUGLAS NEWTON.

IT was not to be expected that the Germans would remain passively acquiescent in the face of the Allied advance ; and it was also inevitable that, when they did attempt to readjust the balance of events, their efforts would be planned in a series of heavy attacks rather in the method of grand assault than that of a counter-stroke. The Germans have no pronounced genius or habit for tenacity in defence—I mean by that the sort of grim immobility in resistance that both the British and French have exhibited both before and since Ypres and Arras — and their dispositions for battle are always based on an aggressive, an aggressive managed with large gestures. Therefore, when they came out against the new fronts of the British and French, it was to be expected that they would come out in a big manner. What remained to be seen was whether new lines swiftly won and but hastily consolidated could stand the enormous strain of the German assault. Within the last week we have had a solution of this point, which, if it is not final—for the German efforts to throw us back are certainly not over yet—is at least as hopeful and satisfactory as any omen in this world of war and wild transition can be. The Germans have launched two great thrusts against the new Western lines— against the French at Biaches, and against the British at Longueval. Both these attempts have been failures — that against the French a complete failure, that against the British hardly less complete.

THE GOLDEN STRIPES OF HONOUR OUR WOUNDED OFFICERS AND MEN NOW WEAR : A SCOTS OFFICER WITH THE NEW "DECORATION" ON HIS SLEEVE.

The attack directed against the French had as its objective those paramount positions south of the Somme near Biaches—Hill 97 and the works of the Maisonnette Farm. Early in the week an assault in the fog gave the Germans the mastery of these points for a time—that is, only until the French counter - attack drove them out. Later in the week, a second powerful assault was sent forward, but met with more drastic repulse. In front of Maisonnette the enemy met with complete failure ; at Biaches they did manage to enter the village, only to be driven out again with heavy losses. Thus this part of the new line remained enduring in spite of Germany, and the French were so little incommoded by the assaults that they were able to make their definite advances elsewhere. The German attack against the British was probably intended to be more imposing. Applying a great force in guns and men, the enemy pushed against the spear-head of our front at Longueval and the Bois Delville, and by their inordinate weight managed to win the wood and the village. When the counter-advance was at the top of the tide, its progress was widely advertised in Germany and among neutrals credulous and incredulous. When the tide turned this advertisement ceased. The tide turned in grim fashion ; the battle, never easy, was fought with a great deal of ferocity, but went steadily in our favour until by degrees we won back most of the ground we had lost, and the

AS THEY APPEARED WHEN ENTERTAINING SOLDIERS IN THE TRENCHES : ARTISTS WHO DID THEIR "BIT" AMONG OUR MEN AT THE FRONT.

The five are, reading from left to right : Mr. Walter Hyde ; Mr. Percy Sharman ; Mr. Arthur Fagge (Piano) ; Mr. Nelson Jackson, the well-known humorous entertainer ; and Mr. Charles Tree. They are now at the Coliseum giving the entertainment they gave in the trenches as a Firing-Line Concert Party, and wear the same muddy clothes, gaiters, etc., they wore while at the Front.—[Photo. by Alfieri.]

position became more or less as it was before the advent of the German effort. It should be noted that other German thrusts—against our new works at Waterlot, for example—broke down before there was the meanest occasion for wiring a victory Berlinwards.

The German counter-effort is given first place here because its failure gives the most auspicious note of the week. At the same time, the German effort has represented but a part of the week's fighting, and the result of the rest is very palpably on the credit side of our account. There has been very useful movement in the West from both British and French lines, and our advance has made ground at many notable points. The British have set themselves the deliberate task of widening out the gap they have forced in the enemy's front. East of Longueval, early in the week, they

German third line, and have again made an entry into the positions in the Bois des Foureaux. At one time we held the whole of this wood, but counter-attacks gave the enemy back the northern fringes, though not the southern, which we still hold, and which we will know how to turn to excellent use when the just time for further advance arises. There has been a great deal of heavy bombardment on this and other fronts, and some raiding, particularly near Fromelles. Everywhere the troops are showing progressive activity, and are working forward in the best of spirits.

At the point, it seemed, where our second big fighting, the plan being reminiscent of the German method of alternation in attack east and west of the Meuse. 'The French,' however, were not con-

"KING ALBERT'S BAND" IN LONDON TO CELEBRATE THE BELGIAN INDEPENDENCE ANNIVERSARY DAY : THE BAND OF THE 1st ROYAL BELGIAN GUIDES.

In honour of the Belgian National Fête, on July 21, the anniversary day of the Declaration of Belgian Independence three-quarters of a century ago, the crack regimental band of the Belgian Army, that of the 1st Regiment of Guides (known also as "King Albert's Band") have been in London to take part in the patriotic celebration at the Royal Albert Hall.—[Photograph by Alfieri.]

forced their way past the Waterlot Farm, to flank the German works at Guillemont Fort. North of Longueval our troops are pursuing the conquest of the remaining high points of the Albert Plateau ; and the front is working towards Martinpuich in such a manner as to encroach dangerously northwest of the German hold at Pozières ; and have, indeed, since fought their way into the village. Between the Bapaume Road and our left flank above Thiepval we have been going forward also ; Ovillers is now entirely in our hands, and we have captured strongly held lines and posts eastward of this village and eastward of the Leipzig Redoubt, which is south of Thiepval. Better still, the British have returned to their attack on the

tent with the German advance of yards. From the point where the French join our lines they have pushed the enemy back over a front of four miles—that is, from the hill north-east of Hardecourt to the river. This advance not only straightens out the line, but carries our Ally well along the light railway east of Hardecourt, and very close up to the Combles-Peronne railway that acts as feeder to the German front. At the same time, the French attacked south of the Somme, on the extreme right flank of the battle, and yet again forced the Germans to give ground. Here they carried in its entirety the first German position from Estrées to the Hill of Vermand-Ovillers. The French have won their advances in spite of heavy attacks made upon them, notably against their new front by Soyécourt and near Chaulnes. All attacks have been frustrated. Moreover, it is well to call attention to the fighting at Verdun. Here the Germans have certainly given indications of lack of drive; and the French—who should be, according to German calculations, exhausted—have been pushing very deliberately ahead in the direction of Fleury. Nearly every day of the week has seen recorded some movement here, and, though these gains have generally been small, they have been final enough to show which way the power of action is setting. The Germans have attacked Verdun in a direction south of Damloup, and they have been broken. Quite one of the outstanding features of the week has been the work of the Allied aviators; numerous aerial combats have seen them successful, and some large bombing expeditions—against Metz and against points of importance behind the German lines—have been brilliantly carried out.

Russia has once more shown her versatility in movement; our Ally has again broken the enemy line, and has again broken it in the Lutsk salient. The fighting brings yet another able Russian commander to prominence, for it is General Sakharoff's army which has driven its way forward in the region of the Styr at its junction with the

Lipa, and is pressing back the Austrians in some hurry along the Galician border. This movement has brought a number of villages, including the town of Berestechko, within the Russian line, and our Ally is going westward in such a manner as to imperil the enemy line southward through

A SERBIAN REGIMENTAL ANNIVERSARY AT SALONIKA : MEN OF THE 1st SERBIAN CAVALRY KEEPING THEIR ANNUAL "SLAVA" ROUND THEIR "CAIRN OF VICTORIES."

The 1st Serbian Cavalry (now equipped as infantry) are seen keeping their yearly "Slava," or festival, in memory of Milan Obilitz, their reputed organiser, who killed a Turkish Sultan in battle in 1389. The troopers are dancing round a cairn of stones each bearing the name of a battle the regiment fought in, crowned by flags of the Allies.
Official Press Bureau Photograph.

Brody to Tarnopol. The enemy is surrendering in wholesale fashion, and is offering a weak resistance so far. Further south, the Russians are also pressing, and have made their way to the Carpathian Passes without adequate check. To the north, Hindenburg has not been able to do anything satisfactory, and our Ally is attacking the German line from Baranovitchi to Riga, and at points has broken into the trench system. In the Caucasus, also, the Russian arms go forward, and have developed their attack on a big front from the Black Sea and Trebizond to a point 100 miles west of Erzerum. The Italians, too, in their sphere have been doing extremely well, and the latest news gives them advances between the Brenta and the Piave, the capture of the Rolle Pass, the storming of the strong Eniser Peak (8000 feet) in the Sexten Valley, and the occupation of the summit in the Upper Piave. From East Africa comes the news that General Smuts has driven the enemy across the Pangani, and that the Usambara railways have fallen into our hands. LONDON: JULY 24, 1916.

READY TO WIN BACK THEIR COUNTRY : SERBIAN OFFICERS AT SALONIKA EXAMINING A NEW TRENCH-MORTAR AND PROJECTILE.

The Serbian Army at Salonika is in a state of efficiency unknown before, completely equipped, drilled and disciplined. Every modern appliance in the way of war *matériel* has been supplied to it by England and France, down to—as seen above—trench-helmets and the newest pattern of trench-mortars for firing air-torpedoes or giant bombs.
Official Press Bureau Photograph.

The Battlefield Chivalry of the British Soldier.

TOMMY BEARS NO ILL-FEELING : GIVING ᴀ WOUNDED GERMAN PRISONER A LIGHT.

A British soldier on the battlefield is here seen giving a wounded German prisoner a cigarette, and lighting it for him. Hundreds of such instances have been told of our men's good-hearted kindness to enemy soldiers on surrender, Germans with whom barely five minutes before, it may be, they were hotly engaged in hand-to-hand fight. No finer testimony indeed to the chivalrous spirit of one and all among our troops at the front could be given than the story which has gone the round of the Press, of how, after the taking of Ovillers the other day, during the Great Offensive, the British victors presented arms to the remnant of the German garrison—men of the Prussian Guard—on surrendering, in recognition of the gallantry of the defence.—[Official Press Bureau Photograph.]

Turkish Prisoners in British Hands.

AT A DETENTION CAMP FOR TURKS: THE COOK-HOUSE; AND BREAD-RATION ISSUE.

The first of the photographs here given shows the cook-house in one of the British internment camps for Turkish prisoners captured in the Dardanelles fighting, on the Tigris, and in the actions on the banks of the Suez Canal. Our Turkish prisoners everywhere accept their lot, not only with characteristic resignation, but also, it is on record, with expressions of contentment at the way they are dealt with. Many, indeed, have admitted that their considerate treatment is a condition of things unknown in their lives before. Turkish prisoner-orderlies parading at a camp during the serving out of the daily bread ration, prepared according to Mahomedan custom, are seen in the lower illustration.—[Official Press Bureau Photographs.]

Turkish Prisoners' Camp Life Scenes.

INCIDENTS OF CAMP ROUTINE : KIT INSPECTION AND ROLL CALL ; TOBACCO BEING SERVED OUT.

Turkish prisoners at a periodical kit-inspection parade and roll-call in camp are seen in the upper illustration, mustered in one of the barracks in which they are quartered. In front of the line, towards the centre, are seen a helmeted group of British officers in charge. Each prisoner wears on his coat his identification-disc with his number on the books of the establishment. From all reports, the most friendly relations are maintained between the British officers in charge and the Turkish prisoners, who take their detention very philosophically—and give practically no trouble. In the second illustration, Turkish prisoner-orderlies are shown with members of a prison camp commissariat staff drawing the tobacco ration.—[Official Press Bureau Photographs.]

Turkish Prisoners' Ways of Passing the Time.

CAMP RECREATION AND FESTIVAL SCENES : A PRISONERS' CONCERT PARTY AND A REHEARSAL.

Testimony to the manner in which our Turkish prisoners appreciate the consideration shown them by their British captors is given by the demeanour of the men shown in both these illustrations. They serve, too, to give an idea of the stalwart physique of the Turkish soldiery, recruited as they largely are from the brawny-limbed, sturdy peasantry of Rumelia, Anatolia, and Syria ; besides in-cidentally reflecting credit on our soldiers who made them captive. A native orchestra at a concert got up in camp by the prisoners themselves is seen in the upper illustration. In the lower, Turks are seen rehearsing dances for the great Mahomedan festival of the Eed, allowed to be celebrated at the prison camps in orthodox religious fashion.—[Official Press Bureau Photographs.]

Italy's Austrian Prisoners: A Few of the Many.

CAPTURED BY THE ITALIANS: AUSTRIANS MARCHING FROM THE FRONT ALONG A LOMBARDY ROAD.

The Italian High Command does not go into details of figures in regard to its prisoners; nor, indeed, as to the numbers of guns or quantities of war *matériel* captured. Taken as they are—both prisoners and spoil—among the recesses of the Alpine valleys and all over the mountain sides, exact enumeration is certainly difficult. The illustration above is the more interesting on that account by being a photograph of one of the many roads from the Italian front through Lombardy. It shows a column of Austrian prisoners which kept on marching apparently endlessly one day along the road. The Austrian losses on the Italian front are known to be immense, amounting in killed, wounded, and prisoners to several hundreds of thousands.—[*Photo. by Record Press.*]

THE BEGINNINGS OF WAR - MACHINES : PROJECTILES.

STICKS and stones thrown by hand were probably the first projectiles used in warfare, and at a very early period a body of men called "Stone Casters" formed a part of the ancient Greek army. The stick as a projectile, in the form of a throwing-spear (Fig. 26), survives to-day amongst savage warriors.

Stones thrown from slings were used by the Gauls against the Romans about B.C. 59, and we find stone shot projected from catapults at a somewhat later date ; whilst, later still, stone missiles were fired from cannon. Catapults and ballistæ for throwing heavy stones were used over a very long period extending from a date prior to the siege of Jerusalem by the Romans to 1303, when Edward I. employed one of these weapons to throw 300 lb. shot at the siege of Stirling. Stones and darts were thrown from cannon by the Arabs at the siege of Niebla, in Spain, in 1257. During the fourteenth, fifteenth, and sixteenth centuries efforts were made to produce cannon throwing the heaviest possible shot, and 300-lb. missiles were frequently used. In the two following centuries, however, the large-bore pieces gave place to smaller and longer weapons calculated to attain greater range and accuracy, the largest shot these used weighing about 150 lb. The change from stone to cast-iron occurred about

Meg," of 1489. Arrows thrown from long-bows were used as far back as B.C. 1058, and continued in use till A.D. 1643. Slings for throwing stones were in existence about B.C. 810. Lead bullets took the place of stones for sling missiles about the end of the fifth century B.C. These bullets, used by the Greeks and Romans, were frequently ornamented with some fancy device or with a word of defiance (Fig. 25), "Receive this," "Desist," or some similar inscription being engraved or cast in the surface of the metal.

We first hear of the use of red-hot shot in B.C. 57, in Quintus Cicero's campaign against the Nervii, when porcelain or earthenware pellets were discharged from a sling in that condition. Red-hot shot from cannon was employed at Cherbourg in 1418, at La Fère in 1580, and at Gibraltar in 1782, the successful defence of the last-named being attributed in a very great measure to its use. A hollow iron shell lined with clay and filled with molten metal five minutes before it was thrown from the cannon, known as Martin's shell, was introduced in 1855, with

FIG. 27.—MEDIÆVAL CROSS-BOW BOLTS.

the object of setting fire to any vessel or building struck by it. Its use was discontinued in 1869. Burning brands attached to arrows were at one time thrown from catapults.

"Wild Fire," a mixture of pitch, sulphur, and naphtha made up in a ball, used to be thrown, when alight, on to an enemy vessel. "Greek Fire," A.D. 668, was a combustible mixture inextinguishable in water, the secret of whose composition is not now known. A chemical known as "Chinese Fire" is said to have developed such fierce heat that it penetrated the breastplates on which it fell. This substance, together with fire-arrows, was used at the siege of Pien-Leang in 1232. Incendiary shells and hand-grenades were used by the Chinese in the twelfth and thirteenth centuries.

FIG. 26.—ANCIENT THROWING-SPEARS : (1) A ROMAN PILUM, 6 FT. LONG, HELD AT a ; AND (2) A GREEK SPEAR 2 OR 3 FT. LONG.

1400, when the French adopted it, though it had been tried somewhat earlier, the English having used iron cannon-balls in 1346 at Crecy. Combinations of lead, cast-iron, bronze, etc., were experimented with over a long period, and cast-iron shells filled with lead are said to have been thrown to a distance of 3½ miles at the siege of Cadiz, in 1596. Early in the fifteenth century stone shot 600 lb. in weight, were used by Mahomet II. at the siege of Constantinople ; and cannon were at one time in existence on the coast of the Dardanelles which were constructed to throw a stone shot weighing 1100 lb. Stone balls were used by the Turks as recently as 1807, when defending the passage of the Dardanelles. An enormous stone shot may be seen in the United Services Museum in Whitehall, where also are specimens of many of the projectiles illustrated here. A granite shot about 325 lb. in weight was the missile of the old Edinburgh cannon. "Mons

FIG. 25. — INSCRIBED WITH WORDS OF DEFIANCE (E.G., "SHOW YOURSELF ") : ANCIENT GREEK LEADEN SLING-BULLETS, B.C. 500.

Figs. 1 to 14 illustrate a variety of missiles thrown from ancient cannon—bar-shot, chain-shot, and linked-shot, all used to damage the rigging and sails of an enemy vessel.

[Continued opposite.]

The Beginnings of War-Machines: Projectiles.

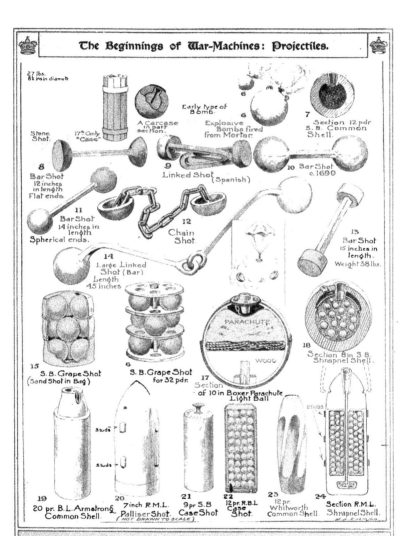

27 lbs.
8½ ins in diameter

Stone Shot.

17ᵗʰ Cenly "Case"

A Carcase in part section.

Early type of Bomb.

Explosive Bombs fired from Mortar.

6

6

7 Section 12 pdr S.B. Common Shell.

8 Bar Shot 12 inches in length Flat ends

9 Linked Shot (Spanish)

10 Bar Shot c.1690

11 Bar Shot 14 inches in length Spherical ends.

12 Chain Shot

13 Bar Shot 15 inches in length. Weight 38 lbs.

14 Large Linked Shot (Bar) Length 45 inches

15 S.B. Grape Shot (Sand Shot in Bag)

6 S.B. Grape Shot for 32 pdr.

17 Section of 10 in Boxer Parachute Light Ball

PARACHUTE

WOOD

18 Section 8 in S.B. Shrapnel Shell.

19 20 pr. B.L. Armstrong Common Shell.

Studs

Studs

20 7 inch R.M.L. Palliser Shot. (NOT DRAWN TO SCALE)

21 9 pr S.B. Case Shot

22 12 pr. R.B.L. Case Shot

23 12 pr. Whitworth Common Shell

STUDS

24 Section R.M.L. Shrapnel Shell.

FROM STONE SHOT TO SHRAPNEL SHELL: PROTOTYPES OF THE PROJECTILES USED IN THE WAR.

(Continued.)

A "carcase" was an early type of incendiary shell. Figs. 15 and 16 show methods of holding together a charge of grape shot for a muzzle-loading cannon; and Fig. 17 a Boxer "star" shell, with its supporting parachute, intended to cause a gradual descent and, consequently, an extended period of light. Fig. 18 is a spherical shrapnel shell. Fig. 20, a 7-inch Palliser shell, shows the studs

that engaged with the rifling-grooves in the barrel, and so caused the shell to revolve and keep "nose first," a specially important detail for the purpose of the Palliser. Fig. 23 shows a Whitworth shell having sloping grooves on its exterior surface to take the rifling. Fig. 24 shows another shell fitted with driving-studs like the Palliser.—[Drawn by W. B. Robinson.]

France's Gratitude to her Sons who have Died for Her.

GIVEN TO RELATIVES OF FALLEN FRENCH SOLDIERS: A MEMORIAL CARD.

Just before the great parade of Allied troops in Paris on July 14, M. Poincaré presented to relatives of fallen French soldiers, as a tribute of national gratitude, a memorial card inscribed with the soldier's name. The card here reproduced is that of the first French soldier killed in the war. In a moving speech to the bereaved relatives, M. Poincaré said: "Two years have passed without shaking French resolution." The verses may be translated thus: "Those who died for their country deserve that to their tomb the multitude should come and pray. Among the noblest names theirs is the most noble. Beside them all glory passes away and droops ephemeral, and, like a mother's, the voice of a whole people lulls them in their grave."—[Photo. by Rol.]

Dealing with German Prisoners in the British Advance.

GERMAN PRISONERS : UNWOUNDED MEN SET TO WORK ; A WOUNDED MAN HAVING HIS NAME TAKEN.

The upper photograph shows some German prisoners captured in the British advance helping with a Red Cross water-cart. In the lower photograph a wounded German is being questioned by an Intelligence Officer, who is taking the names of prisoners as they are brought in. Some of the prisoners who were unwounded have also been employed as stretcher-bearers and in other ways. The prisoners themselves were generally very glad to get water to drink. Describing the capture of some at Ovillers, Mr. Philip Gibbs says : "These men . . . had long been in a hopeless position. They were starving because all supplies had been cut off by our never-ending barrage, and they had no water supply, so that they suffered all the torture of great thirst."—[*Official Press Bureau Photographs.*]

ROMANCES OF THE REGIMENTS : VII.—THE ROYAL FUSILIERS.

A PAGEANT AND A TRAGEDY.

IN the old wars soldiers had more leisure than they enjoy in the field to-day, and the intervals of fighting were often filled up with amusements—not casual, but elaborate. One of the most magnificent of these interludes was organised in May 1778 at Philadelphia by a young officer of the Royal Fusiliers; and under the direction of his genius for pageantry it was brought to splendid success, and provided not only the Army but Philadelphian society with a nine days' wonder. In the city there were many colonists favourable to the British; and even among the disaffected some were not averse to knowing the officers of King George. Howe, it is true, was in possession of Philadelphia, but his triumph had been barren; he was about to retire,

stiff old writer, "took a character of romance and elegant gaiety from the genius of its promoter." The revel opened with a regatta on the Delaware. After the procession of boats, the chief personages landed and marched in very picturesque style to the lists, in a meadow a quarter of a mile from the river. Six Knights of the Blended Rose contended with six of the Burning Mountain, all in fantastic silk dresses, with ribbons, devices and mottoes, lances, shields, and (let purists in romance be calm if they can) pistols ! Perhaps the Burning Mountain thought pistols indispensable and appropriate.

Lord Cathcart, attended by two squires, led the Knights. On his shield he bore a Cupid mounted on a Lion. He proclaimed that he

THE GREAT BRITISH OFFENSIVE : A BATTALION OF LANCASHIRE FUSILIERS, MASSED IN HOLLOW SQUARE,
BEING ADDRESSED BY THEIR DIVISIONAL GENERAL BEFORE ACTION.

The Lancashire Fusiliers have more than once, and at many places (including "Lancashire Landing" at the Dardanelles), made their mark in the war. The first battalion is the famous old 20th Foot, the heroes of Minden.—[Official Press Bureau Photograph.]

the army was soon to evacuate the city, and it was by way of putting the best face on the matter that the revel was set afoot — professedly in honour of Howe, but also, perhaps, for the edification of Washington's shoeless army, which lay in cantonments a few miles away. The pageant-master improved his acquaintance among the belles of Philadelphia, little dreaming that his friendship with one of them would be the indirect means of bringing him, three years later, to the gallows. The reader will already have guessed that the officer in question was none other than the gallant and chivalrous, but most unfortunate Major (then Captain) John André.

André called his festival the "Mischianza" (Italian for "a medley"), and did his best to make it live up to its title. "The affair," says a

appeared in honour of Miss Auchmuty. André, Knight of the Blended Rose, stood forth for Miss P. Chew. He bore as device on his shield two game-cocks, and the motto "No Rival."

The Herald of the Blended Rose now, with flourish of trumpet, proclaimed the Knights' intention to maintain by force of arms the supremacy of their ladies in wit, beauty, and virtue. The Herald of the Burning Mountain responded with defiance; and the two factions closed, shivering lances, discharging pistols, and finally going at it with their swords until the Marshal of the Lists, at the ladies' request, ordered the combatants to desist.

Then to the dance. A house close by had been fantastically decorated for the occasion, and here the revel was continued. Concealed folding doors

[Continued overleaf.

A British Tribute to France's Heroes.

PRESENTED FOR THE WOUNDED OF OUR ALLY, FRANCE: A RED CROSS AMBULANCE CONVOY.

In the upper illustration is seen a convoy of Red Cross ambulance-wagons presented by donors in England to France as a special gift to the French nation and a token of admiration for the heroic stand the Army of our ally is making at Verdun. The ambulances are seen parked on the Esplanade des Invalides, in Paris, where President Poincaré inspected them and in person accepted the gift in the name of the people of France. In the lower illustration part of the interior of the motor repair lorry, which accompanies the ambulance-car section, is seen. One of its sides is let down, as would be the case for workshop purposes, disclosing also a glimpse of the interior with its racks of tools and appliances.—[Photos. by Rol and Meurisse.]

now glided aside, and showed an exquisitely laid supper-table. And at last, as darkness fell, Philadelphia was treated to a display of fireworks such as had not been seen before in America.

André was hugely congratulated upon his skill as an organiser, and the affair brought him into notice. Miss P. Chew, however, was not André's only flame in Philadelphia. He was received everywhere in the best circles of that exclusive old colonial world, and he was particularly intimate with the family of a Mr. Edward Shippen, whose favourite daughter married Benedict Arnold.

That the future Mrs. Arnold was charming all accounts of her agree; but the most curious testimony to the continuance of her fascination is the chance remark of Washington himself—made to Lafayette, strangely enough, that very morning on which Arnold's treachery was discovered. "Ah, Marquis, all you young men are in love with Mrs. Arnold. Ride on, if you like, and tell her not to wait breakfast for me."

For Mrs. Arnold that breakfast was memorable and terrible. In all innocence she had been the link between two men, an American and a Briton, whose downfall was at hand. These were her husband and Major André. Perhaps at some earlier day she brought them together—at any

RUSSIAN OFFICERS OF GENERAL BRUSILOFF'S ARMY VISITING THE SCENE OF SHARP FIGHTING AFTER A BATTLE: INSPECTING AN AUSTRIAN ENTRENCHED AND FORTIFIED DWELLING-HOUSE AT DUBNO.

Photograph by Illustrations Bureau.

rate, it was André's known friendship with Mrs. Arnold which led to his selection by Clinton to meet the traitor Arnold and negotiate with him for the betrayal of West Point to the British.

Arnold and André met by night in a thicket near Haverstraw, some thirty-five miles up the Hudson. There the traitor made over, for a consideration, the plans of West Point and the scheme for its betrayal. On the way back to New York André fell into the hands of the Americans. He had foolishly put off his uniform for a civilian disguise, he carried the proofs of his errand; there was no way out of it, he was a spy.

Suspicion did not immediately fasten upon Arnold, for the plans bore no identifying mark, and André's custodian wrote in all good faith to the traitor telling him of the spy's capture. It was that letter which upset Mrs. Arnold's breakfast-party and compelled her husband to flee in haste to a British ship. It is little wonder that she fainted when Arnold confessed to her what he had been about, how his plans had miscarried, and how his wife's friend of the gay Mischianza days was a prisoner with little hope of escaping a spy's fate.

Washington had a hard struggle with himself to send Major André to the gallows, but his sense of duty prevailed; nor would he yield even so little as to grant the condemned man's petition to be shot as a soldier.

RUSSIA'S HARD-FIGHTING WOMEN SOLDIERS: A GIRL HERO OF SIXTEEN, RECOMMENDED FOR THE ST. GEORGE'S CROSS.

Mlle. Tania, the centre figure here, is a Russian girl of sixteen who managed to get into the Army. She has been in action, and been recommended for the St. George's Cross, the Russian V.C. The soldier on the right is a boy volunteer of fifteen. The soldier on the left is the tallest man in the company to which Mlle. Tania belongs.

Photograph by C.N.

Immelmann's Conqueror in Hospital: Lieutenant "McC."

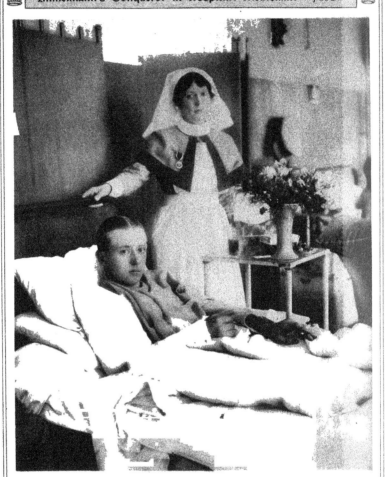

PILOT OF THE BATTLE-PLANE WHICH BROUGHT DOWN IMMELMANN : LIEUT. McCUBBIN IN HOSPITAL.

Second Lieut. McCubbin, the pilot of the British battle-plane whose observer shot down the famous German airman, Immelmann, had never been in an aeroplane before last February. He dived for 2500 feet from a height of about 8000 feet to attack the German, who had just brought down another British machine. Immelmann was shot at very close quarters. In the official reports the victorious pilot was called merely "Lieutenant McC.," but his name was mentioned in a question asked in Parliament. It was not in the fight with Immelmann that he was wounded, but in a later encounter. A bullet entered his shoulder and passed down into his forearm, but he heroically brought his machine and observer to earth, himself collapsing as they landed.—[Photo. by C.N.]

flying Corps Service with the Army in Egypt.

A DESERT DILEMMA AND A CONTRAST: DISABLED IN A SANDSTORM; ABOVE CHEOPS' PYRAMID.

A British observer and pilot belonging to the aviation corps of the Army in Egypt are seen in the upper illustration in difficulties with a disabled aeroplane in the desert east of the Suez Canal, during a sandstorm. Petrol shortage had compelled a descent when nine miles out, while reconnoitring towards the enemy. The airmen had to remain for upwards of nine hours, most of the time in a blinding sandstorm, on the watch through the fog-like gloom until evening. On the storm abating, a party of some two hundred Australians appeared, and hauled the aeroplane back to the nearest camp. In the second illustration is shown an almost unimaginable contrast: an aeroplane flying over the Sphinx and the Pyramid of Cheops.—[Sketches from Egypt.]

flying Corps Service with the Army in Egypt.

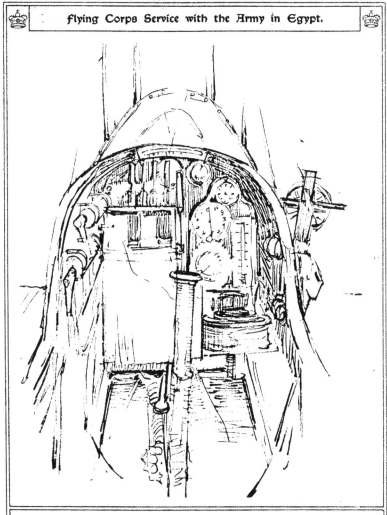

THE PILOT'S COCKPIT: THE "ENGINE ROOM" AND POWER CENTRE OF AN AEROPLANE.

The illustration shows what the sender of the sketch aptly terms the "Pilot's cockpit." It is the cavity in the body of an aeroplane where are placed the indicating instruments, levers, gauges, and machinery details among which the pilot sits, in touch with every appliance, and whence he controls every movement of the 'plane—speed, elevation changes, and so forth. The 'plane sketched was one of those that took part, on June 18, in the aerial attack by a squadron of the Royal Flying Corps on the enemy's advanced Air-base at El Arish, in the desert, a hundred miles east of the Suez Canal. In the brilliantly carried-out operation, the German hangars were all either wrecked inside, burned, or blown up, and eight German aeroplanes destroyed.—[Sketches from Egypt.]

20 — [Part 7 / New Series] — THE ILLUSTRATED

A Captured German Mine-Laying Submarine

1.—THE BRITISH NAVAL ENSIGN FLYING OV
2.—THE "U C 5" IN A BRITI

IT was announced in Parliament on the 20th that th
of the mine-laying type —"U C 5 "—up the Than
fortnight beginning on Wednesday, July 26, between
for admission to the pier. From our photographs
on the top of the submarine. We quote the following
" The German submarine mine-layer ' U C 5,' which
ment next week, was found in distress off the En
jumped into the sea and swam for dear life from th
of the vessel. The last of the explosions was the m
tower and went up forty feet into the air ; the fas
ship from destruction, for the force of the explosio
were blown in the bottom of the submarine, with
of the vessel was full of thick black gases, and m
there, but it was impossible to estimate the dama
German U-boat to the extraordinary fearlessness of
at the bottom of the ship, detached the detonators,
attempt to salve the captured vessel. This work a
brought into port. She lies now in an East Coast h
the German ensign. A coat of grey paint and ' U
at any rate, quite the ship she was before her adv
she received from the explosions. . . . ' U C 5 ' is
across Belgium and assembled at the coast, th

...ing Submarine for Exhibition in London: The "UC5."

HAULING UP THE GERMAN FLAG ON BOARD THE "UC5"; ... CONNING-TOWER; 3.—ONE OF HER MINES.

... the Admiralty proposed to bring a captured German submarine ... alongside Temple Pier on view to the public for a ... and 9 p.m. every day, a small charge being made ... noted that mines to be laid are fixed in position ... article on the subject in the "Pall Mall Gazette": ... view off the Temple Pier on the Thames Embank- ... last April. . . . . After the crew of the submarine ... there followed a series of explosions in the interior ... A lot of hammocks came flying out of the conning- ... conning-tower was left open undoubtedly saved the ... partially expended in the air. As it was, two holes ... that she made water pretty quickly. The interior ... could be seen. There was about two feet of water ... The public owes its opportunity to inspect a real ... who went down as a diver to inspect the mines ... dered them as safe as he could preparatory to the ... seventeen days; the U-boat was ultimately lifted and ... Union Jack flying proudly at her masthead above ... large white letters on her side make her, externally ... inside she still bears marks of the rough handling ... the U-boats which were conveyed in sections by land ... part of her four sections being now clearly visible."

"We Will Not Relax Our Efforts!"

LABOUR DELEGATES AND THE HOLIDAYS: THE CONFERENCE AT CAXTON HALL, JULY 18, 1916.

The Conference of representatives of the principal trades of the country, under the chairmanship of the Right Hon. Arthur Henderson, President of the Board of Education, to discuss the question of postponing the August holidays, was characterised by a fine spirit of patriotism, stimulated by a letter from Sir Douglas Haig, in which he said: "Let the whole British nation forego any idea of a general holiday until our goal is reached." Our photographs show: (1) The platform, with Mr. Henderson in the chair, supported by Mr. Montagu, Minister of Munitions, and Dr. Addison, Parliamentary Secretary to the Ministry of Munitions; (2) Some delegates, including Mr. Arthur Henderson and Mr. Ben Tillett.—[Photos. by L.N.A.]

South Africa's Share in the Great British Advance.

WOUNDED ON THE WESTERN FRONT: GALLANT SOUTH AFRICANS IN HOSPITAL IN ENGLAND.

South African troops now fighting on the Western Front have borne themselves splendidly in the great offensive. "In the heavy fighting of Saturday (the 15th)," said a Reuter message from the War-Correspondents' Headquarters, "the South African Infantry attacked with great gallantry, and went right through a certain wood. They displayed great resource and skill in overcoming the peculiar difficulties of this species of fighting, and have won unstinted praise for their services. South Africa may well be proud of the part her sons have borne in the tremendous struggle." An official despatch of the 15th said : "We have captured the whole of the Delville - Wood." Heavy fighting continued there, with fluctuating results.—[Photos. by Central Press.]

Fruits of Victory: Captured German Armament.

SOME OF THE 100 OR SO TAKEN BY THE BRITISH: GERMAN TRENCH-MORTARS AND A FIELD-GUN.

In the Anglo-French offensive the German losses in guns and lighter armament have been heavy. A Reuter message of the 17th from the British Headquarters said: "It is pretty certain that the enemy losses in guns run into three figures, not including machine-guns." An official despatch of that date gave the totals already collected as "five 8-inch howitzers, three 6-inch howitzers, four 6-inch guns, five other heavy guns, 37 field-guns, 30 trench-howitzers, and 66 machine-guns . . . exclusive of many guns not yet brought in and of the numbers destroyed by our artillery." The French had then taken 85 guns, 26 mine-throwers, and 89 machine-guns, and on the 20th they captured 3 more guns, and 30 machine-guns.—[Official Photographs issued by the Press Bureau.]

British Trophies from the Great Offensive.

CAPTURED "MINNIEWAFFERS": GERMAN WIRE-WOUND WOODEN MINENWERFER.

Captured German *Minenwerfer*, or trench-bomb mortars, taken by our men during the present fighting in Northern France, are shown above. They are made of wood strapped over with closely coiled wire and clamped round, at intervals, with metal bands. They are of big calibre, for large projectiles. Owing to the material used, such pieces cannot stand very many rounds, and have constantly to be replaced. As seen in the illustration, beside the mounted *Minenwerfer* is a relief weapon which was taken at the same time. Wood as a material for bomb-throwing guns was used in war in the East in former times, and every State War Museum in Germany has specimens of the leather cannon used by Gustavus Adolphus in the Thirty Years' War.—[*Photo. by Topical.*]

THINGS DONE : VII.—THE R.A.M.C.

ONE of the unfortunate delusions of the Army is the Royal Army Medical Corps. The form the delusion takes is this—that to some who wished to do their duty, but not to do it violently, the R.A.M.C. appeared to be a haven of rest. The men who thought that know better now. The R.A.M.C. is everything else.

The way wisdom came to these men was with a stretcher, carried at the double over very rough ground and under a most cynical sun. When the men arrived, after distressful periods of time, at the point where human nature demanded and expected to receive a little rest, rest was not. A large, unhelpful man lying inert, and, since this was only training, jeeringly cheerful in a trench where the architecture was all wrong for stretcher-bearers, had to be lifted on to the stretcher—not bumped in, as his uncanny cheeriness tempted one to bump him, but lifted in with a most appalling gentleness. Then that large man had to be carried off. He had to be carried along that idiot trench with finnicky care, by the rounded corners of traverses that permitted the stretcher to get by, and then, when the soul of the stretcher bearer said unto him, "Really, I can't stand this any longer," he had to be carried over the rough ground, through distressful periods of time, and under

THE BERLIN MUNICIPAL ORGANISATION FOR SUPPLYING CHEAP SOUP IN THE STREET: TRAVELLING KITCHENS AND STREET-DISTRIBUTING HAND-CARTS AT A DEPÔT.

For some considerable time past the Berlin City authorities have been sending out vehicles to sell soup and cooked food cheaply to the poorer classes. On one hand-cart seen above is the city heraldic badge — a crimson bear on a white shield.—[Photo. by S. and G.]

RUSSIAN STAFF OFFICERS VISITING THE ALLIES ON THE WESTERN FRONT: AN INSPECTION OF BELGIAN AIR-BOMBS.

The officers, reading from left to right, are: Capt. Prebjiano, Russian Attaché at Belgian Headquarters; Staff-Col. Koudatcheff; Gen. Romanovski; Major Van Crombrugghe, Head of the Belgian Flying Corps; Engr.-Col. Loganoff; Flight-Lieut. Coomans; Comndr. De Haen, of the Belgian Headquarters Staff.—[Photo. by Underwood and Underwood.]

the cynical sun, until the stretcher-bearers' hearts broke and the field dressing-station was reached. After that, and immediately, the bearers went back again over the rough ground and did it all over again with another cheerful fellow, who kept them warm with pointed comment all the return journey. And they went on doing this all day.

When the R.A.M.C. recruit could pause for a moment, and his aching body allowed him to think of something other than long cool drinks and well-applied liniment, his reflections were not as luxurious as he had anticipated. He reflected that this back-breaking, heart-cracking labour would presently be carried on under circumstances not even so pleasant. It would be carried on at a time when the bullets were whining round, and the shrapnel was reaching out for him with greedy fingers, and when "crumps" of all degrees would be after him with a hearty unanimity. And there would be no cover. He would be doing his job at a time when his knees were weak and his back was water, and the dry and coppery taste that filled his mouth and throat and got into his lungs made him feel inclined to swoon. As he thought of those things, the R.A.M.C. man wondered what form of congenital lunacy had enabled him to

[Continued overleaf.

"No Admittance Except on Business!"

AT THE FRENCH FRONT—A BOYAU WIRE-NETTING BARRIER; TO STOP TRESPASSERS AND GERMANS.

A wire-netting *grille*, forming a gateway in one section of a *boyau*, or communication-trench, in the French lines at the front, between the support-trenches and the advanced fire-trenches, is seen in the above photograph with a sentry on duty there interrogating a comrade on the other side of the barrier. To prevent its being climbed over, strands of barbed wire have been attached to the transverse pole, as can be seen. Ordinarily, the gateway is intended to prevent unauthorised persons passing, to stop soldiers and others from trespassing beyond their sections. In case of the enemy getting into the *boyau*, the barrier would be an obstacle to hold up a party while the defenders fired on them through the netting.—[*Photo. by Photopress.*]

conclude that the job of the R.A.M.C. was a "soft" one.

And, when he had thought his thoughts in full, he took up his stretcher and did some more, not with a cloying sweetness, but with a stout heart. He had tackled the task, he was going through with it in spite of sweat and "crumps." And he is going through with it now, with his lip stiff and his chin out. That is the way of the R.A.M.C. For hard work and sheer grit the corps stands second to none. Just tot up the casualty lists, every man in them having been brought out of the line and brought home and looked after by the R.A.M.C.; and just tot up the list of R.A.M.C. "V.C.'s"—no other corps in the Army can equal them there.

Hiking a wounded man out of the firing-line, giving him first aid, carrying him through the shell *barrage* to the field dressing-station, and then taking him by motor, train, and ship from general hospital to clearing hospital, from clearing hospital to base hospital, and then on to the nursing homes and hospitals of England, is only part of the R.A.M.C. job. Their job is concerned with disease as well as casualties, with prevention as well as cure. They start before war, labouring with an immense scientific energy to make war as innocuous as possible. They are out in a general offensive against the conditions that beget disease; they tackle the water supply that may bring enteric, but must not; they see to sanitation that may lead to fevers and infection if not well organised; they are the apostles of cleanliness, which is the foe of all ungodly illness, including the hated gangrene and other unspeakable things. By inoculation, by splendid laboratory work, by the application of scientific systems of filtration, by their rigid attention to and inspection of camps, billets, and barracks, and the men in camps,

IN MESOPOTAMIA—ASSAILANTS THAT TROUBLE BOTH MAN AND BEAST: THE FLY PLAGUE—DONKEYS STANDING IN SMOKE TO AVOID THE FLIES.

Photograph by C.N.

billets, and barracks, they have brought down the waste of war to a minimum, and have made, on the whole, the soldier's life a not unreasonable one.

And the things they cannot check or prevent—and the bullet of Brother Boche is one of the things they cannot check or prevent—they fight with an equally scientific manner in the arts of healing and building up. The wounded soldier is handled in a manner at times little short of miraculous as he travels back from the point of wounds through the various hospitals to that home of convalescence where his full recovery is assured. The brilliant flexibility of the R.A.M.C. in grappling with modern hurts in the most modern fashion is astounding. Nothing baffles. Brain shock and shattered nerves are cured just as capably as broken limbs and shattered bodies. Faces that in the old days of war were left in the almost unspeakable deformity of wounds are now made whole. In the same way science is applied to the old terror of septic poisoning. A new method of wound-irrigation—the discovery of an Englishman—has supplanted old forms of dressing for certain cases, and recovery has usurped the place held so grimly in past days by gangrene. Science with its miracles works through the R.A.M.C., and the R.A.M.C. works with all the ardours of science.—W. DOUGLAS NEWTON.

WITH THE TROOPS IN MESOPOTAMIA — THE FLY PLAGUE; SOLDIERS ON A TIGRIS TRANSPORT-STEAMER ASLEEP UNDER THE GAUZE NETTING SUPPLIED FOR NIGHT USE AGAINST MOSQUITOES.

Photograph by C.N.

Annamites in France: Troops from Indo-China.

MEN OF THE FRENCH COLONIAL ARMY SERVING IN FRANCE: ANNAMITE TROOPS AT ST. RAPHAEL.

The upper photograph, taken at the Gallieni Camp at St. Raphael, where the Annamite troops from French Indo-China are quartered, shows some of them at work there, attending, apparently, to one of their field-kitchens. From the lower photograph it may be seen that they are provided with modern and scientific transport equipment, in the form of motor-lorries, from which boxes of supplies or munitions are being unloaded. Annam became a French protectorate in 1884, and French troops occupy part of the citadel at Hué, the capital. The internal affairs of the country are administered by native officials under the control of the French Government. France maintains a European force in Indo-China and also native troops under French officers.—[Photo. by Rol.]

With the Annamites in France: Camp Cookery.

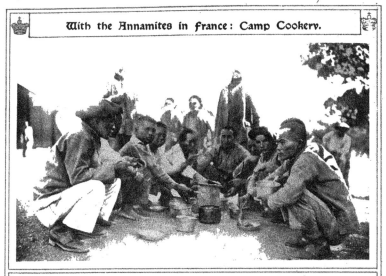

AFTER THE "LAMP-SHADE" HAT, THE CHASSEUR *BÉRET*: ANNAMITE SOLDIERS IN FRANCE.

As mentioned on the previous page, the French colonial troops from Annam, in Indo-China, after their arrival in France, discarded their native head-gear, consisting of a conical hat like a "lamp-shade," and received new caps of a kind of Tam-o'-Shanter shape such as are worn by the French Chasseurs Alpins. Some of the Annamites are seen wearing these caps in the above photographs, which are interesting as showing the physical type of the men, and their camp arrangements in the matter of cookery and meals. They are using, it may be noted, the ordinary European spoon and fork. Their faces give an impression of cheerfulness and docility. As in the case of the two previous pages, the photographs were taken at the Galliéni Camp, St. Raphael.—[*Photos. Rol.*]

Men from the Far East Come to Fight for France.

IN THEIR CONICAL "LAMP-SHADE" HATS : TROOPS FROM ANNAM MARCHING TO CAMP IN FRANCE.

In their native country, the Annamite troops wear conical hats, made of straw or bamboo fibre covered with grey cloth, and in shape resembling an ordinary electric-light lamp-shade. They also use fans in the hot weather, as shown in a photograph given in our issue of July 5. They were wearing these conical hats when they arrived in France, and when they marched to camp at St. Raphael, as seen in the above illustration. Later, however, they were provided with caps, or bérets, of a pattern similar to those worn by the French Chasseurs Alpins. Their fans have been entirely discarded since they reached Europe. A contingent of Annamites, it may be recalled, took part in the great march-past of Allied troops in Paris on July 14.—[Photo. by Rol.]

The Great Anglo-French Offensive: The Battle Area.

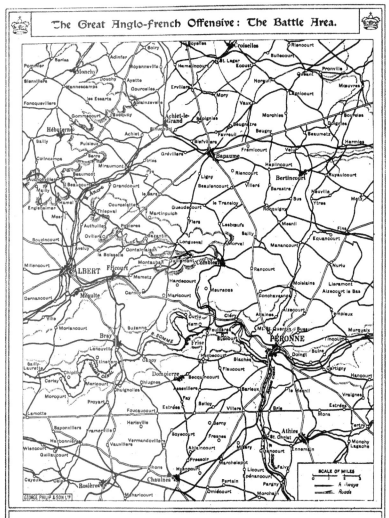

THE BATTLE OF THE SOMME : WHERE BRITISH AND FRENCH TROOPS HAVE ADVANCED.

The battle that is still raging north and south of the River Somme began, it will be remembered, on July 1 with a general advance of the British troops between Gommecourt and Montauban, and of the French troops on their right flank, further south, between Hardecourt and Fay. In the first two days our troops captured the strongly fortified villages of Montauban, Mametz, and Fricourt, and afterwards La Boiselle and Contalmaison. The French took Frise, Dompierre, Bussu, Becquincourt, Fay Herbécourt, Feuillères, Belloy, Estrées, and Biaches. On the 20th they captured the whole German 1st line from Barleux to Soyécourt. In the attack on the German second line, begun on July 14, the British captured Longueval, Bazentin, and Ovillers, and later advanced north of Longueval.

British Honours for a Great Malay Ruler.

HONOURING A MUNIFICENT ALLY: THE INVESTITURE OF THE SULTAN OF JOHORE WITH THE G.C.M.G.

The upper photograph shows a close view of the Investiture of the Sultan of Johore with the G.C.M.G. (Grand Commander of the Order of St. Michael and St. George). The ceremony was performed by the Governor of the Straits Settlements, Sir Arthur Young, G.C.M.G., at Johore, on May 11. At the outbreak of the war, the Sultan placed the Johore forces at the disposal of the Straits Government, and he has lately given the munificent sum of £28,000 to purchase aircraft for the British Army. The Sultan Ibrahim was born in 1873 and succeeded his father in 1895. As Crown Prince he visited Europe in 1890 and as Sultan in 1904-5. He is a keen sportsman and motorist, and is a member of the R.A.C. Johore is an independent State, under British protection.

WOMEN AND THE WAR.

SINCE women have taken a prominent part in all sorts of public services, life all round has become much more pleasant. The magistrate who made such complimentary remarks about the "conductorette" the other day was really expressing the general opinion about the "footwoman" and the van-woman, the lift-woman and the page-girl, the commissionairess in her smart braided uniform, and all those other "war workers" in unaccustomed professions who have now become an accepted fact of life.

Women seem to bring an interest and enthusiasm to bear on their duties which suggest the idea that work to them has the zest of play. The attitude of the average man, on the other hand, however polite he may be, is invariably one of boredom towards his work. Probably it is a pose rather than an actual fact, but as people— and at any rate women —have an objection to being made to feel that they are regarded as nuisances, the new woman worker, with her ingratiating smile and polite manners, has firmly established herself in the public affections.

Some people have already begun to ask what is going to happen when the war is over. Shall we go back to the lift-man who whirls you up to the top landing and then suggests by his manner, if not by his words, that it is your fault and not his; or the conductor who seems to take fiendish delight in stamping on your feet and spoiling the blocking of your best shoes?

ENGLISH LADIES DOING RED CROSS WORK IN FRANCE: MISS CHISHOLM AND THE BARONESS DE SERCLAES.
The Red Cross ambulance - wagons in the background tell their own tale of the useful work being done by the ladies in our picture, both of whom are English, the Baroness de Serclaes being an English lady by birth.—[Photo. by Sport and General.]

Is the impish page likely to supplant his pleasant little successor; and will the managers of large establishments revert to the stolid commissionaire to the exclusion of that worthy's distinctly picturesque war-time substitute? Above all, what will women themselves have to say on the subject? These and many other knotty problems are amongst the things that will have to be dealt with after the war, when the general "straightening out" process is likely to be a very complicated affair. Experienced people, however, seem inclined to the view that now that women have had a chance of proving their industrial value things will never go back to their pre-war status. Meantime, the new woman worker enjoys her duties as much as the public appreciates her presence.

The war, which has brought about a wider and a more general appreciation of women's capabilities, has incidentally led to quite a number of interesting "discoveries"—or what some term discoveries—concerning women themselves. For instance, women have proved, to the astonishment of not a few men, that they are quite good engineers, and the result is that a brand-new profession is to be thrown open to them. The announcement is more important than on the face of it it appears, for in this case opportunities for practising it will continue after peace has been restored.

AT WORK FOR THE ARMY AND NAVY: MEMBERS OF THE WOMEN'S VOLUNTEER RESERVE CULTIVATING WASTE LAND.
These ladies are busily employed on waste land at Finchley, to be used, when fit, for growing vegetables for our soldiers and sailors.—[Photo. by Central Press.]

Impressed by women's engineering efforts in war-time factories, a certain number of men have

[Continued overleaf.

"Pigs in Clover": A Scene in Sussex.

A JUDGE'S DAUGHTER WHO WORKS LOYALLY ON A SUSSEX FARM: MISS TRAYNER FEEDING PIGS.

To the woman of to-day, so admirably eager to "do her bit" in the labour crisis brought about by the war, no work comes amiss, and nothing, to her, is "common or unclean," as our very unconventional picture shows. Miss Trayner is a daughter of Lord Trayner, LL.D., Judge of Court of Session, Scotland, and is here seen feeding pigs on The Women's Co-operative Farm at Heathfield, Sussex. Very contented seem the porcine protégés of their new keeper, and they are probably preferable in some ways to the human bipeds exhibited to a wondering world as "Pigs in Clover" in one of the late "Frank Danby's" clever novels. Miss Trayner is very thorough in her new work.—[Photo. by F. R. James.]

determined to start works for the construction of aeroplane-engine parts, and the works are to be staffed by women. Whether the scope of the work is extended after the war, is in the hands of

MARY, DUCHESS OF HAMILTON, AS FARMER: HER GRACE FEEDS THE CHICKENS.
Mary, Duchess of Hamilton, widow of the twelfth Duke, has a model poultry farm at Easton Park, Wickham Market, Suffolk, where every detail is carried on upon the most up-to-date principles. Our picture shows her Grace feeding the chickens at Easton.
Photograph by Photopress.

the workers themselves, upon whom, in the last resort, the success or failure of the enterprise must necessarily depend. An interesting point about the scheme is that it is intended for educated women, preferably the widows and daughters of military and naval officers.

Amongst the various duties now undertaken by women, not the least interesting are those connected with work in the postal censor's department. This particular form of work, by the way, has revealed the fact that the numbers of women in this country who possess a useful knowledge of German is much greater than the number of men similarly accomplished, and the department in question is full of women to whom the war has given an opportunity for serving their country in an exceedingly useful and necessary way. For some reason or another, women in the past seem to have taken a fancy to the tongue-tormenting language of the Hun, with its multisyllabic words and arbitrary rules on gender. Perhaps one reason may be that few women learn Latin, and the Southern European languages, therefore, come to them as strangers, whereas there is a strong similarity between

common words in German and common words in English. Women, too, have shown themselves to be remarkably quick at picking up a working knowledge of Dutch, Flemish, and Swedish. It is no uncommon thing to find fair students immersed in foreign grammars on the top of motor-buses. For the time being, at any rate, it is even more interesting to learn a new tongue than to read all about the doings of impossibly vicious Dukes and blameless damsels.

Censor-girls with a gift for writing could produce marvellously interesting books concerning the follies, frailties, and virtues of mankind—and womenkind to boot—were it not for the strict secrecy that officialdom imposes upon them. They know all about the war weariness of Fritz, longing only for the peace that will enable him to return to his Gretchen, interned in comfort, well fed, while he bears the brunt of battle. The duplicity of Heinrich, from whom three plump Fräuleins receive letters of love in rotation does not escape their all-seeing eyes. In addition, they are up to all the dodges for conveying interesting information through texts, and dinner menus, and other seemingly harmless things.

An enormous increase of work is one of the results of the war as it affects the telegraph department of the Post Office. Here, too, women are largely employed. In fact, for all the lighter parts of telegraphy women are often better than men; and while they are scarcely up to the punching necessary with the Wheatstone transmitter, at ordinary machines their

A DUCHESS AS FARMER: MARY, DUCHESS OF HAMILTON, WITH HER DAUGHTER AND GRAND-CHILDREN.
Our photograph shows Mary, Duchess of Hamilton, with her daughter, the Marchioness of Graham, who was married to the heir of the Duke of Montrose in 1906, with two of the children of the Marchioness, Lord Ronald and Lady Mary Graham. The Marchioness of Graham takes a very practical interest in gardening.—[Photo. by Photopress.]

natural lightness of touch and quickness of hand secure for them an undoubted advantage over the mere male.   CLAUDINE CLEVE

War-Workers in the Women's Procession in London.

CHEERED BY THE WAR SECRETARY; MUNITIONERS IN THE PROCESSION; AND MR. LL. GEORGE.

The first photograph shows a party of munition-workers wearing mouth-coverings in the Women's War Procession held in London, on July 22, by the Women's Social and Political Union. In the second photograph is seen Mr. Lloyd George, the new Secretary of State for War, with Mr. Herbert Samuel, on a balcony of the War Office. They cheered the women munition-makers and some with shell-cases raised them aloft in acknowledgment. The third photograph shows a car containing tableaux of war-work. On it were women shell-makers demonstrating how part of their task is done. The section representing the work of women in munition-making received the heartiest welcome from the crowd.—[Photos. by Topical, C.N., and Central Press.]

Thirty feet Underground, and fortified with Concrete.

SAFE FROM SHELLS, BUT NOT FROM RUSSIAN VALOUR: AN AUSTRIAN OFFICERS' DUG-OUT.

This illustration offers striking testimony to the heroic intrepidity and impetuous dash of the Russian onset during General Brusiloff's sweeping advance across the Austrian trench-lines in the Great Offensive, so brilliantly carried through by our Ally on the Eastern Front. The Austrian dug-out, the entrance to which is seen here, was in the lines stormed by the Russians without giving the enemy opportunity to rally. It was thirty feet below ground and was used as living quarters for Austrian officers, at a depth where they could count on being secure against the heaviest high-explosive shells. It was specially strengthened with a concrete roof and walls. One of the Russian captors is seen in the' photograph emerging from its recesses.—[Photo. by Illustrations Bureau.]

Wanton Vandalism with a Cunning Purpose.

UTILISING THE RUSSIAN RESPECT FOR CHURCHES: AN AUSTRIAN DUG-OUT UNDER AN ALTAR!

There is little to choose as to wanton vandalism between Germans and Austrians in regard to their methods of dealing with sacred buildings—churches and cathedrals. The illustration affords an Austrian instance of a church on the Galician front being made a screen for a trench dug-out, excavated in the foundations immediately under the high altar. One idea in the minds of the enemy in choosing the church is obvious. From the very opening of the war and consistently since, even during the great retreat of last summer, the Russians have carefully refrained from firing on churches. Again, here, from the intact state of the church, shown after the Russian capture of the place, the Russians turned their guns aside and spared the building.—[Photo. by Illustrations Bureau.]

A Football that Headed a Charge.

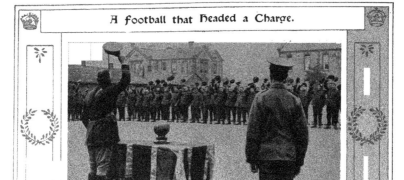

THE EAST SURREYS' FIGHT WITH THE PRUSSIAN GUARD : A KICK-OFF FOOTBALL HONOURED.

In the upper illustration the East Surreys at Kingston Barracks, and wounded from the military hospital, are seen cheering, led by Colonel H. S. Treehy, D.S.O., their "chief," at the presentation of the historic football which Captain Nevill, of the regiment, kicked off in action with the Prussian Guard during the Great Offensive. The football is on the flag-draped table before the Colonel.

Below, Colonel Treehy is shown holding up the football as he addressed the men : "The gallant officer who kicked it off," he said, "fell in front of the German trenches . . . It will be a fitting memorial of the devotion and sacrifice of the battalion who played the game so well and served so heroically our God, our King, and out Country."—[Photos. by L.N.A.]

LONDON: Published Weekly at the Office, 172, Strand, in the Parish of St. Clement Danes, in the County of London, by THE ILLUSTRATED LONDON NEWS AND SKETCH, LTD., 172, Strand, aforesaid; and Printed by THE ILLUSTRATED LONDON NEWS AND SKETCH, LTD., Milford Lane, W.C.—WEDNESDAY, JULY 26, 1916.

The Illustrated War News, Aug. 2, 1916.—Part 8, New Series.

The Illustrated War News

THE FUNERAL OF THE NAVAL BOY HERO, JACK CORNWELL: LEAVING EAST HAM TOWN HALL.

Photograph by C.N.

THE GREAT WAR.

By W. DOUGLAS NEWTON.

THERE are two things obvious in the fighting, not merely of the West, but of the whole circle of war—and these things are such as to engender a distinctly happy feeling. The first of these is that the enemy has already had time to gauge the scope of the Allied offensives, and has stiffened his fronts to the best of his ability to check them. The second is that he has failed to check them. Exactly a month has passed since the opening of the Western offensive; close on two months since the opening of the Eastern offensive—time enough to reorganise and re-strengthen the fronts. All the same, the Western Allies press inward and the Eastern Allies press inward. At no time have the Central Powers been able to call a halt.

The fronts are moving forward with a sense of inevitability, and this sense of inevitability is founded on the strongest practical basis — the practical basis of an overwhelming artillery strength overwhelmingly supplied with shells. With these means to hand, the reduction of the enemy is automatic. It is perhaps slow, because it means that each line of works must be reduced, the defenders forced to fight on the same plane and terms as the attackers — or on slightly worse terms — with the regularised victory of the attackers and the taking over of the shell-prepared ground following. The method is, after all, an apt adaptation of the German plan of attack on Verdun; and as the Germans were able to force advances in spite of the most heroic resistance of the French, so the British, the French, and the Russians are able, and will continue able, to force advances in spite of the Germans. There are differences, however, between the present aggres-

SHOT BY THE GERMANS IN BELGIUM : CAPTAIN CHARLES FRYATT, OF THE CAPTURED G.E.R. LINER "BRUSSELS."

The shooting of Captain Fryatt, after a court-martial for an alleged attempt to ram a German submarine, has aroused intense indignation. Captain Fryatt commanded the Great Eastern Railway's steamer "Brussels," captured by German war-ships on June 23. In correspondence regarding his trial with the United States Ambassador, Sir Edward Grey said : " His Majesty's Government are of opinion that his action was perfectly legitimate. His Majesty's Government consider that the act of a merchant-ship in steering for an enemy submarine and forcing her to dive is essentially defensive, and precisely on the same footing as the use by a defensively armed vessel of her defensive armament in order to resist capture, which both the United States Government and His Majesty's Government hold to be the exercise of an undoubted right."—[Photo. by Illus. Bureau.]

sion and the German attempt on Verdun. These differences are in favour of the Allies. The Allies are attacking not only on fronts wider and less cramped geographically, but they are attacking from points as widely apart as the Somme and the Lipa—that is, the Allies are not attacking an enemy able to resist without distraction, as the French could resist at Verdun, but are attacking an enemy who has to pay particular attention to Poland and Galicia as well as the Somme, and who must keep a general, uneasy eye on other points of concentration also ; I mean, he must watch events at Trent, in the Balkans, and in Turkey. The fruit of this distraction of power is already apparent. It is the reason why the Anglo-French advance has been able to do so much more than the German advance has been able to do at Verdun, though our advance has covered only a month to Verdun's six months of fighting. It explains why German resistance has been ineffectual before the determination of our troops, who have so far been able to attain their objectives in spite of the most anxious efforts of Germany ; whereas the Germans before Verdun were not always able to attain their objectives, though they put as much power, and perhaps more, into their efforts. Germany is unable to hold the Allies because she cannot meet them on the equal and practical basis of war—that is, the basis of gun-power and man-power. The only way to stop us—each of the Allies—is to face our concentrations with equal concentrations. This Germany is obviously unable to do. She has frittered away her strength in her successes ; she has extended her line until that line has drained her ; she has won a burden of territorial booty that weighs too heavily on her present strength. She is, in fact, now reaping the harvest of her victories.

She is not, of course, beaten yet—nor, perhaps, nearly beaten—for, if her fighting has been ineffectual in the past few months, it has been at least fiercely brave. In the West we have had a week's experience of the bitterest fighting, though from Germany's point of view it has been unavailing. These encounters have fallen mainly to the share of the British, and the battle has been waged about that point of strategic worth known as the village of Pozières. The enemy clung to this spot with the utmost tenacity. They had reason. It was the last bar of considerable fortification between our advancing troops and the crests of the high ground. If the British won Pozières, they would have a more open *terrain* between them and Hill 160—a short space along the Bapaume road—and, Hill 160 taken, our men would then have control of the summits that dominate the stretch of country between here and Bapaume. Pozières was defended furiously. But it was taken. After three days of the most ferocious battling, our Territorials and units of the Anzacs came beneath the crest of the hill. At the same time, our front was extended along the plateau beyond Pozières cemetery towards Thiepval, and so a threat is held out that may send the whole German line back beyond the latter village. During the week, too, and in the closest hand-to-hand fighting, our troops have worked forward at Longueval, in

THE NEW SERBIAN MINISTER IN LONDON : M. YOVAN M. YOVANOVITCH.

M. Yovanovitch has been appointed to represent Serbia at the Court of St. James's in place of the former Minister, M. Boschkovitch.—[*Photo. by Vandyk.*]

the Wood of Delville, and in the Guillemont area. The fighting has been that of consolidation rather than that of deliberate attack, and it has had to encounter heavy German resistance, yet it has been pressed so successfully that the whole of Delville Wood has been wrenched from the Brandenburgers who were called upon, as a last resort, to hold it ; and the last houses of Longueval have been won back by us. These gains, with continued gains beyond Pozières, mark the paramountcy of our will in the fighting. The new joint advance of French and British on a front extending from Delville Wood to the Somme, and to a depth reaching to the outskirts of Maurepas, is but an entr'acte of events.

The French have been quieter on their Somme front—indeed, ominously quiet. They have resisted in excellent fashion some enemy thrusts, and have proved that their front can stand any strain applied to it. Their own movements during the week gave them a group of heavily fortified houses south of Estrées and certain trenches north of Vermand - Ovillers, together with a number of guns, machine-guns, and prisoners. On the rest of the French line there has been a certain amount of activity, and among such minor incidents a successful trench raid by the Russians against the Germans in the Champagne country is worth noting. At Verdun the balance of events favours the French. The few German attacks have been easily broken, while our Ally continues to creep forward in the Fleury area.

The Russians have had

THE BRITISH SPORTSMEN'S GIFT OF A HUNDRED AMBULANCES TO THE ALLIED ARMIES : "ANZAC" WOMEN CHAUFFEURS.

Thirty-five of the hundred motor-ambulances which the British Sportsmen's Ambulance Fund is providing for service on various fronts have been recently handed over by Lord Lonsdale, President of the Fund, at Carlton House Terrace. "Anzac" Women chauffeurs in uniform are shown above.—[*Photo. Sport and General.*]

a notable week, and have included 'in it the serious discomfort of the three main enemy Powers. They have struck two very shrewd blows, one in Europe and one in Asia, and each of these blows has won them towns of singular importance in the scale of war. The European victory is the fruit of General Sak-

THE PUBLIC FUNERAL OF THE BOY HERO OF JUTLAND BATTLE : JOHN CORNWELL'S COFFIN-PLATE.

Owing to his mother's lack of means, the body of John Travers Cornwell was first laid to rest in a common grave in Ilford Cemetery. It was removed and, by Government order, laid in a specially presented grave with a State funeral ceremony. The coffin nameplate, with the motto, "Faithful unto Death," is shown here.—[Photo. by S. and G.]

haroff's offensive on the Lutsk salient. Engaging in his third great battle in the region of the Boldurka, Slonuvka, and Styr, he has won his third victory in magnificent fashion, has pressed forward over these three rivers, and has taken Brody in his stride. Brody in itself, though on the direct railway to Lemberg, is not of violent importance, but the advance here is overhanging the Austro-German defence on the Strypa, and threatening it in a way it has not been threatened before. Pressing forward some twenty-five miles along this line, the Russians will be cutting one of the feeder railways serving, from Lemberg, von Bothmer's front. And Lemberg itself lies in peril from the menace of the swift advance. The victory, too, may give General Sakharoff an occasion to swing his right flank against the line defending the marches to Kovel. The position of the enemy in the face of this threat is not pleasant, and it is made less comfortable by the fact that the line of battle has spread northward until, on a front of eighty miles—that is, as far as the railway running from Kovel to Rovno—the Russians are breaking into the Austro-German line, are forcing their way across such important streams as the Stokhod, and are netting men and guns in lavish fashion. The whole of the enemy line is endangered in Poland and Galicia, and any moment may see a drastic and fateful retirement. The threat to the Galician front, that has held out staunchly up to this, is increased by the reassumption of movement from the Russian wing acting on the Dniester. Here the floods have held our Ally for some time, but at last General Lechitsky has gone forward again, has flung his forces towards Stanislaus, and has carried ground in brilliant fashion. At

the same time, the Russians are not idle in other sectors of their front. They are keeping von Hindenburg busy enough, and are holding their lines from Riga to Baranovitchi ; while on the Carpathians they already fight their way to the summits of the passes.

The Russian Asiatic campaign shows equal merit. After the Grand Duke's patient wait in Armenia, he has struck again. From Trebizond and Erzerum the attack passed onward, until, in an amazingly short space, all resistance was cleared away, and Erzingan fell in a manner almost nerveless. The brilliance of the victory must not be lost in the rapidity and smoothness of the movement : it was Staff work of the first order that gave such effectual and uncheckable results. The fall of the main Turkish depot town gives the Russians the entire command of Armenia, and it does more than this—it gives them the gates of all the roads that lead to the heart of Turkey. The advance is already moving towards Sivas, and Sivas is a pivotal point of all the Ottoman East from the Black Sea to the Persian border, and from that to Mesopotamia. It seems probable that we are at the dawn of a new phase in the East, and the action of the reorganised Serbian Army, which has attacked and driven its Bulgarian enemy from strong hill positions on the Greek border, may be the first hint of that new phase. The Balkans have been quiet, but that is not a proof they will be quiet for ever.   LONDON : JULY 31, 1916.

THE PUBLIC FUNERAL OF THE BOY HERO OF JUTLAND BATTLE : HIS SHIPMATES' TRIBUTE.

On July 29 the Admiralty accorded a public funeral with naval honours to the remains of Boy John Travers Cornwell, whose superb heroism was specially mentioned in Sir John Jellicoe's despatch. His boy shipmates sent the wreath seen above.—[Photo. by S. and G.]

To Clear the Way for our Invincible Infantry.

"SUPER-DREADNOUGHT" PROJECTILES FOR THE GREAT BRITISH OFFENSIVE : A 15-INCH SHELL.

The enormous size and bulk of one of the big shells with which, day after day, our gunners in the Great Offensive, are bombarding the enemy's fortified positions and clearing the way for our heroic infantry to attack, can be well realised by comparing the shell in the above illustration with the figure of the man close to it. One can understand the blank amazement and sheer terror with which such projectiles fill the enemy during our bombardments when these shells plough up their trench - lines, as recorded in the numerous letters and diaries found on dead Germans, or taken from prisoners, and published in the papers. The Empire may well be grateful to the munition - workers who work day and night to make such projectiles.—[Official Photograph.]

The French Victories on the Somme: Captured Guns.

SPOILS OF THE ALLIED OFFENSIVE: SOME OF THE NUMEROUS GERMAN GUNS TAKEN BY THE FRENCH.

These guns represent only a fraction of the large number taken by our gallant French allies. Summing up the results of the first phase of the battle on the French side, up to July 10, Mr. H. Warner Allen wrote recently, quoting a semi-official account: "In less than a fortnight the French troops, on a front 16 miles long, with a maximum depth of 6½ miles, have carried 50 square miles of fortifications. The booty amounts to: 85 guns (several of large calibre), 100 machine-guns, 26 *Minenwerfer*, 256 officers, and 12,000 men, besides large quantities of material." The French have since made further captures. On the 20th, for instance, they took 5 guns, 30 machine-guns, and 2900 prisoners. —[*Photo. by Rol.*]

The Chief Post of Danger in Artillery Work.

AN ARTILLERY OBSERVER'S "CROW'S-NEST"; AN OBSERVATION-POST IN A TREE—THE FIRST PLATFORM.

A tall tree, especially in summer time, when the foliage conceals anyone within it, forms an excellent observation-post, though it is, of course, like any other such post, liable to destruction by the enemy's shell-fire. The duty of a "spotter" is always perilous. A British artillery officer, describing his work in a letter home, writes: "At length the position is ready and the guns can be brought up and coaxed into the pits made for them. . . . Forward of such a gun-position would be an observing-station. About observing-stations it would not be wise to say much lest this letter should fall into alien hands. Observing-stations are the chief posts of danger in modern artillery work, and the most careful guard is kept on their secrets."—[Photo. by Boudoin.]

The Kind of Men Fighting for Us.

FOUR HEROES: TWO MILITARY CROSSES; A D.S.O.; AND ONE WHO SACRIFICED HIMSELF.

Lieut. Archibald S. C. Maclaren, R.F.C. (first portrait), has won the Military Cross for descending to within 100 feet and destroying a German aeroplane just starting, and a Fokker in its hangar. Capt. W. A. Grattan-Bellew, R.F.C. (second portrait), won the M.C. for attacking, on three occasions, first eight enemy 'planes, then four, then three more, destroying several and returning safely. Capt. Stuart Grant-Dalton, R.F.C. (third portrait), has the D.S.O. Seeing a British 'plane down in enemy territory, he descended and rescued the pilot. Corpl. H. Cowlin, London Rifle Brigade, was wounded and dropped his bomb, fuse alight. To save his comrades, he flung himself on the bomb, which burst and killed him.— [Photos. by Central Press and Photopress.]

The Annamites in France Receiving Steel Helmets.

PARADED FOR INSPECTION: ANNAMITE INFANTRY WEARING THE NEW "SHRAPNEL-PROOF" HELMETS.

The French Oversea possessions are all furnishing contingents for service in Europe. Annamites from the Far East, battalions of whom serve in Tonkin and Annam, are seen in these illustrations. In the upper, infantry are being inspected after having the native conical bamboo hats replaced by steel helmets. In the lower, a lieutenant is examining the fit of the helmets. Algerian Turcos, Moroccans, and Soudanese (as we have previously illustrated) are in the French battle-line. The suggestion that we should freely utilise the fighting races in British African colonies, notably Zulus and Basutos, has been recently made in Parliament by Commander Wedgwood, M.P., just back from seeing how our "black" troops are fighting in East Africa.—[French War Office Photograph.]

THE BEGINNINGS OF WAR - MACHINES : WAR-SHIPS.

AMONGST the earliest fighting vessels of which we have any record are the Egyptian galleys of Rameses III., 1200 B.C., though his predecessor, Rameses II., is known to have carried on several naval campaigns. These vessels were propelled by oars operated by rowers, with sails as an auxiliary power, and steered by means of oars or paddles situated aft on either counter. In some of the earliest Egyptian illustrations of these boats a man is shown posted in a " crow's-nest," or look-out station at the top of the mast.

In later years, galleys having two or more rows or banks of oars were used, the rowers pulling the higher rows being seated higher and further inboard than those operating the oars projecting from the vessel's side lower down. A galley having two banks of oars was called a " bireme," and one having three banks a " trireme." The fighting men were stationed on a platform above the heads of the rowers, a forecastle being erected at the bows and a poop at the stern, above the level of this platform, to accommodate the catapults and other " ordnance." The archers were also stationed on these, whilst the slingers occupied the top.

Fig. 1 shows a galley such as the Romans used in their invasion of Britain, and Fig. 2 an Attic trireme of the middle of the fourth century B.C. The length of this vessel was about 125 feet, to which must be added about 10 feet of " beak," or ram— a strong, pointed projection at the vessel's stem designed to rip open the side of a vessel attacked. Sails were used when the wind was favourable, but only oars when the vessel was in action, as rapid manœuvring was impossible with the primitive form of sail-rigging then in use.

The Romans had very powerfully propelled vessels of this class even at a very early date, a quinquereme (a vessel having five banks of oars or else five men to each oar) being used by them in the first Carthaginian War, in 256 B.C. This craft carried 300 rowers and 120 fighting men. A similar vessel of about A.D. 50 employed 400 rowers.

A MEDITERRANEAN WAR-GALLEY : THE BEAK AND FORWARD FIGHTING "CASTLE."

IN THE GALLEY-SLAVE PERIOD : A MALTESE GALLEY OF THE EARLY EIGHTEENTH CENTURY.
The Mediterranean galleys continued in use till the middle of the eighteenth century. C C are " castles " for fighting men, fore and aft.

The Roman galleys carried a " corvus," or crow—an ingenious " boarding " device in the shape of a long gangway hinged to the bottom of the mast, and lashed to it in a vertical position until the enemy vessel was reached, when the end of the gangway was allowed to fall on the enemy's deck to provide a passage for the attacking force, whilst the spike or beak projecting from the under-side of the board at its outer end embedded itself in the enemy's deck.

The first British attempt to provide a Navy was that made by Alfred the Great towards the end of the ninth century, when the incursions of the Danes became so troublesome that merchant - vessels were organised as a defence force. A Danish vessel of this period is shown in Fig. 3, and a Norman vessel such as carried William the Conqueror to England in 1066 is shown in Fig. 4.

In the reign of King John a considerable naval force was accumulated, and this force destroyed the French fleet at the battle of Damme in 1213. Four years later, a large English fleet under Hubert de Burgh again defeated a French squadron, this result being partly due to the fact that the English ships were provided with large quantities of quick-lime, which blinded the enemy when the English attacked with the wind behind them. Fig. 5 shows the type of vessel used at that period, which did not carry cannon of any description.

Sans Merci, an early thirteenth-century ship, first carried the Royal Standard to sea, emblazoned on the vessel's mainsail.

The middle of the fourteenth century saw the end of the galley as a first - line fighting unit, and larger vessels propelled by sails took its place.

Fig. 6 shows a fifteenth - century vessel on which deck - cannon were used, though the archers had not as yet disappeared. The first ship built by any English monarch for fighting purposes only was a vessel of this type, the Regent, constructed by Henry VII. in 1485. Some writers call her the Great Harry.
[Continued opposite.]

The Beginnings of War-Machines: Early War-Ships.

1 ROMAN GALLEY c. 110 A.D.

2 DIAGRAMMATIC DRAWING OF AN ATTIC TRIREME. 4TH CENTURY B.C.

5 DANISH WARSHIP c. 876 A.D.

4 NORMAN WARSHIP 11TH CENTURY (AS RESTORED BY JAL).

5 EARLY 15TH CENTY ENGLISH WARSHIP (NO CANNON)

6 ENGLISH 15TH CENTURY (EARLY CANNON + BOWMEN)

7 TUDOR SHIP "HENRI GRACE A DIEU" (PORT HOLES) c.1520.

8 LATE 16TH CENTURY ENGLISH WARSHIP

9 THE "SOVEREIGN OF THE SEAS" 1637.

10 A THREE-DECKER OF THE NELSON PERIOD

FROM THE ANCIENT GREEK TRIREME TO NELSON'S THREE-DECKERS: THE EVOLUTION OF WAR-SHIPS.

(Continued.)

This may, therefore, be correctly termed the first ship of the Royal Navy. In the next illustration (Fig. 7) we see the "Henri Grace à Dieu," a two-decker built by Henry VIII., provided with port-holes through the vessel's sides. The invention of the "port-hole" revolutionised naval armament, in that it made possible the use of a number of superimposed gun-decks and consequently a very

much heavier broadside. Fig. 8 shows an Elizabethan vessel such as those used against the Spanish Armada. The first three-decker constructed in England was the "Sovereign of the Seas" (Fig. 9), afterwards renamed the "Royal Sovereign," which appears to have resembled in general external features the main points of the three-decker of Nelson's time shown in Fig. 10.

A Russian Military Funeral in France.

HONÓURING THE FIRST RUSSIAN OFFICER TO FALL IN FRANCE: A FUNERAL IN CHAMPAGNE.

These photographs were taken at the funeral of the first Russian officer to lay down his life for France on French soil. He was mortally wounded during a raid on German trenches, and was buried in a village cemetery in Champagne. The first photograph shows the procession, headed by two Russian "popes" (priests), one of whom (in the lower photograph) is pronouncing a valediction.

It may be recalled that a Reuter message from Paris of July 16 said: "The newspapers report that the Russian troops in France have received their baptism of fire on the Western front, and that they recently attacked the enemy's trenches and brought back a number of German prisoners, who seemed dazed at finding themselves in the hands of the Tsar's soldiers in France."—[Photos. by C.N.]

The Tsar's Emissary Inspects Russians in France.

INSPECTING RUSSIANS IN FRANCE FOR THE TSAR: GENERAL BELAIEFF LEAVING A DUG-OUT.

The correspondent who supplies the above photograph writes : " General Belaieff, head of the Russian General Staff, was sent by the Tsar from Petrograd to inspect and review the Russian brigade in France. General Belaieff is here seen inspecting the Russian trenches in Champagne." It was reported from Paris on the 17th that a new contingent had landed at Brest, to proceed to the front after a period of preparation in camp. The previous contingents, it will be remembered, landed at Marseilles. Part of the Champagne front is known as the Russian sector, and the Russians have already been successful there, as mentioned on the page illustrating the funeral of the first Russian officer to fall in France.—[Photo. by C.N.]

ROMANCES OF THE REGIMENTS : VIII.—THE 6TH ROYAL WARWICK.

THE GHOST OF SERGEANT DAVIS.

FOUR years after the '45, when Guise's Regiment, nicknamed "Guise's Geese," now the Royal Warwickshire Regiment, was stationed at Castleton of Braewar, in Aberdeenshire (the village, by-the-bye, where Robert Louis wrote "Treasure Island"), a certain Sergeant Arthur Davis fell a victim possibly to the Highland dislike of the English troops, but chiefly, it is believed, to the cupidity of the wild clansmen. He disappeared, and for years no clue to the mystery was found. Davis was known to have gone out alone with a fowling-piece. He had money and some valuables about him, and Scott, who was interested in the affair and wrote a short account of it long after, believed that robbery was the sole motive for the murder. Be that as it may, Davis vanished, leaving no trace, on Sept. 28, 1749.

The matter was almost forgotten, when in 1754 it was suddenly revived by the extraordinary story told by Alexander Macpherson (or Macgillias), a farm - servant at Inveray, not far from Braemar, whose evidence led to the arrest of Duncan Terig, *alias* Clark, and Alexander Bain Macdonald, two Highlanders, who were tried on June 10 at Edinburgh for the murder of Davis. Macpherson, the chief witness, who spoke only Gaelic and gave his evidence through an interpreter, deposed that one night, two

NOT COUNTED IN THE BRITISH DESPATCHES : A GERMAN GUN TOO MUCH DAMAGED FOR REMOVAL.

Sir Douglas Haig stated in a recent despatch that, although an ever-increasing number of captured German guns had been brought in from the front during the Great Offensive, many more had been left on the field as being so damaged as to be not worth while removing.

Official Press Bureau Photograph. Crown Copyright reserved.

GALLANT "ANZAC" GREETS GALLANT INDIAN : AN INDIAN OFFICER D.S.O. BEING CONGRATULATED OUTSIDE BUCKINGHAM PALACE.

An interesting touch of Imperial sentiment attaches to this snapshot, taken outside Buckingham Palace after a recent investiture of war honours by the King. It shows Captain Badan Singh, of the 34th Poona Horse, on leaving the Palace after receiving the D.S.O., being congratulated by an "Anzac."—[*Photo. by Topical.*]

years after the murder, when he was in bed in his cottage, an apparition came to him and commanded him to rise and follow it out of doors. Macpherson, fancying that his visitor was his friend and neighbour Donald Farquharson (it must have been a substantial-looking ghost, for the Farquharsons are fine men), did as he was bid. Once outside, the ghost introduced himself as the late Sergeant Davis, of Guise's Regiment, and requested Macpherson to go and bury his mortal remains, which lay concealed at a place he pointed out, on a moorland tract known as the Hill of Christie. The shade of Davis further requested Macpherson to take with him, as assistant sexton, Donald Farquharson aforesaid.

Next day the obedient Sandy went to the place specified, where he duly discovered the bones of a human body, in no very good state of preservation, as was only to be expected. Evidently he fought shy of his task, for he did nothing. That night the Sergeant again appeared, considerably hurt, and upbraided Alexander for his breach of faith. Macpherson very prudently asked for some information as to the murderers, whereupon Davis named the prisoners at the bar. Macpherson now resolved to do his duty, summoned Farquharson, and with his help buried the remains.

[Continued overleaf.

A French Theatre near the Guns: "The Théâtre du Front."

DESIGNED BY THE FAMOUS ARTIST GEORGES SCOTT: A THEATRE FOR FIGHTING-MEN.

The "Théâtre du Front" is a great institution with the play-loving *poilus*, although the scenes cannot always be put upon the stage with such charm as that suggested by our photographs. With its gracefully proportioned proscenium, decorated with the national Tricolour and medallions bearing the dates 1914, 1915, and a suggestive space for the current year, it has a pretty effect and must recall to the French soldiers the gaities of their beloved Paris. Easily put together and taken down, it is as conveniently portable as it is artistic. It was designed by that clever artist M. Georges Scott, with whose admirable work readers of both the Paris "L'Illustration" and the "Illustrated London News" are pleasantly familiar.—[*French War Office Official Photographs.*]

Farquharson was next called, and corroborated Macpherson's story in every particular known to him.

Further corroboration was given by Isabel Machardie (a lady with a typical Braemar name), who slept in the same house as Macpherson and in the same room, for accom-

MOVING UP TO SHELL THE GERMAN THIRD-LINE TRENCHES: A BRITISH FIELD-ARTILLERY BATTERY GOING FORWARD.

The field-artillery battery shown here is one whose shells have been raining down on and destroying the German first and second line trenches. The gunners are now seen on the move forward to come into action ahead and shell the German third-line trenches.

Official Press Bureau Photograph. Crown Copyright reserved.

modation in Highland shielings was not palatial. Isabel testified that on the fateful night she saw the figure of a naked man enter the house and go towards Macpherson's bed. It came in in a bowing posture, and frightened Isabel so much that she drew the bedclothes over her head. She could not identify the ghost, whose lack of apparel, by the way, does not seem to have been noted by either of the two gentlemen concerned. In the morning she asked Macpherson what it was that had troubled them the night before, and he replied that she might be easy, for it would trouble her no more.

So far, so good; but the Court was inclined to treat the case for the prosecution as rather ludicrous. More suspicious was the alleged fact that some of Davis's valuables had been seen in the possession of Messrs. Duncan Terig, *alias* Clark, and Alexander Bain Macdonald, the panels at the bar. The defence naturally fastened on the ghost story as excellent material for cross-examination, and the wits of the Parliament

House, as is their way, got in their fine work upon it.

COUNSEL (*cross-examining Macpherson*): What language did the ghost speak?

MACPHERSON (*who knew no English*): As good Gaelic as I ever heard in Lochaber.

COUNSEL: Pretty well for the ghost of an English sergeant."

This was the trump-card for the prisoners. The jury thereupon acquitted them both, although the Court, their counsel, and solicitors were perfectly convinced of their guilt. Scott criticises counsel's point as unsound, remarking that, admitting the apparition, we know too little of the other world to judge whether all languages may not be alike familiar to those who belong to it. Sir Walter believed that Macpherson, unwilling to play the direct informer, got up his story to save his face. But such a passion for justice to an English soldier is improbable in a Highlander of that date. Three years had elapsed after Macpherson saw the ghost before proceedings were taken, and nothing would have been done but for a retired Army officer named Small, who forced on the case. Small was so angry with Lockhart, prisoners' counsel, an ardent Jacobite, that next day he drew his sword upon him in Parliament Close. For this he was committed by the Lords of Session,

THE FOOD SUPPLY OF OUR TROOPS IN ACTION: REGIMENTAL PARTIES LOADING UP RATIONS AT A "DUMP"

Official Press Bureau Photograph. Crown Copyright reserved.

and was only released on making an abject apology. There in farce ended one of the most curious cases in the annals of Scottish justice.

Music after Victory: The Skirl of the Pipes.

AFTER THE CAPTURE OF LONGUEVAL : THE BAND OF THE BLACK WATCH PLAYS TO THE TROOPS.

The capture of Longueval was a feat of military importance, as well as the occasion of splendid courage on the part of our gallant troops, and there was every reason for the band of the Black Watch further to hearten their comrades on their return by the strains of their stirring national music. The subject is worthy of the brush of an artist, as well as the realisation of the scene by the camera. The beautiful, peaceful background, with trees, would have appealed to Corot ; and the gallant show of brave troops Meissonier would not have disdained to immortalise on canvas. The grim mouth of a trench emphasises the pastoral peace of the landscape, and the martial figures complete a remarkable camera-picture.—[Official Photograph ; issued on behalf of the Press Bureau.]

An Arm which is Now Coming into Its Own in the West.

OUR CAVALRY GETTING THEIR DAY ONCE MORE : DRAGOON GUARDS CHARGING.

Dragoon Guards charging the enemy, with their sabres held ready to thrust when they get to close quarters, are shown in the upper illustration. It was very much like that, with sabres out, that the troop of Dragoon Guards pressed forward when they made their dashing and highly successful attack the other day on German infantry in a cornfield in the cavalry fight on July 14 between High Wood and Longueval, in company with a troop of Indian cavalry. The Indian horsemen, as a "Times" correspondent relates, went at the enemy with the lance ; the Dragoon Guards with the sabre. In the lower illustration a patrol of British cavalry scouts is seen setting off to reconnoitre. — [Official Press Bureau Photograph. Crown Copyright reserved.]

Now Beginning to Join in the Great Offensive.

OUR CAVALRY RESUMING THEIR RÔLE : A PATROL WHILE ENGAGED IN A MUSKETRY SKIRMISH.

Men of a cavalry section on detached duty, part of them dismounted and sent forward on foot to engage an enemy force with musketry a little way in advance, are seen in the first illustration. The troopers shown here are waiting in rear of the attackers, in charge of the horses of their dismounted comrades, to see after the horses until the others return, or the order be given to ride on ahead up to the firing squad for the attacking party to mount again where they are. In the second illustration a dismounted party is seen doubling out in advance with their carbines, just after getting down from their horses, which have been left with the squad of their comrades, as the photograph shows, to the right in rear.—[Official Press Bureau Photograph. Crown Copyright reserved.]

An Arm Now Coming into Its

READY TO REPEAT THE LESSONS OF AUG

Our British cavalry are now at last, it has become evident, on the eve of once more taking the field in force and giving the
enemy a taste of their quality, as they did on more than one occasion in the autumn of 1914. That our horsemen will come
into their own with equal *éclat* in the coming days may be taken for granted. In proof of that we have the official stor

on the West: British Cavalry.

G FORWARD OVER ROUGH GROUND.

happened the other day. The little "scrap" in the cornfields near Contalmaison on July 14, when Dragoon Guards and
cavalry rode down with sabre and lance a well-posted force of the enemy with machine-guns and cut them up badly,
ily returning with prisoners, may be taken as a sample of what is in store for the enemy.—[*Photo, C.N.*]

In the Attack on the German Second Line.

AUTOMATIC RIFLES THAT ARE DOING USEFUL SERVICE: THE LEWIS AND THE HOTCHKISS.

A trench incident during the battle in front of Ovillers, in Sir Douglas Haig's attack on the German second-line positions, is shown in the upper illustration. Ovillers was very strongly fortified, and was stubbornly held for some time by a battalion of the Prussian Guard. A British soldier is seen firing with a Lewis automatic rifle, which can discharge three hundred and more aimed shots a minute. Weighing only twenty-nine pounds, it is easily portable by infantry. It is an air-cooled weapon, and is "fed" in action, as seen above, by means of a "drum" of cartridges attached over the breech-mechanism. In the lower illustration a cavalry trooper is firing with a Hotchkiss automatic rifle.—[Official Press Bureau Photographs. Crown Copyright reserved.]

British Cavalry Scout against German Airman.

USING A HOTCHKISS AUTOMATIC RIFLE FROM A SHELL-HOLE: AN UNEXPECTED ATTACK.

German airmen at the front are well advised to fly high, as they are reported to be doing consistently. In many places, expert marksmen are to be found lying in wait, on the look out to wing them. This often happens in localities where there are no anti-aircraft guns available in the immediate neighbourhood. Our illustration shows a place where unsuspected danger for an enemy airman, flying probably unawares till too late within range of musketry, is found lurking on occasion. The British cavalryman shown using a Hotchkiss automatic rifle is a member of a scouting party and has sighted a German aeroplane within range. He is making use of a high-explosive shell-hole in the road as cover.—[Photo. by C.N.]

On a Battlefield in the Great Offensive.

HOW BRITISH SOLDIERS BIVOUAC IN DUG-OUTS IN CAPTURED GERMAN TRENCHES.

How our troops in present-day warfare bivouac on their field of battle is well suggested in this pair of illustrations. Some of our heroic men now in the midst of the Great Offensive are seen resting on the scene of their victories; during an interval between attacks burrowing in the former dug-outs of the German trenches while shells of the German reply artillery fire are bursting all round.

The rabbit-hole-like formation of some of the dug-out entrances is noticeable in the upper illustration. In the second, the concreted roof over one entrance may be observed—incidentally also the wrappings over the muzzles of our man's rifles, which serve to provide protection against rain or heavy night dews.— *[Official Press Bureau Photograph. Crown Copyright reserved.]*

Heroes of the Maple Leaf: On the Canadian Front.

WITH THE GALLANT CANADIANS: A BATTALION HEADQUARTERS; AND MINE-SHAFT AIR-PUMPING.

The upper photograph shows the solid construction of the sand-bag defences at a battalion headquarters on the Canadian front. Outside the dug-out will be noted an ingeniously constructed garden seat which, in shape, is reminiscent of Hyde Park. In the lower photograph some French Canadians in the trenches are seen employed in pumping air into a mine-shaft. The Canadian troops, it is hardly necessary to recall, have displayed magnificent fighting qualities ever since they first went out to the Front. Their heroic deeds in more than one battle near Ypres are not, and never will be, forgotten. It was stated recently that the Canadian Minister of Militia, General Sir Sam Hughes, would be arriving in London before long.— [Canadian Official Photographs. Government Copyright reserved.]

THINGS DONE : VIII.—THE ARMY ORDNANCE CORPS.

IF you have a large American imagination, and can dream dreams of the biggest kind of Store doing a trade beyond the visions of millionaires in every kind of goods from howitzers to tablets of soap ; if you can screw your imagination up a trifle more, can see this Biggest Emporium on Earth keeping the books for six or more million customers, and delivering its goods, carriage in advance to Mombassa as easily as Aldershot, and to the Tigris as easily as to Tyneside, and doing this not by way of exception, but as a regular everyday-of-the-week habit — if you can grasp just the broad and magnificent effect of this Largest Universal Provider bar None, then you are just beginning to know something of the work of the Army Ordnance Corps.

It is hard to realise the A.O.C.—in fact, there are quite a number of people who have to be told of its existence. This is because the Corps remains in the background — too busy to come forward, maybe — and also because many are inclined to give credit to the Army Service Corps for the blessings the A.O.C. send. This is unfair.

CAROUSING IN THE HOUSE OF GOD : GERMANS DESECRATING A CHURCH ALTAR—A PICTURE POST-CARD.

WRITTEN BY A GERMAN EVIDENTLY PROUD OF IT : THE ADDRESS SIDE OF THE PICTURE CARD ABOVE.

The picture post-card of which both sides are here reproduced, illustrates a flagrant case of quite needless desecration of churches by the Germans. The card was taken from a prisoner of the 21st Bavarian Reserve Regiment.

correct entry), the rest of him is all A.O.C. Boots, puttees, clothes, kit, first-aid dressing, buttons, shoulder-plates, cap, rifle, cartridges—all the civilisation of him comes from the Biggest Stores on earth, which are the A.O.C. stores—unlimited.

The A.O.C. lives a hurried life in its vast central depôts trying to keep pace with all the wants of the Army, trying to keep its stocks up to " Great Reduction Sale " standard. But even that is not enough. It ties itself into knots all over the country; and wherever you go, to the towns that ship munitions, to the towns that victual troops, to the camps and the barracks and the billeting centres, you will find in each the little knot—that is, the A.O.C.— working miracles daily, keeping the stores and the equipment of fighting men up to fighting trim, and doing it all with a sleight of hand that makes it seem so simple that the soldier grumbles when anything goes wrong.

And supply isn't enough. The A.O.C. has the bump of economy largely developed. The A.O.C. repairs, makes worn equipment good, makes new lamps out of old. They have the war-saving

The A.S.C. only carries the goods ; it is the A.O.C. usually finds the goods to carry. All equipment and stores, from gun-parts to " housewife," are provided by the A.O.C., and, more often than not, packed and despatched by the A.O.C. Take a soldier to pieces, and though his body is certainly his own and hasn't been indented for on an A.O.C. memo in the recognised A.O.C. style (" Body, private of the line, one "—would be the

habit in the large way that brings balm to the soul of Chancellors of the Exchequer. To-day armies do not scrap those things that seem past repairing, as in the bad days of old. They simply send those things along to the A.O.C.; the A.O.C. again performs miracles, and returns the things as new. There are whole battalions of the A.O.C. enlisted to do the science of economic renovation on discarded things. Cobblers—many of them serenely

[Continued overleaf.]

The Great Offensive: Indian Cavalry and Cyclists.

INDIANS WHOSE TURN IS NEAR AT HAND: LANCERS; AND A CYCLIST SECTION.

In the upper illustration a detachment of Indian cavalry in France, "somewhere" close to the fighting front during the Great Offensive now so successfully breaking through the German defence lines, are seen at a halt. They are wearing, it will be noted, the steel helmet worn by all in action or about to go under fire. They carry long bamboo lances, the typical arm of our Indian horsemen, in the handling of which in action no cavalry in the world can surpass them. The Germans on the Western Front are likely to find our Indian horse no less redoubtable antagonists in hand-to-hand fight than the dreaded Cossacks of our Russian ally. Indian cyclist riders are shown in the lower illustration.—[Official Press Bureau Photograph. Crown Copyright reserved.]

over age—deal with all the boots an army of millions wears out or kicks out. Tailors do the same for old uniforms; harness-makers do the same for old kit. Indeed, you cannot, with the greatest ingenuity in the world, make anything altogether useless in this war. Cycle-smiths, sail-

WITH ALTAR AND CHANCEL DAMAGED BY SHELL-FIRE : THE CHOIR OF A BOMBARDED CHURCH IN ARTOIS.

Photograph by C.N.

makers, carpenters, tinsmiths, motor-mechanics, wheelwrights, armourers, and the rest, have all been drafted into the A.O.C. to make whole the things that have been broken. The organisation is marvellous. Nothing is scrapped that can be mended. The great motor-repair depôts deal with broken-down lorries as surely and as completely as they deal with Staff automobiles that have encountered shells not wisely but too well. Battered cycles are no longer thrown into ditches, but taken to those who know their ways, and are repaired. From field-guns to fountain-pens the A.O.C. ranges in its passion for replacement and repair.

The officer and the private of the A.O.C. are specialists each of their kind. The officers generally find themselves destined by their curious attainments to the ranks of the Corps, the privates are enlisted from their trades. Being specialists, they lend themselves and their services to the battalions who have not their talents, and so the armourer-sergeants that mend the rifles of the line are sergeants of the Ordnance Corps.

Rifles and guns and shells come naturally under the A.O.C.'s wide vision of industry. Woolwich

has been its sanctuary since the time of autocratic Kings and old and curious prints, for the old and curious prints are in existence to prove that the A.O.C. existed in early days as the workers in explosives and the makers of guns. As early as 1418 there was a " Clerk of the Ordinance," and since then he has sometimes been a clerk and sometimes a General, a civilian at times and at times a soldier, and the A.O.C. has led a worried life with a variety of masters. Still, it has always done well enough, and it has always worked hard. In peace it not only provided for armies who must live and fire off musketry courses and run through suits of clothes, but it had to prepare for war. The whole means of war had to be stored and set by, so that when war came the armies could fight; so that when recruits came and reserves were called up they could be instantly equipped and sent out to battle, or to training for battle. And while there is a war there are no trading limits to the Corps. Where there are men needing bayonets or buttons, to those men must the Corps send the goods. The whole German Empire is ringed round with the Branch

WRECKED IN THE BATTLE OF THE SOMME : THE RUINS OF THE VILLAGE CHURCH AT FRISE.

Frise, which lies just south of the Somme, between Bray and Péronne, was one of the first villages captured by the French in the great Franco-British offensive on the Western Front.

Photograph by Rol.

Establishments of the A.O.C.; and possibly the German Empire, with its eye on this fact, is very much in earnest in its desire for military Tariff Reform. W. Douglas Newton.

Picking Up the Wounded — and After.

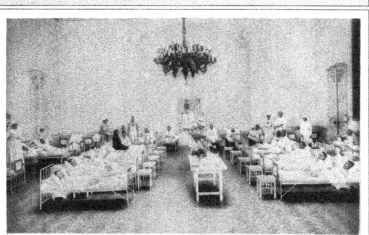

SCENES OF MERCY: THE R.A.M.C. IN THE WEST; THE ANGLO-RUSSIAN HOSPITAL AT PETROGRAD.

Our first photograph shows the R.A.M.C. at work in the West, picking up soldiers who have been wounded in the "Great Push" which has lately been of such engrossing interest, and of such unquestionable value to the Allied Forces. The Red Cross ambulance wagons are seen in an environment of broken trees and shattered walls inevitable in war, amid which the Royal Army Medical Corps does its splendid work. Our second photograph shows Lady Muriel Paget (in grey, on right), in one of the wards of the Anglo-Russian Hospital, in the Dmitri Palace, Petrograd. Lady Muriel Paget is Honorary Organising Secretary of the Anglo-Russian Hospital, 32, Victoria Street, S.W.—[Photo. No. 1, Official, issued on behalf of the Press Bureau; No. 2, by Steinberg, Petrograd.]

Striving for "A Speedy and Decisive Victory": The C.-in-C.

LEADER OF THE BRITISH OFFENSIVE: SIR DOUGLAS HAIG (RIGHT); WITH GENERAL RAWLINSON.

It is appropriate now to recall Sir Douglas Haig's appeal to munition-makers to forego the August holiday promised instead of Whitsuntide. After expressing the Army's high appreciation of the self-sacrifice of the workers at home, he said : ". The continuous supply of ammunition is a vital factor. . . . Let the whole British nation forego any idea of a general holiday until our goal is reached. A speedy and decisive victory will then be ours ! " He is also reported to have said, in an interview, to Senator Henry Bérenger : " The supreme decisions of the war are on the battlefields of the West ; it is there that we must impose a peace that is worth the price we shall have paid for it."—[Official Press Bureau Photograph taken during the British Advance.]

Victors of the Somme: Two famous French Generals.

ORGANISERS OF THE FRENCH OFFENSIVE ON THE SOMME : GEN. FOCH (RIGHT) AND GEN. FAYOLLE.

General Foch, who did such brilliant work in the Battle of the Marne and in subsequent operations, has had the chief direction of the great French offensive. "General Fayolle," writes Mr. H. Warner Allen, "commands the army of the Somme, which is one of the group of armies commanded by General Foch. General Fayolle had reached the age limit before the outbreak of war, and was actually on the retired list. . . . While General Pétain, the hero of Verdun, has followed step by step General de Castelnau in his commands and promotions, General Fayolle has . . . followed in the steps of General Pétain. He held a command in the French offensive in Artois in May last year, and in Champagne in September."—[French War Office Official Photograph.]

A German "O. Pip"—Somewhat Out of Repair.

DAMAGED BY OUR FIRE IN THE ADVANCE : A GERMAN OBSERVATION-POST IN MAMETZ WOOD.

The capture of the Mametz Wood was announced in a British official despatch of July 12. Writing on the same day, of this "battle of the woods," Mr. Philip Gibbs said : "Some of these places are but a few shell-slashed trees serving as land-marks, but Bailiff Wood, Mametz Wood, Bernafay Wood, and Trones Wood are still dense thickets under heavy foliage hiding the enemy's troops and our own, but giving no protection from shell-fire. It is for these woodlands on high ground that our men have been fighting with the greatest gallantry . . . these woods are the way to the second bastion of the German stronghold." Among our own troops artillery observation-posts are nicknamed " O. Pips."—[Official Press Bureau Photograph. Crown Copyright reserved.]

A Cornish Link with the Past Retained in War-Time.

A PICTURESQUE OLD CUSTOM AT ST. IVES: THE "OLD HUNDREDTH" AT THE JOHN KNILL OBELISK.

More than a hundred years ago one John Knill, a prominent citizen of St. Ives, left a sum of money to perpetuate his memory by the erection of an obelisk and the distribution of sums of money every five years. The ceremony was carried out again last week, children and aged widows dancing round the memorial and singing, to the playing of a fiddler. Various sums of £5 and £10 were distributed, and the "Old Hundredth" was sung, as shown in our photograph. It is interesting to notice that the coat of arms on the obelisk bears a lion rampant, as does the coat of arms of the Sir John Knill of to-day, who was Lord Mayor of London in 1909-10; but the Lord Mayor's coat of arms has also the fasces, token of authority.—[Photo. by C.N.]

WOMEN AND THE WAR.

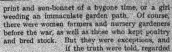

THOUGH women have been working on the land ever since Eve first learnt what was really meant by "division of labour," it took a European war and a whole lot of "high-explosive" speeches about scarcity of food and the necessity of preserving our export trade in edible commodities, before the British farmer could be brought to realise that the employment of female labour on his farm would not immediately set him on the path that leads to ruin. But then farmers are a conservative class; a class, moreover, who have brought grumbling to the level of a fine art; so that perhaps it is not to be wondered at that when the cry of women for the land was first raised they were amongst its most bitter opponents. Even now, though a great many of them are quite ready to enlist the services of women, there are not a few who hint darkly at reduced turnip supplies or an inferior crop of mangel-wurzels as though it were directly due to their presence; and it only needs a little encouragement for them to attribute the poor plum prospect to the same cause.

The late President of the Board of Agriculture said some time ago that turnips were as important as shells. The country, however, was rather slow to realise that women could be as useful in helping to grow the one as they had proved themselves capable of making the other. The popular notion of women in relation to work on the land prevalent before August 1914 seems to have been limited to a dairymaid in the flowered

THE DAY OF THE WOMAN DOCTOR : AN M.D. IN HER UNIFORM.

Not so long ago the woman doctor was, as it were, fighting for recognition, but the war has brought the value, and need, of her services equally to the front. Forty qualified ladies have been chosen for regular service in Army hospitals. It is the first time women have been thus requisitioned. The uniform chosen for them is practical but not unfeminine—except in the very desirable detail that it is well supplied with pockets !—[Photo. by Photopress.]

print and sun-bonnet of a bygone time, or a girl weeding an immaculate garden path. Of course, there were women farmers and nursery gardeners before the war, as well as those who kept poultry and bred stock. But they were exceptions, and if the truth were told, regarded as rather eccentric specimens of their sex. The woman farm-labourer, versed in the rudiments of general farm-work, was practically unknown.

But many prejudices have been laid aside during the last twenty months or so, and there has now sprung up in the country a corps of land Amazons armed with hoe and rake, and scythe and pruning-knife, ready to go where duty and the farmer calls, and their usefulness is not by any means limited to waging war on dock and nettle, "or doing a little weeding," or keeping flower-beds tidy. The land army is out for "business" in the strictest sense of the word, and there are few branches of farming or horticulture, ploughing not excepted, in which it is not ready to lend a hand. Some of its members are employed in the care of live stock, others have shown that the manipulation of the plough and the harrow are not beyond the capacity of an intelligent, though female, human being. Market-gardening has claimed others : the number of lady expert pea and bean pickers, fruit - grafters, and vegetable-packers is growing more numerous every day. Others, again, devote their energies to rearing poultry, or the money-making goat, or occupy themselves in the multifarious duties connected with dairy-farming ; from all of

WOMEN CHEMISTS : TWO CLEVER WORKERS IN THEIR LABORATORY.

These ladies, Miss E. J. Smith (right) and Miss Markham (left), are seen conducting the final tests in the manufacture of a certain disinfectant. They control large works and hope to obtain a Board of Trade certificate to use a certain process in the production of a disinfectant used in the trenches. Miss Smith is a B.Sc. in engineering, of Edinburgh University, and Miss Markham took Honours in Chemistry at Oxford.—[Photo. by L.N.A.]

[Continued overleaf.]

Women Fruit-Farmers in Hertfordshire.

PLEASANT; PROFITABLE; PATRIOTIC: ON A FRUIT-FARM AT LETCHMORE HEATH, NEAR ST. ALBANS.

A large land-owner in Hertfordshire, Mr. Phillimore, has converted many acres of his property into a typical fruit-farm, and, what is specially typical of these war-days, only girls are employed on the land. They live a thoroughly healthy and pleasant life in the open air; do their work well; and have their meals in huts. Our first photograph shows some of them planting acres of ground with fruit-trees, and looking healthy and happy in their new work and unconventional dress. No. 2 shows one of the girls putting on her puttees for a comrade; and in No. 3 we see some girls bringing in material for cuttings to be made in their huts. The experiment has been made with girls largely drawn from East London, and has proved very satisfactory.—[Photos. by Photopress.]

which it will be seen that there is no place for the dilettante worker in the ranks of the land army.

As a witty cartoonist recently pointed out, "Marian, Marian, utilitarian," is the exact antithesis of "Mary, Mary, quite contrary," of other days, whom she has entirely or almost entirely superseded. She is an outcome of the war, though her services are not necessarily restricted to its duration; and, as befits the stern necessity that called her into being, she is animated with a severely - like business spirit. You see her on the land in her "war" dress of breeches and gaiters, which, strangely enough, becomes her just as well as the more conventional skirt of peace time. She deals with soils and turnips and cattle-food mixtures with the same skill that she used to lavish on wood-carving or golf, and her work, like that of her munition - making sister, is of infinite value to the country. Her job is not in any sense a "soft" one. To get up at four and work steadily at hoeing, picking, pitching, planting, and packing, or any other farmwork for ten hours a day and sleep on a straw mattress in a barn at the end of it, is no light feat for women accustomed to the ordinary comforts of well-run homes—for the land army is by no means recruited solely from the industrial classes. College gradu-

ates, women of leisure, daughters of professional men, women who have given up lucrative employment at their country's call, are amongst those who have thrown aside the frock of peace for the brown drabbet overalls of war. Some of them have volunteered for the holiday season, others until the declaration of peace; to not a few the work offers a prospect of a comfortable livelihood derived from new potatoes and cabbages and cucumbers all in a row, long after the need for munitions has ceased to exist.

Experts are always telling us that England must grow more food, and "Marian" is now held in such esteem in official circles that the Board of Agriculture has been emphasising the need for her permanent presence in the ranks of the land - worker. A good deal of the valuable work she has already done would have been impossible had it not been for the initiative and energy of the National Political Reform League, who organised the National Land Council as soon as it became apparent that there would be a call for women's services in this direction. Patriotic landowners made a generous response to the request that they should admit women to work on their farms in order that later on they might be fit to replace Hodge at the harrow. CLAUDINE CLEVE.

A NEW USE FOR A GOLF CLUB HOUSE : QUEEN MARY'S NEEDLEWORKERS, AT WOLDINGHAM.

Members of that most excellent society, "Queen Mary's Needlework Guild," have done invaluable work for the wounded, and our photograph shows a number of them busily engaged in the Golf Club House at Woldingham making swabs, bandages, dressings, and garments for our wounded in the various war hospitals.—[Photo. by Underwood and Underwood.]

"'I'M GOING A-MILKING, SIR,' SHE SAID" : DAIRY-FARMING BEING TAUGHT AT AN ESSEX SCHOOL.

Women's work on the land has passed into an accepted fact brought about by the war. The Essex Women's War Agricultural Association, of which Lady Petre, of Thorndon Hall, Brentwood, is president, is doing useful work in this direction. Our picture shows a class of boys and girls assembled for their first lesson in milking a cow, which stands patiently enough with an air of sleepy superciliousness which is not without its amusing side. The work, however, is very practical and useful in the present shortage of labour.—[Photo. by Alfieri.]

Honouring the Boy Hero of the Great Sea-Fight.

"THIS GRAVE SHALL BE THE BIRTHPLACE OF HEROES": THE FUNERAL OF JACK CORNWELL.

The upper photograph shows bluejackets carrying wreaths, and the lower one the procession in the High Street, East Ham, on July 29, when John Travers Cornwell, of H.M.S. "Chester," whose heroism in the Battle of Jutland was mentioned in Admiral Beatty's report, was reburied in Manor Park Cemetery. East Ham was his native place. Six boys from the "Chester," who were in the battle, carried wreaths from the ship. Among many other floral tributes was one from Admiral Beatty. The coffin was covered with the White Ensign. The Bishop of Barking conducted the service. At the graveside, Dr. Macnamara, Financial Secretary to the Admiralty, in a moving address, said : "This grave shall be the birthplace of heroes."—[Photos. by Central Press and News Illustrations Co.]

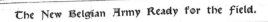

The New Belgian Army Ready for the Field.

ARTILLERY TYPES : ANTI-AIRCRAFT GUNS AND AN EX-PRUSSIAN-GUARD GUN.

A Belgian battery of 75-mm. (2·9-inch) anti-aircraft guns, with their field carriages, are seen in the upper illustration. They are mounted on special pedestals, on which the guns are swivelled so as to be readily trained to point to any quarter right round the horizon. In the lower illustration is shown an ex-German field-gun of 105 mm. (4-inch), one of the larger-calibre field-pieces originally served out to the batteries of the artillery of the Prussian Guard, and turned over to the Belgian Army by the French, who captured several batteries of such pieces, brand-new and intact, in Champagne. They constitute a valuable addition to the new artillery with which the reorganised Belgian Army is already amply provided.—[Photos. supplied by Topical.]

The New Belgian Army Ready for the Field.

ARTILLERY TYPES: 75-MM. (2·9-INCH) MORTAR, AND 210-MM. (8-INCH) HOWITZER, MADE IN ENGLAND.

The gun in the upper illustration is a 75-mm. (2·9-inch) mortar of a new and powerful pattern, with which the Belgian Army, now fit and "ready to go anywhere and do anything" in the regaining of its native land, has been supplied. Such pieces are available for use either in the trenches or for holding or attacking fortified village positions like those the British have been victoriously fighting among in the Great Offensive during the past month. These mortars can be easily man-handled on their light trolley carts, as seen. The gun in the lower illustration is a Belgian 210-mm. (8-inch) howitzer, of the latest type, one of a number of these hard-hitting weapons which have been constructed in England specially for King Albert's Army.—[Photos. supplied by Topical.]

A Giant Mine on the Western Front.

LIKE A QUARRY, OR A VOLCANO: A CRATER FORMED BY THE EXPLOSION OF A BRITISH MINE.

This might be taken at first glance for a picture of a man clambering up the side of a quarry, or exploring a volcano—it is the photograph of a part of one side of a mine-crater on the Western Front after being blown up. The figure helps in giving an idea of the enormous depth and area of the cavity resulting from an explosion. A letter in the papers recently described the blowing-up of an exceptionally huge mine, for which it had taken many days' labour to excavate the galleries. It spoke of the anxiety of our men in the trenches, during its being dug, lest the enemy should find out prematurely what was going on. As things turned out, their anxiety proved unfounded. The enemy remained totally unaware of its existence until it was exploded.—[Photo. by C.N.]

The Illustrated War News, Aug. 9, 1916.—Part 9, New Series.

The Illustrated War News

THE ARMY BEHIND THE ARMY: ROYAL ARSENAL BOYS IN A HOLIDAY CAMP.

Photograph by Alfieri.

THE GREAT WAR.

By W. DOUGLAS NEWTON.

THE week has been fully occupied with the heavy and exacting fighting of consolidation, rather than with the more striking incidents of large offensive. The week, then, has appeared quieter, though in practical fact the work accomplished by the troops is undoubtedly more trying than that necessary to win sweeping advances. It is work necessary for events, and under cover of this reticence in report the next great fighting is being matured. The battle in the West has worked forward on natural lines to that point which may give us our biggest gain. The enemy has been driven through his vast intricacies of trenches, and has reached his final effective hold in this sphere —along the crest of hills running from Thiepval, north-east of Pozières, through the Bois des Foureaux, past Longueval and the wood of Delville, by Guillemont and the Bois des Trones, to Hardecourt and the fringes of Maurepas. He has still the commanding positions, and his salients push, at some places, well into the Allied line.

The work of the week, then, has been mainly concerned in reducing the salients, straightening out the Franco-British front —notably between Guillemont and the Somme — concentrating in the newly captured positions for the next step, and generally accumulating force necessary to remove the Germans from their last holds on the Albert plateau. The whole intention of this can be observed in the engagements of the week. The movement, so capably carried out at the beginning of the week, making more regular the Guillemont-Somme front

AN IRISH THEOLOGICAL PROFESSOR FALLEN ON THE BATTLEFIELD : THE REV. D. O. SULLIVAN.

The Rev. D. O. Sullivan, a Professor at St. Brendan's Seminary, Killarney, whose death in action in France has been reported among recent casualties, was Roman Catholic Chaplain to the Loyal North Lancashire Regiment. With them he was serving when killed.—[Photo. by News Illustrations.]

gave—to the French particularly—a good advantage of ground, including the strong positions in the Wood of Hem and in and about the Monacu Farm. The attack appears to have been halted deliberately on the outskirts of Maurepas, the French feeling it not to their gain to carry the powerfully held village at this moment. At the same time, the British joined in the push as far as they had the opportunities, and straightened out any kinks north of the French. North of Bazentin-le-Petit, too, our men also made steady if small encroachments towards the ridge line in the direction of Martinpuich, and the week closed with a brave attack by the Anzac and new army troops, in which a new dent from 400 to 600 yards deep and 3000 yards wide was hammered into the German line north and west of Pozières. Here, and at most points of the Allied sphere of offensive, the Germans have been held off, in spite of the fact that some of their attacks have been handled with the greatest determination.

A note of extreme auspiciousness in the whole tale of the Western fighting has been marked turn of the current at Verdun. For some time past it has been apparent that the German effort has suffered from vitiation here, undoubtedly because of events on the Somme and in the East. Not only has the German assault lacked dynamic fervour, but the French have been creeping back over the ground the Germans spent so many lives and so much energy to win. The return towards Fleury has been constant during the past few weeks, and now the French have won back most of the

FRENCH ARMY PHOTOGRAPHS IN LONDON : THE OPENING OF THE GEORGIAN GALLERIES EXHIBITION, BY M. PAINLEVÉ, MINISTER OF EDUCATION.

The collection, which is exceedingly interesting, comprises some six hundred photographs of life on the Front and of Verdun since the bombardment began, taken by the Photographic Section of the French Army. The exhibition, which is held at Messrs. Waring and Gillow's Georgian Galleries, Oxford Street, is free, and will be open for some weeks.
Photo. by Newspaper Illustrations.

village, and have taken all the trenches as far as and including the grim Thiaumont Work and the approaches of Hill 320. When it is remembered how much importance the enemy attached to Fleury, how anxious they showed themselves to get this position — which they considered was a pistol directed at the heart of the Verdun defences—and how tenacious they have been in holding to the place, we can measure something of the real power of the blow that the French have struck at the enemy. It is not belittling the heroic French to say that their work and our work on the Somme, no less than the work of the Russians in the East, have helped to win at Fleury. It is, indeed, more important to realise that fighting so remote as that at Albert

then, shows not only that practically all their efforts have gone for nothing, but that they are without the means to uphold their honour in spite of all that depends upon it. The fighting at Verdun may develop in a greater intensity yet— there are signs that this will be so—but the French victory at Fleury is as striking a sign of Allied power and German weakness as those signs shown at the Somme and in the Lutsk salient.

The Russians are encountering the force of a desperate and accumulated resistance on their European fronts, and their pace has accommodated itself to the necessity of breaking German counter-efforts before sweeping forward again. The fighting in the Lutsk salient is of the liveliest nature, and, though the enemy is doing the best he can,

A MEMORIAL TO LORD KITCHENER, JACK CORNWELL, AND MEN OF THE H.A.C.: THE BISHOP OF STEPNEY
SPEAKING AT THE UNVEILING.
The Lord Mayor, Colonel Sir Charles Wakefield (seated to the right), unveiled on August 4, in the churchyard of St. Botolph's, Bishopsgate, a Gothic cross in memory of Lord Kitchener and also of Jack Cornwell, the boy hero of Jutland Bank, and of fallen officers and men of the Honourable Artillery Company.　The Bishop of Stepney gave a short address.—[Photo. by Sport and General.]

and that in Poland has had a very palpable effect at a point where the Germans had staked so much. Since the Germans committed themselves so deeply at Verdun, it has always been obvious that a German setback would have a greater moral repercussion than a defeat to the French—that is, that the French had accomplished so much in their defence that the fall of the fortress had ceased to be vital; while the Germans had staked so much that anything less than a complete victory meant to them the gravest military and moral defeat of modern times. The fact that the Germans have been unable to hold on at Fleury,

he has not been able to prevent a progressive encroachment before Kovel, and the gains across the Stokhod—no more than twenty-one miles from the menaced town—have been consolidated and held. On the southern flank of this salient, where the Russians have been able to press a new advance into Galicia beyond Brody, our Ally shows a tendency to force his way to the north of Lemberg, and has already brought the fighting to the Sereth, where villages, woods, and prisoners have fallen into Russian hands.　During the week, too, the Austrians under von Bothmer were driven back across the Koropiec, and the Russians were able to gain the further bank. The success was small, but it is of a kind that might easily lead to something bigger as the Austrian centre grows more embarrassed from the pressure to the north.

The appearance of the Turks in some force at outposts some eighteen miles east of Suez Canal was an event more dramatic than disturbing. This force of some 14,000 strong appeared at Katia — where there have been certain cavalry incidents in the past—and at Romani, a little to the west of Katia. Here the British positions over a front of eight miles were attacked, in a way that seems unsubstantial. The Turks met with a crushing reverse. Lured into the sandhills, they were attacked and routed in centre and flank, with the loss of over 2500 prisoners. During the fighting the ships of the Royal Navy rendered excellent help by firing on the enemy from the Bay of Tina. Fourteen thousand Turks could not have hoped to make a very pronounced impression on the powerful line of defensive works

FOR THE REBUILDING OF DEVASTATED FRENCH TOWNS AND VILLAGES: AT THE EXHIBITION IN PARIS—A MODEL COTTAGE.
Under the auspices of the French Government, in anticipation of the driving out of the German invaders before long, an exhibition has been opened in the Tuileries Gardens, in Paris, of model houses and cottages to replace the destroyed homes of the former inhabitants.—[Photo. by Newspaper Illustrations.]

that guard the canal, and certainly the number was hopelessly inadequate — in the face of the troops we must have in this area—to do anything of purpose at all. The mission of the 14,000, however, was probably rather strategical than tactical, and is an example of Germany's

delicate Egyptian front, and to preserve the main German armies from contact with those troops. In this it must now be counted a failure. We have already, it is obvious, taken full stock of the Turkish chances against Suez and Egypt, and our dispositions to mar those chances must have been made before, or at least at the same time as, the Western offensive was planned. The feat of transporting 14,000 troops across the desert from El Arish is, no doubt, a great one; but the feat is more likely to stand as a record than as a regular habit.

The East African phase of the great offensive continues in its condition of unabated victory. General Van Deventer, one of the most brilliant of mobile fighters, has forced his way down to the Central Railway by three roads from Kondoa Irangi, beating the Germans on all of them, and has cut the line by his occupation of Dodona. Further to the east the defence is being swept out of the country about the Usambara railway, the port of Pagani has been occupied, and the enemy hustled southward. On Lake Tanganyika, the Belgian force, working along in capital fashion, has seized the last and most important of the lake ports. With their capture of Ujiji, the Belgians have taken the lake

FOR THE REBUILDING OF DEVASTATED FRENCH TOWNS AND VILLAGES: AT THE EXHIBITION IN PARIS—
A TOWNSHIP OF THE FUTURE IN MINIATURE.
The Exhibition in the Tuileries Gardens, in Paris, has been made as complete as possible by the inclusion of models not only of dwellings of every kind, but also of towns and villages in miniature.—[Photo. by Newspaper Illustrations.]

rather frantic endeavour to distract us anyhow and at all costs. The assault, then, must be regarded as a holding movement. By it the enemy hopes to tie down prodigal numbers of troops on this

terminus of the railway that runs from Dar-es-Salaam, and have thus helped considerably to cripple German mobility and supply in the doomed colony. LONDON: Aug. 7, 1916.

A "Kitchener's Man" as France Sees Him.

A CELEBRATED FRENCH ARTIST'S PORTRAIT. "TOMMY, LE VAINQUEUR DES 'HUNS.'"

The July battles of the British "New" Army in the Allied Offensive in the West have proved, in the language of the prize-ring, an "eye-opener" to friends and foes alike. To the enemy the irresistible fighting qualities of our troops have proved a revelation admittedly startling, if not, indeed, staggering, to German moral. To the French they have been a discovery surpassing the highest expectations. The smashing-in of the German front; the storming of the tremendously fortified villages in hand-to-hand fight; above all, the smashing blows dealt to the redoubtable Prussian Guard at Contalmaison, and Germany's next best troops, the "Iron" 3rd Brandenburg Army Corps, at Pozières, have won the hearts of all France.—[Drawn by J. Simont.]

A Game as Respite from "The Great Game."

SOLDIERS AND SPORTSMEN : BELGIAN AND BRITISH OFFICERS IN A POLO MATCH AT THE FRONT.

Although the old story which attributed to the Duke of Wellington the epigram that the Battle of Waterloo was won upon the Eton Playing Fields has long passed into the limbo of exploded legends, the spirit of sport has been very evident in the present great war, British officers, in particular, seizing upon their rest time to indulge their taste. Our pictures show a polo match being played on the Belgian Front between British and Belgian officers. There are "brave men" in the teams, but none of the "fair women" who shared in the glories of the historic ball in Brussels on the eve of Waterloo. Yet the scene is typical of the spirit in which the war is being carried on by our gallant Army and its Allies.—[Official Photographs issued by the Press Bureau.]

The Allied Attack in the West: Gunners off Duty.

BETWEEN BOMBARDMENTS: BRITISH SERGEANTS AT MESS; AND FRENCH HAVING COFFEE AND MUSIC.

In the upper of these two Illustrations a party of British artillery sergeants, off duty for a brief spell, are seen having a meal in their field mess quarters, *al fresco*, in a corner among the ammunition-boxes, a short way in rear of one of the places "somewhere at the Front," at which our artillery batteries daily shell the enemy while the Great Offensive steadily goes forward. In the lower Illustration we have a bivouac scene close in rear of the French artillery line; some of the French gunners having coffee during a spell off between their turns of battery duty. In the boiler-casing one of the soldiers is playing a lively tune on a piano, salved from an abandoned dwelling-house close at hand.—[Photos, by *Official Press Bureau and C.N.*]

The King's Visit of Inspection to Cambridge.

AT A UNIVERSITY WHICH HAS OVER 12,000 MEN IN THE SERVICES: HIS MAJESTY AT CAMBRIDGE.

The upper of these photographs, taken during the King's visit to Cambridge on August 3, shows his Majesty, accompanied by Col. H. J. Edwards, C.B., in the grounds of King's College, where he inspected a company of cadets engaged on the lawn in preliminary instruction in rifle drill and musketry. In the lower photograph the King is conversing with some of the Dons. Among those presented to him were the Vice-Chancellor, the Master of Trinity, the Provost of King's, the President of Queen's, and the Masters of Clare, Peterhouse, Christ's, and Emmanuel. After visiting Clare and King's, his Majesty drove to Trinity and inspected the University O.T.C. and some cadets. Later, at the 1st Eastern General Hospital, he saw many wounded.—[Photos. by C.N.]

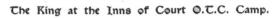

The King at the Inns of Court O.T.C. Camp.

GREETING WOUNDED SOLDIERS AND THEIR NURSES : HIS MAJESTY'S INSPECTION AT BERKHAMSTED.

The King's unflagging interest in the welfare of his soldiers, both those who have fought and those preparing to fight, is once more illustrated in these photographs, as in those on another page taken a few days later, at Cambridge. His Majesty went down to the camp of the Inns of Court Officers' Training Corps at Berkhamsted on August 1, and was received there by Colonel Errington.

He witnessed a sham fight, inspected the trenches made by the corps, and saw them go through various training exercises. At the camp the King also spoke words of kindly greeting to a number of wounded soldiers and the nurses in attendance on them. His Majesty was attended by Brig.-General W. W. Bird, Col. Clive Wigram, and Major R. H. Seymour.—[Photos. by Newspaper Illus.]

THE BEGINNINGS OF WAR-MACHINES: STEAM WAR-SHIPS AND IRONCLADS.

THE introduction of steam-power about 1832 caused a great change in naval design. The paddle-steamer H.M.S. *Salamander* appeared in that year, and was followed by a number of similar war-vessels. Paddle-steamers did not, however, long hold a place as fighting vessels. The paddles themselves were so placed as to be easily damaged by gun-fire, and their engines were, of necessity, above the water-line, and vulnerable.

In 1843, H.M.S. *Rattler* was built, and given a screw-propeller. Her success led to the general adoption of the screw, but it was five years later before the screw was applied to the line-of-battle ship. Although satisfactory iron ships were built in 1832, iron was not adopted by the naval authorities for fighting craft till eighteen years later, when wooden beams in certain war-ships were replaced by iron. Six years later still, iron-built war-vessels were produced. These were the floating batteries *Thunderbolt*, *Erebus*, and *Terror* of the Crimean War.

As the best position for engines of a screw-propelled vessel is in the lowest part of the ship, the conversion of old sailing-vessels on that system was fairly simple, the engines and boilers replacing the ballast (Fig. 8). A certain number of vessels were converted from sail to steam—or rather, had steam-propulsion added to their existing sail-power.

In 1858 the British authorities recognised the fact that the French Navy was becoming dangerously strong as compared with our own, and steps were taken to balance matters. In view of the situation to-day, it is interesting to recall that the German Press of 1859 first drew serious attention to our laxity in this matter. Indeed, it was in some measure due to the agitation started by German newspaper articles that the British public became awake to the situation.

The introduction of explosive shells, the destructive power of which was first put to the test by Russia in the fight with the Turkish vessels off Sinope in 1854, necessitated better protection than that afforded by the old "wooden walls." Armoured vessels came into existence as a result. The first sea-going ironclad, *La Gloire*, was built by the French in 1859. Great Britain's first effort in this direction was the *Warrior* (Fig. 1), launched in 1860. The French vessel displaced about 5600 tons, and steamed nearly 13 knots; the English ironclad displaced 6100 tons, and steamed over 14 knots. Both were protected by iron side-armour 4½ inches thick, which experiments had shown could not be penetrated at 800-yards range by the projectiles thrown by a 68-pounder, then the most powerful gun at sea, if the plate were backed by 18 inches of teak (see Fig. 3). The *Warrior* carried a crew of about 700 men, and cost about £356,700 to build—a small sum compared with £2,500,000, the cost of a modern battleship. The armour-plating in the *Warrior* and in many subsequent vessels only covered a portion of the ship's side, and consequently gave protection to a comparatively small part of the hull. This fault was inevitable, owing to the restricted use of plating made necessary by its enormous weight. In later years, when hardened steel took the place of iron, this defect was remedied. The resistance of a hardened steel plate being equal to that of an iron plate of double its thickness, a vessel was able to carry twice the superficial area of the improved plating without adding to weight.

In 1861 H.M.S. *Minotaur* was laid down, and fitted with armour extending from stem to stern (Fig. 6); and four years later, H.M.S. *Bellerophon* followed: an iron-built vessel, also protected throughout her full length (Fig. 7). In 1869, 9-inch armour was used in the *Hercules*, and 14-inch in the *Dreadnought* of 1875. The American Civil War led to the production of a peculiar type of vessel for use in the river estuaries, called a "monitor," mounting one or more heavy guns in a revolving turret heavily armour-plated (Fig. 4). The vessel itself was constructed with a very low "freeboard," and consequently was unsuitable for high-sea work. Its hull was so deeply submerged as to be fairly safe under gun-fire.

FIG. 8.—A WOODEN WAR-SHIP, SHOWING THE HOLD-SPACE WHERE THE ENGINES WERE PLACED: PART OF THE MID-SHIP SECTION OF H.M.S. "RODNEY."

The "Rodney" was built as a sailing two-decker in 1833. In 1860 she was "converted" into an auxiliary screw-steam man-o'-war.

[Continued opposite.

The Beginnings of War-Machines: Steam and Ironclads.

EVOLUTION OF ARMOURED WAR-SHIPS : EARLY BRITISH IRON-CLADS AND AMERICAN "MONITORS."

(Continued.)

The frigate "Merrimac" was converted into an ironclad during the same campaign by the erection on its deck of an armour-plated fort, the vessel's masts and sails being entirely removed (Fig. 5). From 1875 onwards until about 1889, the power of the gun increased more rapidly than the resistance of the armour, and, as a result, vessels were built (such as the "Inflexible," 1881) in which the central turret, containing the guns, was protected with armour 24 inches thick, whilst the bow and stern of the vessel were left unprotected. This unsatisfactory method was discontinued about 1889, when hardened steel-plating so reduced armour weight that it became possible for a vessel to carry practically complete protection, a condition of the first importance.

In Egypt in War-Time: A Question of Supplies.

AT CAIRO: VEGETABLES FOR THE GARRISON AND PETROLEUM FOR THE PEOPLE.

In the upper illustration is shown a daily scene at Cairo station in connection with the provisioning of the garrison. Fresh vegetables are brought in regularly by train from outlying native villages and market gardens, coming packed in crates or baskets (as seen here), of date palm leaf stalks. At the station the crates are stacked on carts, as shown, and taken to the commissariat and barrack depots. Another war-time incident at Cairo is recorded in the lower illustration. The authorities decided, for very good reasons, to take control of the petroleum supply. The issue now takes place at the Cairo police-stations at officially fixed minimum prices. Natives are seen obtaining supplies, which may soon be as rigidly regulated there as here.—[Photos. by Topical.]

An Egyptian Officer fallen for His Country.

AT CAIRO STATION—THE MILITARY FUNERAL: THE GUARD OF HONOUR AND GUN-CARRIAGE.

On this page are shown two scenes at the recent military funeral, specially held at Cairo, of an Egyptian artillery officer, Lieut. Helmi, who fell in action with the Turks on the Suez Canal some time ago, and was provisionally buried at Suez. He was mentioned in General Maxwell's despatches for gallantry in action. The body was disinterred lately and removed by rail to Cairo for final sepulture there. In the upper illustration an Egyptian military band with a guard of honour of the deceased officer's regiment are seen outside Cairo railway station waiting for the arrival of the train from Suez. In the lower illustration the funeral procession is seen starting from Cairo station, with Lieut. Helmi's coffin under the Egyptian national flag.—[Photos. by Topical.]

ROMANCES OF THE REGIMENTS : IX.—THE WORCESTERSHIRES.

LIEUTENANT WILD AND MARSHAL MORTIER.

THERE were cruelties enough in the Peninsular campaigns, but, as a general rule, the soldiers of that day had not forgotten the ordinary laws of war, and a prisoner, however hard his lot, did not run much risk of being murdered in cold blood, after the manner recommended, approved, and practised by the *soi-disant* supreme War-Lord of to-day. The captive might even receive such consideration as he could hardly expect, and find himself treated as a friend. Such was the experience of Lieutenant Wild, Adjutant of the old 29th Regiment in Spain, who was wounded and taken prisoner at Salamanca. Out of that misfortune arose one of the pleasantest episodes of Wild's career, a little adventure which he always delighted to recall, for it brought him the acquaintance of Marshal Mortier, Duke of Treviso — the man who fell a victim long afterwards to one of the shots fired at Louis Philippe from Fieschi's infernal machine.

The first courtesy shown to Wild by his captors, as he was being taken up country to prison, was an invitation from the officers to march with them at the head of the column, in order to escape the dust.

Marshal Mortier had his own notions about the way to treat an unfortunate enemy. When the party reported to him at the garrison town, he invited the officers to dine with him the same evening, and added : " Bring your English prisoner with you." Wild, for all the good treatment he had hitherto received, was naturally a little surprised at this mark of distinction, and at the same time rather put about, for he was not exactly in the best possible form to make the appearance he would like. Kit he had none, except what he had been taken in, and that was battle-stained and travel-stained, and for the most part in rags. He had not a decent shirt to his back.

The French officers, however, were kindness itself, and insisted on giving him all that he required. The dinner was magnificent, as befitted an entertainment given by a Marshal of France, and

JAPAN'S HONOUR TO A JAPANESE OFFICER KILLED AT THE BATTLE OF JUTLAND : THE FUNERAL PROCESSION ON THE WAY TO THE CEMETERY.

The Emperor of Japan, on learning that Commander Shimooura, of the Japanese Navy, had perished at the Battle of Jutland, ordered a special funeral service to be held for him at the pavilion in Aoyama cemetery. The principal Japanese Admirals, including the famous Admiral Togo, officially attended the service.

[Continued overleaf.

SPREADING THE NEWS AMONG THE RUSSIANS OF THE ALLIES' SUCCESSES ON THE WESTERN FRONT : THE COLONEL OF 5TH SIBERIAN COSSACKS READING AN OFFICIAL TELEGRAM TO HIS MEN.

The news of the British and French victories on the Western Front has been specially communicated by telegrams from the Russian Main Headquarters to the troops in the field everywhere. Commanding officers are instructed to read the telegrams at the head of their regiments on parade.—[Photo. by *Illustrations Bureau*.]

The Italian Front: Sniping on a Mountain-Side.

USING AN ALPINE SHEPHERDS' SHELTER FOR CONCEALMENT: A SNIPER'S WELL-CHOSEN POST.

An Italian sniper posted in a selected coign of vantage high up on a mountain side in the Alps is seen in the illustration. The place is one of the Alpine shepherds' faggot and brushwood shelters, such as are met with everywhere in the Higher Alps in localities whither the sheep and cattle herdsmen drive their charges for the animal summer pasturage. Generally, as here, such shelters are on the edge of some thicket, near a hollow where a mountain spring trickles out, affording a ready water supply, the place also providing grateful shade from the heat of the noonday sun. There is always a good view obtainable over where the animals are grazing below in the open. Nothing seems suspicious about such shelters at first glance, as Italian snipers know.—(Photo. by L.N.A.)

everything passed off most agreeably. And there was a great surprise in store for Wild. When the guests rose to retire, Mortier bade the French officers leave their prisoner with him ; and, when they had gone, Wild was thunderstruck to find himself addressed by the Marshal in excellent colloquial English.

" Well, and where do you come from ? " said Mortier.

" From beyond Rochdale, in Lancashire," said the Lieutenant.

He could not have made a happier opening. Mortier smiled, and, to the prisoner's further amazement, continued—

" Well, and how 's Dick Crompton ? "

Mortier was amused to learn that the Lancashire worthy in question was at that moment town-major of Lisbon, and the conversation flowed into an easy channel of Rochdale local gossip, in which the Marshal showed himself extraordinarily well posted.

Wild went back to prison, where he remained for some time ; but he was at last enabled to escape through the favour and connivance of the jailer's daughter. At first he wandered about the country, but at length he fell in with some *contrabandista*, and with their aid regained the British headquarters. He got his captaincy and retired on half-pay, to marry a very beautiful girl

THE INFURIATED VANDALISM OF THE BAFFLED GERMANS AT VERDUN : JOAN OF ARC'S CHAPEL AMID THE CATHEDRAL RUINS.

Since the end of June, the Germans, apparently out of sheer savagery at finding themselves baffled by the heroic defenders of Verdun, have been firing day after day deliberately at the ancient Cathedral, which is now a heap of ruins. The last part to remain fairly intact amidst the surrounding destruction was the Chapel of Joan of Arc.

French Official Photograph.

and take up the not very distinguished profession of publican in Manchester. There he fell on evil days, and died in a debtors' prison.

In his native county he found not a few persons who were able to explain Marshal Mortier's interest in him and his curious know-

VERDUN'S MEMENTO OF THE FRANCO - GERMAN WAR OF 1870 : THE MONUMENT ERECTED IN MEMORY OF THOSE WHO FELL IN THE SIEGE.

The monument (as in existence on July 8) is in the Garden of the Bishop of Verdun's residence, near the Cathedral. The cross stands on shells of the pattern used during the siege in 1870 when Verdun held out for months after Sedan and only surrendered after Metz had fallen, when the last hope of relief had gone, and the garrison was at the last gasp.—[*French Official Photograph.*]

ledge of Lancashire and its people. The Marshal was the son of a Lyons merchant, and had been sent by him to a Manchester academy, and later was attached to various business houses in the city to obtain insight into English methods. It has been said that he served as a clerk in the firm of Sylvester, but his position was always that of a pupil without salary. He made himself very much at home in Lancashire, and had a large circle of acquaintances, among whom was that Captain Crompton whose name he sprung at random upon Wild, scarcely hoping, perhaps, to get an immediate and particular answer, or to learn that Crompton too was, comparatively speaking, so near at hand. When the Peninsular War began, Mortier left Manchester and joined the French Army, where his talents very soon brought him the coveted baton.

Mortier's meeting with the Lieutenant of the 29th (now the Worcestershire) Regiment is one of those coincidences which a careful novelist would hardly dare to invent. But, fortunately, it does not fall within the province of fiction.

On the French Front: An "Inspection" and Spoils.

YOUNG FRANCE, AND THE FRUITS OF FRENCH HEROISM: A BOY'S CURIOSITY; AND CAPTURED GUNS.

The upper photograph shows a kindly French soldier lifting up a little French boy for a peep down the barrel of a "great big gun," while another eager youngster stands by awaiting his turn. To all boys a gun is a thing of wonder and romance, and now young France is, of course, more deeply interested than ever in the big guns which, in the hands of their brave elders, are delivering "la patrie" from the invader. In the lower photograph are seen some German guns captured in recent French victories on the Somme. Many such trophies have already been placed on view at the Invalides in Paris. More recently, it may be recalled, the French have also won successes at Verdun, taking many prisoners.—[Photos. by Wyndham and C.N.]

French Spoil from the Somme Battles.

THREE PATTERNS OF GERMAN HAND-GRENADES: "CRAPAUDS"; "PIGEONS"; AND ORDINARIES.

Three distinct patterns of German hand-grenades are shown on this page. They are part of the immense quantity of war matériel captured by the French during the series of battles on the Somme with which our Allies opened the Great Offensive on the Western Front. In the first illustration are seen hand-grenades of a type called, from their peculiar shape, "crapauds," or toads; somewhat like flat flasks, studded round the edge with detonating knobs. Another type called "pigeons" by the French, with torpedo-propeller-shaped tails to ensure the bomb coming down head-first on to its detonating-stud, are shown in the second illustration. The third shows captured boxes of ordinary German hand-bombs fitted with club-handles.—[French Official Photographs.]

Guns in the Great Offensive: A British Giant.

ONE OF THE BIG PIECES OUR ARTILLERY ARE USING: MOVING UP INTO POSITION.

A squad of men are seen here, at a place "somewhere" on the Western Front, where the British Offensive is being pressed hard, hauling one of our bigger guns to its firing-point by main force. The ponderous gun-carriage is on rails. Man-power could hardly stir it were it on ordinary ground. The giant weapon may be taken as a sample of the heavier guns which we are using success-

fully to destroy and "smother" the tremendously strong German fortified positions all along the front of the British advance. Before the war such monster pieces were only to be seen on board battle-ships, as turret guns, or specially mounted at certain of our principal fortresses abroad such as Gibraltar and Malta. To-day they are important features of the Great Push.

A Word from the Western Fro

A MESSAGE FROM MARS — PICARDY VERSION : NEW GIANT BRITISH " TH

There are dumps and dumps at the front—both commissariat dumps and ordnance department or artillery dumps—places by t
roadside, as near to the actual firing front as it is advisable to go, where transport and munition vehicles deposit their loa
Some gigantic projectiles in daily use by our gunners are shown at an artillery dump ; the enormous dimensions of t

"To Willie with Compliments."

BOLTS OF VICTORY"; AND A READY METHOD OF JUDGING THEIR SIZE.

projectiles being readily realisable by a comparison with the size of the sergeant seen lying down beside the nearest shell. It bears a message of the sort gunners often chalk on their shells. The German make use of similar dumps in rear of their lines, one of which, as a recent official communiqué recorded, was blown up by bombs dropped by our airmen.

French Shell-Making for the Allied Offensive.

INSIDE A MUNITION-FACTORY: LARGE-CALIBRE HIGH-EXPLOSIVE SHELLS IN THE MAKING.

The upper illustration shows a shell for a French large-calibre gun, intended to take a bursting charge of high-explosive, having the interior surface of the metal turned and polished smooth. The process is one of vital importance. Unless the interior of the shell has an absolutely smooth surface there is risk of premature bursting from friction owing to the sensitive nature of the explosive composition, either during the transport of the shell to the front, or on being fired while in flight, possibly just after leaving the gun's muzzle, when the consequences could hardly fail to be disastrous to the men at the gun. A shell turned so as to fit to the thousandth fraction of an inch the bore of its gun is seen on the lathe in the second photograph.—[*French Official Photographs.*]

French Gun-Making for the Allied Offensive.

IN A MUNITION-FACTORY: A GUN READY; AND A TUBE-INGOT UNDERGOING A FURNACE PROCESS.

In the upper Illustration one of the heavy guns in process of construction for the French Army is seen while still at the works of its makers, at a French munition-factory engaged on gun-foundry work. Similar French guns are already in action at the Front. The one seen here is a 340-mm. (or 13'4-inch) weapon, weighing 66 tons and 50 feet long. It fires a high-explosive shell, 1300 odd lb. in weight. In the lower Illustration is seen a solid, forged ingot of steel, weighing upwards of six tons, which is intended to form the inner tube of a large-calibre French gun. It is shown being super-heated in a furnace in one of the foundry shops, held in place meanwhile by an enormous chain.—[French Official Photograph.]

Avenues of British Shells "Somewhere" at the Front.

"MADE IN ENGLAND": SOME OF THE FORMIDABLE PROJECTILES OUR GUNNERS ARE USING.

It is more than highly probable that some time before the illustrations on this page meet the eyes of any of our readers, the British munition-factory-made big shells seen here will have been sent on their errand to blow up German trenches in the "Great Push." They were photographed at a "place"—as lawyers say, and a few years ago argued over in the Law Courts for weeks on end—that is "somewhere" very near the front, where Sir Douglas Haig is attacking. The sight of them, at any rate, ought to encourage our munition workers who have so patriotically given up, first their Whitsuntide and now their August Bank Holidays. Yet the insatiable gunners everywhere want more and ever yet more—and will get them!—[Official Press Bureau Photograph.]

The Western Front Offensive: French Commanders.

MEN OF THE HOUR: THE LEADER ON THE SOMME AND A VETERAN COMRADE.

In the motor-car are seen seated together two French Generals associated with the operations of the Great Offensive in Picardy. One, the officer in field-blue uniform, second from the right, with the open map on his knees, is the man who counts at the front in that quarter, the officer in charge of the attack on the Somme, General Fayolle. The other (on the right), the white-haired, elderly officer in general's everyday uniform, is General Balfourier.. He succeeded the famous General Foch in the command of the 20th. Army Corps, which General Balfourier led victoriously in earlier battles of the first year of the war, and in Champagne last year. He is now leading the 20th Corps in fresh successes; while every day proves more and more the capabilities of General Fayolle.

THINGS DONE: IX.—THE ROYAL FLYING CORPS.

THE Royal Flying Corps is the last word in war, but it has not finished all that it has to say yet. The R.F.C. is still finding new things to do, and not only does it rise to every occasion, but it sometimes drops to them. A very short yesterday ago its main concern in life was scouting, ranging for the guns, and an occasional flutter in bombs. To-day it is turning itself into a species of flying infantry, and is charging into battle with the rest of the troops, to the damage to German feelings, with machine-gun fire at close quarters.

From the moment that men began to fly it was apparent that the R.F.C. would have to come into existence. The vision of the bird is so much more august than the vision of the earth-walker, and so much more useful. The R.F.C., then, grew up out of that portion of the Army connected with the faculty of seeing as much as possible of what the enemy did not want seen— that is, it grew up out of the old balloon section of the Royal Engineers. It came into being for observation purposes, then—and, indeed, practically all its functions and feats have developed out of this faculty.

The enormous range and the comparative immunity of the aeroplane gave war its new science. The aviator who passes many miles back

PREPARING SHOULD THE CALL COME FOR HIM TO JOIN HIS ROYAL BROTHERS: PRINCE HENRY IN THE ETON O.T.C.

Prince Henry, the King's third son, who is at Eton, is a member of the Eton College branch of the Officers' Training Corps.—[Photo. by Vandyk.]

over the enemy's lines can bring information of dispositions, of points of concentration and lines of route, of depôts of reserve, positions of guns and ammunition parks, and can gauge with his trained eye the enemy's means and strengths in resistance as well as his developments for attack. He can do this with such accuracy that Commanders-in-Chief know in this war things the Commanders-in-Chief never really knew before. The present Commander can be certain where the old Commander only guessed. In this way the aeroplane has robbed war of much of its romantical element of surprise; in this way it is the aeroplane which has bound down war with entanglements and trenches. Both sides can know what is going on on the enemy's side. Both sides take rigid precautions.

The aviator — whom you will not call an "airman," it is not done—has for his first task that of observation. He learns, with a range and vision not possible to cavalry or cyclist or automobile scouts, all the facts possible about the enemy. The science of doing this well is still developing. Not merely does the observer's novel bird's-eye view call for special method of examination and appreciation of the top of things rather than their profiles, but it calls for special

[Continued overleaf.

A CELEBRATED JOCKEY WOUNDED IN ACTION, AND NOW IN ENGLAND FROM THE FRONT: STANLEY WOOTTON AT WINDSOR.

In the photograph are seen, resting during the heat of an afternoon in the paddock, Lt. Stanley Wootton, who has been wounded recently and has received the Military Cross ; Dr. Rosenthal ; and Frank Wootton.—[Photo. by S. and G.]

The Allied Attack in the West: French Aeroplanes.

ESCADRILLE, OR AIR-SQUADRON, FIGHTING : AEROPLANES PHOTOGRAPHED FROM CONSORTS IN MID-AIR.

These illustrations show French aeroplanes acting in "escadrille," or squadron formation—in each case one machine is seen in flight as photographed from one of its consorts. The escadrille system of air-fighting is one that the Allies largely favour, and its tactical employment has met with universal success. In practically every case where our own and the French airmen, so acting together, have encountered the enemy, the outcome has been in the highest degree encouraging. Both for air-battle purposes over the enemy's lines and for bomb-dropping expeditions to raid German camps and fortified positions and munition-factories, the escadrille attack method has proved its efficacy. Below the aeroplanes are seen long, whitish-grey streaks—trench lines.—[Photos. by Alfieri.]

rapidity in reconnaissance, special coolness, and special judgment and courage in choosing the just heights of flight for each scouting effort. That is, the observer in an aeroplane must be able to note everything on the earth's surface, in spite of the most cunning concealment, record what he has noted on the just place of the map before him with a method which will make it recognisable, or signal it back to the gunners in a way to make their fire infallible — and he must do all these things swiftly, while the pilot drives the machine at a great pace, and frequently in an erratic manner, to avoid the eager attention of Archibald, the anti-aircraft gun. Added to this skill in seeing and recording vital things, the R.F.C. observer must be able to take photographs of enemy positions at the right time and at the right places to give the best negatives.

Arising out of this habit of finding out facts, there arises the brisk business of dealing with those who would check the growth of knowledge. Here the science of aviation has developed on fighting lines, and will probably develop much further. Fighting passed from the slower observation planes when it was found that the R.F.C. had a pretty skill in fighting. The fast Fokker monoplanes were brought in, to make up in speed what the Germans lacked in native fibre. In our turn, fighting planes were linked to the observation planes to meet the Fokker, so that now the steadier reconnaissance machines go to their work with an escort of fighting planes to meet and

destroy the fighting destroyers. The German aviator, who sneered at and rigorously avoided such "gallery-play" as looping-the-loop, has more than once found that a British (or French) aviator whom he considered at his mercy has looped the loop, secured a position to strike, and has struck. In the same way, too, the method of fighting has developed to the uneasiness of observation balloons. At one time "kite-balloons" had a sporting chance of being dragged to ground safely when an aeroplane went for them. The aviator had only bombs wherewith to shatter them, and to bomb a balloon is not easy. Now the aviator just burns a balloon with a shot from an incendiary pistol.

In the realms of active aggression the R.F.C. is developing healthily and swiftly also. It can hit with its own power. It can bomb the depôts that feed and maintain the enemy's line on a war footing; it bombs and breaks the railways over which troops must pass to the front; it destroys and scatters troops and gun trains and commissariat columns using the roads; it spends many industrious hours this way in disturbing and irritating the delicate system of communications and supply that mean everything to an efficient defence. And it does this in a fashion that the Germans do not attempt. For the R.F.C. makes its bombing raids with large numbers of machines, acting in concert in a way the Germans have not yet found themselves able to act.

W. DOUGLAS NEWTON.

THE NEW CHIEF SECRETARY FOR IRELAND: THE RIGHT HON. H. E. DUKE, P.C., K.C., M.P. Mr. Henry Edward Duke was born in 1855, and called to the Bar in 1885. He sat in Parliament for Plymouth from 1900 to 1906, and represented Exeter since 1910. He is Chairman of the Royal Commission on Defence of the Realm losses. — [Photo. by Vandyk.]

PERMANENT UNDER-SECRETARY FOR IRELAND PRO. TEM.: SIR ROBERT CHALMERS, K.C.B. Sir Robert Chalmers was appointed Governor of Ceylon in 1913. He took over the duties of Permanent Under-Secretary for Ireland during the Dublin rising, and will continue in that post for the present.
Photo. by Elliott and Fry.

THE BISHOP OF LONDON'S RECENT VISIT TO THE GRAND FLEET: THE BISHOP AND SIR JOHN JELLICOE ON THE QUARTER-DECK OF THE FLAG-SHIP. On July 23 the Bishop held a special Confirmation Service on board the Grand Fleet flag-ship. — [Photo. by Alfieri.]

Work of the Splendid Russian Force in France.

IN STEEL HELMETS : RUSSIAN TROOPS IN FRANCE TRENCH-DIGGING.

The upper photograph shows a trench-digging party of the Russian force in France, with picks and shovels over their shoulders, on the march to their quarters. In the lower photograph some of them are seen at work on their trench-digging operations. The fine physique and soldierly bearing of the men are very evident from these illustrations. It will be noted that they are wearing steel helmets similar to those adopted in the French Army. They wear the same uniforms as the French troops, except for the little blouse that is associated with the Moujik costume. Some other photographs of the magnificent Russian brigade, which is now actively engaged on the French front, are given on the two succeeding pages.—[Official Photographs issued by the French War Office.]

In the Russian Trenches on the French Front.

WITH THE RUSSIAN BRIGADE IN FRANCE : A FIRST-LINE TRENCH ; AND A GENERAL INSPECTING.

In the upper photograph is seen part of a trench occupied by Russian troops in France. The lower one shows the Russian General making a tour of inspection. The delegates of the Russian Duma who recently visited Britain, France, and Italy reported : " With feelings of the liveliest joy we visited in France the camp of our Russian warrior brethren at ———, where our Russian officers and men are preparing soon to take a share in the common fighting cause. . . . We know that their numbers will grow ; we know with what fraternal feelings France and their French comrades regard them, and with feelings of pride we saw these glorious, confident young Russian troops in our kindred France."—[Official Photographs issued by the French War Office.]

Evidence of a Russian Success in France.

RUSSIAN KINDNESS TO PRISONERS: A WOUNDED GERMAN HELPED BY TWO RUSSIAN SOLDIERS.

As mentioned in our last issue, the fact that the Russian troops in France had been in action, and received their baptism of fire on French soil, was reported in a Reuter message of July 16. It was added that they "brought back a number of German prisoners, who seemed dazed at finding themselves in the hands of the Tsar's soldiers in France." Later, an official French communiqué, issued on July 28, stated : "In Champagne, in the district of Aubérive, a reconnaissance carried out by Russian troops penetrated into the enemy's trench, which was cleared with grenades. The Russians brought back some prisoners." Our photograph shows a typical instance of the kindness with which the Russian soldiers treat a captured foe, especially when he is wounded.—[Photo. by C.N.]

Campaigning in East Africa: E.A.M.R. and K.A.R.

WHERE BRITAIN HAS "THE VERY BEST COLOURED TROOPS IN THE WORLD": EAST AFRICAN SCENES.

The upper photograph shows, in the words of the correspondent who sends it, "the exterior of the fort in the German town of Aruscha, to which the railway does not run, in spite of what the maps in the papers show. E.A.M.R. (East African Mounted Rifles) have just ridden in and off-saddled on the village green." In the lower photograph are seen some native troops, of the King's African Rifles, with a British officer (in the centre foreground), on the march. In the House of Commons a few days ago, Lieut.-Commr. Wedgwood, who had just returned from that country, said: "We raised in East Africa perhaps the very best coloured troops in the world." He claimed that we could raise 2½ millions there, and strongly urged more extensive use of African troops.

The British "Push": Road-Work and Artillery Aiming.

WHILE THE INFANTRY ADVANCE: ROAD-MENDING; AND DIRECTING ARTILLERY BY WIRELESS.

The upper of these two photographs, both of which were taken during the great British advance on the Western Front, shows some big motor-lorries unloading stones for making up the roads as our troops advance—a very important and necessary task as the roads are frequently torn up by shells. In the lower photograph a British artillery officer, speaking through a megaphone, is seen giving his battery the order to "Open Fire!" after receiving information regarding a target by wireless from some of our spotting aircraft. By his side is seated a member of the Royal Flying Corps. Aerial observation for the artillery is done by scouting aeroplanes, and by kite-balloons, which keep permanent watch.—[Official Photographs issued by the Press Bureau.]

WOMEN AND THE WAR.

The nursery lisps out in all they utter;
Besides, they always smell of bread-and-butter.
—*Byron.*

Like a well-conducted person,
Went on cutting bread-and-butter.—*Thackeray.*

THIS is no time for the bread-and-butter miss. Among all the old Victorian ideas, good and bad, that the war has demolished, none has gone with a greater crash than the notion that a woman, if she is not to be " unsexed," must stick to a certain routine of duties, and, above all, be indoors (preferably in bed) at an orthodox hour. What can people still not more than middle-aged think of the revolution in woman's life that the last twenty months or so has brought about? Social values have had to be violently readjusted. Mrs. Grundy is dead and buried under a tomb mountains high. The occupations still considered " not proper for girls "— other than those that call for exceptional physical strength—are very few in number. The woman's army daily extends its activities in some new direction; there is no demand that its members are not ready and willing to meet. It is said that there is a woman at the front who spends her working hours nailing down soldiers' coffins. Could there be a more striking instance of women's determination to stifle all personal feeling and inclination at the call of national necessity?

Two years ago, if anyone had suggested that women should replace the Army cooks in a military camp, they would have been written down as imbecile or worse. Even the most revolutionary would have dismissed the idea as unthinkable. To-day the phenomenon is looked upon not only as commonplace, but as absolutely the right and natural thing. Army cooks have been obliged in increasing numbers to relinquish the ladle for the bayonet, and exchange the safety of

WOMEN AND THE WAR: THE GIRL MILLER.
The war is steadily stamping out the old fallacy of the weakness of women, whether physical or intellectual, and is opening up for them channels of work unthought of in pre-war days. Our photograph shows some girls in a Yorkshire mill in their neat white working garb, filling sacks with flour.—[*Photo. by C.N.*]

the cook-house for the uncertainties of life at the front, and their place is being taken by members of the Martha battalion of the Women's Army. There are hundreds of them engaged in the work of attending to the " stomach " on which the Army marches, which is just as important now as it was in Napoleon's time.

Not far from London there is a military camp inhabited by 4000 convalescent soldiers. Their digestive welfare is entirely in the hands of women, whose natural aptitude for " looking after " something finds an outlet in devising all sorts of new and savoury ways of cooking the prosaic rations prescribed by the Government authorities. Perhaps the male cook is wanting in imagination; maybe a man can never enter heart and soul into what is supposed to be an essentially womanly task; but, anyhow, the men are quick to appreciate the imaginative sympathy that prompts the preparation of unaccustomed puddings and savoury dishes from the " trimmings " purchased with the few pence per man allowed over and above the more solid part of the " ration." " Them girls seem to know what a feller likes " is about as far as the verbal expression of their gratitude for these extra attentions goes; and with it the girls are more than content.

The woman Army cook, like the soldier, lives under military discipline. She has her uniform— a Norfolk coat and skirt of brown frieze, flannel shirt and tie, brown shoes and felt hat, with a khaki overall and cap for working hours. She has to get up early and work hard all day, for cooking, when the number of meals to be prepared runs into thousands, is by no means a light recreation, but arduous work of a kind that is not to be lightly

[Continued overleaf.]

A "Flour" Girl—New Style.

WOMEN'S WORK IN WAR-TIME: THE "MILLER'S DAUGHTER" OF TO-DAY.

Quite as remarkable as it is valuable is the readiness with which the woman worker of these war-days has adapted herself to callings in many cases quite opposed to her previous experience. Picturesque, too, is the subject of our photograph, a young worker in a Yorkshire flour-mill, clad in a manner suggesting Rosalind, and placing a sack of flour in its place, to be hauled up in due course. We cannot see in the picture the "dark round of the dripping wheel," but the "meal-sacks on the whiten'd floor", are there, and the well-poised figure of the worker offers a pleasant illustration of one of the unconventional products of the war in the world of labour. Scarcely a day passes without bringing new proofs of feminine versatility and eagerness to take its share of the new duties.—[Photo, C.N.]

undertaken. The Military Cooking section of the Women's Legion, which provides the Army cook— new pattern—have neither the leisure nor the desire to deal with any but serious workers. After the applicant has served a probationary period of a month, she signs an agreement to serve for a year or the duration of the war, whichever is less.

The Army kitchen is not the only stronghold to capitulate to all-conquering woman. The mess-room, where her presence in peace time was only tolerated on an occasional "Ladies' Night," has had to yield to the necessities of war, and the mess-waitress has been added to the already long list of war-workers. There are any number of messes all over the country where young women are learning to acquire the correct degree of dignity and impassiveness necessary for the perfect waitress. In clubs, where women have been installed as attendants for some time, Fritz's war-time substitute has proved such a success that her permanent retention is declared to be strongly probable.

Perhaps the most striking example of departure from the fetters of red tape during this war has

authorities at home. They were declined. France and Belgium, however, saw things in a different light. A month after war was declared, a women's hospital unit was working in Belgium, and the Women's Hospital Corps had established itself, its

ENGAGED IN RESEARCH : FRENCH RED CROSS WORKERS.

The war has proved, both here and on the Continent, how able, as well as devoted, are the nurses of all countries. Our photographs show French Red Cross workers deeply engaged in research work for the benefit of "cases."—[French Official Photograph.]

offer of help having been accepted by the French Government, at Claridge's Hotel in Paris. The papers gave it columns of praise, and the medical people at home began to think they had been mistaken, and, not long after, the Corps was working under their auspices. Their ideas have enlarged a good deal since those early days. There is now a military hospital in Endell Street with 500 beds, and the whole of the medical and administrative staff are women. There are other military hospitals, too, to which medical women have been appointed in different capacities, where they are graded according to military rank, but only for purposes of pay.

Now a further interesting development has taken place. The War Office, for the first time on record, has invited women to apply for appointments in regular Army hospitals. A large number of them have already been appointed. The work of medical women has not been confined to military institutions. It covers a wide field of activity. Their efforts have been loyally supported by people of the most widely divergent views, but it seems only fair to add that the Women's Hospital Corps was in the first instance the work of Suffragists.   CLAUDINE CLEVE.

A PRIVATE SECRETARY TO MR. LLOYD GEORGE : MISS F. L. STEVENSON.

Among the unconventional innovations which the Right Hon. David Lloyd George has instituted is the encouragement of the woman worker, upon a scale hitherto unparalleled. Mr. Lloyd George, knowing how ably and loyally the Empire is being served by women, has taken Miss F. L. Stevenson, of whose capability and zeal he has been able to judge while she was serving under him when he was Minister of Munitions, to act as one of his principal private secretaries at the War Office—a compliment to women which they will be slow to forget.—[Photo. by L.N.A.]

been given, curiously enough, by the War Office. When the war was yet young, British medical women offered their services to the military

"Iron Rations" for the Enemy.

ONE REASON WHY OUR ADVANCE CONTINUES UNCHECKED: BIG SHELLS FOR THE BIG GUNS.

The British offensive in Northern France owes its success largely to the big shells, as seen above, with which our munition-workers are keeping our artillerymen well supplied. Where they fall the German trenches cease to exist, save as flattened hollows and tumbled mounds of earth. The massive bulk of the projectiles is apparent by comparing the shell in the upper illustration with the men slinging it for loading. Its ponderous weight may be surmised from the stout tackling needed to support the shell. The legend, "Iron Ration," chalked on the shell in the second illustration, is an appropriate specimen of battlefield wit in the circumstances.— [*Official Photographs issued by the Press Bureau. Crown copyright reserved.*]

The Machine-Gun as an Arm for Cavalry.

CAVALRY UNDER NEW CONDITIONS : A LEWIS GUN-TEAM GOING INTO ACTION IN OUR ADVANCE.

These photographs, taken during the British advance in the West, illustrate some of the activities of our cavalry. They show a Lewis gun-team, consisting of eight mounted men and a horse carrying the gun, going into action recently. Our cavalry have latterly had some chances of operating in their own traditional manner. It will be remembered that a short time ago some detachments of the Dragoon Guards and the Deccan Horse were able to ride forward in open country, near Delville Wood, when they charged a body of German infantry in a cornfield. It was the first cavalry action in the old style on the Western Front since October 1914, and seemed to promise a change from trench-warfare to open fighting.—[Official Photographs issued by the Press Bureau.]

An Effective Reply to the German Machine-Guns.

BATTLE-FRONT EPISODES: INDIANS WITH A HOTCHKISS AUTOMATIC RIFLE; AN INDIAN BARBER.

The enemy's former preponderance in machine-guns is being met by our increasing employment of automatic rifles that can fire upwards of three hundred shots a minute. Automatic rifles are also more readily portable than machine-guns. One man can race forward with an automatic rifle for a considerable distance, where it takes three men to get over the ground with a machine-gun and its apparatus. The machine-gun has then to be put together again; the automatic rifle is ready. An Indian soldier with ammunition-supply attendants is seen in action in the upper illustration. A scene behind the lines is shown in the lower illustration: one of the Indian regimental barbers at work.—[*Official Photographs. Crown copyright reserved.*]

"Sarch 'is Pockets!" Prisoners in British Hands.

THE FIRST STEP WITH GERMAN PRISONERS: SEARCHING MEN CAPTURED DURING THE ADVANCE.

The upper photograph shows some British N.C.O.s searching German prisoners, and in the lower one they are making sure that the captured men have nothing dangerous concealed in their caps. There is a story told in Cornwall of the old wrecking days, that a stranger once inquired: "What do you do when you find a person apparently drowned?" and the answer was, "Sarch 'is pockets."

The object of searching prisoners is only to see that they have no arms or explosives concealed about them, and not to deprive them of personal effects. Their gratitude at being allowed to keep souvenirs and belongings was mentioned recently. The number captured is increasing. An official despatch of the 6th mentioned several hundred prisoners.—[Official Photos, issued by Press Bureau.]

The Illustrated War News

FRENCH CIVILIANS BEING HARDENED INTO SOLDIERS : GYMNASTICS AT A TRAINING SCHOOL, VINCENNES.

Official Photograph issued by the French War Office.

THE GREAT WAR.

By W. DOUGLAS NEWTON.

THE week is certainly Italy's. The fall of Gorizia after a few days of brilliantly planned and handled fighting is a splendid achievement under any circumstances. Under the present circumstances it is even more notable. It is the outward and dramatic sign that Italy is, with the other Allies, one in plan and power; and that Italy, in spite of the extreme difficulties of her campaign, in spite of a disturbing circumstance like the Austrian offensive in the Tyrol, has yet the tenacity, elasticity, and striking force to hold to the determined scheme of concentric offensive, even as France, Russia, Britain, and Serbia are ready to hold to it.

We can be exceedingly glad with the triumphing Italians because we have always recognised the trials of the task that was before them. Our Southern Ally has had, from the outset, perhaps the most difficult of all campaigns to face. The Austrians, at every point, have had the best of defence systems, for the frontier was drawn by Austria to take in a series of almost impregnable positions. Italy has not merely been fighting uphill, but up mountains, from the moment she entered the war; and it was only the swift ability of our Ally's Command in the first days that enabled them to neutralise their adverse circumstances by a rapid jump-off into Austrian territory. The Gorizia position is one of the difficulties in point. Gorizia itself is in the valley, and it might have been entered by the Italians at any time during the last few months. Gorizia, however, is surrounded by an amphitheatre of mountain positions that must be turned before the town could be entered with any degree of security and finality. During the months of the war the Italians have been working a dogged way forward to that point from which the mountain positions could be effectually turned.

The patient, wearying, and heroic months bore good fruit; but there came a time when it seemed that all the work would be undone at one bitter stroke. This was the moment when the Austrians began to thrust with such keenness from the Trentino down through the frontier passes and out towards the Venetian Plain. The ideal of this offensive was undoubtedly to spoil the labours on the Isonzo for ever. The assault was dangerous. It threatened to cut right across the communications of Italy's north-eastern army. If it had done so, Gorizia would not have fallen. We can see, both by the power of this threat and the swiftness and certainty with which it was checked, what high and real ability there is in the Italian Command. We can see this even more in the way the Italian forces have recovered and reorganised after that assault, and have, with unexpected rapidity, returned to the offensive and carried the defences of the Isonzo in their rebound. It is possible that Austria could not realise that such power remained after the heavy battles in the Tyrol. If so, the Higher Command of the Central Powers has been again at fault, as they were at fault about Russia, France after Verdun, and the British Army all the time.

The Italian victory was finely and compactly planned. The strength of the fighting developed on Aug. 8, when the advance forces, notably the cyclists of the Bersaglieri, began to push forward in the Monfalcone area, over-running the enemy works on Hills 85 and 121, and capturing some 3600 prisoners. On the 9th the assault had worked up admirably on both wings, and the key positions on Monte Sabotino (to the north) and Monte St. Michele (to the south) were carried, the bridge-heads of Gorizia thus falling into Italian hands. From that point our Ally advanced with great sureness, took the town itself, with its ammunition depots, guns, and some prisoners, and pressed well east of the town until they had reached and were fighting on a line Rosenthal-Vertoiba. The cavalry came into action and did some dashing work, and the whole impression of the fighting is that the Austrians were woefully shaken and disordered after their defeat. Over 12,000 prisoners fell to the Italians in the capture

WITH THE SALONIKA ARMY: GAS-HELMETED SOLDIERS IN THE TRENCHES.

Official Photograph.

of the town, and the fall of so important a centre does not make the position of the Trieste defences at all healthy. One of the very few avenues of supply has gone. Stimulated by their victory, the Italians are bound to go on, also adding their invaluable co-operation to the growing embarrassment of the Central Powers, especially to Austria,

NOT A BIG GUN! A NEW SEAPLANE PACKED FOR TRANSPORT IN ENGLAND.
Photograph by Topical.

the weaker partner of the Central Powers. And indeed there are many signs of Italy's determination. Already, over the week-end, the attack had pressed to the second line of Austrian defence, Italian arms are hammering in a predominant way at the defences of Tolmino, the whole of the painful Doberdo plateau has come under Italian command, and the capture of Monte San Michele with that of San Martino gives our Ally a strong position on the Carso.

Austria has certainly had a terrible week, for Russia has opened out again and added enormously to her discomfort. Both General Lechitsky and General Sakharoff have been swinging their lines to the peril of the Austrian defence, and have gained ground on von Bothmer's flanks in alarming fashion — to say nothing of their inevitable gains in prisoners. The movement on the southern flank is, at this moment, the most valuable and important. General Lechitsky's troops, who had been held up by the rains, have, in spite of bad conditions, resumed the forward march, and, with that quickness we have learned to expect from the new Russian attack, have swung forward on a big front. They drove the enemy out of the important positions at Tysmienica, smashed past the railway

junction at Chryplin, and reached the River Bystryca at a point almost in the environments of Stanislau. It was expected that the strong defences on the Bystryca would give some trouble, but, in surprising fashion, the Austrians continued their retreat, and the Russians were able to enter Stanislau not merely without fighting, but without finding any damage done to the defences. With Stanislau fallen the advance was not halted, and the Russians set themselves to attack and embarass the enemy by striking at those vital points of communication and retreat, the railway junctions. They are now pressing towards Halicz, and have already secured an important stretch of line and some high ground near Monastergyska. Here the advance indubitably cuts in behind von Bothmer's sturdy defence on the Strypa, and from this wing his position was rapidly becoming precarious. With the Russian advance on the north the Austrian chances of resistance developed on most malignant lines. Sakharoff managed to hammer Bothmer's left flank until he had forced it across the Sereth, and moving towards the Lemberg-Odessa line, bent the Austrian front back woefully, as well as threatened to get across yet another of the avenues of retirement. It was not unexpected, then, that von Bothmer's attack should at last crumble, and that, at this late hour, he should make up his mind to go back

FRENCH MUNITIONS: SHELL-TRAINS ON THE WESTERN FRONT.
French War Office Official Photograph.

in order to escape envelopment. In this condition of mind the Russians gave him all the necessary help, and on Aug. 12 the Austrians began to fall back from the Strypa, our Ally following them across it with such urgency that soon the whole thirty-five mile front, running from a point north-west of Tarnopol to the Dniester was on the move. Village after village was captured, and all the ground which had been so strongly fortified, and which has been held so powerfully since the winter of last year, has been overrun. At the same time, lower down on the map, the Russians have captured the important village of Nadvorna, on the railway, and twenty-two miles south of Stanislau, and are pushing along into enemy territory. The brilliance of the Eastern command is, perhaps, on the eve of its most glorious achievements.

Meanwhile, it is well to point out that both Italy and Russia are receiving co-operative help from the Balkans. The signal for movement seems to have been set at Salonika. The Serbians had already initiated the offensive by turning the Bulgars from their hill positions below the Greek border. Now the Allies, particularly the French, guns have joined in the crescendo of fighting, and the troops have gone in where the guns paved the way. The result was admirable. The Franco-British force advanced, occupied Hill 227, south of Doiran, and the station five miles east of the town, and so made their mark for a starting-off point for anything that is to come after. The movement has not been

AUSTRALIANS ON THE WESTERN FRONT : MACHINE-GUNNERS RETURNING FROM THE TRENCHES.
Official Photograph.

if it is weakened we still hold the threat of cutting up through Serbia, and pushing right up against the most intimate frontiers of our enemies in a linked line that would join with Russia and Italy. This to say nothing of the threat to separate Bulgaria and Turkey from their central partners.

Our troops in the West have continued the fighting of consolidation, and have been widening the ripple of advance round Pozières, as well as fighting south-west of Guillemont. The gains have been regular, and in some cases of really emphatic utility, and we are gradually working our way into positions of command on the hill-tops that will give us an excellent advantage for the next planned push. On their line the French have done magnificently. They have again opened out in a smashing attack north of the Somme, and have, with the force of their blow, driven their way into the enemy third line from Hardecourt to the height of Buscourt by the Somme. They have, in this, captured all the trenches and fortified positions on a front of four miles and to a depth of penetration varying from 600 to 1000 metres. In this attack the village of Maurepas was entered ; the new front is also carried to the southern slope of Hill 109, along the Maurepas-Clery road, and on to the saddle west of Clery village. At Verdun the days are still

AUSTRALIANS ON THE WESTERN FRONT : BRINGING UP A HEAVY GUN.
Official Photograph.

much so far, but it is one that is bound to disturb the enemy, and again, particularly, the Austrian enemy. The enemy front cannot be weakened here, whatever the need of men elsewhere, and the reward of the French. The Germans make no impression in spite of attacks ; on the other hand, the French have scored further advances in the Thiaumont sector.   LONDON: AUG. 14, 1916.

A Memorial to fallen Heroes, at Hampstead.

THE CALVARY IN HAMPSTEAD GARDEN SUBURB : WOUNDED SOLDIERS VIEWING THE MEMORIAL.

The Garden Suburb at Hampstead has sent many residents to the war, and a worthy tribute to the memory of those who have already given their lives for their country has been erected in the central square. Beneath the sacred Figure on the Cross is a stone on which are inscribed the names of the fallen men. Their relatives bring, day by day, tributes of flowers, and among those who reverently visit the spot are groups of wounded soldiers, as seen in our photograph. No doubt the kindly act of the residents of this Suburb will initiate many more tributes of the kind. The originators of the movement deserve the hearty thanks of all relatives and friends of soldiers who have fought and fallen.— [Photo. by Photopress.]

Duke of Connaught: British Prince and Indian Chief.

INSPECTING STONY INDIANS: "CHIEF" THE DUKE OF CONNAUGHT, AT ALBERTA.

Picturesque, unconventional, and impressive, was the investiture, at Alberta, on July 15, of H.R.H. the Duke of Connaught with the insignia and costume of a Chief of the Stony Tribe of Indians. The ceremony took place on the racecourse, in the presence of H.R.H. the Duchess of Connaught and Princess Patricia, who spoke with some of the Indian Chiefs and Braves, their squaws and papooses. Our first photograph shows the scene on the racecourse, and our second the Duke, wearing his "bonnet" as Great Mountain Chief—Teenchaka Eeyaka Oonka—of the Stony Tribe. Chief George McLean and Mr. N. K. Luxton read Addresses, to which the Duke made appreciative replies, the Rev. Dr. John McDougall acting as interpreter.

Canadian Representatives in the Grand Fleet.

ONE WAY IN WHICH THE DOMINION HELPS AT SEA: TWO CANADIAN SUBMARINES.

When the notorious German cargo-carrying submarine, "Deutschland," made her noisily advertised appearance in Baltimore Harbour, U.S.A., it was widely trumpeted among neutrals by the German Press and also by certain hyphenated American newspaper writers in the United States, that the "Deutschland's" voyage across the Atlantic was a record performance in every respect. "Germany," declared one writer, "has performed what the rest of the world declared to be impossible!" As a fact, not only had British submarines been navigated to Australia before the war, but Canadian-built submarines had since the war began crossed the Atlantic to British waters for service with the Grand Fleet. Two Canadian submarines are seen above, lying alongside a dockyard wharf.—[Photo. Topical.]

Direct Hits on German Guns at Pozières.

EVIDENCE OF GOOD SHOOTING BY THE BRITISH ARTILLERY: GERMAN GUNS KNOCKED OUT AT POZIÈRES.

These photographs, taken during the British advance, show the shattering effects of direct hits obtained by our guns on some of the enemy's at Pozières, where there was very heavy fighting before the position was finally carried, on August 4, by Australian and English troops. On the subject of our artillery's work here, Mr. Philip Gibbs writes : "One thing must have disheartened the German troops. . . . The British guns, which should have been worn out, and the British gunners, supposed to be exhausted, went on firing. They went on all yesterday, as on the day before, and more than a month of yesterdays, with their long, steady bombardment. . . . Long-range guns were reaching out to places far behind the German lines."—[Official Photographs issued by the Press Bureau.]

"Anzac" Gunners at Work in Hot Weather.

STRIPPED TO THE WAIST, LIKE NELSON'S SAILORS : AUSTRALIAN GUNNERS IN THE BRITISH ADVANCE.

The Australians are not slow to discard superfluous clothing in hot weather, and in their *déshabillé* they work their guns with magnificent vigour. They did the same in Gallipoli, and doubtless they do the same in Egypt, where they have lately been distinguishing themselves, as on the Western Front, near Pozières. Our photographs, taken during the British offensive in France, show (above) the gunners with a shell ready to insert in the gun ; and (below) ramming it home. A British despatch of August 5 stated : "North of Pozières a local attack last night, in which the Australians and troops of the New Army took part, was completely successful." Further successes were announced on the 9th.—[*Official Photographs issued by the Press Bureau.*]

THE BEGINNINGS OF WAR - MACHINES : HAND FIREARMS.

ALTHOUGH the successful use of hand fire-arms for throwing projectiles dates from some time in the fourteenth century, devices coming within this category were used in very early times for stampeding cattle and horses. These weapons took the form of iron tubes covered with wood, and lashed round with hemp, hides, or similar materials. They were loaded with alternate layers of powder and inflammable balls. The charge was ignited at the muzzle, and the flaming balls went off one after another like those of a " Roman - candle " of to - day.

One of the earliest " hand cannons," throwing a solid ball as a ballistic projectile, is that illustrated in Fig. 1. This device comprises an iron barrel attached to a wooden stock, the latter to be placed on the shoulder

A.—AN EIGHTEENTH - CENTURY FLINT - LOCK :
THE BLUNDERBUSS.

when the weapon was fired. The application of a lighted match to the touch-hole near the breech end of the barrel discharged the piece, which was loaded from the muzzle. Weapons of this type came in about the middle of the fourteenth century. A later type, with a more suitable stock,

charge in a hand-gun by the application of fire to the old type of touch-hole soon led to attempted improvements in firing devices. The first result was the " matchlock," in which a " serpentin " or pivotted " hammer " held in its " nose " an inflammable substance. This, when the trigger was pulled, became ignited by passing contact with a " slow match," kept burning in a suitable position on the barrel. On the hammer continuing its fall, it finally applied the fire to the touch-hole. This was one of the first devices by means of which guns could be fired by merely pulling a trigger. The sixteenth - century arquebus (Fig. 6) is provided with a firing device of this type. The form of ignition was very unreliable, particularly in wet weather. At the Battle of Dunbar, 1650, the firearms of the English were for that reason practically useless.

The remedy for this trouble was found in the employment of flint and steel. The wheel-lock, produced at Nuremberg early in the sixteenth century, was one of the first reasonably successful devices for effecting the discharge of firearms by

B.—AS USED IN NAPOLEON'S ARMY : A FRENCH WATERLOO MUSKET.

appears in Fig. 2. Fig. 3 shows a similar weapon whose stock takes the form of a battle-axe head. In view of the crude nature of the firearm, it was probably a more destructive weapon as battle-axe than as a gun. Fig. 4 shows a " handgonne " adapted for use on horseback. An iron rod in this case takes the place of the stock. A hole through the after-end of this rod accommodated a cord which, passing round the neck of the horseman, supported the breech end of the piece, the muzzle being carried in a fork on the saddle-bow. In the reign of Henry VIII. a pistol-shield (Figs. 5a and 5b) was invented, and a number of such were made by command of the King. It was a weapon of offence and defence, a crude form of breech-loading pistol being attached to a shield, with its muzzle projecting through the shield. The breech was inside the shield, which also afforded cover for the user.

The difficulties attending the ignition of the

C.—AN EARLY NINETEENTH - CENTURY INVENTION :
A SEVEN - BARRELLED FLINT - LOCK CARBINE.

this means. A toothed steel wheel was caused to revolve by means of a spring when the pull of the trigger released its retaining pawl, or catch. Whilst the wheel was rapidly revolving, a piece of flint was brought into contact with its teeth, the resulting stream of sparks falling on the priming powder communicating with the touch-hole. The spring was wound up when the piece was reloaded.

After the " wheel-lock " came the " flint-lock " (shown in Fig. 14). A piece of flint, held in the nose of a spring-operated hammer, struck a slanting blow on the vertical portion of a hinged lid covering a priming-pan containing powder. The blow caused the lid to fly open, and the sparks resulting from it fell on the powder in the priming-pan, which communicated with the charge inside the barrel through a horizontal touch-hole. This form survived to some extent until 1857, when the " Brown Bess," was superseded by the Enfield muzzle-loader fired by a percussion-cap — the first really reliable form of ignition.

[Continued opposite.

The Beginnings of War-Machines: Hand Firearms.

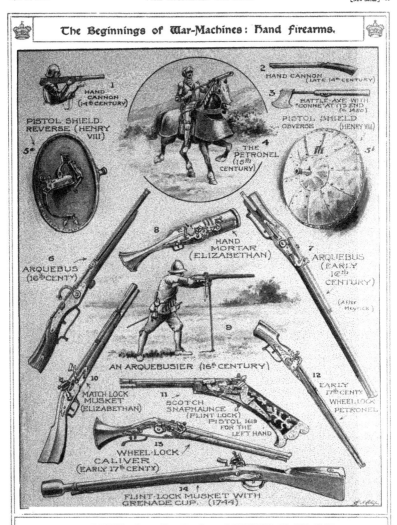

FOUR CENTURIES OF MUSKET EVOLUTION: PREDECESSORS OF THE RIFLE.

Continued.]

It remains to-day, although it is now placed in the cartridge instead of being on an outside nipple at the breech end of the barrel. The performance of early weapons as "arms of precision" was unsatisfactory down to the days of "Brown Bess." That weapon's effective range was supposed to be 200 yards, but no reliance could be placed on its accuracy except at very close quarters. Soldiers usually reserved their fire until they could see the whites of their enemy's eyes. The erratic flight of the ball from the old smooth-bore musket was caused by the escape of gas between the spherical ball and the barrel of the weapon, known as "windage," and this defection remained until the adoption of "rifling" permitted the use of a long and partly cylindrical bullet.

The Tale of Bricks and the Tale of Water.

BRICKS AND WATER: ROAD-REPAIR; AND SOLDIERS' WATER-SUPPLY DURING OUR ADVANCE.

In the upper photograph some of our men are seen collecting bricks in a captured village, for repairing roads. The lower one shows how water for the troops is stored in the trenches, in butts strongly protected by timber and sand-bags. In an interesting account of the "Army behind the Army," Lord Northcliffe wrote recently, after a visit to the British front: " Presently we come to the roads where one sees one of the triumphs of the war—the transport which brings the ammunition for the guns and the food for the men, a transport which has had to meet all kinds of unexpected difficulties. The last is water, for our troops are approaching a part of France which is as chalky and dry as our South Downs."—[Official Photographs issued by the Press Bureau.]

Black Watch Pipers; and a "Flying Pig."

DURING OUR ADVANCE: THE BLACK WATCH ON THE MARCH; AND LOADING A TRENCH-MORTAR.

The upper photograph shows the Black Watch marching back from the trenches headed by their pipers; the lower one, some British soldiers loading a trench-mortar, the shell of which is known at the front as "a flying pig." The pipers of the Scottish regiments have shown their accustomed heroism in this war. Describing an attack by Highlanders at Longueval recently, Mr. Philip Gibbs wrote: "They were led forward by their pipers, who went with them . . . . into the thick of the battle. It was to the tune of 'The Campbells are Coming' that one regiment went forward. . . . Then the pipes screamed out the 'Charge,' the most awful music to be heard by men who have the Highlanders against them."—[Official Photographs issued by the Press Bureau.]

ROMANCES OF THE REGIMENTS: X.—THE 27TH BENGAL INFANTRY.

THE GOD "NIKALSAIN."

A LEGENDARY glory has gathered about the name of more than one British soldier in India, but to John Nicholson, of the 27th (and later of the 41st) Bengal Infantry, divine honour have been paid, for the natives he impressed by his prowess in the field and by his iron rule as an administrator came at length to regard him as a god. He went out to India to join the Army when he was only seventeen, and two years later, in 1841, he played a memorable part in the defence of Ghazni, Afghanistan, thus laying the foundation of that career which, cut short at thirty-four, placed him in the foremost rank of our Anglo-Indian heroes.

After his arrival in India young Nicholson set himself to study the native languages, but these peaceful pursuits were interrupted by orders for his regiment to form part of a force that was to relieve the 16th at Ghazni, which lies eighty-five miles south-west of Kabul. The fortress was weakly held, and had already been more than seriously threatened by the Afghans, who were in a most unsettled state. Things rapidly went from bad to worse, and in bitter December weather the enemy reappeared in force before the walls of Ghazni, and, pouring in through a breach dug for them by their friends inside the town, drove the garrison into the citadel. Then began a period of great misery. Food was scarce, the hours of duty interminable, and the defenders were constantly sniped by the Afghan

FALLEN FOR THE EMPIRE IN GERMAN EAST AFRICA: A MEMORIAL STONE ERECTED BY COMRADES.

This memorial stone has been erected in memory of the men of one of our mounted corps serving in East Africa, who fell in action at Longido in November 1914. Comrades of the same squadron provided it, and set it up at the foot of the German position.

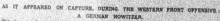

AS IT APPEARED ON CAPTURE, DURING THE WESTERN FRONT OFFENSIVE: A GERMAN HOWITZER.

This is one of the German heavy guns referred to in the despatches as pieces there had not been time to bring in as yet.—[Official Press Bureau Photograph.]

marksmen, whose long jezails outranged the smooth bores of the Sepoys. In January the British were practically starved out, and, two months later, were fain to make terms. They were to march out with the honours of war, and occupy new quarters in the city. On March 6 they evacuated the citadel, with colours flying, under promise of a safe conduct to Peshawar when the snows in the passes should have melted.

But there was no faith in the Afghan of that time. Next day the British force was set upon by a crowd of fanatical natives, who stormed the houses where the English officers and their native troops had found shelter. For two days Nicholson and Lieutenant Crawford, with two companies of Sepoys, fought for their lives in a burning building, defending room by room as the flames forced them to retire. They were without food and water, and were worn out, but they contrived with their bayonets to dig through the back wall of the house and drop down into the street. Thence they made their way to the quarters held by the other survivors. These were crowded with men, women, and children in a terrible plight, for the place was constantly harassed by the big guns of the citadel. But they held out until March 20, when they surrendered for the second time, receiving, with mistrust, further fair promises of good treatment. Nicholson was most reluctant to give in. Three times he drove the

[Continued overleaf]

A Peeress's Kindly Thought for Mothers.

"MOTHERS DAY": LADY BYRON ENTERTAINS MOTHERS OF FIGHTING MEN TO TEA.

It was an admirable and most kindly idea that a "day," August 6, should be set aside for some special mark of recognition of mothers, upon whom the anxieties and sorrows of the war have fallen heavily enough. As Coleridge says: "A mother is a mother still, The holiest thing alive," and the mothers of the Empire have borne their burdens bravely. Our photographs show Lady Byron and some of her friends, entertaining to tea in the grounds of Byron Cottage, Hampstead Heath, a number of mothers of the "boys" who are doing, or have done, such splendid service to their country. The sad-coloured dresses of some of the guests tell their own story. It is well to know that they, too, are in the thoughts of the nation in this time of stress.—[Photos. by C.N.]

Afghan guard before him at the point of the bayonet before, with tears in his eyes, he bade his men yield and flung his sword at the feet of his captors. For nearly a year—tortured, threatened, and robbed—the survivors of the Ghazni garrison were kept in captivity. But even in this desperate pass Nicholson showed that mastery of the native mind which was his supreme gift. He alone of the party was not robbed of every article of value he possessed. He managed to keep a little locket containing his mother's hair. He did this not by craft or by persuasion, but simply by those downright methods which the Oriental understands and respects. When Nicholson was ordered to give up the trinket, he flung it at the sirdar's head. The act might have cost him his life then and there ; but no. "He seemed," writes Nicholson, "to like it, for he gave strict orders that the locket was not to be taken from me."

thrashings to which their divinity treated them in return for their devotion. The more Nikalsain thrashed his ardent worshippers, the more they loved and venerated him. The sect grew and flourished.

A man of his time, the priest of the Nikalsainis had his eye not only upon religion, but upon the main chance. He worried Sir James Abbott, a friend of Nicholson's, for the gift of an old top hat, which that official, somewhat mystified, at length gave him. Thereby hung a queer tale. One day a native shopkeeper rushed into Abbott's office and complained that the fakir had come begging to his door, and, being refused, produced the ancient tile, which he set upon the ground and dared the tradesman to advance and outrage the *sahib-log* by treading upon it. To avoid so dire a contingency, the poor merchant parted with a rupee towards the funds of the Nikalsaini. This

A FRENCH PRISON - SHIP FOR CAPTURED GERMANS : WASHING - DAY ON BOARD.

Numbers of the German prisoners in France are found useful employment on harbour works and in coast reclamation. They are housed in cargo-steamers hired by the French Government at various ports.—[*Photo. by C.N.*]

That act was an earnest of the Nikalsain to be, that Deputy Commissioner of a Punjab district who, at the age of twenty-seven, was feared and adored, and by his wise though stern justice did more than any man to exalt and confirm the authority of the British name in India. His subjects invested him with, perhaps, more than his fair share of the fame he had won in the late Sikh war, and acclaimed him as the supreme conqueror. From that it was an easy step to apotheosis.

A Gosain, or Hindu devotee, saw in Nikalsain a new incarnation of Brahma, and began to preach the gospel of the Deputy Commissioner's godhead. He was joined by other believers, and they instituted a new sect, the Nikalsainis. Every day they prayed, with characteristic fervour, to the new Avatar, and refused to be discouraged by the

subtle combination of religion and profit was too much for Abbott. He required the devotee to withdraw from the district. He did so, but only to seek Nicholson at Derajat and resume his pious efforts. Again Nicholson rewarded him with the proverbial alternative of halfpence, and he went home, a little subdued, but still faithful to his belief.

Brigadier-General Nicholson's glorious and tragic fate before Delhi forms one of the most romantic passages of Lord Roberts's memoirs. Death did not extinguish the Nikalsain legend, and in Northern India the natives still whisper his name with awe and affection. To favoured eyes he is believed to be visible even yet, and among Indian minstrels there lingers a ballad to his honour.

The Queen's Tribute to East End Patriotism.

CHATTING WITH RELATIVES OF SOLDIERS: HER MAJESTY INSPECTING STREET ROLLS OF .HONOUR.

. The informality and kindliness of the Queen's visit to South Hackney on August 10, to inspect local Rolls of Honour, were immensely appreciated by the people. Her Majesty left her car and talked personally with relatives of men who have answered the country's call, and placed flowers beside the Rolls. Our photograph was taken in Palace Road, from which 111 men had volun-

tarily enlisted out of a total of 77 houses. The Queen, who was attended by Lady Mary Trefusis and Sir Edward Wallington, also visited Rolls of Honour in Balcorne Street, Havelock Road, Frampton Park Road, and Eaton Place. This excellent system of recording local patriotism was instituted by the Rev. B. S. Batty, Rector of St. John of Jerusalem, South Hackney.—[Photo. by C.N.].

With the British Troops at Salonika.

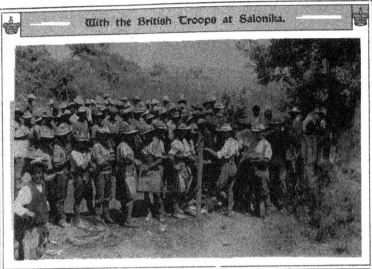

KILTS—WITH BROAD-BRIMMED HATS; AND A SYLVAN SURGERY: SUMMER SCENES AT SALONIKA

With the upper photograph, showing some of the British troops at Salonika, the following description is supplied : " Why the Greeks smile. The crowd of customers. Note the unusual combination of kilts and broad-brimmed hats." Apparently the men are making purchases at a Greek store, but as to the nature of the goods history is silent. Of the lower photograph, it is stated : " This great hollow sycamore is used as a surgery by the doctor attached to ———— Divisional Headquarters." Recent news from Salonika has concerned chiefly the successful resumption of fighting by the Serbians, but Mr. Ward Price wrote on the 5th : " For the first time for many months the British were engaged in bomb and bayonet fighting on this front."—[Official Photographs. Crown copyright reserved.]

Puggarees and Sun-Helmets in Vogue at Salonika.

A SPELL OF TROPICAL HEAT FOR OUR TROOPS AT SALONIKA : ROLLING PUGGAREES FOR SUN-HELMETS.

The upper of these two photographs, taken recently at Salonika, shows the method of rolling a 9-yard-long muslin puggaree for a sun-helmet. In the lower one is seen the process of rolling it round the helmet. " It is an insidious characteristic of the climate of Salonika," says Mr. Ward Price in a recent despatch from thence, " that in a hot summer like this it has most of the characteristics of the tropics, but, owing to its being situated in Europe, life is organised as if nothing more torrid were to be expected than an English June. Sun-helmets, smoked spectacles, puggarees, and light drill clothes have all had to be adopted as the thermometer has climbed relentlessly higher."—[*Official Photographs. Crown copyright reserved.*]

The Might of Britain's New Artillery: One o

HOW THE BRITISH ARTILLERY BLASTS A WAY FOR THE INFANTRY THROUGH TH

Our big guns, of the type shown in the above photograph, make havoc in the German trenches and enable the troops to break through. Describing recently the work of the British artillery near Poziéres and Guillemont, M. Marcel Hutin, the well-known French writer, said : "The great 15-inch guns fire with extraordinary precision a 1700-lb. shell, containing a new secret and terrible

Our Big Guns in Action During the Advance.

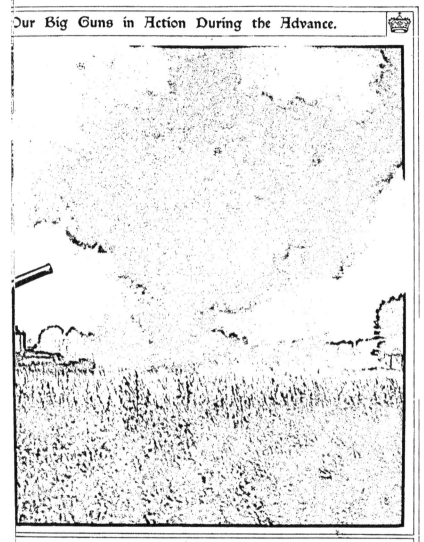

RMAN LINES : A LONG-RANGE MONSTER PHOTOGRAPHED AT THE MOMENT OF FIRING.

xplosive, to a distance of seven miles, and can fire one shell per minute. The aim is regulated with remarkable precision by eroplane and wireless . . . these huge guns are really mobile weapons. I saw men lay, take up, and lay down again across the ountry in a few hours railway lines sufficient for moving these enormous guns rapidly forward."—[Official Photo. issued by the Press Bureau.]

Italian Alpine Warfare in the Eternal Snows.

IN THE MOUNTAINS WHILE COMRADES TRIUMPH ON THE ISONZO: ITALIANS IN CADORE AND TRENTINO.

The upper photograph shows an Italian blockhouse in Cadore at a height of over 8000 ft., and the lower one some tents and huts at a mountain position in the Trentino at an altitude almost as great. The magnificent Italian victory on the Isonzo has eclipsed for the moment the wonderful feats of the Alpini in Italy's more mountainous fronts in Cadore and the Trentino. In the latter district it will be remembered that the Italian troops successfully withstood a great Austrian offensive in May, and on June 16 began a victorious counter-offensive there, driving the enemy headlong back into the mountains. Much of the fighting in the Trentino and Cadore has to be conducted amid the perpetual snows, the snow-line in the Alps ranging from about 7500 to 9000 ft.

Italy's Victorious Advance: A Mountain March.

TROOPS OF THE TRIUMPHANT ITALIAN ARMY: A COLUMN APPROACHING THE GARIBALDI SHELTER.

An interesting account of the Italian campaign in the Alps was given recently by a "Times" military correspondent. "The Italians," he writes, "were the first people in Europe, except the Swiss, to organise mountain warfare scientifically, and in their Alpine Groups they possess a force unrivalled for combat in the higher mountains. . . . Over nine-tenths of Italy's frontier the war is Alpine, and . . . Italian soldiers have brought the art of mountain fighting to a degree of perfection never attained before. . . . The time allowed for big things in the Alps by big armies is strictly limited. . . . There are winter defences to be made in snow, and summer defences in earth and rock. . . . The barbed-wire chevaux-de-frise are often covered by snow in a night."

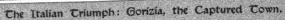

The Italian Triumph: Gorizia, the Captured Town.

"THE AUSTRIAN NICE" TAKEN BY THE ITALIAN ARMY ON AUGUST 9: VIEWS OF GORIZIA.

The upper photograph shows a general view of Gorizia from the height of Podgora, and the lower one some buildings in the town, with the castle beyond. An Italian official communiqué of August 9 said: "This morning our troops entered the town of Gorizia. . . . Up till now we have taken about 10,000 prisoners, and more are coming in." This important and long-looked-for victory has been hailed with the utmost enthusiasm throughout Italy. Gorizia, which lies on the left bank of the Isonzo some 36 miles from Trieste, has been called "the Austrian Nice," from its mild climate, picturesque surroundings, and fertility in flowers and fruit. It is essentially Italian. In the old part is the castle of the former Counts of Gorizia, now a barrack.—[Photos. by C.N.]

A Somme front Snapshot: The fog of War.

A GERMAN ARTIFICE FOR COVERING A DAY-TIME ATTACK: A SMOKE-BOMB BURSTING.

The German smoke-bombs are largely used to cover day-time attacks with the bayonet where the trenches are only a short distance apart. A photograph taken quite close to one of the bombs at the moment of its explosion is given here. Ordinarily they are thrown by trench-mortars, which lob them over to burst on impact just in front of the trenches opposite, near the points selected for assault. A number are fired simultaneously, extending over the whole space to be attacked in a line of bursting bombs. The dense, black smoke created is spread wider by means of a chemical powder intermingled with the bursting charge, which acts in the middle of the dense column thrown up and widens the area of smoke-fog caused by the shell.—[*French War Office Photograph.*]

FOOTNOTES TO ARMAGEDDON: I.—THE CHARMED LIFE.

A "WOUNDED" was in a bath-chair on the sea-front. He looked weak and painfully ill. This is his story.

From the beginning of his fighting days he seemed to be set aside for breathless experiences. His battalion was shelled when they arrived in billets at the front, and they picked this man out—with a certainty that the worst had happened—from amid the shattered beams and broken bricks of a house. One big beam, large enough to crush to death the strongest man, was across his stomach. But it had stopped before it touched him. The débris upheld it and he was safe. In fact, there was scarcely a bruise on him when they got him out.

Going into the trenches for the first time the man before him and the man following him in single file were shot. He was not touched. When he had been in the trenches a few days a "crump" blew in his section of the parapet. The man with him was killed outright, he himself was buried to the hips, and the crumping continued for several minutes. When the dust and smoke had finally settled and his comrades could get at him, they found his clothes badly tattered, but himself cheerful and unhurt.

The next thing that happened to him was a bomb. It came over the parapet in a solid German manner, and fell between his feet. He guessed he was a dead man then. The trenches were particularly narrow here, and he was hemmed in by a traverse. He

TAKING OUT ONE OF THE AEROPLANES PRESENTED BY FRANCE: A SERBIAN AIR SQUAD AT SALONIKA.

To complete the war equipment of the re-organised Serbian Army, the French have supplied the forces at Salonika with aeroplanes, in the handling of which Serbian airmen are trained regularly. They make constant practice flights.—[Photo. by Illustrations Bureau.]

had, also, no more than a second or so to do his thinking. He threw the man who was with him flat, and sat on the fellow's back and waited. It seemed he waited for a million years, but the bomb went off all right. There was an explosion that nearly made him insane, and a wildness of smoke. He felt a great blow on his chest, and he guessed that this time his luck had fizzled. But it had not. He picked an ugly piece of iron out of the khaki of his chest, and found a large, unlovely bruise underneath. Nothing more. He was so little shaken that he did not even think of leaving the trench.

He began to think that, after all, he wasn't born to be strafed. He acted on the idea. He did daring things. He went out across No Man's Land in a number of raids, and one, at least, should have ended him. This was a raid that didn't "function." Something had upset the Germans in front, and they were irritable and alert. The party had no sooner reached the wire when the star-lights went aloft in unattractive numbers, and the German machine-guns began to work overtime. There were a good many casualties to the British party, but some of them got back. The man was not among that number. At the moment the Germans opened fire he found himself right in the line of one of the machine-guns. He felt bullets snatching and whipping at his clothes even as he dropped prone. Fortunately, he dropped into a shell-hole, and the main

[Continued overleaf.]

ENABLING AMMUNITION AND STORES TO KEEP UP WITH THE BRITISH ADVANCE IN THE "GREAT PUSH": A LABOUR BATTALION ROAD-MAKING.

The navvy Labour battalions raised by Colonel John Ward, M.P., as units of the London Regiment, are doing notable "spade-work" at the Front, close in rear of the firing-line.

Official Press Bureau Photograph.

On the Battlefield in the British Offensive.

WOUNDED GERMAN PRISONERS: A PARTY GOING TO HOSPITAL—A SOLDIER DISTRIBUTING WATER.

In the upper illustration a party of wounded German prisoners, able to walk, are seen arriving at a British advanced dressing-station, from the trenches in which they were captured. A general glance at their uniforms suggests that they are men of several different regiments. In the lower illustration we have a characteristic instance of the kindly nature of the British soldier. The scene is at one end of a captured trench, and the Germans shown have not long been prisoners. Some of their captors are in the background keeping guard until the prisoners can be moved away. Red Cross attendants are at work among them, while one of our men is taking round water. The humaner instincts survive the ordeal of war.—[Official Photograph issued by Press Bureau.]

stream of bullets swept over and clear of him. The shell-hole protected him only while he remained still. The Germans were firing along the ground to destroy the illusions of any man who thought that to hug Mother Earth was to be safe. Two or three times the man tried to crawl out of his hole and get away; each time bullets whipped very close to him, even snapped through his clothes again. Day came and he was still in his hole, alone, and in a dangerous position. He remained quiet as long as he could, but his anxiety made him venturesome. He tried to get back to the shelter of the British parapets once more. The Germans saw him with uncanny celerity, and they spent an athletic day trying to lob bombs into his shell-hole. The German was not trained on the playing fields of England, so that most of his full-pitchers were wides, but some were not. After bombs had exploded with an air of finality in the shell-hole there came such an immobility about the spot that the British in the trenches concluded that the man had been killed. But he clambered back over the parapets that night. He was Homerically hungry, and super-Homerically thirsty. There were bullet-holes or marks in every garment—exterior and interior — and the smoke of the bombs had made his eyes sore. But he was untouched. It would take a good deal of time to chronicle all the things that man survived, the number of times he seemed to be scheduled for wounds and death—and came out

unscratched. He was blown up by shells once or twice. He took part in an offensive or two and turned up with the remnants of his platoon, unbowed and unbloody. He had a long duel with a particularly brilliant sniper and had beaten him. A bullet should have passed through his head in a dug-out, only at that critical moment he happened to be leaning forward to read a difficult word in a letter from Blighty. He carried a message, at one time, over a patch of shell-trap

MR. LLOYD GEORGE'S REVIEW OF A CANADIAN DIVISION : GENERAL SIR SAM HUGHES LEADING THE CHEERS FOR THE WAR MINISTER.

Mr. Lloyd George's first review as War Minister took place at the camp of a Canadian Division in England. The Canadian War Minister, General Sir Sam Hughes, accompanied him.—[Photo. by C.N.]

that had killed the three messengers who had tried the task before him. He had been in a working party that had been caught by a machine-gun. The swing of the machine-gun stopped just as it killed the man next him. He had been in a trench that had been isolated by a barrage and had lived well beyond the limits of his iron ration and the water-supply—and had survived where others did not. He had been a member of an indomitable regiment that had mustered a sergeant, a lance-corporal, and three privates after a terrible fight, and he was one of the privates.

He had hobnobbed with Death as no other man had ; he should have been slain or wounded a thousand times, it seemed. And had not even been touched. His adventures and escapes were almost epic. There was something immense and transcendent about them.

And yet here he is in a bath-chair, on the sea-front, weak, and painfully ill. He has been invalided home with an attack of summer influenza. W. DOUGLAS NEWTON.

TROPHIES TO BE ON VIEW IN ENGLAND SOON : A FEW OF THE GERMAN GUNS CAPTURED BY US DURING THE RECENT FIGHTING.

These are a few specimens of the guns taken from the enemy in July, some of which, it has been stated in Parliament, are being brought to England for public exhibition. Those shown are field-guns, with, near the centre, a position-gun.

Official Press Bureau Photograph.

The Enemy and his Limbless Soldiers.

IN BREST-LITOVSK HOSPITAL : CRIPPLED AUSTRIANS PRACTISING WALKING WITH ARTIFICIAL LIMBS.

The hospital authorities in Germany and Austria are taking specially devised measures with regard to the training of their maimed and permanently crippled soldiers in the use of the appliances supplied to the men to make good as far as possible the loss of their limbs. A special surgical commission at Berlin and Vienna has had the matter in hand since early in the war, and has held exhibitions of the appliances. These illustrations, from a German paper, show wounded men, Austrians, being taught how to walk with artificial legs at the War Hospital at Brest-Litovsk, in Poland. They are seen practising in a regular drill to lift their artificial feet over undulating surfaces and obstacles (as on a road), and to maintain their balance while using the limbs.

On the Italian Front: Close-Action Artillery.

SHORT-RANGE PIECES FOUND EXCEPTIONALLY EFFECTIVE; PATTERNS OF TRENCH "BOMBARDS."

There is necessarily a certain sameness not only of methods of warfare but also in the apparatus employed on all fronts, in consequence of the universality of trench-fighting. Whether among the Russians on the Riga front (where, as far as is known at the time of writing, no general advance in force has taken shape); at Ypres; in Champagne; or with the Italians in the Trentino, practically identical appliances are in use. The two illustrations here show two kinds of mortars, or small howitzers, which the Italians use for trench-fighting. "Bombards" is the name given them. In the upper illustration is seen a bombard of 210-mm. (9 inches) with an artillery officer by it; in the lower is another type of Italian bombard.—[Photo. by H. Manuel.]

On the Italian Front: Close-Action Projectiles.

USEFUL TYPES: A WING-HEADED SHELL AND AN AIR-TORPEDO IN A GUN.

It is largely by aid of the kinds of projectiles shown here that the Italians on the Isonzo front, particularly, are succeeding in forcing their way forward across the entrenched Austrian positions on the plateaux towards Trieste. The advance has necessitated the taking of trench after trench by bombardment at close quarters followed by direct attacks. The nature of the ground has precluded hitherto the onsweeping tactics that the French and ourselves find practicable in the West. In the first illustration Italian artillerymen are seen carrying a wing-headed shell for a large-calibre trench-mortar. In the second, an air-torpedo of the ordinary pattern is seen ready loaded in a trench-mortar of the *minenwerfer* type.— [*Photos. by H. Manuel.*]

Flies and Films: Salonika Front Incidents.

WAR APPLIANCES: A MOSQUITO-CURTAINED AMBULANCE LITTER—A CINEMA CAMERA.

In the upper illustration is seen a field-ambulance litter, mule-drawn, and of a special design, used on the Salonika front. The long shaft-poles with slightly turned-up lower ends are so devised for getting over rough ground where wheeled traffic is impossible owing to the lack of made roads. The litter itself, slung on the poles so as to remain horizontal, has all openings draped with gauze netting to keep out the flies and mosquitoes which swarm everywhere. In the lower photograph one of the cinematograph operators at the front, some of whose films are being shown in England, is seen with the Salonika army taking a picture of quick-firing gun shooting through a trench loop-hole. The operators repeatedly run risks.—[Official Photographs.]

"P. G."—But Not Persona Grata!

GERMAN PRISONERS OF THE FRENCH: PLACING CLOTHES IN A DISINFECTING-CHAMBER.

The number of German prisoners taken by the French in the first push in Picardy was over 6000. Nearly 3000 more were captured on the 20th, and the total has since increased. At Verdun some 1700 were taken on August 4. They are very well treated by our chivalrous Allies. Lord Northcliffe writes: "The authorities at home seem to hide our German prisoners. In France they work, and in public, and are content with their lot, as I know by personal inquiry of many of them. Save for the letters 'P.G.' (*prisonnier de guerre*) at the back of their coats, it would be difficult to realise that comfortable-looking, middle-aged Landsturm Hans, with his long pipe, and young Fritz, with his cigarette, were prisoners at all."—(*Official Photographs authorised by the French War Office.*)

WOMEN AND THE WAR.

WOMEN in these days are divided into two classes—those who wear khaki and those who don't. But usually, since most women are doing some sort of work just now, the distinction between them is only dress deep. Mufti, whether its wearer is in trousers or skirt, does not necessarily symbolise the slacker. The khaki woman is, of course, rather a more picturesque figure than her less conspicuous though equally useful colleague. But, her work apart, she serves another and a quite important purpose, for she is a constant reminder that this war, at any rate, is not only a man's game, and she is, as it were, the outward and visible symbol of the practical genius which women have brought to bear on the unexpected problems with which they have been confronted during the last two years.

Nowadays the petticoated platoons of the khaki brigade are accepted as a matter of course. It was otherwise when they made their first public appearance. Ignorant people smiled a superior smile at "the women who can't keep away from apeing men," and prophesied their speedy disappearance. That was in the early days of the war, before it had been acknowledged that women were of "invaluable use to the State." Jeers notwithstanding, the numbers of those who joined the ranks of the khaki women increased every day. Now they are counted by thousands, and there is no job, from washing dishes at a hospital to driving a motor - ambulance, that they

are not ready and willing to undertake. Probably the best testimony to their efficiency is the ever-increasing demand for their services, and particularly in regard to canteen work.

STRENUOUS WORK FOR WAR-HELPERS: WOMEN IN THE GAS-WORKS.

In the absence of men who have joined the colours, from the Somerset parish of Chew Magna, women-workers have taken up their strenuous tasks in the gas-works, under the supervision of a manager. Mrs. Summers and her daughter open and refill retorts, although the heat is terrific.
Photograph by Photopress.

It was only four or five weeks after the declaration of war that the appearance of companies of women, dressed in a neat khaki uniform of Norfolk coat and skirt, leather belt, brown shoes, spat-puttees, and felt hat, marching through the streets of London first startled steady-going citizens, and gave them a faint inkling of the active part women were to play in the struggle. They were the Women's Volunteer Reserve, founded under the auspices of the Women's Emergency Corps (whose activities have already been described) by the Hon. Evelina Haverfield, and they claimed to be ready to help the State in any direction in which it might require their service. Starting as a comparatively small body, the Corps has now eight London companies, forty branches throughout the country, four battalions in Canada, and a membership of over 10,000.

Recently the newspapers have been emphasising the need for the services of voluntary workers in hospitals and in other directions, and a list of the activities of the W.V.R. shows how wide is the field in which workers are needed. There is ambulance work, for instance. If it should happen, and it has happened over again in

SPORTSWOMEN AND WAR-WORK: LADIES IN A DEPÔT FOR CONVALESCENT REMOUNTS.

The value of sport as a training for the "great game" has been proved a thousand times at the Front, and it has also been shown in cases such as that illustrated, where a group of ladies, obviously good sportswomen who know how to "dress the part," are seen cheerily carrying saddles, bridles, and so on, to clean, and looking businesslike and smart, as sportswomen should.—[Photo. by Alfieri.]

[Continued overleaf.

A War-Time Transformation in Eaton Square.

A BELGRAVIAN MANSION FOR THE WOUNDED: THE COUNTESS OF DUNDONALD'S HOSPITAL.

The Countess of Dundonald generously bought No. 87, Eaton Square, equipped it as a hospital, and is maintaining it with the co-operation of those who have given beds. The hospital is being conducted by the Hon. Margaret Amherst, a sister of the Baroness Amherst of Hackney, and the staff of the Norfolk 116 V.A.D., who, by special permission, have transferred their services to the London area. Miss Amherst is a Lady of Justice of the Order of St. John of Jerusalem in England. The mansion makes a lordly home for the gallant wounded inmates. The Countess of Dundonald was, before her marriage, Miss Winifred Bamforth-Hesketh, only child of the late Mr. Robert Bamforth-Hesketh, formerly 2nd Life Guards, of Gwrych Castle, Abergele, North Wales.—[Photo. by C.N.]

London, that a hospital wants the services of a chauffeur and an ambulance-van for the transportation of stretcher cases, the Corps will, on request, very quickly supply both. Or, again, wounded soldiers are constantly being entertained by hospitable people who, however, are not always

ENTERTAINING THE WOUNDED IN THE COUNTESS OF DUNDONALD'S HOSPITAL : "SISTER " THE HON. MARGARET AMHERST PLAYS TO THE PATIENTS.

The Countess of Dundonald generously purchased and equipped No 87, Eaton Square, and is maintaining it as a hospital for wounded soldiers, with the co-operation of friends who have given beds. The Hon. Margaret Amherst is conducting the hospital, aided by her staff of the Norfolk 110 V.A.D. Miss Amherst, who is a sister of the Baroness Amherst of Hackney, and a Lady of Justice of the Order of St. John of Jerusalem in England, gives her patients much enjoyment by playing to them when time permits. — [Photo. by C.N.]

able to provide the necessary conveyances for their guests. Such an emergency has been met by the Corps over and over again. Here are a few more of their activities. They have regularly carried bales of medical supplies and other hospital accessories for the central workrooms of the British Red Cross Society, they have transported food for the Belgian Refugees Food Fund, and there is a town " somewhere in England " that remembers with a rather amazed gratitude the complete calmness and indifference to personal danger shown by the local stretcher squad of the W.V.R. when " called out " for duty on the occasion of a quite considerable Zeppelin raid. They have helped on " Flag " days, and acted as stewards at the various in-aid-of entertainments which have, for the time being, become almost a feature of our national life; and cleaning Admiralty cars or carrying despatches to and from aircraft stations have been included in their duties.

Canteen work is a branch of activity the importance of which is being repeatedly urged by people interested in the physical and moral welfare of those who are engaged on work of national importance. The

country can't do without the workers, and the workers can't do without the food and recreation necessary to keep them fit. So the W.V.R. has canteen squads who work in relays from 9 p.m. every night until 7 a.m. next morning in the Y.M.C.A. canteens at Woolwich Arsenal, as well as in other munition areas throughout the country ; and, afterwards, not a few will hurry off, after a hasty breakfast and a necessary wash, to a long day's work in office or classroom.

Now that everyone, even the owner of a small backyard, is a horticulturist on a small scale, and vegetable-growing is fast developing into a national hobby, the woman gardener is coming to her own. The W.V.R. has taken under its wing hospital gardens in various towns throughout the country, and has secured on the outskirts of London a large plot of ground, the vegetables grown on which are sent regularly to different ships of his Majesty's Navy. A motor garage for instructional and repairing purposes has recently been started by the organisation at 12, Cromwell Mews, and is run on a co-operative basis for the benefit of the workers, all of whom are Corps members. This brief sketch of the activities of the Women's Volunteer Reserve—who, by the way, may be known from other khaki women by the bronze letters W.V.R. they wear on their shoulder—though by no means a complete list of everything that has been achieved or is in course of being carried out, does serve to show that the Corps lives up to the article of its constitution as " an organisation of trained and disciplined women ready to assist the

"OYEZ! OYEZ! OYEZ!" AN EAST ANGLIAN GIRL AS TOWN-CRIER OF THETFORD.

The Town Council of Thetford, in the absence of her father, who has joined the Army, have appointed Miss Florrie Clark, who is only fifteen, to be Town-Crier and official bill-poster. Our photograph shows her at her work.—[Photo. by C.N.]

State in any capacity." The Colonel commanding is Mrs. W. M. Charlesworth, and the headquarters are at 15, York Place, Baker Street.—CLAUDINE CLEVE.

The Lord Mayor of London and the Wounded.

SIR CHARLES WAKEFIELD ENTERTAINS WOUNDED SOLDIERS—AND GENERAL MACKINTOSH.

Sir Charles Wakefield has shown in many ways the interest taken by him in the war and the troops. He has paid a visit to the Front, and seen for himself the brave men who are facing death with so fine a patriotism. On Saturday, August 12, he gave a pleasant proof of his goodwill by entertaining at The Karsino, Hampton Court, a thousand wounded men drawn from the hospitals in and round London. It proved a very cheery fête, the men taking a lively interest in the amusements provided for them, and being specially appreciative of the geniality with which the Lord Mayor, in all the civic dignity of feathered hat, furred robes, and chain of office, entered into a competition with General Mackintosh in a "cocoa-nut shy."—[Photos. by G.N.]

Testing the Wind by a Miniature Balloon.

TESTING ATMOSPHERIC CONDITIONS FOR ARTILLERY FIRE: A FRENCH AEROLOGICAL SECTION.

In the upper photograph a miniature balloon, which at first sight resembles a big football, is seen being sent up by a French aerological section, in order to test the strength and direction of the wind for the guidance of a "320" battery of artillery. The lower photograph shows the process of inflating the balloon. It has been found that the projectile from a gun does not travel always on exactly the same line, but that its course is subject to deflection by the condition of the wind. Consequently the information as to the state of the upper atmosphere obtained by the use of these little balloons is of great value to the gunners. The illustrations show the highly scientific methods of the French artillery.—[Official Photographs authorised by the French War Office.]

German Striplings Among Prisoners Taken by the French.

EVIDENCE OF AGE AND PHYSIQUE OF GERMAN TROOPS: PRISONERS GUARDED BY ALGERIANS.

These photographs afford testimony to the fact that many of the German troops opposed to the Allies in the West are youths of the 1916 class. It is not, of course, the case that the German armies are generally composed of such material, as many German prisoners are of more mature age and finer type. Those shown above were captured in the battles of the Somme, and have been taken to work in the quarries of Royanmoix. They form a striking contrast with the stalwart Algerians seen guarding them in the upper photograph. A French communiqué of August 12 stated regarding recent fighting at Maurepas: "The number of unwounded prisoners counted up to the present number 1000."— [*Official Photographs authorised by the French War Office.*]

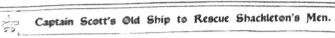

Captain Scott's Old Ship to Rescue Shackleton's Men.

A NEW ATTEMPT TO RESCUE SHACKLETON'S MEN ON ELEPHANT ISLAND : THE "DISCOVERY" SAILS.

The upper photograph shows the "Discovery," Captain Scott's old ship, leaving home waters for Elephant Island, in the Antarctic, where some members of Sir Ernest Shackleton's expedition were left. The lower photograph shows men at work in the "Discovery's" rigging. She has been sent out by the Government at Sir Ernest's request, being placed at their disposal by the Hudson Bay Company, and fitted out at Devonport. Three previous rescue attempts by Sir Ernest were unsuccessful. The first was made in a whaler from South Georgia ; the second from the Falklands in a vessel lent by the Uruguay Governmen ; and the third in the schooner "Emma," which left Chile on July 12. Badly damaged, she reached the Falklands early this month.—[Photos. by Topical.]

The Illustrated War News, Aug. 23, 1916.—Part 11, New Series.

The Illustrated War News

THE COMMANDER OF THE HOME FORCES IN IRELAND: LORD FRENCH INSPECTING WOUNDED AT CORK.
Photograph by C.N.

THE GREAT WAR.

By W. DOUGLAS NEWTON.

A POINT that is worth peculiar attention is this new sterility of the German effort. The certainty with which the enemy finds himself incapable of doing things is a distinguished and attractive feature of the present phase of fighting. The Germans have before failed to do the things they had planned—they failed to break through at Ypres, and they failed to break through on the Dvina, for example. At no moment in their contemporary history, however, have they failed—as now—with such unanimity in every particular of their circumferent war. They are advancing nowhere, and at no point are they able to check the Allied advance. They cannot balance events. They cannot set an advance in Poland against our advance in the Champagne, as they did last year. They cannot set the invasion of Serbia against their failure to break the Russian line, as they could last November. They can show nothing in their favour.

THE ALLIES' COMBINED OFFENSIVE : THE SECTION IN FLANDERS AND NORTHERN FRANCE HELD BY THE BELGIANS AND BRITISH ; AND THE POZIÈRES DISTRICT. The Belgian position extends between the Ypres district and the sea ; the British from Ypres to the Ancre, north of Albert.

Their defence systems have been broken in Russia, Italy, at Verdun, and on the Somme, and when those systems have been reorganised with every ounce of strength and material, they have been broken again with the ease of deliberation. And as they cannot hold the Allies in line, they have been unable to stop the Allied advance by counter-assault. On all the fronts these counter - moves have been initiated, on all the fronts they have been disintegrated ; and the Allies have gone forward.

THE ALLIES' COMBINED OFFENSIVE : THE FRENCH BATTLE-LINE FROM THE SOMME TO SWITZERLAND, AND THE PLACES WHERE FIGHTING IS PROCEEDING NEAR PERONNE AND VERDUN. The French line connects with the British on the north bank of the Somme, a little to the north and north-west of Amiens.

Germany is experiencing, for the first time in the war, the attribute of complete negation.

During the period under consideration we have had marked occasion to perceive this state of things. For the major portion of the week the entirety of the Allied ring has been in that condition of hiatus which is the natural and expected state between powerful advances. Russia, after her great blows on the Sereth and at Stanislau, has been gathering herself for new blows. Italy, after that spring that carried her beyond Gorizia, has been accumulating her strength for fresh progress. The Anglo-French on the Somme, after their advances to the crests running from Pozières past Maurepas to the Somme, have been working deliberately for the stroke that will drive the Germans well below the crests. Here, surely, was the time for the German and Austrian reserves—reserves which, we know, have been hurried to all points of fracture—to drive back at their enemies and force them off their fields of victory. In no place have the Germans and Austrians been able to reap the fruit of this occasion, or even to hold out an efficient defence against the advances of consolidation. On the Sereth and Stanislau wings the Austro - Germans can only fight desperately for their lives, while they do not even hold the Russians, while in the centre General Bezobrazoff has made ground and taken prisoners. The Italians hold their gains and push steadily across the mountains to Trieste, and six waves of attack against the lines of the Somme not only failed to force a gap in the Allied front, but failed to halt for a moment a plan that sent new waves of British and French over the German trenches from Guillemont to Maurepas, from Maurepas to the Clery road. Most ominous of all ominous facts, this, that shows that, in the three months of her most desperate need, Germany has been able to do nothing.

It must be said that for one moment there was a hint the Germans might do something. Largely grouped attacks gave them an entry into some of those trenches west of Pozières which the British had lately captured. But so confident was the British Command of its own strength and dispositions that they were able to prophesy the German hold as temporary. The prophecy was good, for in less than a day the Germans were out of the works, and our men had them soundly. At the same time we had not curtailed our inclination to work forward at all points, and thanks to the grimly deliberate work of our men from trench to trench, we were soon able to establish ourselves on practically all the heights of the easy plateau for which we had been fighting. As the *Times* points out, the enemy now holds only one point of ground

A SPLENDID EXAMPLE OF AUSTRALIAN PATRIOTISM : PRIVATE THE HON. STANIFORTH SMITH—EX-ADMINISTRATOR OF PAPUA.

A notable example of the high patriotism of all in the Oversea Dominions is afforded by the case of the Hon. Miles Staniforth Cater Smith, of Victoria, Australia, Administrator of Papua. He has resigned his appointment, and enlisted as a private in the Commonwealth Forces for the Front.

Photograph by Walshams.

Thiepval is threatened from the rear via Courcelette, and Martinpuich is endangered both by the face and the flank of our advance between Pozières and the High Wood.

Moreover, we are driving forward a wedge that browbeats Guillemont and its strong defences, and, with the French, are pushing south of that place in a manner which shows the likelihood of flanking it as well as moving on to Combles. The initial movement of the fighting which is giving us this command of the line, was that undertaken with the French on Thursday and Friday. The battle, however, developed in a profound manner until, during the week-end, our gains had assumed great and excellent proportions. This fighting entailed engagements not only on the Guillemont-Maurepas front, but in the entire eleven-mile arc from Thiepval to Guillemont. On most points our gains were striking. At Guillemont we have pushed our way into the outskirts of that strong place, and hold as well the railway station—and the quarry, a point of specific importance ; here, too, our line has progressed half-way to Ginchy. We have also won our way to the western edge of the High Woods, and have gained the orchards north of Longueval, besides encroaching deeply beyond

"FIRST AID" FOR TEMPORARILY DISABLED GUNS : ONE OF OUR "HEAVIES" ON A TRAVELLING-WORKSHOP LORRY.
Official Photograph issued by the Press Bureau.

higher than our general level, and that is a point between High Wood and Delville Wood. At the same time we have pushed along the hills until

Pozières on both sides of the Pozières-Bapaume road. North of Pozières we have pushed well beyond the Mouquet Farm, on a front of a mile and a half, and have captured the dominant south-east ridge of Thiepval : so that, with our command of the slopes north of ·Pozières, we now look down upon the enemy to the east and north-east. With these admirable gains we have made a big haul of prisoners. There is an inclination—led by a whole Saxon detachment—to surrender without waiting for the fighting.

These tactics of the salient are also apparent in the movements of the French. In the advance in which our men co-operated the front was carried beyond a line of German trenches to reach at certain points the Guillemont-Maurepas road. South of Maurepas the French alone were able to take over the whole line on a front of a mile and a quarter to a depth of 500 yards, until, indeed, the new front was well east of the Maurepas-Clery road. These advances hem Maurepas from both flanks, and presage its fall under the enfilading fire of the new, sharp salient. South of the Somme the French were also active, for on the same day—Wednesday—they carried a strong system of German trenches over a front of 1300 yards. At Verdun counter - attack has availed nothing. The brilliant French go on brilliantly. The end of the week saw the whole of Fleury once more in their hands, and the course of the week saw them working steadily to the capture of position after position in the Thiaumont region.

The Russian fighting has been concerned, mainly, with the breaking of Bothmer's wings on the Sereth and in the Stanislau area. Bothmer has been fighting stubbornly on a line he has been able to straighten for the betterment of his wings, but at the same time he has not been able to hold off our Ally. Now Brusiloff has the Austro-German force in retreat again, and has forced them out of their fine lines on the Zlota Lipa, south of Brzezany, and is driving them west. Further south the Russians are across the Western Bystrzyca,

and are going ahead beyond Solotwina. South again they are driving in to the Jablonica Pass, and are holding out a threat to Hungary beyond the Carpathians. Finally, the end of the week

THE ALLIES' COMBINED OFFENSIVE : THE SPHERE OF GENERAL BRUSILOFF'S OPERATIONS ON THE SOUTHERN SECTION OF THE MAIN RUSSIAN BATTLE-LINE.

Count Bothmer's Austro-German army is in front of Lemberg, and the Austrian General Boehm-Ermolli near Lutsk and Kovel. General Sakharoff is striking at the enemy from Brody, and General Lechinsky from Stanislau, with General Shcherbacheff's Central Russian Army between.

shows them to have broken the German defences on the Stokhod, and to have broached forward there beyond the village of Tobol. A good week for Russia too.

In reply to the Allied movement in the Balkans, the Bulgarians have stirred themselves with energy, have attacked, and have been bitterly repulsed on a line running along the Greek border from Doiran to Florina. The French were able to force some works and establish themselves on Tortoise Hill, near Doldjeli, a point of importance. The Italian front has pressed on over the Carso.

The Secretary of the Admiralty announced on Monday : " The German High Sea Fleet came out " (on Saturday) " but learning from their scouts that the British forces were in considerable strength the enemy avoided engaging and returned to port." Our losses were two light cruisers by submarine attack; the enemy lost one submarine and another was " rammed and possibly sunk." LONDON : AUG. 21, 1916.

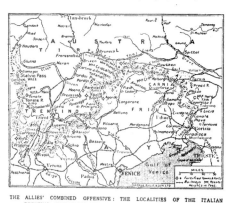

THE ALLIES' COMBINED OFFENSIVE : THE LOCALITIES OF THE ITALIAN TRENTINO OPERATIONS AND THE GORIZIA-TOLMINO BATTLE-LINE.

The Italians on their Isonzo Front hold Monfalcone and Gorizia beyond the river, also the western bank at Monte Nero. In the Trentino the Italians are near Rovereto.

The German fashion in "Tin Hats" for the Trenches.

WITH LOW BACK BRIM, CUT-AWAY FRONT, AND VENTILATION HOLES : INFANTRY IN STEEL HELMETS.

The type of steel helmet worn by the German troops has, of course, often been illustrated before, but this photograph shows its peculiar shape so much better than any that have previously appeared that it certainly justifies a return to the subject. The German helmets differ a good deal both from those of our own men, who call them "tin hats," and from those worn by the French. While ours are wide-brimmed and comparatively shallow, like inverted basins, the German type fits more closely to the head, and curves down behind over the back of the neck, like the back of a fireman's helmet. Over the forehead in front it is slightly cut away, and in the crown are two little ventilation holes, one on each side.— [Photo. by Topical.]

Troops from the Far East Serving in France.

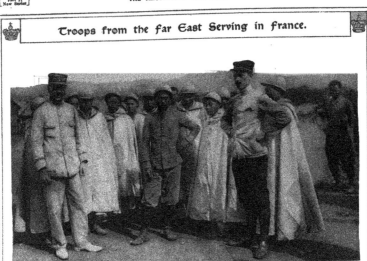

ANNAMITES OF THE FRENCH COLONIAL ARMY IN FRANCE: EQUIPMENT AND MEALS.

The upper photograph shows the smart and thorough equipment of the Annamite troops who have been brought from the Far East to fight for France on French soil. It will be noted that they have been provided with the French steel helmet, and also with waterproof cloaks. In the lower photograph some are seen at a meal, which they are evidently enjoying. Like our own native troops in India and Africa, the Annamites are officered by Europeans. They are of Mongolian race, though differing somewhat from the Chinese. Their food consists largely of rice, quantities of which are imported from China and Cochin-China, in addition to that grown in Annam. The country became a French protectorate in 1884.—[Official Photographs authorised by the French War Office.]

Annamites in France Practising their Religion.

RELIGIOUS OBSERVANCES AMONG THE ANNAMITE TROOPS IN FRANCE: THE HOUR OF PRAYER.

The Annamite soldiers serving in France are, of course, enabled to practice their religious observances just as they do in their own country. It is not stated to what form of faith the particular men here shown belong. The majority of the people of Annam are Buddhists, while there are also a certain number of Confucianists. Christianity has also made considerable headway in the country, through the efforts of missionaries. In an article on Annam in "Everyman's Encyclopaedia," it is stated : "The religion, borrowed as is all the rest of the culture from China, is chiefly Buddhism. There are some 420,000 Roman Catholics. Extreme reverence is shown to the dead, and ancestor-worship is in great vogue."—[*Official Photographs authorised by the French War Office.*]

The Attempted Turkish Invasion of Egypt.

THE ARRIVAL OF TWO THOUSAND PRISONERS AT CAIRO : MARCHING THROUGH THE STREETS.

The main body of the Turkish prisoners taken at the coast battle of Romani, in the desert beyond the Suez Canal, on August 5, arrived at Cairo during the afternoon of August 6. They numbered some two thousand in all, officers and men, and were marched through the streets to the place of temporary detention, the Kasr-el-Nil Barracks, escorted by British troops. The column was headed by the band of the Welsh Regiment. A second batch of five hundred Turks came in the same evening. Our upper illustration shows the leading sections of the prisoners column on its way from the railway station, headed by part of the escort. In the lower illustration the leading files of the prisoners are seen passing through a street in Cairo.—[Photos. by Record Press.]

The Attempted Turkish Invasion of Egypt.

OUR PRISONERS : UNWOUNDED TURKS MARCHING THROUGH CAIRO ; WOUNDED BORNE IN AMBULANCES.

According to a Cairo correspondent of the "Daily Telegraph," the Turkish prisoners who marched through the city were mostly men who were fairly well drilled and of good physique. They were all, however, very dirty-looking and unkempt, after their desert marching before the battle. They were wearing all sorts of patched garments. The majority of them were barefooted, but a number, relates the correspondent, had on canvas shoes like tennis shoes. Some wore fezes, others of the prisoners had on the queer-shaped "Enverieh" sun-helmet, invented, or introduced, by Enver Pasha, and named after the then War Minister. The wounded prisoners were brought to Cairo by a Red Cross train, and taken to hospital in British Army ambulances.—[Photos, Record Press.]

THE BEGINNINGS OF WAR-MACHINES: HELMETS, ARMOUR, AND SHIELDS.

THE adoption of steel helmets in the present campaign imparts considerable interest to a review of the various types of protective armour used by fighting men in days of old. We find one of the earliest records in the British Museum bas-reliefs representing Assyrian foot soldiers about 700 B.C. Amongst others, a soldier of Sennacherib's army is shown wearing a coat and leggings of what appears to be chain-mail. In the Louvre Museum is an Assyrian horseman's helmet with cheek-plates, which dates from the same period. Bronze helmets and breast-plates were used by the Greeks and Etruscans about 200 B.C.

Body-armour may be roughly divided into three classes, viz., chain-mail, scale-armour, and plate-armour. The first of these was made by interlacing metal links or rings so as to form a protection against any weapon inflicting a wound larger than the clearance space through the links. The space

FIG. 13.— A THIRTEENTH-CENTURY SOLDIER IN SCALE-ARMOUR — THE SYSTEM OF ARMOURING.

was so small that the shaft of an arrow would not pass through it. Armour of this class was worn prior to the Norman Conquest, but by rich men alone, as its cost of production was very high. Each ring or link of which it was composed was beaten from a solid

FIG. 14.—TRELLISED-COAT MAIL (LEFT); RINGED MAIL (CENTRE); CHAIN-MAIL (RIGHT).

lump of iron and rivetted up, the art of wire-drawing being unknown until some time in the fourteenth century. The rivets completing the links are clearly shown in the chain-mail illustration—Fig. 14. In another type of " ringed armour," shown in the same figure, the rings are sewn in rows on a leather coat. The " Trellised " coat illustrated with it—constructed by interlacing thongs of leather, with rivets in the intervening spaces — though not strictly chain-mail, is really a more or less efficient substitute, which could be produced at a much lower cost. Scale-armour (Fig. 13) was produced by attaching rows of small metal plates to a leather, or quilted, garment in such a manner that the

FIG. 15. — ARCHER'S ATTENDANT WITH " PAVISE " (LEFT); A " TARGITER " OF THE LONDON SIXTEENTH .. CENTURY CITIZEN FORCES.

edges of the plates over-lapped and a metal surface was consequently always presented to the point or edge of an adversary's weapon. At the

same time, the garment itself was sufficiently flexible to allow free movement to its wearer.

Plate-armour came into general use in the latter part of the reign of Edward II., but the older chain-armour was for some time worn with it, as a leg protection, the plate-armour consisting of " helm " " breastplate " and " gauntlets " only.

Improvements in hand weapons about the middle of the twelfth century led to the adoption of the helm or " heaume," a metal head-covering worn over a hood of mail. Many varieties of this device were used through the Middle Ages. A comparatively modern example of the headpiece is the nineteenth-century sapper's helmet (Fig. 8), designed to protect the head of its wearer against damage through falls of earth during mining operations.

The steel helmets used by the British and French infantry to-day are very like the cup-shaped helmet (Fig. 3) and the archer's helmet (Fig. 1), the former of these dating from the thirteenth century. The resemblance, however, ends with the shape, as the remarkable strength of the metal of which the modern helmet is made is the result of very recent improvements. Its resistance to indentation or fracture is so high that it will give efficient protection against a blow which would have demolished the older type. Breastplates do not as yet form part of the modern soldier's equipment, but several are in existence which are said to be bullet-proof. Provided this effect can be attained without overloading the wearer, no doubt the use of body armour will be to a certain extent revived. It will, however, probably never regain the popularity it lost when the invention of gunpowder caused it to be relinquished. The hardest metal in use at that date was so soft that a ball from an " Arquebus " or " match-lock " would penetrate any armour whose weight was not too much for a man to carry. Fig. 12 shows a breastplate which has been severely damaged by a round-shot, or cannon-ball.

(Continued opposite.

The Beginnings of War Machines: Armour.

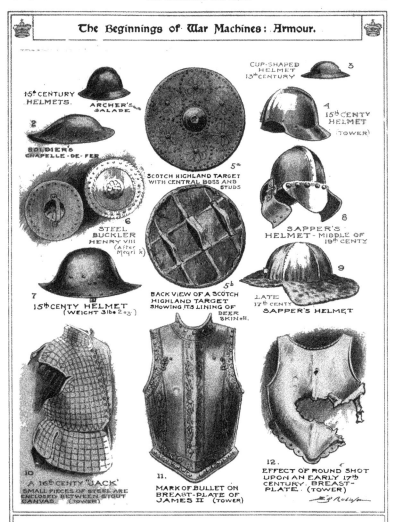

CUP-SHAPED HELMET 13th CENTURY 3

15th CENTURY HELMETS. ARCHER'S SALADE

2

SOLDIER'S CHAPELLE-DE-FER

4 15th CENTY HELMET (TOWER)

5a
SCOTCH HIGHLAND TARGET WITH CENTRAL BOSS AND STUDS

6
STEEL BUCKLER HENRY VIII (After Meyrick)

8
SAPPER'S HELMET - MIDDLE OF 19th CENTY

9

7
15th CENTY HELMET (WEIGHT 3lbs 2oz)

5b
BACK VIEW OF A SCOTCH HIGHLAND TARGET SHOWING ITS LINING OF DEER SKIN etc.

LATE 17th CENTY SAPPER'S HELMET

10
A 16th CENTY 'JACK' SMALL PIECES OF STEEL ARE ENCLOSED BETWEEN STOUT CANVAS. (TOWER)

11.
MARK OF BULLET ON BREAST-PLATE OF JAMES II (TOWER)

12.
EFFECT OF ROUND SHOT UPON AN EARLY 17th CENTURY. BREAST-PLATE. (TOWER)

HEAD AND BODY PROTECTION IN BATTLE: PROTOTYPES OF EXPEDIENTS REVIVED IN THE WAR.

[Continued.]

Shields, bucklers, and targets were used in England over a very long period of history, commencing before the Roman invasion and ending about 1748, when a Highland regiment in Flanders was allowed to carry targets similar in pattern to the one shown in Figs. 5a and 5b. The shield, though used in the Highlands in tribal fights, did not form part of the military uniform. The Scottish shield was carried on the forearm by means of loops, as shown in Fig. 5b. The buckler (Fig. 6) was a smaller affair, and was held in the hand, at arm's length. King Henry V. provided his archers with a large shield (Fig. 15) called a "pavise," carried by an attendant, behind which the bowman could shelter from the missiles of his enemy, and shoot undisturbed.

Art in War: French Humour at Salonika.

DESCHAMPS

is

REMPART DE ZEITENLIK

BY A FRENCH ARTIST SERVING IN THE RANKS AT SALONIKA: A CARICATURE BY M. JOLLIOT.

There are many artists and men of letters on active service in the French Army, both on the Western Front and elsewhere. At Salonika the artistic element is sufficiently important to have made it possible recently to hold an exhibition of drawings and paintings, done by prominent artists serving in the ranks of the French forces. The above caricature, by M. Jolliot, was one of the exhibits. As regards its subject, we must leave the drawing to speak for itself, as no explanation of it has been supplied beyond the words in French that appear upon it, doubtless in allusion to some topical joke familiar to the men on the spot. The skill of the drawing, however, is obvious to anyone.—[Official Photograph issued by the Press Bureau.]

"The Poilu" fashioned in Salonika Trench-Clay.

BY A FRENCH SCULPTOR SERVING IN THE RANKS AT SALONIKA: A PLAQUE BY M. BALICK.

As mentioned on the opposite page, an exhibition of drawings and paintings by prominent artists serving in the French ranks was held recently at Salonika. Sculpture was also represented, as witness this clever plaque entitled "The Poilu," fashioned from the clay of the trenches by M. R. Balick. During the summer the troops at Salonika have had a certain amount of leisure to pursue their particular hobbies. In the hot weather the French military authorities there introduced a very sensible system of periodical rests. Batches of ten men at a time were released from military duties for ten days, and spent their time as though on holiday, reading, smoking, and so on. Doubtless the artists took advantage of the respite.—[Official Photograph issued by the Press Bureau.]

ROMANCES OF THE REGIMENTS: XI.—THE 14TH BENGAL LANCERS.

THE CAPTURE OF SAIFOOLLAH DEEN.

THE capture of Saifoollah Deen, styled " General " Saifoollah Deen, one of the very choice Afghan rascals who fought against us in the war of 1879, is the subject of one of the most grimly humorous stories in Major Maitland's lively diary, " To Caubul with the Cavalry Brigade." Saifoollah had been one of the leaders at Char Asiab, which was fought on Oct. 6, 1879, and on the 21st Major Mitford was ordered to search certain villages and bring in the worthy General, who had been a fugitive ever since the action, and was wisely making himself very scarce. Saifoollah's probable whereabouts had been made known

USED AT GALLIPOLI, SHOT-TORN THERE, AND NOW TO DO
SERVICE AT SALONIKA: AN ENGINE UNDER REPAIR.

Official Photograph. Crown Copyright Reserved.

by a Kisil Bash, Ibrahim Khan, who had his own private reasons for wishing to see the General captured, and to this Ibrahim, a considerable character in his way, fell the congenial duty of acting as guide to Major Mitford, who took with him thirty men of his own regiment, the 14th Bengal Lancers. In the first village they tried, they had no success, and in the next they seemed likely to fare no

WITH THE SALONIKA ARMY : THE NEW PIER AT STAVROS.

Official Photograph. Crown Copyright Reserved.

better. The leader, with Ibrahim, and six dismounted men, entered the place and searched it thoroughly, in vain ; and, completely thrown out for the moment, stood in the courtyard of the headman's house, wondering

what to do next. Suddenly Mitford had an inspiration. Hearing the sound of women talking, he called in a loud voice to Ibrahim, " Where are the women's apartments ? The General wants to see the zenana."

This astounding proposition from a British officer knocked the excellent Ibrahim metaphorically flat. He stared open-mouthed at his commander, and imagined, perhaps, that the chief had taken leave of his senses. But already the ruse had worked. Indignant female voices betrayed the position of the zenana, and thither the search party made their way, led by the poor headman in person, under the gentle persuasion of a revolver held to his ear. As they went up a narrow stair, Ibrahim received orders to call out to the women to veil themselves, and no harm would come to them. But the dove-cote was terribly fluttered, and a chorus of screams greeted the arrival of the intruders. The beauties, to the impious eye of the beholder, presented only a huddled mass of feminine apparel, with a foot visible here and there. The narrator however, hints that they were not too frightened to take a sly glance at their visitor, and he swears to a flash or two of bright eyes.

[Continued overleaf.]

The Murder of Captain Fryatt Not forgotten by the Army.

AN EFFECT OF CAPTAIN FRYATT'S DEATH ON BRITISH TROOPS : SIGNIFICANT SHELL-INSCRIPTIONS.

The judicial murder of Captain Fryatt by the Germans has had a deep effect on the British Army at the front, as did that of Nurse Cavell, of which it was said that her death was worth an Army Corps to this country. Now, however, the Army is better able to give effect to its indignation, and Captain Fryatt's memory will act as a spur to their resolve. Deducing German motives for the crime from an article in the "Kreuz Zeitung," Mr. Charles Tower writes : "Captain Fryatt was murdered with the deliberate intention of exasperating British public opinion and of enabling the Pan-Germans, Annexationists, and anti - Bethmannites to cry, 'England will never forgive us now ; we must fight her to the last drop of blood.' "—[Official Photograph issued by the Press Bureau.]

But beauty was not in the bill that day for the British officer. The one woman whom he was privileged to see unveiled was of a most finished and perfect ugliness. As this good lady barred a door, which her visitor was curious to open, he bade her make way, and Ibrahim interpreted the order first in Persian and then in

WITH THE SALONIKA ARMY: ROYAL ENGINEERS LAYING A LIGHT RAILWAY.
Official Photograph. Crown Copyright Reserved.

Pushtoo, without result. Madam sat tight, gibbering and making most horrible grimaces. Budge she would not.

Words being in vain, Major Mitford resorted to action, and the occasion scarcely being one for ceremony, he used none, but picked the fair one up in his arms and set her down on the heap of trembling femininity in the corner. More screams and curses, Babel and confusion; but the way was now clear, and the ladies a negligible quantity.

The door was kicked open, and revealed a small, dark chamber in the wall. At first nothing could be seen, but gradually Major Mitford made out a white figure crouching in the far corner. He presented his revolver, and said, "Come out, or I 'll fire."

The inmate of the retreat mumbled something in Persian, which the officer failed to catch. Ibrahim, interpreting, explained that the person inside said he was lame, and could not obey. Further, he begged that his visitors would kindly go away and shut the door, as the light hurt his eyes. The plea did not prevail; for

Major Mitford had now a strong desire for the retiring gentleman's better acquaintance. He knew that at Char Asiab the gentle Saifoollah had been wounded in the foot. A lame man with an objection to publicity had therefore points of peculiar interest.

Certain cogent arguments soon brought the gentleman into clear visibility, whereupon Ibrahim, who loved to air his English before a native audience, fit, if few, set all doubt at rest with the fervent exclamation—" This your man, Sir; this your damn rascal ! "

The "damn rascal" it was, and if any further doubt existed, it was soon dispelled by an examination of his foot, which bore a half-healed bullet-wound. Saifoollah's stay in his seductive refuge was not prolonged. Someone found a pony in the village, and on this he was set for his journey to Headquarters. To make the story quite complete in its irony, the pony turned out to be the prisoner's own. The party left the village amid a storm of objurgations from the old lady and her fair charges, who might well weep for the unreturning brave, for they

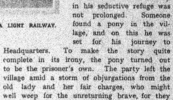

WITH THE SALONIKA ARMY: WHERE THE BRITISH LINE RUNS DOWN TO THE SEA.
Official Photograph.

had seen the last of the gallant "General" Saifoollah Deen.

In due time he was found guilty of complicity in the murder of Cavagnari, which earned him a short shrift and a long drop.

Some of Russia's 366,000 Austro-German Prisoners.

TAKEN BY THE RUSSIANS IN THE RECENT GREAT OFFENSIVE : TYPICAL AUSTRIAN GROUPS.

Russia's toll of prisoners taken in the recent fighting has reached an enormous figure. An official Petrograd communiqué of the 16th stated : "The total captures by the troops of General Brusiloff during the operations from June 4 up to August 12, in which period the winter fortified lines of the Austro-Germans, stretching from the River Pripet up to the Roumanian frontier, were captured, are as follows : . . . in all—7757 officers and 350,845 rank and file, 405 cannon, 1326 machine-guns, 338 mine and bomb-throwers, and 292 powder-carts." Considerable additions have been made since. A communiqué of the 17th said that General Bezobrazoff had captured a further 198 officers and 7308 men, with many guns, and over 14,000 shells.—[*Photos. by Kirushoff.*]

General Brusiloff's Victorious Advance in Galicia.

THE LEADER OF THE RUSSIAN LEFT-WING ARMY GROUP: GENERAL LECHITSKY.

General Lechitsky's army group, according to an official Petrograd message, captured between June 4 and August 12, 102,717 prisoners, 127 guns, and 464 machine and trench guns. The General, a man of sixty, has passed most of his career with the Siberian Army, which is continually undergoing war-training. He commanded the Siberian Rifle Division in the war with Japan; then the First Guard Division at Petrograd, and the 18th Army Corps. In June General Lechitsky overran Bukovina to the Carpathians, breaking up the Austrian Southern Armies. More recently he struck north and captured Stanislau, and the enemy's Dniester River positions, outflanking the centre army of Austro-Germans under Count Bothmer.

General Brusiloff's Victorious Advance in Galicia.

THE LEADER OF THE RUSSIAN RIGHT-WING ARMY GROUP : GENERAL SAKHAROFF.

The total of Austro-German prisoners and war spoil officially credited to the group of Russian armies under the leadership of General Sakharoff, for the period of General Brusiloff's offensive between June 4 and August 12, amounts to 89,215 officers and men, 76 guns, and 351 machine and trench guns. General Sakharoff is at the head of the troops operating against Count Bothmer's left wing. He commands the right wing of General Brusiloff's main force, corresponding to General Lechitsky's left-wing group of armies. General Sakharoff has been acknowledged as an officer of exceptional capacity ever since the Russo-Japanese War, when General Kuropatkin, Commander-in-Chief in Manchuria, chose him as Chief of the Staff to the armies in the field.

WITH THE AUSTRALIANS ON THE WESTERN

While the "Anzac" infantry regiments on the Western Front have been adding fresh laurels to the immortal fame they won at the Dardanelles, on the battlefields of Northern France during the Great Offensive, and notably at the capture of Pozières, their gunners have been no less profitably employed in the same district. The photograph shows a heavy position-gun of one of the

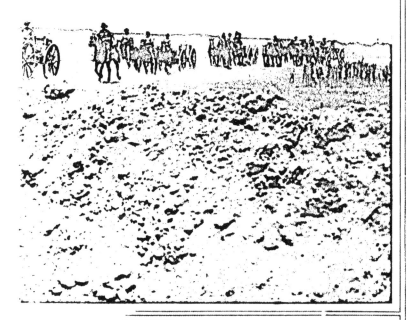

HARD-HITTER.

valuable aid by shelling German entrenched positions far in advance. If we hear less, ɛ recent battles, they are taking their full share equally with the infantry, of whose whole Empire is proud.—[*War Office Photograph issued by the Press Bureau.*]

At Verdun: A Recently Captured German "Albatross."

NOTING NEW FEATURES: GENERALS JOFFRE AND NIVELLE VIEWING THE FLYING-MACHINE.

An informative acquisition for the constructive branch of the French Military Air Department was made lately by the bringing-down within the French lines at Verdun, of a new type of German Albatross biplane, practically undamaged. In the upper illustration it is shown being examined by General Joffre himself. General Nivelle, the highly talented officer in charge of the Verdun forces, is seen beside the Generalissimo, to whom novel points of the engine mechanism are being explained. General Joffre is readily recognisable in the dark undress Staff uniform he always wears. In the second illustration the three French aviators concerned in the capture are seen being congratulated by the Generals.—[French War Office Photographs.]

After the Storming of a Somme Position by the French.

IN A CAPTURED VILLAGE : A WRECKED GERMAN RAILWAY LINE AND AN ENGINE LEFT DERELICT.

The actual taking of trenches and gains of ground apart, one highly useful and satisfactory piece of work effected by the Allied offensive in the West is the disintegration of the network of railway lines which intersect the German front-line positions. They are laid to enable reinforcements to be moved rapidly between threatened points, and keep up a continuous supply of munitions as these arrive at the main railway junctions in rear, from Krupp's and elsewhere in Germany. The upper illustration shows how one such light line was laid through a village recently captured by the French, and its wrecked state after the preliminary bombardment. In the lower is noted the fate of a German engine disabled and left standing on the line.—[French War Office Photographs.]

Nearly 3,000 Years Old: "Finds" at Salonika.

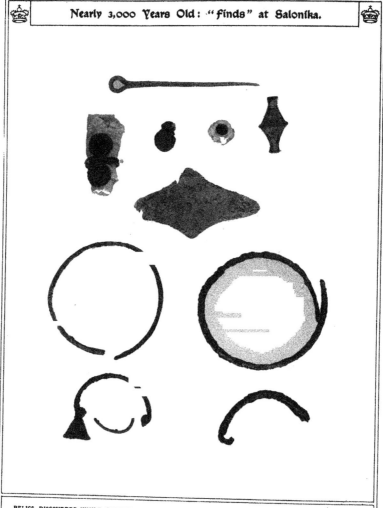

RELICS DISCOVERED WHILE DIGGING BRITISH TRENCHES NEAR SALONIKA: ORNAMENTS 2700 YEARS OLD.

These ornaments, found in ancient graves while trench-digging near Salonika, are said to date from the eighth century B.C. The objects are (reading from left to right, beginning at the top)—a gold spike, bronze spiral ring, earthenware bead, china bead, gold ornament, gold ornament with design impressed, bronze bracelets, and bronze safety-pin. Describing the museum mentioned on the opposite page, Mr. Ward Price continues: "The best things came from a tomb which one of our working parties dug into near Langaza Lake. It contained a skeleton bedecked with ornaments of gold and bronze of a pattern unusual in Greece, though found in middle Europe, which may prove to be a link of some archaeological importance."—[Official Photograph issued by the Press Bureau.]

Archaeology in War: "Finds" at Salonika.

UNEARTHED WHILE TRENCH-DIGGING, AND KEPT FOR GREECE: ANCIENT INCISED POTTERY.

"The country around Salonika," writes Mr. G. Ward Price, "is rich in archaeological remains, and has never been properly explored. The Allied Armies decided to take steps to preserve the relics that they found, for the benefit of the Greek Government. . . . A well-known English professor of archaeology was here already as a lieutenant in the R.N.V.R., and he was put in charge of a collection of British finds which he is arranging as a local archaeological museum in the White Tower." A British cyclist officer at Salonika writes: "The road by which we came was before the war absolutely unknown to all but about three archaeologists; some of the most perfect and invaluable things have been found there. . . ."—[Official Photograph issued by the Press Bureau.]

FOOTNOTES TO ARMAGEDDON: II.—WIRE.

THE Verey flare made a creepy daylight over "No Man's Land." The watching men stared avidly, greedily using every moment of the brightness.

"No mistake about *that*," said the Lieutenant, when the light had sunk into blackness once more. "The whole happy family outside the bags. Did you see 'em? As numerous as a battalion; neither in profile nor deportment are they like wire - entanglement supports?"

The Subaltern said ruefully, "Well, *they* don't seem short of wire, do they? From the size of that party, they are rolling in wire. Opulent beasts! Let 's take it out of them with a little *strafe*."

"Shall I give 'em a couple o' trays, Sir?" said the machine-gunner, thinking this was his cue. "Got a line on 'em, dead sure." The machine-gunner was looking affectionately along his gun to that point, now invisible in that deep darkness that is before the dawn, where the large German working party was renewing its entanglements with a detestably lavish supply of wire. A couple of minutes' work from his gun, and there would be no German working party. The machine-gunner, like the Subaltern, would like

DURING THE ADVANCE IN THE WEST: AN AUSTRALIAN SIGNALMAN MENDING HIS APPARATUS.

Official Photograph.

to balance matters by a few emphatic moments of shooting. It would relieve the feelings. The Lieutenant said, thoughtfully, "Wait."

They waited. It was very unpleasant to wait while the Germans piled up defences. It was almost against nature to wait when one was on a sure target. But they waited. They heard muffled sounds from the other side of "No Man's Land" — the soft shuffling of nervous men, now and then the gentle "clop" of muffled mallets, now and then the tang of cut wire, now and then the gentle crash of things dropped to the ground. The Subaltern was impatient and angry.

"Listen to the brutes," he whispered. "For heaven's sake, let Johns give them a tray or two. That 's another knife - rest over the bags—that 's the fifth I 've counted. Positively wallowing in wire, they are. Let 's take the pride out of them, Smith."

Lieutenant Smith again said "Wait." But now he said it with something sharp in his voice. The Subaltern thought there was a chuckle in it—almost. He couldn't understand it. He thought that the heads of full Lieutenants had surfaces that tended to impenetrability. The machine-gunner was resigned. He thought he

[Continued overleaf.

DURING THE ADVANCE IN THE WEST: AUSTRALIAN TRAVELLING - KITCHENS IN THE FIELD.

Official Photograph.

The British Offensive: Scenes Now Often Witnessed.

GERMAN PRISONERS: ARRIVALS AT A DETENTION-CAMP—AND OUR MEN'S CHIVALRY.

The activities and spheres of labour of the Army Service Corps are admittedly manifold; extensive and peculiar. They include, as the upper photograph shows, the carting of German prisoners from the front to the first-line detention-camps. There the prisoners, as batch after batch are brought in, remain until a sufficient number have been collected and a convenient opportunity arrives for sending them further to the rear, to be entrained for their ports of embarkation for England. The illustration of British soldiers tossing cigarettes to their captives testifies to the kindly, chivalrous spirit of our men. The reverse of such an incident—German soldiers so behaving to British captives—is, unfortunately, unimaginable!—[Official Photographs; supplied by the Press Bureau.]

saw now why it was we hadn't won the war so soon. They waited, and presently the Lieutenant got down from the firing-step—his line of route was obviously set towards the dug-out.

"If anything extra happens," he said to the sentry, "call me before you fire." The Sub-altern followed him backwards more in anger than in sorrow. The Subaltern was protesting softly.

"There is a proverb all about waiting," said the Lieutenant to his junior. "Bear it in mind, old dear. Consider it well—and let me go to sleep. Waiting sometimes pays."

But this did not appear to be one of those happy times. When morning came the German trenches looked loathly. Barbed wire had grown up there like a species of weed. Knife-rests had accumulated with abominable profusion. The luxuriance of those entanglements was disgusting. The Lieutenant looked at them assiduously throughout the day. And now and then the angry Sub. thought he chuckled. The Sub. thought that the Lieutenant's attitude towards the whole business was fundamentally dangerous, and when the Lieutenant said to him, apropos of nothing, that "they" were not bad fellows, "Saxons, you know," the Sub. wondered whether he should report to H.Q. that his senior officer was mad. As the day went on his conviction deepened, and he could hardly keep away from the H.Q. telephone. For in the afternoon the Lieutenant had chosen a working party, a large working party, for that night. The Sub. said, "Hullo, has our wire come along, or is it coming along?" And to that the fool Lieutenant had answered, foolishly, "Perhaps."

The Lieutenant laughed at the Sub. when the latter tried to talk wisdom and mere sense, and the Lieutenant got over the parapet with

deuce . . . . He tried to tell himself that what he was hearing couldn't be mallet - strokes, or the noise of men busy over wire. It was all idiotic. The Lieutenant came tumbling back before dawn. He was chuckling. So were his men. The Sub. was too dignified

THE SOMME OFFENSIVE: A FRENCH ARTILLERY OBSERVATION - OFFICER AND HIS PORTABLE SEARCHLIGHT.

to ask questions. But he thought the Lieutenant rather incompetent, on the whole.

In the morning the Saxons woke him. The Saxons were very bad-tempered. They were yelling. Also they were wasting much good ammunition against solid parapets in the way the Teutonic mind does when it is really hurt. The Sub. went to the fire-step at the double, and gazed at nature and the Saxons through his periscope. At first, the most amazing thing about the Saxon trenches was the illusion that they were without entanglements. All that beautiful wire, all those beautiful knife-rests, had vanished. The second amazing thing was that they had all crossed over "No Man's Land" in the night. All that beautiful wire, all those knife-rests—were before the British trenches. The Lieutenant was behind the Sub. There was no mistake about his chuckling now.   W. DOUGLAS NEWTON.

ENEMY WAR-DOGS: KENNELS BEHIND THE LINES ON THE EASTERN FRONT.

his working party. The Sub. thought he was living in a world of dreams and lunatics. What the deuce was the good of going out "there" empty-handed? What the

The Physiognomy of the 20th Century Hun.

FACIAL TYPES OF GERMAN PRISONERS : MEN OF RECENT BATCHES FROM THE SOMME.

These are typical German prisoners in France recently brought in to one of the detention-camps, from the battlefields on the Somme. One of them, it will be noted, has still on a German steel trench-helmet. The German prisoners in France wear the uniforms they arrive in as long as the garments are wearable, the only mark or badge to show that they are captives being the letters "P.G." (*prisonnier de guerre*), which are affixed or stamped on the backs of their coats. They are well housed in huts behind barbed-wire barriers, are well fed, and have plenty of tobacco supplied them. Occupation is provided for them on public works of various kinds, according to the sort of labour required in each neighbourhood.— [*Photo. by Wyndham.*]

For Wives of Soldiers Travelling by Train.

"THE MARSHALL GUEST-ROOM," WATERLOO ROAD Y.M.C.A. HUT : AT THE OPENING.

A "Wives' Room," for wives accompanying soldiers to Waterloo Railway Station or meeting them on arrival, was opened on August 15 at the Y.M.C.A. Hut in Waterloo Road by Lady Lloyd, wife of Major-General Sir Francis Lloyd, commanding the London District. In the new room (known as "The Marshall Guest-Room") teas will be obtainable, and there will also be facilities for doing needlework. In the upper photograph are seen (reading from left to right) : Mrs. T. R. Marshall, the donor of the hut (in a black hat and standing) Lady Lloyd, and Major-General Lloyd. In the lower illustration a soldier and his wife and family are seen at tea. Similar rooms, it is hoped, will be provided near other railway termini.—[Photos. by S. and G.]

An Appropriate Figure on a Bombarded Church.

AN ALLY OF GERMANY? A STONE DEVIL GLARES AT FRENCH TROOPS MARCHING TO THE TRENCHES.

There is something peculiarly appropriate to the surroundings in the figure of the stone devil in the above photograph, which was taken recently during the French operations on the Somme. The French soldiers marching along the road below are on their way to the trenches. As they pass the ruined church, wrecked, no doubt, by bombardment, they look up, smiling at the grotesque image leering down at them from the broken wall. The demon has the air of gloating over the general devastation and the prospect of further bloodshed. He is not unlike the Devil in Raemaekers' cartoon, shown as Germany's Ally, who remarks that his name would not benefit the business, but that his partners are quite competent to conduct it themselves.—[Photo. by Topical.]

From the New Country to the Old: Canadian Colours.

FLAGS FROM WINDSOR, ONTARIO: COLOURS, TO BE SAFEGUARDED IN WINDSOR, BERKSHIRE.

Our first photograph shows an interesting procession from the Town Hall, Windsor, to the Parish Church, in the old High Street, which has in its time witnessed so many historic scenes. The Colours of the 99th Essex County Reserve Battalion, Canadian Expeditionary Force, are being carried to the church, there to be deposited for safe keeping during the war. The Battalion was mobilised in the City of Windsor, Ontario. The Mayor and Town Council took part in the ceremony of the 16th inst., and our second photograph shows an interesting group, taken outside the Town Hall, in which are seen the Mayor of Windsor, Lieut.-Colonel T. B. Welch, Commanding, and the two lieutenants carrying the Colours.—[Photos. by Sport and General.]

At the Italian Front: A Tribute to the Alliance.

HOW THE STORMERS OF GORIZIA KEEP FIT :— FOOTBALL MATCH—AND A BRITISH LINESMAN.

This pair of illustrations, depicting incidents at a football match at an Italian camp recently, have a curious and instructive interest. They show something of the physical capabilities of the Italian soldier—the match taking place under blazing sunshine, in grilling heat. Northern Italy in July and August is as torrid a place, perhaps, as any on the continent of Europe. One can understand something of the powers of endurance of the stormers of the heights at Gorizia in as hot weather as this summer has seen. From another point of view the illustrations are of interest as showing how one of our own soldiers' favourite camp games finds favour with the soldiers of one of our Allies. A love of sport "makes the whole world kin."—[Photos. by S. and G.]

WOMEN AND THE WAR.

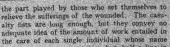

CHARITY begins at home. The proverb is as true to-day as it ever was, but it all depends on the definition of home. Our horizon has now to be widened to sweep in not only the whole British Empire, but France, Russia, Serbia, Belgium, and all the rest. For these are all "home" for the purposes of war and charity.

An industrial magnate in the North is credited with the remark that "the women are going to pull the country through this war." His generous overstatement of the case is most probably due to the fact that his conversion to the value of women's help in matters industrial, dates from the time the nation utilised their services to help make munitions of war. Not that women have any intention of posing as the saviours of England. And though women cannot fight for their country, and are not yet in a position to help in its government, no history of the war will be complete that does not include a record of their activities.

Never before in the history of the world have women's efforts in all directions met with greater encouragement or, on the whole, more generous recognition, and the opposition in the early days against the dilution of labour has collapsed under the pressure of war necessity. Everyone knows that women have done splendid work in munitions factories throughout the country. Equally important has been

WOMEN ON THE LAND: A WOMAN-WORKER IN KENT.

Now that crops are being cut all over the country, and men-workers are for the most part doing gallant work in a very different field, it is no uncommon thing to see, as in our photograph, taken in Kent, a woman sharpening her scythe. The help of the women-workers in the rush of harvest-time is proving of great value to farmers all over the country.—[Photo. by Photopress.]

the part played by those who set themselves to relieve the sufferings of the wounded. The casualty lists are long enough, but they convey no adequate idea of the amount of work entailed in the care of each single individual whose name occupies but half a line in the newspaper. Hundreds of thousands of women are employed in hospital work, and the British Red Cross Society appeals for thousands more.

Women have taken their responsibilities seriously in this war. "Home" boundaries have been widely extended. The certainty of encountering disease, difficulty, and danger has merely spurred women on to greater effort to help our Allies in the different theatres of action. Unfortunate Serbia, Russia (now marching, as we are convinced, to victory), martyred Belgium, and France have all good cause to be grateful to Englishwomen.

Of all the hospitals organised by private enterprise probably none have done better or more valuable work than those known as the Scottish Women's Hospitals for Foreign Service. War had no sooner been declared than the National Union of Women's Suffrage Societies, in common with other suffrage bodies, suspended its political activities. Ever since, its great organisation and resources have been devoted to war relief work. The Scottish Federation of the Union decided on hospital work, and the Scottish

"SWEET GIRL."—GARDENERS: AT OTFORD CASTLE FARM, KENT.

The war has translated the charm of poetry into prosaic but very practical and useful fact, and our photograph shows a group of girls, including two Girton girls, who live in an oast house in Kent, sleep under canvas, and work hard in the hop-gardens during the day. The variety in their working garb is picturesque, and the workers distinctly "give satisfaction" to their employer.—[Photo. by Photopress.]

[Continued overleaf.

"The Harvest Truly is Plenteous."

"THE LABOURERS ARE FEW": WOMEN-WORKERS ON THE LAND IN TIME OF HARVEST.

There is every promise of a good harvest, and women have come forward to take the place of men who are at the front, and this, in no mere holiday-making humour, but in real earnest, working hard and giving complete satisfaction to farmers. In our first photograph a woman-worker is seen riding, man-fashion, one fine horse and leading another. In the second picture the farmer's daughter, Miss Luke, is herself driving the machine, and a soldier in khaki is at the side. Mr. Luke, of Aldboro' Hatch Farm, Essex, has arranged for a number of soldier helpers. His daughter is an expert reaper and is shown cutting a large field of wheat. The versatility of the woman-worker as elicited by the war is little less than wonderful.—[Photos. by C.N.]

Women's Hospitals for Foreign Service, which a month or two ago had been responsible for 1300 beds and received subscriptions amounting to over £104,000, are the result of their labours.

The first hospital started at Calais undertook, by special request of a famous Belgian surgeon,

GOLF COURSES IN WAR-TIME : FROM PLAY TO WORK.
In addition to its original purpose, the golf course at Sandy Hook is now in part utilised as a poultry farm, and for the growth of potatoes and other vegetables. The labour is largely supplied by boys on holiday and by girls, or women. Our photograph shows a greenswoman and a girl mowing one of the greens.—[Photo. by Alfieri.]

the charge of a typhoid annexe, and the hospital gained the distinction of having the lowest death-rate of any similar institution in the place. The epidemic coming to an end, the activities of the hospital staff were transferred to another sphere of work.

The woeful lack of all medical requisites in Serbia was not the least of the drawbacks against which its people had to contend, and Serbia in consequence has received a very large share of the attention of the Committee of the Scottish Women's Hospitals. The first unit was sent there at the beginning of 1915. Others soon followed. One of them, by the way, was detained by the Government for a fortnight at Malta to help cope with the rush of wounded from the Dardanelles. But the enemy occupation of Serbia necessitated a hasty change of plans, and the evacuation of hospitals already established. Down through Serbia to the coast marched the *personnel* of some of the units. The distance was over two hundred miles, most of it had to be done on foot, and it took six weeks in bitter cold weather to do it. Of the other units, one was

captured by the Austrians, and its members treated as common prisoners of war. Another fell into the hands of the Germans. After a good many hardships, both succeeded in reaching England once more. From all of which it will be seen that some of the workers attached to the Scottish Women's Hospitals have had their share of adventure—a good deal of it under conditions the reverse of agreeable. Because Serbia was invaded it did not mean that Serbia had no further need of such help as the Scottish units could give it. Streams of Serbian refugees, flying before the invading enemy armies, went to Corsica. The French Government have found accommodation for some 5000 refugees, and a Scottish unit is in charge of their medical affairs.

There is, too, a unit at Salonika. It is there, by order of the French military authorities, attached to the army operating in the Balkans. As the occasions on which a voluntary hospital has been ordered to accompany an expeditionary force are very few in number, the unit is naturally proud of the honour conferred upon it, and the implied compliment to the organisation it represents. There is another hospital at Royaumont, in France. Originally intended for a hundred patients, it was

GOLF COURSES IN WAR-TIME : WOMEN-WORKERS WEEDING A SAND-HILL.
It is no light task which these women-workers have set themselves, for the coarse bent which they have to exterminate is of the hard-and-wiry kind of grass common to waste and, and might almost be held as peace parallels to the wire "entanglements" in the war area.—[Photo. by Alfieri.]

enlarged to double its former size, at the urgent request of the French medical department, whose enthusiasm and admiration for the staff is wholehearted and sincere.   CLAUDINE CLEVE.

Home Work for a Rare "Bird," the Conscientious Objector.

CONSCIENTIOUS OBJECTORS USEFULLY EMPLOYED : MEN OF THE N.C.C. ON A MILITARY ROAD.

In order to utilise the services of conscientious objectors, it will be remembered, the military authorities formed a Non-Combatant Corps, to be employed on various kinds of useful work. Our photographs show some of the men employed on the construction of a military road in East Anglia. Others of the corps have been sent to France, where the first batches arrived early in May.

"At present," wrote Mr. Philip Gibbs shortly afterwards, "they are engaged on railway work ; but afterwards, if they are strong enough, they will be put to stiffer work. ' 'It is part of our faith,' said one of them, 'that it is wrong to take human life. If we became combatants we should deny our faith.' " Another said : "It 's not cowardice that brings us here."—[Photo. by L.N.A.]

No Man's Land: A Section of the Long Stri

WHERE THE DEAD ARE OFTEN UNCLAIMED: "NO MAN'S LAND"—PHOTOGRAPHE

"No Man's Land" is, of course, the ground that lies between the front trenches of the opposing armies. It varies in v at different points, and in some places—as here—it is only a few yards across. This long strip of tortured soil that v across Northern France and Flanders is an outcome of the modern system of trench warfare. Its position is shifted, of course,

₂uted Territory between the Opposing Trenches.

WHERE THE HOSTILE TRENCHES ARE SEPARATED BY ONLY A FEW YARDS.

advance, and it is a scene of utter desolation. Ordinarily, no one can appear in it in daylight and hope to live ; only at do men crawl across it stealthily, or make sudden rushes to raid the enemy's trenches. Bodies of those who fall there often n for weeks and months unclaimed and unburied.—[Official Photograph authorised by the French War Office.]

A Soldier's Unconventional Wedding.

MARRIED IN A MILITARY HOSPITAL : A SAPPER'S WEDDING AT BARRY ISLAND, GLAMORGANSHIRE.

St. John's Military Hospital, Barry Island, reverted to its original purpose for a time on Saturday last. Before its conversion for the occupation of wounded soldiers, it was a Wesleyan Chapel, and on Saturday it was the scene of the wedding of Sapper W. H. Crockett, R.E., and Miss Mitchell. Our first photograph shows the bride and bridegroom and their friends leaving the altar for the vestry ; our second, nurses and patients lined up outside the building ready good-humouredly to "strafe" with confetti the newly married couple. Staff, nurses, and patients all showed the friendliest interest in the wedding, and patients in cots formed a novel "Guard of Honour" outside the building. The hospital has already dealt with two thousand patients.—[Photographs by Topical.]

The Illustrated War News, Aug. 30, 1916.—Part 12, New Series.

The Illustrated War News

THE LATEST ALLY OF THE ENTENTE : HIS MAJESTY KING FERDINAND OF ROUMANIA.

Photograph by Mandy.

THE GREAT WAR.

By W. DOUGLAS NEWTON.

ALTHOUGH the week has been, in the main, devoid of major encounters, it has, none the less, been full of events that are interesting and stimulating enough as signs of the uncheckable volatility of the Allies. There has been this quickening movement all over the world, and at every point that movement has been of our commanding. Not merely in the West have we fought German attacks to the standstill, and then pushed forward ourselves with an unexcited imperturbability; not only in the East has movement being going on as Russia breaks the Austro-German spirit, and forces her advances; but there has also been fighting in the Asiatic East—a new blow by Russia against a Turkish point of self-congratulation; there has been a pronounced and significant development in the Balkan East, where the Armies of all the Allies have joined up to present a new weapon, fused in unity, to the fronts of the enemy; there has, in that Italy which was for a time Austria, been steady movement; in East Africa there has been that progress which is leading to the last acts of the German comedy of occupation; and, finally, on the sea, truth has again got the better of a German success, and an enemy victory over two of our light cruisers has proved to be the sort of victory the Germans gain by losing a capital ship like the *Westfalen*, and a submarine, if not two, into the bargain. In the entire ring of war where is the decisive German success? —unless we name the safe arrival of the submersible *Deutschland* such a one? And then—what is one small *Deutschland* among so much?

The success that gave the British the Thiepval-Pozières-Longueval hill crests has had its natural

AT THE FRONT DURING THE BRITISH ADVANCE : THE GERMANS SHELLING OUR WIRE ENTANGLEMENTS.

While our gunners are destroying the German trenches by bombardments, the enemy reply with similar artillery fire on our trench lines. One of their objects is to clear away the British wire entanglements, in view of counter-attacks. *[Official Photograph. Crown Copyright Reserved.]*

OFF DUTY AFTER THE TAKING OF GORIZIA : AN ITALIAN OFFICER AND HIS PET PUPPY.
Photograph by C.N.

reaction in German anxiety, and the enemy has spent a determined week trying to win those heights back. The fighting may not possess much of the dramatic air that lies in great success, but it has been of fierce and terrible nature. The enemy appears to have come on with great, if unavailing, resolution time and time again. At points the fringes of the assault did penetrate into our works, notably south of Thiepval and at the advance posts near High Wood, but even these footholds availed nothing, and reflex movements on the part of our men not only drove the attacks off, but carried our line further forward, so that we have now straightened out most of our salients on the heights, have advanced until we are well within five hundred yards of Thiepval, and have pushed forward in other areas, the Pozières zone particularly. The whole tendency of this fighting is to reduce the Thiepval defences, and to cause the collapse of the whole of this very strong sector of the enemy line. When that is done it may be found that a big German front, running up towards Arras, will be in a position of considerable difficulty, and that a great deal of genius will have to be employed to hold the German scheme of defence in the West together. That the Germans place particular value on their dispositions in the Thiepval bend needs no more evidence than that shown by the calibre of their effort here during the week-end. No less a force than that of the redoubtable Prussian Guard was flung against our new hold south of the village. The attack was bitterly determined; but, thanks to the steadiness of two fine county regiments—the Wiltshires and the Worcesters, the assault was a failure. At the same time, attacks of an almost equal intensity were driven against our front in the Guillemont sector. These were broken. The attack on the latter front was an attempt to regain a valuable point of ground captured by the British in an advance on Friday. The advance gave us command of several hundred yards of works on the eastern and north-eastern fringes of Delville Wood north-east of Guillemont. It is a bite into the enemy line that places our front in valuable position, since it now tends to overhang Guillemont and its precarious defences.

On their front the French have been meeting with equanimity the heavy buffets of counter-offensive. The whole of their line north and south of the Somme has had to face these engagements, and, on the whole, the French have broken up the German advances admirably. As with

notably heavy. Indeed, in a war of almost incessant movement the Western Allies are forcing the pace for their enemies in a manner that must be intensely detrimental to their strength and their morale. There has been some violent fighting both on the Champagne and Fleury fronts, but the final results of the encounters have been to the advantage of the French, particularly at Verdun.

The first item of Eastern news concerns the reawakening of the southern wing of the Caucasian campaign. Here, during an offensive in the beginning of August, the Turks were able to force the Russians back to a depth of thirty miles, capturing the towns of Mush and Bitlis in their stride. The Russians turned their attention from the Erzinghan zone, where they had a great deal in hand, and reorganised their troops on the

A WAR-HONOURS CEREMONY IN MOROCCO: GENERAL LYAUTEY DECORATING SOLDIERS
ON THE DAY OF THE FÊTE NATIONALE.

The French Fête Nationale was observed in Morocco by a presentation of war decorations to soldiers of the local army corps from the front. General Lyautey, the Resident-General, performed the ceremony at Rabat before a large gathering of Moroccan notables.

the British, the French had to suffer penetration at several points of their front; near Soyécourt was one such break, but the lines were soon made good at the affected points, and the French, in return, have been gaining advances all the week—in the Guillemont-Maurepas zone, near Cléry, and even about Soyécourt. They have captured trenches and prisoners and guns, and have still forced their way forward until, their work in the Maurepas sector being so good, they were able to take in a sweep those houses of the village of Maurepas that they did not already possess, and push east and south on a front of a mile and a quarter, to a depth of 200 yards. Here, elsewhere on the French line, and at all points of the British line, the casualties of the enemy have been

Lake Van front. The result is to hand. The Russians have won forward again, Mush has fallen, and so powerful was the drive that the Turkish forces were handled with extreme severity. An entire battalion and the great part of another fell intact into Russian hands, and in all 2300 prisoners were taken. Our Ally will no doubt press on to Diarbekr, and thus not merely straighten his line, but menace in a very thorough manner the Mesopotamian and Persian communications, particularly the Nisibin railhead of the Bagdad railway. There is every sign of this forward movement, for under the threat of advance Bitlis has been evacuated, while the harried Fourth Turkish Division is falling back on the Tigris and its base at Mosul.

The forces of Russia in Europe are still meeting with very obstinate resistance, though there are signs that General Brusiloff is gathering his strength for a deep blow, as there are also signs that this appearance of endless supplies of reserves is making the enemy timid. There has been no particular movement in the major portion of the Polish or Galician line, though in the Carpathians it is obvious that our Ally is working to control the summits, and has already brought the advance guards into play, and by this means dispersed the enemy holding the ground west of Nadvorna, occupying the village of Guta. Already the sources of the rivers Bystritza and Bystritza - Nadvorna in the Rafalov area have been reached, and the enemy's resistance subdued. This progress in the Carpathians is interesting. It may prove to have meaning not only for Hungary, but, as I write, comes a report that Roumania has joined the Allies.

The condition of Roumania and the Balkans generally is certainly worthy of a great deal of attention just now. It is vain to prophesy anything about a peninsula so enigmatical, but we can watch the very definite things that appear to be happening there. Of Roumania herself it is best to adopt a waiting attitude, noting, by the way, that her vote for military purposes has just been expanded from £8,000,000 to £24,000,000, that some drastic changes have been made in her higher military commands, and that Berlin and Vienna show an attitude of nervous anger towards the Danube State. Of the

SETTING AN EXAMPLE TO YOUNG ITALY : THE DUKE OF AOSTA'S HEIR DIGGING A GUN-PIT.

Prince Amadeus of Savoy, who is also known as the Duke of the Puglie, has taken his place in the ranks as a gunner.
Photo. by Brocherel.

A BOY PRINCE OF THE ITALIAN ROYAL HOUSE AT THE FRONT : PRINCE AMADEUS OF SAVOY, CORPORAL OF ARTILLERY.

The sixteen-year-old Prince Amadeus of Savoy, eldest son of the Duke of Aosta, is doing his part as a corporal of artillery on the Isonzo front. His father commanded the corps that stormed Gorizia, and has won high distinction as a leader.
Photo. by Brocherel.

critical fronts in Greece much more can be said. Here the situation has taken on a more determined complexion by the entry of both Italian and Russian contingents into the army of the Allies holding the front at Salonika. At the same time there has been fighting of varying and curious quality. This fighting was caused by a Bulgarian offensive ; this in answer to the Allied move that gave us command of certain positions near Doiran. The offensive against the Serbs on the left wing was legitimate enough, even if it failed ; but the movement upon the Greek posts of Seres, Kavalla, and the like brought about a grave situation. Certain of the Greek posts resisted, and so great was the outcry in Greece that the Germans had to call off their acquisitive ally. The movement toward Kavalla has apparently stopped, and, the Bulgar assault on the left wing tiring, the Serbs at once turned to counter-assault. They are pushing up into the Moglena Mountains, and have so far driven back the Bulgars half a mile in the Ostrovo sector. The British cavalry has also been active, and has blown up bridges on the right wing, notably those on the Angista that carried the Salonika - Drama Railway. With the fall of Kilossa and the march of General Smuts's troops on Dares - Salaam, the German hold on the Central Railway of German East Africa seems virtually at an end, and on the face of things it seems improbable that the East African campaign can last many weeks longer.

LONDON : AUG. 28, 1916.

A "Poilu" as Disciple of Izaac Walton.

RECREATION AFTER WAR'S ALARMS : A FRENCH SOLDIER WITH ROD AND LINE ON THE MARNE.

Occasional periods of rest and recreation are essential for men engaged in the nerve-racking work of war, in order to maintain the efficiency of mind and body. There is no more peaceful occupation than fishing in a quiet river on a summer day ; and here we see a French soldier, temporarily off duty, thus whiling away a free hour at a village in the Department of the Marne. His rod is of the home-made type, but that would not detract from his enjoyment, and it may be hoped that he had good sport. Both the church and the bridge, it will be noted, bear signs of having suffered severely from bombardment, and form a strange contrast with the *insouciance* of the angler, intent only on watching for a "bite."—[*French War Office Official Photograph.*]

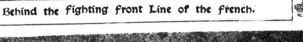

Behind the Fighting Front Line of the French.

CAMP BANDSMEN WITH INSTRUMENTS MADE BY THEMSELVES; AND A SHELLED HEADQUARTERS.

In the upper illustration an improvised band for entertainments in camp is shown, with instruments contrived by the men themselves from odds and ends—flutes, flageolets, violins, and two 'cellos constructed with packing-cases. The second illustration shows a ruin that still remains to mark the track of the German invaders in the advance on Paris of August and September 1914, which was stopped by the Franco-British victory on the Marne. We see here the ruined remains of what was before the war a beautiful country house. The German Crown Prince made it his temporary head-quarters, and other German officers lived there until shelled out by the French themselves, whose projectiles reduced the mansion to a wrecked condition.—[French War Office Official Photographs.]

War-Harvesting in France—Soldiers and Peasants.

HARVEST TIME ON THE SOMME AND THE MARNE : PEACE—AND WAR.

Our first photograph shows one of the contrasts which are so often the outcome of the war—French soldiers encamped in the Somme district, near a village from which the peasants have been obliged to flee, taking up their work in the fields, cutting the corn that is ripe and ready to harvest. Their tents are seen in the background, under the shade of the trees. In the second photograph one of the old peasants left in the Marne district has ceased work for the moment to watch the passing of a military convoy. Here, again, the contrast is striking, and drives home with the vigour of realism the stern lesson and strange transformations brought about by the great struggle now at its height in the pastoral districts of France.—[French War Office Official Photographs.]

The Resurgence of the Serbian Army.

IN THEIR NEW EQUIPMENT—INCLUDING STEEL HELMETS : SERBIAN TROOPS AT SALONIKA.

The Serbian Army, after being reorganised and refitted, recently took the field again at Salonika, and have already had some notable successes. They are naturally burning to drive the invader from their country. A French official communiqué of August 23 from Salonika stated : " Along the entire mountain front west of the Moglenitza the Serbian troops are developing their offensive.

On the extreme left they reoccupied by a vigorous counter - attack Hill 1506. . . . Hot fighting continues on the Serbian left, north of Lake Ostrovo, where the Serbians are holding the Gajund Well." The upper photograph shows a Serbian regiment leaving for the Doiran front. In the lower one some Serbian soldiers are seen in bivouac.—[Photos. by Underwood and Underwood.]

With the Russians on the Eastern Front.

GOING INTO ACTION AND ENTRAINING MUNITIONS: MEN OF THE VICTORIOUS RUSSIAN ARMIES.

Our correspondent who sends these two photographs from the Eastern front states, regarding the upper one, that it shows Russian troops going towards the trenches. It will be noted that some of them are carrying large planks, possibly to be used as bridges for crossing trenches; while the heavy smoke in the background indicates that some action is in progress. In the lower photograph some Russian soldiers are seen busily engaged in loading a train with munitions of war. At the moment of writing the centre of interest in the Russian campaign has shifted from Galicia to the Caucasus. Russian communiqués of August 24 announced the capture of Mush, near Lake Van, with some 2500 Turkish prisoners.—[Photos. by Korsakoff.]

THE BEGINNINGS OF WAR-MACHINES: RIFLES AND BREECH-LOADERS.

THE invention of rifling for firearms dates from the middle of the sixteenth century; but, although used for sporting weapons at an earlier period, rifled arms were put to no serious military use until the end of that century. In the beginning of the seventeenth century rifles were used by certain Danish and Bavarian troops, and some French cavalry units were armed with them about 1680. Although the advantages of the rifle in point of accuracy and range were recognised, it did not, for some time, become popular as a military weapon. The difficulty of forcing the tight-fitting bullet required down the barrel against the grooves, so retarded the loading operation that a slow rate of fire was unavoidable, compared with that of the old smooth-bore musket, whose bullet dropped easily down into its place. This trouble was responsible for the non-adoption of the rifle for service use until about the end of the eighteenth century. The final triumph of rifling was probably due to the experience gained in hunting rather than in fighting, accuracy of fire being of more importance than rapidity in sporting work.

The hunter's rifle used for military purposes in the American War of Independence gave practical proof of its immense advantages, and went some way towards causing its adoption by other nations. Napoleon armed some of his troops with the rifle, but gave it up, as he considered that the firing was too slow. After the American War the British authorities formed the Rifle Brigade and armed it with the Baker rifle (Fig. 1). This weapon fired a spherical lead bullet. It was sighted up to 200 yards, and was rifled with seven grooves. Great difficulty, however, was experienced in loading the weapon, and a wooden mallet was provided with which to drive down the bullet.

Fig. 2 shows the Brunswick rifle, issued to the Rifle Brigade in 1836. This was a percussion rifle of a very large bore, more than twice that of the present Service weapon. Fig. 6 shows the bullet used, which is peculiar in that a projecting band runs round it to fit the two grooves in the barrel, the spiral of which gives the turn in thirty inches. Many attempts were made from time to time to overcome the loading difficulty by providing a ball which would slip easily down the barrel, and would have a tight fit during the discharge of the piece. In one of these, by M. Delvigne (Fig. 4), the diameter of the powder-chamber was reduced, and the bullet was expanded by forcing it with the ramrod against the shoulder thus formed. This method, however, so deformed it that its accuracy was impaired. Poncharra, in 1833, improved upon the Delvigne system by enclosing the bullet in a greased patch, and placing it in a wooden cup. Greener's compound bullet (Fig. 3) is another example of an attempt to produce an expanding bullet. In this case the force of the explosion was employed to drive a tapered plug into the body of the bullet.

The introduction of the Minié rifle (Fig. 7)

FIG. 14.—SYSTEMS OF RIFLING IN BRITISH ARMY WEAPONS.
The left-hand three, reading from top to bottom, represent the Enfield (five-grooved) system; the Lancaster oval-bore system; the Metford system. The right-hand three represent, in similar order, the Enfield (three-grooved) system; the Whitworth hexagonal-bore system; and the Henry system.

marked the abolition of the spherical bullet. From this time onwards conical and semi-cylindrical bullets were universally adopted. The Minié bullet (Fig. 9) had a loose iron centre, which the force of the explosion drove into its base, and in that way expanded it to fit the grooves. The Minié bullet was the first really satisfactory expanding bullet for a muzzle-loader, as it could be made small enough to fall easily into place when the weapon was loaded, and at the same time was fairly "gas tight" during discharge. The Minié rifle was introduced into the British Army in 1851, but was not generally issued. A number of regiments, however, had it in the Crimean War. In the Kaffir War (1846-1852) our troops were armed with a number of Lancaster rifles, whose bullets were cast with two wings to fit the grooves.

The Enfield rifle (Fig. 8) was the last muzzle-loader used by the British Army. With its disappearance departed the expanding bullet difficulty. The breech-loading system eliminated the necessity for ramming a bullet down the rifled barrel. The "needle gun" (Fig. 12), adopted by Prussia in 1841, led the way in breech-loading military rifles. The breech was closed by a bolt, through which passed a spring-operated needle, which, when released by the trigger, pierced the base of the cartridge, and ignited the charge by striking a disc of fulminate. The escape of gas and flame was, however, very serious, and the rifle was consequently difficult, not to say dangerous, to use. The advantage, however, that it gave of extremely rapid fire, was so marked that no muzzle-loader could compete with it.

[Continued opposite.

The Beginnings of War Machines: Rifles; Breech-Loaders.

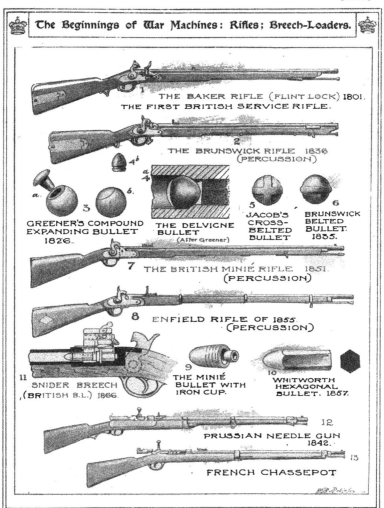

THE BAKER RIFLE (FLINT LOCK) 1801.
THE FIRST BRITISH SERVICE RIFLE.

THE BRUNSWICK RIFLE 1836
(PERCUSSION)

GREENER'S COMPOUND
EXPANDING BULLET
1826..

THE DELVIGNE
BULLET
(After Greener)

JACOB'S
CROSS-
BELTED
BULLET

BRUNSWICK
BELTED
BULLET.
1835.

THE BRITISH MINIÉ RIFLE 1851.
(PERCUSSION)

ENFIELD RIFLE OF 1855.
(PERCUSSION)

SNIDER BREECH
(BRITISH B.L.) 1866.

THE MINIÉ
BULLET WITH
IRON CUP.

WHITWORTH
HEXAGONAL
BULLET. 1857.

PRUSSIAN NEEDLE GUN
1842.

FRENCH CHASSEPOT

THE EVOLUTION OF THE MODERN RIFLE: MUZZLE AND BREECH LOADERS AND BULLETS.

Continued.] In 1866 the French adopted the Chassepot (Fig. 13), a bolt-operated rifle somewhat similar to the "needle-gun." The first breech-loader used in the British Army was the "Snider" (Fig. 11), which was actually the old Enfield rifle converted to a breech-loader. The gas trouble was overcome in the Snider by the use of a metal cartridge-case which was not pierced by

the striker, the percussion-cap in the base of the case remaining in position after the discharge. This system of cartridge construction is now universal. In 1871 the Snider rifle was superseded by the "hammerless" Martini-Henry of .45-inch bore, which gave place in 1891 to the Lee-Metford small bore (.303-inch) magazine rifle.

One of the British Aerial Watch

CRAFT OF WHOSE DOINGS THE PUBLIC HEAR LITTL

A squadron of five of our British airships is seen here while engaged in carrying out evolutions in company, in a certain area "somewhere in England." Although, certainly, the public at large necessarily hear comparatively little of the proceedings of our British dirigibles, these vessels have their allotted duties of a special nature to perform in various localities, and the work appointed

eeping Squadrons on a Cruise.

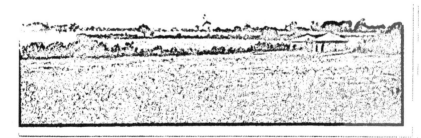

HOUGH THEY ARE CONSTANTLY ON DUTY: BRITISH AIRSHIPS.

o them is satisfactorily carried out. It is generally understood that one of the duties allotted to some of our airships is to cruise off hore, in association with patrol-boats and destroyer flotillas, along the coast, particularly in the vicinity of selected districts or places where it is suspected that enemy submarines may be lurking submerged, in wait to attack passing British vessels.—[Photo. by C.N.]

ROMANCES OF THE REGIMENTS : XII.—THE COLDSTREAM GUARDS.

THE LENNOX AFFAIR.

DURING the early part of the year 1789, military society, and, in fact, society generally, found abundant material for gossip and discussion over the peculiar imbroglio which arose between the Duke of York, Colonel of the Coldstream Guards, and Lieutenant-Colonel Lennox, of the same regiment. The King had just recovered from one of his mental illnesses, and at a dinner given to celebrate the happy event, Lieutenant-Colonel Lennox, a Tory, proposed Mr. Pitt's health. This gave great offence to his Colonel-in-Chief, who resolved to give Lennox a bit of his mind, but took the strangest and most roundabout way of doing so, with unfortunate results. Hence the following queer and involved story, very characteristic of the solemn fooling of duelling days. Soon after the dinner, the Duchess of Ancaster gave a masked ball, at which the

after parade Lennox returned to the attack in the orderly room. The Duke declined to give his authority for the words alleged, but said he was quite ready to answer for his conduct in the manner usual between men of honour. He wished to derive no protection from his rank : when not on duty he wore a brown coat, and he hoped that Colonel Lennox would consider him merely as an officer of the regiment. Lennox replied that he could not consider his Royal Highness as any other than the son of his King.

Lennox thereupon wrote a circular letter to every member of D'Aubigny's Club, asking whether such words had been used to him. If no reply was received within seven days, Colonel Lennox said he would take it as evidence that no such words had been spoken. No member had any recollection of any such affair ; and so, when the

AN OPERATION MUCH APPRECIATED IN HOT WEATHER: BRITISH SOLDIERS AT THE FRONT ENJOYING A BATH.
Official Photograph. Crown Copyright Reserved.

Duke of York was present. Seeing a gentleman, whom he took for Lennox, speaking to the Duchess of Gordon, his Royal Highness went up to him and said that recently at D'Aubigny's Club Colonel Lennox had put up with words which no gentleman should have endured. As it happened, the person whom the Duke addressed was not Colonel Lennox, but Lord Paget, who, in the usual kind friend's way, made it his business to pass the amiable remark on to the person most concerned. He took care to add that he was sure, from voice and manner, that the person who had spoken to him was the Duke of York.

The fat was now in the fire. At the next field-day, Lennox publicly asked the Duke what were the words in question, and by whom they had been spoken. The Duke replied by ordering the Lieutenant-Colonel back to his post. But

seven days were up, Colonel Lennox sent the Earl of Winchilsea to the Duke, to call upon him either to give up the name of his false informant or afford the satisfaction of a gentleman. The Duke replied by naming Lord Rawdon as his friend, and the two seconds proceeded to arrange a meeting.

This took place on the morning of May 26, 1789, on Wimbledon Common. The distance was twelve paces, the parties to fire at a given signal. Lennox fired, and his bullet grazed the Duke's side-curl. The Duke did not return the shot. Lord Rawdon then interfered, and said matters had gone far enough. Lennox remarked that his Royal Highness had not yet fired, to which Rawdon replied that his Royal Highness had no intention of firing. The Duke had come out merely to give Colonel Lennox the satisfaction he desired ; he bore no animosity. Lennox

[Continued overleaf.

The Terror of German Fokkers.

PHOTOGRAPHED FROM A COMPANION AEROPLANE IN MID-AIR: ONE OF OUR NIEUPORT "CHASERS."

A Nieuport aeroplane—one of a class of aircraft that has been, and is now, doing exceptionally valuable work for the Allies as a "chaser" all along the Western Front and off the Belgian coast—is shown in flight, starting off to bring to action a German machine which it has in sight. The photograph was taken from a companion aeroplane. Apart from its remarkable speed and general handiness, a feature of the Nieuport which makes it a magnificent fighting craft—and deadly to German Fokkers, as events for some time past have proved—is the mounting and training arrangements of its gun. All the British, French, and Italian aircraft are marked with tricolour badges. All the German and Austrian 'planes bear black crosses, of Iron Cross design.—[Photo. by C.N.]

begged that the Duke should fire, but the request was refused and the reason repeated. Lord Winchilsea thereupon approached the Duke, and said he hoped that his Royal Highness would not object to say that he considered Colonel Lennox a man of courage and honour. The Duke replied that he should say nothing, and repeated his former reason for not firing. If Colonel Lennox was not satisfied, he might fire again. Lennox said he could not possibly fire again at the Duke, if the Duke refused to fire at him. In face of such a deadlock, there was nothing for it but that the parties should withdraw from the field.

There it might well have ended, but Colonel Lennox was still very sore, feeling that, as his opponent had not fired at him, his honour had not been properly vindicated. He accordingly called a meeting of the officers of the Coldstream Guards and invited them to decide whether he had behaved in the recent dispute as became

AN ARMY FARRIER AT THE BRITISH FRONT DEALING WITH A REFRACTORY SUBJECT: SHOEING A MULE.
Official Photograph. Crown Copyright Reserved.

an officer and a gentleman. Considering who the parties were, the officers may be pardoned if they issued a rather Delphic deliverance. The debate was long, and was once adjourned; but at last the following resolution was carried: "It is the opinion of the Coldstream regiment, that subse-

difficulty of his case, not with judgment." The affair had a further development at the next King's Birthday Ball at St. James's Palace. It was fated to be a ball of only one dance, for the Queen broke it up by a sudden withdrawal, on a complaint of the Prince of Wales that he was tired, not with the dance, but with dancing in such company. He refused to let his sister, the Princess Royal, who was his partner, be turned through a certain figure of a square dance by one of the other dancers; and that although the Duke of York, the Princess Augusta, the Duke of Clarence, and the Princess Elizabeth had made not the slightest objection to dance the figure with the chance partner of the moment. "I never," said the Prince, "will countenance insults given to my family, however they may be treated by others." He might have rested content with the Duke of York's willingness to endure the supposed obnoxious partner, for the Duke, though most concerned in any possible "insult," was not the person most insulted. He may even have intended reparation for his own recent folly; for the guest at whom the Prince of Wales's petulance was maliciously aimed was none other than Colonel Lennox, who had to endure this further annoy-

A BRITISH MACHINE-GUN SECTION AT THE FRONT *EN DÉSHABILLE*: BRINGING UP LEWIS GUNS BY HAND-CART.
Official Photograph. Crown Copyright Reserved.

quent to the 15th of May, the day of the meeting in the orderly room, Lieutenant-Colonel Lennox has behaved with courage, but, from the peculiar

ance. He at once exchanged into the 35th, then quartered at Edinburgh, where he was received with open arms, and became a popular hero.

The Intelligence Department in East Africa.

GETTING NEWS OF THE ENEMY: A BRITISH OFFICER, WITH NATIVE GUN-BEARERS.

A British officer belonging to one of the forces operating under General Smuts in East Africa is seen here, accompanied by his party of "gun-bearers." Officers attached to various columns are sent forward into the bush on reconnoitring expeditions that last often for days. They take gun-bearers, and baggage-carriers with supplies and light camping gear. The officers generally go to work in pairs, but sometimes singly, usually sending back natives to headquarters with intelligence, or, if the information be urgent and especially important, returning themselves. It is largely by the individual work of officer-scouts that the dispositions of the enemy are discovered, enabling the general rounding up of the Germans to be effected as it has been with unvarying success.

King George's Most Recent Visit to the Front.

HIS MAJESTY AND PRESIDENT POINCARÉ BEFORE THE CAMERA; AND H.M. WATCHING AUSTRALIANS.

In our first photograph the King, President Poincaré, Sir Douglas Haig, and General Joffre are seen in France, with the camera making its record of the historic if informal meeting which has had such happy results on the cordial relations of the Allied armies. In the second picture, his Majesty is shown intently watching Australians at trench drill, bayonet work being of the first importance in that form of warfare. The brave Australian Contingent has no warmer admirer than the King. Such representations of actualities as these are of permanent interest and value, no previous wars in history having been recorded in such undeniably faithful fashion.—[Official Photographs. Crown Copyright Reserved.]

The Most Recent Visit of King George to the Front.

HIS MAJESTY AT A SOLDIER'S GRAVE; AND AT CHURCH WITH HIS TROOPS.

Our first photograph records one of many very human and very touching incidents in the recent visit of King George to the battle-fields of France. His Majesty is looking at "a little, little grave, an obscure grave," but it is the grave of an unnamed hero, one of the gallant men who have answered the call of their country at the cost of their lives, and this feeling permeates the whole of the picture. Close to the King, on the left, is H.R.H. the Prince of Wales. The second photograph is of his Majesty attending church service among his troops, showing by his presence his keen appreciation of the fine spirit which his Army has shown throughout the long and arduous campaign.—[*Official Photographs. Crown Copyright Reserved.*]

The King at the front: His Majesty's Inte

THE KING IN A GUN-PIT DURING HIS RECENT VISIT TO THE FRONT: HIS M

During his visit to the front the King saw many of the British guns in action. Describing his activities on August 14, Mr. Phi Gibbs writes: "There was a 'big shoot' in progress on the Wytschaete trenches, and before watching its general effect the K. watched the work of some of our 'heavies'—9'2 and 6-inch guns—and went down into the dug-out of one of the batteries. .

in the Work of the British Heavy Artillery.

INSPECTING ONE OF THE HEAVY BRITISH HOWITZERS WHICH HE SAW IN ACTION.

After spending some time with the battery, the King went to the observation post and watched the bombardment of the enemy's trenches. Over a short line it was terrific in intensity. . . . The field-guns were firing in salvoes from hidden positions. . . . The heavies were sending out their great shells . . . . The King was intensely interested.''—[Official Photograph. Crown Copyright Reserved.]

Italy's Triumph at Gorizia—Ready to fire.

HIDDEN IN A HOUSE : AN ITALIAN GUN WELL SCREENED DURING THE PREPARATORY FIGHTING.

The Italian triumph at Gorizia was the result of as cleverly planned and as ably executed a surprise on a grand scale as the annals of war record. Towards the middle of July, it is stated, General Cadorna learned that the Austrians were transferring the bulk of their forces on the Isonzo to the Trentino, for a reinforced counter-offensive. With the utmost secrecy, by night marches, and along roads screened at exposed places by day, he massed his main forces, unsuspected by the enemy, in front of Gorizia, and attacked forthwith, breaking through the weakened Austrian defence lines at vital points. How one of the Italian guns, brought there unknown to the enemy, was concealed inside a house, the illustration shows. [Photo. by the Italian General Headquarters Photographic Section.]

Italy's Triumph at Gorizia—Just Before Attacking.

IN A FRONT ITALIAN TRENCH AT PODGORA HILL: A GAS-MASKED SENTRY.

For the grand attack on Gorizia, the Italian main forces were brought together in front of the Austrian positions and massed in hiding-places and excavated tunnels until the order to attack was given. In the foremost Italian trenches the troops to lead the assault waited in a state of the completest readiness, and the sentries intently watched the Austrian lines in front from loopholes and every other place whence secret observation was possible. In the illustration an Italian trench-sentry, steel-helmeted and wearing his anti-gas mask (with a relief sentry, similarly ready for any emergency), is seen with his eyes fixed on the enemy at Podgora Hill on the morning of August 6, just before the onset.—[*Photo. by the Italian General Headquarters Photographic Section.*]

Another Royal Act of Forethought for the Wounded.

"QUEEN MARY'S WORKSHOP," BRIGHTON : HER MAJESTY'S GIFT ; AND A D.C.M. PRESENTATION.

Viscountess Falmouth, as representative of the Queen, opened the "Queen Mary's Workshop" the other day at the military hospital, Brighton Pavilion. The workshop has been founded by her Majesty for the training of disabled soldiers in various skilled industries—as electrical engineering, carpentering, and typewriting, etc. The upper illustration shows Lady Falmouth, in the course of the ceremony, presenting Colonel Campbell, who is in charge of the hospital, with a framed portrait of the Queen. The second illustration shows the presentation of the D.C.M. by Major - General Sir Francis Lloyd, on behalf of the King, to Sergeant Grimble, 10th Battalion Royal Yorkshire Regiment, for gallantry at Armentières in 1914, where the sergeant lost both legs.—[Photos. by S. and G.]

With the Allies in the Balkans: Salonika Scenes.

ON THE SALONIKA FRONT: A FRENCH AVIATION CAMP; AND A BRITISH DETENTION CAMP.

Interest in the operations on the Balkan front has been greatly stimulated by the news of the arrival of Russian and Italian troops at Salonika. With the British, French, and Serbians already there, the number of the Allies represented in the Balkan forces was thus increased to five, and a detachment of Albanians has since arrived. The upper photograph, of a French aviation camp near Salonika, shows the care with which the Frenchmen tend the trim little flower-beds with which they have surrounded each tent. Some are worked into legends, such as "Gloire à notre France éternelle," round the nearest tent, in the right foreground. The lower photograph shows a place of detention for persons suspected of espionage at Stavros.—[French and British Official Photographs.]

FOOTNOTES TO ARMAGEDDON: III.—THE NATURE OF THE BEAST.

A LARGE fellow came forward, moving as a stodgy shadow in the semi-darkness of the dug-out. His hands were aloft in the latest Hun fashion.

"Don't shoot," he cried in a voice amiable but a little nervy, and accented in German. "As one says to your policemen, 'I'll come quietly.'" The British officer clicked his torch alight.

A redundant German Captain, gold-spectacled and frequent in chin, blinked and smirked under the impact of the bitter white beam. The Britisher was glad at the sight of him. He couldn't face very much trouble—not in his condition — and this one did not look the troublesome sort.

"Are you alone here?" the Britisher demanded. "Don't lie. We're prepared for all tricks—now. Try any on and it will be unpleasant."

"Quite alone," cried the German fervently. "Actually—I have no right to be here . . . I am glad you are an officer."

"You would find it the same if I were a private. The art of private assassination in a dug-out is not a British accomplishment."

The fat German smiled promptly — a large, humane, ingratiating smile. "No—no, of course not. I did not intend to imply such a thing. But war — that is assassination on a general scale, is it not? And in the excitement — well, privates might not be so disciplined as men of culture."

The British officer looked at the fellow carefully. Was the man's national egoism making him unconsciously ironic? No, he did not think it was that. Again he recognised with relief that the fellow was not as other Germans. There was

THE MOTOR OUSTING THE MULE FOR MILITARY TRANSPORT IN INDIA: A LORRY GOING AT THIRTY-FIVE MILES PER HOUR.

THE DEVELOPMENT OF THE MECHANICAL TRANSPORT CORPS ON THE INDIAN FRONTIER: A LINE OF CARS AND LORRIES.

a large benevolence about him. Not that of good-humour and good-spirits so much as that of kindliness and humanity. The Britisher guessed that the German Captain was a "dug-out"; a fat, easy, middle-aged man hoicked by war from some gentle calling. Probably from a professorship. The fellow certainly looked as though he might have been a professor in some drowsy backwater, a professor of philosophy, or social economics — something with fine dreams, not cruel action, in it.

"This discipline you speak of," he said cuttingly to the German; "we don't find culture has done very much for your people — officers or privates." The fat, dreamy Captain expressed himself, facially, in a manner to convey sorrow, agreement, and disgust.

"You are right," he said, as one chewing food distasteful to the palate. "That is the evil and the horror of war. That is why I hate it so very much. As you have taken me prisoner, I can say to you very fervently, I am glad to get out of the whole vile wallow of it."

"Oh, you hate it," said the Britisher, feeling that the conversation was unreal and unnatural.

"I have always hated it"—the German drew himself up with a touch of pride. "You see, I am a humanitarian, a philosopher. I have studied a great deal in these matters, and thought over them deeply all my life. The business of warring and killing is, to men of my type, not merely unlovely, it is useless. It is against all the laws and ideals of civilisation and progress. I have, in fact, written a small pamphlet on this matter. If you knew Germany,

[Continued overleaf.

The Surprise in the Balkan Campaign.

THE RUSSIAN LANDING AT SALONIKA: THE BRITISH BAND; GENERAL SARRAIL'S INSPECTION.

As stated by the Press Bureau despatch, the first draft of Russians landed at Salonika on July 30. They were enthusiastically welcomed, officers and men of the Allies at Salonika—British, French, and Serbians—being on the quay to cheer the new-comers; while guards of honour were mounted, and British and French regimental bands played the Russians ashore. In the upper illustration a British military band, wearing shorts, is shown playing as the Russians pass across the quay. In the lower illustration General Sarrail, the Allied Generalissimo at Salonika, accompanied by the Russian General and his Staff, is seen inspecting the Russians, several of whom are wearing decorations won in Poland and Galicia.—[Official Photographs. Crown Copyright Reserved.]

Sir, you would know that there are many men of my way of thinking. There is a growing opinion among intellectual and thinking men against this useless and abhorrent warfare. I am one of those in the van of that movement. We will end war and killing, you will see, Sir. We are the men who will

MILAN'S HEARTY WELCOME TO THE PRESIDENT OF THE BOARD OF TRADE: THE CROWD WATCHING MR. RUNCIMAN'S ARRIVAL AT THE CHAMBER OF COMMERCE.

Photograph by Record Press.

reshape Germany in a greater and more humane mould."

"Yet here you are at war, killing," suggested the Britisher, anxious to bring the conversation to a more practical level.

"There are forces that command us in spite of our ideals," said the German. "Our following is small and unorganised. Still, as you see, I have evaded as much of this strife as possible." His gentle, his dreamy face smiled. "It was not merely cowardice which kept me down here, or which makes me glad to be a prisoner."

"Which reminds me," jerked the Britisher. "Will you walk towards the steps. Keep clear of me, and keep in front." . . . The German smiled serenely.

"I assure you you need not fear me. I have told you of my mind." His beaming eyes, now accustomed to the torch-glare, now, as he moved, able to penetrate to the British officer, seemed to gaze closely.

"Keep clear of you . . . I assure you . . . but you are wounded."

"Go on," said the Britisher.

"But you are wounded," said the German

more slowly. His eyes did not seem to be so beaming. "And that torch is in your right hand . . . in your right hand."

"Go on," cried the Britisher grimly.

"And your left hand—why, you haven't a pistol. You haven't a pistol." He stopped. He stared at the Britisher, his serene features curiously set.

"You heard me. Go on. No tricks."

"Wounded. No pistol." The attitude of the German crouched abruptly. "Wounded—no pistol." His upheld hands wavered for a moment. Then——

"Schweinhund!" he roared. His placid face was lit with a fire of appalling and animal ferocity, his right hand darted downward to the automatic in his holster. His shoulder bunched and he lunged forward.

The Britisher crouched, met lunge with lunge. The Britisher's hand swept upward with the peculiar and deadly movement that gives a trench dagger full play. The German Captain dropped his pistol and clutched at the fatal wound in his throat.

The British officer looked down at the dead body with a surprised curiosity. He wondered if the man had been a liar. An idea occurred to him, and he went through the fellow's pockets. His haul of literature on universal

THE PRESIDENT OF THE BOARD OF TRADE ARRIVES IN MILAN TO DISCUSS ANGLO-ITALIAN COMMERCIAL QUESTIONS: MR. RUNCIMAN (HAT IN HAND) LEAVING HIS CAR AT THE CHAMBER OF COMMERCE.—[*Photograph by Record Press.*]

peace and goodwill among men was amazing. No, the fellow hadn't been a liar. The nature of the beast had been too strong for him, that was all.   W. DOUGLAS NEWTON.

The Surprise in the Balkan Campaign.

AT THE LANDING OF THE RUSSIANS AT SALONIKA : THE RUSSIAN GENERAL IN COMMAND.

The central figure of the three officers facing the reader is the Russian General at the head of the contingent which has landed at Salonika. Another Russian officer is seen to the reader's right. The officer to the left, half-turned towards the camera, is a French Field-Officer, a Lieutenant-Colonel of the Infanterie de Marine, as the anchor badge on his képi and collar denotes. The officer in dark uniform, with his back turned while he is watching the Russian troops defiling down the gangway from the transport on to the quay, is a Russian. The soldiers are seen coming off the ship in full marching kit, carrying their rifles, and with their great-coats worn in the Russian service fashion on campaign, *en bandrol* over the left shoulder.—[*Official Photograph. Crown Copyright Reserved.*]

The Scene of a Six Months' Battle: Verdun.

WHERE THE FRENCH HAVE BEEN GAINING GROUND: VERDUN—THE STATION AND AN ARMY POSTMAN.

The upper photograph shows Verdun station as it appeared recently. The buildings appear to be mainly intact, though grass and flowers are growing on the permanent way. The lower illustration is an interesting snapshot, also taken in the neighbourhood of Verdun, which gives a vivid glimpse of the conditions under which the gallant French troops live within range of the enemy's artillery.

An Army postman, going his rounds to deliver the letters to soldiers defending a fort, is seen in the act of taking cover while a German shell is on its way, and awaiting the effects of the explosion in an attitude of very natural suspense. The French have been steadily regaining ground at Verdun. They recently recaptured Fleury, and repulsed counter-attacks. —[French War Office Official Photographs.]

On the Somme Battlefield—With the french.

IN ACTION : KEEPING UP THE BIG-GUN SHELL SUPPLY ; AND MACHINE-GUN SHOOTING AT 30 'YARDS.

French artillerymen are shown in the upper illustration wheeling up to where their gun is firing a load of 240-mm. (or 9'4-inch) shells, on a truck running on rails from the battery magazine to the gun station The railed track leads through a timbered tunnel at the rear of the trenches, and one of the artillerymen has with him a pet terrier. The second illustration shows a steel-helmeted French soldier in a front trench working a machine-gun, as stated, within thirty feet from the Germans, at whom he is firing through a loophole. The French Army use the Hotchkiss machine-gun, an air-cooled weapon fed by a rigid metal clip of cartridges. The recoil action and mechanism are worked by the blast set up by the powder-gases of the cartridges.—[French War Office Official Photographs.]

French Ornamental and Memorial Art in War.

THE RED CROSS IN FLOWERS AND A BLOCKHOUSE AS MONUMENT: IN THE MARNE AND THE MEUSE.

The upper of these two photographs shows a first-aid dressing station and dispensary in connection with a French camp in the Department of the Marne. The Red Cross has been carried out in the style of ornamental gardening with which the French soldier, both on the Western front and in the Balkans, is fond of whiling away his leisure time. Another example of this kind of floral ornamentation appears on another page of this issue, showing tents at a French aviation camp near Salonika, each surrounded with borders of flowers, some of them formed into inscriptions. The lower photograph shows a French blockhouse in the lines of the Meuse, on the side of which is engraved a memorial to a fallen officer.—[Official Photographs authorised by the French War Office.]

Having a Well-Earned Rest—The "Heroine of Loos."

THE HEROIC FRENCH GIRL WHO RESCUED BRITISH SOLDIERS BY SHOOTING GERMANS : MLLE. MOREAU.

Mlle. Emilienne Moreau, whose fame as the "Heroine of Loos" is world-wide, is seen here on the sands at Trouville, where she is having a rest with her mother and brother and sister. A number of friends are specially staying at Trouville with her also. Mlle. Moreau was, a few weeks ago, publicly decorated by the British Ambassador in Paris with the British Military Medal and that of the Order of St. John of Jerusalem. Previously she had been decorated with the French Military Cross. A girl of seventeen, during the battle of Loos she saw some Germans firing on the British from a cellar. She courageously went to the rescue, and shot two of the enemy with a revolver, killing three more with hand-grenades. Mlle. Moreau is seen on the right.—[Photo. by C.N.]

WOMEN AND THE WAR.

A POPULAR writer once said that " men hunt, fish, keep the cattle, or raise corn, for women to eat the game, the fish, the meat, and the corn." What he probably had in his mind, though he was too polite to say so, was that men, and men only, were fit to do the useful work of the world. But the stern logic of recent events has killed that theory beyond hope of resurrection. Its epitaph was written by Mr. Asquith the other day when he said, " The women of this country have rendered as effective service in the prosecution of the war as any other class of the community," and no one would accuse Mr. Asquith of going out of his way to emphasise the value of women's work in its relation to the State.

Since women have proved—because they have at last had a chance—that they really do possess practical genius, men have been so busy patting them on the back that it will be a difficult matter for them to reconcile themselves to being treated as merely " ordinary," instead of superwomen,

A NEW BUSINESS FOR WOMEN : PIANOFORTE-TUNING.
Not tuning only, but manufacturing of pianos, is among the various kinds of employment which women have taken up successfully. Our photograph shows a woman learning to tune a piano.—[Photo. by L.N.A.]

Skilled work and trained brains are no mean gifts to offer in the service of the country, but their value is apt to be a good deal minimised if they happen to be employed in an unsuitable direction. That the number of misfits was not greater was due in large measure to the Women's Service Bureau, organised by the London Society for Women's Suffrage, at 58, Victoria Street, S.W.

It is the society's contribution to national necessity, and a very valuable contribution too. As far as women's work is concerned, I suppose its effects are more valuable and far-reaching than any other institution of the kind in London. It is run on lines of sheer common-sense, and the results of its labours will continue long after peace has been signed.

Its aims are fourfold. In the first place, acting on the round-peg-for-the-round-hole principle, it begins by enrolling the services of educated women who are able and anxious to help in these critical times, and then seeks to " place " them where their particular qualifications

NOVEL WORK FOR WOMEN : THE CULTIVATION OF BACTERIA.
The cultivation of bacteria demands scrupulous care, and women are being employed to tend the sprays on filter-beds in the Midlands. They wear high boots of rubber, and rubber coats and skirts.—[Photo. by Topical.]

once more. There is no doubt about it, women have stood the test of the last two years very well. There are no signs of slackening.

will be of most value to the country. Unlooked-for needs demand emergency measures, so the Bureau makes arrangements by means of short

[Continued overleaf.

Glasgow's Memorial Tribute to Lord Roberts.

A REPLICA OF THE CELEBRATED CALCUTTA STATUE : UNVEILED BY THE GREAT SOLDIER'S DAUGHTER.

The Countess Roberts, the elder daughter of the great soldier, unveiled the equestrian statue of Earl Roberts which has been erected in Kelvingrove Park, Glasgow. Among those who attended the ceremony were Lord Derby, Under-Secretary for War, Field-Marshal Viscount French, General Sir Ian Hamilton, the Duke and Duchess of Montrose, the Marquess of Ailsa, and Lord and Lady Lamington. A notable feature in the proceedings was the presence, grouped in front of the statue, of some hundred and forty veteran soldiers who had served with or under Lord Roberts in various of his campaigns. They included veterans of the Indian Mutiny, the Abyssinian War of 1868, and the Afghan campaigns of 1878-80 and the historic march to Candahar.—[*Photo. by C.N.*]

courses to supply the call for semi-skilled workers in aircraft and munition factories. It lends a hand, too, in the task of sending out women to take part in the work of caring for the sick and wounded overseas; and, lastly, it gives women an opportunity for full and thorough instruction in professions and trades

GIRL FARMERS IN ESSEX: FEEDING THE PIGS.
The Hon. Edward Gerald Strutt, who controls his brother's, Lord Rayleigh's, farms at Terling, has trained young women to look to the herds and do other farm-work, in place of men called to the colours. Our photograph shows some of them at Ringer's Farm.
Photo. by Sport and General.

where there is a prospect of a permanent or temporary shortage.

The Bureau, by the way, works partly in conjunction with the Labour Exchanges, and the number of women who have taken advantage of its good offices runs into many thousands. Roughly speaking, there is no form of work, whether paid or voluntary, with which its officials are not capable of dealing; and, as an instance of its hydra-headed activity, it may be mentioned that some of its clients are at present serving as tram-conductors, lift-girls, clerks, agricultural labourers, forage and munition workers, railway and munition workers, as well as in many other occupations.

Not the least interesting development in regard to women's work has been the enlistment in increasing numbers of their services in aircraft factories. In this direction the Women's Service Bureau can claim the credit of having started the first school in the country where women can be taught oxy-acetylene welding — a branch of aircraft work that requires great care and accuracy. Here again the women have proved once more that they are equal to any call that

may be made upon them, and the demand for workers from the school is in excess of the supply. Other classes exist for micrometer-viewing, with instructions in reading from drawings; gauging and measuring, for the inspection of the parts of aircraft, as well as those for instruction in lathe-work (turning and fitting and filing of metals); and, if only sufficient funds were available, the work could be greatly extended.

It is certain that women will have to continue to work after the war. So, with an eye to the future, the authorities at Victoria Street have made a thorough and exhaustive inquiry into the possible shortage in professions and trades, and new openings in industries hitherto chiefly carried on by enemy countries. As a result, it seems clearly established that if women are not allowed to come to the rescue we shall in the future, unless the Hun is to regain his old place in the trade world, be reduced to wearing clogs, reverting to the hour-glass, suffering toothlessness with—as good grace as we can command, and in general leading a quite uncomfortable sort of existence. The Bureau, however, is doing its best to brighten the prospect by founding scholarships for women which will enable them to train in these and other professions or trades, and is thus throw-

TAKING THE PLACE OF MEN WHO HAVE "JOINED UP";
GIRL FARMERS IN ESSEX.
Girls and women are doing men's work on Lord Rayleigh's farms in Essex. They are billeted in Terling, and work in overalls and breeches and soft felt hats. Lord Rayleigh's brother, the Hon. Edward Gerald Strutt, has trained them. The girls in our picture are putting the corn up in shocks.—[Photo. by Alfieri.]

ing open to them additional opportunities for undertaking work that is patriotic as well as profitable.　　　　　CLAUDINE CLEVE.

The Most Desolate Region of the Somme Battlefield.

WHERE OVILLERS WAS: A CAPTURED GERMAN TRENCH IN THE CHALK; AND THE VILLAGE RUINS.

No section of the German line captured by our troops presents a more utterly desolate appearance than that near Ovillers-la-Boiselle, which has been practically obliterated. After visiting the scene, a "Times" correspondent wrote: "The whole earth's surface, before and around, is torn with shell-holes and seamed with lines of trenches, all white, because the soil here is chalk. . . . Opposite, a few ragged stumps, fragments of tree-trunks . . . with bits of splintered lower branches sticking from them, stand gaunt against the sky and mark where Ovillers used to be. . . . We went down across the torn and blasted earth to the white line of what was once the German front line trench. It is a trench no more. . . . The parapet is strewn all over the ground."—[Official Photograph.]

France's Immense Stock of Huge Projectiles.

AN ARTILLERY RAILWAY STATION "DUMP": SHELLS BY HUNDREDS—ONE COMPARED WITH A MAN.

These two illustrations almost stagger one by the impression they convey both of the immensity of the supply of ammunition needed at the front, and of the enormous size of the projectiles in use. Yet the railway *entrepôt*, or intermediate storing place, seen in the upper illustration, is only one of many. The giant shell of the second illustration (400-mm., or 15.7-inch calibre) is a typical specimen, as to size, of the huge projectiles that are being fired every day all along the Allied front. The shells seen in the upper illustration, stacked on the ground beside the railway track, are never left there for many hours. Trains from the front arrive and carry off tons of them, while as many fresh trains from the munitions-factories arrive and replace the shells.—[*French Official Photograph.*]

A British Anti-Aircraft "Fowling-Piece."

FIRING A BATTALION'S DISCHARGE OF BULLETS: A LEWIS GUN ON WHEEL MOUNTING.

The rifle-like shape and handiness of the Lewis magazine-gun make it readily adaptable for employment as an anti-aircraft weapon, apart from its other manifold battlefield uses. In the illustration a Lewis gun, and its drum-shaped cartridge-supply attachment above the breech, is shown with the tripod mounting fixed on an ingeniously contrived stand, devised in order to enable the weapon to deliver an all-round fire. The Lewis fires 300 shots a minute. Rotation is obtained by means of the wheel-base which enables the gunner to follow the evolutions of an aeroplane. There are two wheels, one (on which the gun-tripod rests) revolving above ; the other by way of support or counter-balance, below, buried in the ground.—[Official Photograph. Crown Copyright Reserved.]

The Splendid Fighting Spirit of the Serbian Army.

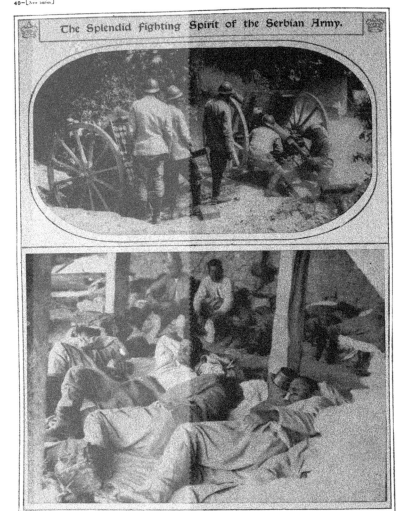

ENTHUSIASTIC : SERBIANS WORKING A "75"

Recent news from Salonika stated that the Serbians, now re-equipped and full of fight, were dislodging the Bulgarians from hill after hill in the Moglena sector. A French communiqué of August 27 stated : "West of the Vardar. . . . five successive (Bulgarian) attacks conducted with extreme violence were shattered by the Serbian artillery fire." The upper photograph shows Serbian

MALARIA PATIENTS EAGER TO FIGHT AGAIN.

artillerymen, in their new French helmets, working a "75." In the lower one are Serbian malaria patients in a field-dressing station, who at their own special request were not sent to a base hospital, because they wished to remain near the front and get back into the fighting. This incident illustrates the splendid spirit that animates the Serbian Army.—[*Official Photographs.*]